Bernard McGinn—Associate Professor of Historical
Theology and History of Christianity, University of Chicago
Divinity School, Chicago, Ill.

John Meyendorff—Professor of Church History, Fordham
University, Bronx, N.Y., and Professor of Patristics and Church
History, St. Vladimir's Seminary, Tuckahoe, N.Y.

Seyyed Hossein Nasr—Professor of Islamics, Department of
Religion, Temple University, Philadelphia, Pa., and Visiting Professor,
Harvard University, Cambridge, Ma.

Heiko A. Oberman—Director, Insititue fuer
Spaetmittelalter and Reformation, Universitaet Tuebingen, West
Germany.

Alfonso Ortiz—Professor of Anthropology, University of
New Mexico, Albuquerque, N. Mex.; Fellow, The Center for
Advanced Study, Stanford, Calif.

Raimundo Panikkar—Professor, Department of Religious
Studies, University of California at Santa Barbara, Calif.

Jaroslav Pelikan—Sterling Professor of History and Religious
Studies, Yale University, New Haven, Conn.

Fazlar Rahman—Professor Islamic Thought, Department of Near
Eastern Languages and Civilization, University of
Chicago, Chicago, Ill.

Annemarie B. Schimmel—Professor of Hindu Muslim Culture,
Harvard University, Cambridge, Mass.

Sandra M. Schneiders—Assistant Professor of New
Testament Studies and Spirituality, Jesuit School of Theology,
Berkeley, Calif.

Huston Smith—Thomas J. Watson Professor of Religion,
Adjunct Professor of Philosophy, Syracuse University, Syracuse, N.Y.

John R. Sommerfeldt—Professor of History, University of
Dallas, Irving, Texas.

David Steindl-Rast—Monk of Mount Savior Monastery,
Pine City, N.Y.

William C. Sturtevant—General Editor, Handbook of North
American Indians, Smithsonian Institution, Washington, D.C.

David Tracy—Professor of Theology, University of Chicago
Divinity School, Chicago, Ill.

Victor Turner—William B. Kenan Professor in
Anthropology, The Center for Advanced Study, University of
Virginia, Charlottesville, Va.

Kallistos Ware—Fellow of Pembroke College, Oxford;
Spalding Lecturer in Eastern Orthodox Studies, Oxford
University, England.

John and Charles Wesley
Selected Prayers, Hymns, Journal Notes, Sermons, Letters and Treatises

EDITED, WITH AN INTRODUCTION
BY
FRANK WHALING

PREFACE
BY
ALBERT C. OUTLER

PAULIST PRESS
NEW YORK • RAMSEY • TORONTO

Cover Art
The artist, LIAM ROBERTS, was born in Ireland and now lives in New York. After
attending the National College of Art in Dublin for five years, he studied at the Academy of Fine Arts in Florence, at the Royal Academy of San Fernando in Madrid, and
at the Academy of Fine Arts in Rome for one year each on scholarship.

Design: Barbini, Pesce & Noble, Inc.

Copyright © 1981 by
The Missionary Society of St. Paul
the Apostle in the State of New York

Library of Congress
Catalog Card Number: 81-82207

ISBN: 0-8091-0318-4 (cloth)
       0-8091-2368-1 (paper)

Published by Paulist Press
545 Island Road Ramsey, N.J. 07446

Printed and bound in the
United States of America

CONTENTS

CONTENTS

ACKNOWLEDGMENT

The editor wishes to record grateful thanks to a number of friends and colleagues who offered encouragement and advice in the preparation of this volume, namely Professor Frank Baker of Duke University, Professor Franz Hildebrandt of Edinburgh, Professor John Kent of Bristol University, Reverend Dr. Henry Rack of Manchester University, Reverend David Tripp of Manchester, Professor Philip Watson of Coulsdon, and the curator of the archives section of the Rylands Museum in Manchester. I am grateful, as always, to my wife and family for their support. My thanks are due too to Mrs. Kathryn Cousins for her practical help, and to Richard Payne of the Paulist Press for his unfailing friendship and assistance.

Editor of this Volume

FRANK WHALING was born at Pontefract, Yorkshire, England, on February 5, 1934. He was educated at the King's School Pontefract, Christ's College Cambridge, Wesley House Cambridge, and Harvard University. He has degrees in history and theology from Cambridge, and a doctorate in comparative religion from Harvard. He has won a number of academic awards including the Peregrine Maitland Studentship from Cambridge and the John E. Theyer Honor Award from Harvard.

Dr. Whaling served as a Methodist minister at the Birmingham Central Hall, England (1960–1962), as a Methodist missionary in Faizabad and Banaras in North India (1962–1966), and at Eastbourne, Sussex (1966–1969). He has spoken on the Wesleys and on American and British Methodism to a number of audiences and conferences, especially American, and was keynote speaker and lecturer at the Indiana School of the Prophets in 1975.

Frank Whaling is presently a member of the largest British divinity faculty at New College in the University of Edinburgh where he is coordinator of the Edinburgh University Religious Studies degrees and Religious Studies Unit. He is also chairman of the Scottish Working Party on Religions of the World in Education, codirector of the Edinburgh/Farmington Project in Religious Studies, and a member of the Shap Working Party, as well as a member of the New York International Center for Integrative Studies.

Dr. Whaling has published a number of articles in journals such as *Sikh Sanskar, Indian Journal of Philosophy, Forum, Scottish Journal of Theology, Irish Theological Quarterly, Journal of Religious Studies,* and *Journal of Religious Education.* He has written or edited a number of present or forthcoming books including *An Approach to Dialogue: Hinduism and Christianity; The Development of the Religious Significance of Rama in North India; Contemporary Approaches to the Study of Religion; Christian Theology and World Religions; Contemporary Issues in Religious Education in Britain and the United States;* and *Think Globally or Perish.*

Frank and Patricia Whaling were married in 1960. They have two children, John aged 14, and Ruth aged 10. Mrs. Whaling has expertise in the area of education.

Author of the Preface

ALBERT C. OUTLER, long-time historian of Christian thought and veteran ecumenist, is now Emeritus Professor of Theology at Southern Methodist University in Dallas, Texas—having already served on the theological faculties of Duke and Yale Universities. His education was at Wofford College (B.A., 1928), Emory University (B.D., 1933) and Yale University (Ph.D., 1938). His interest in the traditions of Christian Platonism (in which, he believes, John Wesley stands) was generated by early studies in Greek philosophy and in Origen, Clement of Alexandria and St. Augustine (he was editor of Volume VII of *The Library of Christian Classics*). His "discovery" of John Wesley as an underdeveloped figure in the history of Christian thought and of Christian spirituality came in the late 1940s and led to his being assigned the editorship of the Wesley volume in *A Library of Protestant Thought* (1964). He was also one of the moving spirits in the planning and preparation of the critical edition of *The Works of John Wesley*, now being published by The Clarendon Press; his editorial assignment in this project is a four-volume bloc of *The Sermons*. He was a delegate to the Second World Conference on Faith and Order, in Lund, Sweden, in 1952 and was Vice-Chairman of the Third Conference, in Montreal, 1963. In the decade between, he served as Co-Chairman of Faith and Order's Commission on Tradition and Traditions. He was an appointed Methodist delegate to the Third Assembly of the World Council of Churches (New Delhi, 1961) and to the Fourth Assembly (Uppsala, 1968). He also served as one of the three principal Methodist delegated-observers to the Second Vatican Council (1962-65). His books include *Psychotherapy and the Christian Message* (1954), *The Christian Tradition and the Unity We Seek* (1957), *A Methodist Observer at Vatican II* (1967), *Who Trusts in God: Musings on the Meaning of Providence* (1968), and *Theology in the Wesleyan Spirit* (1975). Much more numerous are his scholarly articles and book reviews. A list of these (up to 1975) may be seen in the bibliography published in *Our Common History as Christians: Essays in Honor of Albert C. Outler*, ed. by John Deschner, Leroy T. Howe and Klaus Penzel (1975). His record of major lectureships in the United States and abroad runs to thirty-six; his honorary degrees number twelve. His lifelong avocation in psychotherapy has reinforced his interest in the spiritual life and an adequate contemporary understanding of its human dynamics.

PREFACE

It will not be immediately self-evident to all that John and Charles Wesley belong in a series like *The Classics of Western Spirituality*. Neither man was a "saint" (save, of course, in the Pauline sense) and neither made much of religion as a withdrawal from this world or of spirituality as ecstasis or rapture. Together they set a movement in motion that has had its fair share of the godly and devout but with fewer spiritual giants than some others. But if "spirituality" can be construed as "life in the Spirit", "life from God, to God and with God", life in its full range from first repentance to final glory, then the spiritual vision of the brothers Wesley may qualify as "classical". For this, most assuredly, was their shared understanding of "true religion". It has not always been emphasized in "Western spirituality", that a conscious awareness of the vital presence of God in all things and events may still comport with intense activity in "this world" and also with a high level of rational self-consciousness. Both concerns were united in the Wesleys—pre-eminently in John, whose personal, spiritual "peak experiences" were few and far between. He was quite conscious of this and was being utterly candid with Elizabeth Ritchie (and us) when he wrote: "I am very rarely led by impressions [i.e., spontaneous impulses] but generally by reason and by Scripture. I *see* abundantly more than I *feel*". Within six months of the most intensely "spiritual experience" he ever recorded (one of a surprisingly small number) he also reported, with equal forthrightness, an *Anfechtung* in which he doubts that he was, even then, a Christian or that he ever had loved God truly (cf. Journal, Jan. 4, 1739; see also his remarkable letter to Charles, June 27, 1766).

There can, however, be no doubt that "life in the Spirit" and

PREFACE

"the fruit of the Spirit" were the deepest and most nearly constant concerns of both brothers, from childhood till death. They had grown up with the Holy Scriptures and the Prayer Book as a second language, in an atmosphere steeped in the great spiritual classics cherished by their parents (especially such books as Henry Scougal's *The Life of God in the Soul of Man* [1677], Lorenzo Scupoli, *The Spiritual Struggle* [attributed, by the Wesleys and others in those days, to Juan de Castañiza], Lewis Bayly, *The Practice of Piety* [1613], Richard Allestree, *The Whole Duty of Man* [1657], Henry Hammond, *A Practical Catechism* [1645]). At Oxford, they had graduated to other spiritual classics, chiefly in the Anglican tradition (Jeremy Taylor, *Holy Living and Holy Dying*, William Law, *A Serious Call to a Devout and Holy Life*), to à Kempis and other Roman Catholic mystics (Fénelon, De Renty, Bourignon) and in 1732, to the *Theologia Germanica*. In 1730, with others in "The Holy Club", they were exploring the fountain-head of Eastern Orthodox spirituality—e.g., Clement of Alexandria, Macarius, the Cappadocians, Ephrem Syrus and others. The fruits of these explorations were summed up in a university sermon in 1733 (recently discovered and not yet published); its theme is the entire love of God above all else and the love of all creatures in God.

In Epworth, there had been the daily round of family devotions. In Oxford, the brothers, with their friends, observed a regular spiritual discipline that was consciously modeled on conventional traditions: ejaculatory prayers on the hour, collects at 9, 12 and 3, meditations at 6, searching self-interrogations concerning inner spiritual states, and prayers chosen from a rich miscellany (an example of which appears in John's very first publication, *A Collection of Prayers for Every Day of the Week*, 1732). John took this twin-stress on ritual *and* devotion with him to Georgia, where he set out, rather aggressively, to become the spiritual director of the entire colony. His failure in this venture left him more discouraged with himself than with the venture. Thus presently, when he became the freely acknowledged leader of the Methodist Revival, he turned this into his cherished role of *spiritual director*—first to groups in Bristol and London, and thereafter to a veritable network ("connexion", he called it) of small groups all over Britain (see his explanation of the role in his *Doctrinal Minutes*, Aug. 3, 1745). In a different way but to the same end, Charles became chief Psalmist to the movement, and it was no accident that the Methodist people learned at least as much doctrine from Charles' hymns as they did from John's preaching. What is crucial is that it was the same basic doctrine!

This is how, for John, the written word came to function as supplement to the oral; it also explains why almost everything in the Wesley corpus (including *The Christian Library* and *The Arminian Magazine*) was aimed at the spiritual nurture of these men and women "in connexion with Mr. Wesley."

Given all this, it is easy to see why the task of choosing an *ideal* anthology from John Wesley's prose and Charles' poetry is quite out of the question. What is clear, however, is that no proper anthology focused on "spirituality" could afford to omit John's *Plain Account of Christian Perfection* or a representative sampling of Charles' *Hymns.* The *Plain Account* . . . is John's most important single essay. "Perfection" was, as all agree, his most distinctive doctrinal emphasis; and the *Plain Account* . . . gathers up into itself all that he ever said on the subject that is of real importance.

It may be important, however, in reading the Wesleys, to realize how intently but almost without full awareness, they were working with a distinctive *pneumatology* that has no exact equivalent in "Western spirituality" up to their time. This distinctive emphasis on the person and work of the Holy Spirit separates them, at least by nuance, from the Puritan, Moravian and Lutheran pietists before their time and from all Pentecostalists and "holiness associations" after them (who have so often invoked their authority). Their doctrine of *perfection* as the perfection of intention and love had a sub-surface prehistory in Anglicanism (in obscure men like Robert Gell and Thomas Drayton); there are echoes of it in medieval Catholicism (as in Fénelon and William of St. Thierry). But the brothers Wesley placed it as the capstone of their vision of the entire "order of salvation" and made it turn on an especially vivid sense of the pervasive and personal reality of the Holy Spirit in all human experience—in conscience, faith, reason and moral agency. So wide and vital is the role and range of prevenient grace (which, for the Wesleys, was always identified as the special work of the Holy Spirit). In religious experience, this means that conscience is always in order to repentance (understood as self-knowledge rather than remorse), just as repentance, then, is in order to faith, as faith is in order to hope and love, as, finally, love is in order to that holiness and true happiness for which we were created in the first place. This also means that "Christian Perfection" is perfection in love—to God above all and to neighbor as a spiritual consequence. Such a doctrine presupposes both the sovereignty of grace *and* the participation of the human spirit, always and only in *re*-action to the actions of the Holy Spirit.

Within such a perspective, there is a marked absence of the sort of forensic view that has pervaded Western "soteriology" in general and the Lutheran and Calvinist traditions in particular. It is, however, worlds away from any of the notions of self-absorption that are characteristic of unitive mysticism (as in Eckhart) or from any human initiative (Pelagianism).

What was not always made clear was that this particular vision of Christian existence was more "Eastern" than "Western". The result was that the idea of "perfection" of love "in this life" seemed far more self-evidently valid to the Wesleys than it did to their critics (or even to the Methodists—then and subsequently).

This theme is as pervasive in Charles' hymns as in John's preaching (and always radically pneumatological):

> Spirit of faith, come down; reveal the things of God
> And make to us the Godhead known, and witness with the
> blood.
> 'Tis thine the blood to apply and give us eyes to see:
> Who did for every sinner die, hath surely died for me.
> . . . . .
>
> Inspire the living faith which, whoso'er receives
> The witness in himself he hath and *consciously* believes;
> That faith that conquers all and doth the mountains move,
> And saves who'er on Jesus call, and perfects them in love.

Or, again:

> . . . .
> Finish, then, thy new creation; pure and spotless let us
> be.
> Let us see thy great salvation perfectly restored in thee.
> Changed from glory into glory, till in heaven we take
> our place,
> Till we cast our crowns before thee, lost in wonder, love
> and praise.

PREFACE

For the phrase "changed from glory into glory, . . ." cf. Danielou-Musurillo, *From Glory to Glory: Texts from Gregory of Nyssa* [1962].

Here then, in the Wesleys, we are dealing with their shared vision of the *ordo salutis*. It is like and yet unlike their own Anglican tradition through which it came to them; it is like and unlike the pietism which influenced them so strongly; it is like and unlike Western mysticism, since its sources are in an older and farther tradition. But there is also something forward looking in Wesleyan spirituality: its stress upon inwardness ("heart religion") and its complementary stress upon the *fides caritate formate* that issued in a strenuous moral and economic discipline. It carries within it an implicit theory of social revolution that is non-violent and conservative, a faith in the human future based on an unfaltering optimism of grace.

The literary styles of the two Wesleys have their respective merits: John's prose is lean and graceful; Charles' poetry packed with lively imaging. And speaking practically, they shared a remarkable mission in eighteenth century Britain—a revival of popular spirituality that found its outlet in preaching, praying, singing—and powerful social change! Neither the virtues of their style nor the memories of their mission will, however, quite warrant their careful study in our later age, living as we do in the face of a very different human future. It is their *message,* in which so much of the *fides historica* is summed up in a fashion fit "for plain people" that may still command attention when faithfully presented. In one way, a collection like this (and others like it) may be examined as if it were a museum, a re-presentation of an epoch long ago. But in the way that matters most, it is also a living resource. It reflects one of those significant disclosures of sovereign grace in the work of two brothers through whom that grace has been actualized for millions—and still may be for millions more.

Albert C. Outler

FOREWORD

John and Charles Wesley were two of the greatest Christians of the modern (or any other) age of the Church. Charles Wesley is famous as probably the finest hymn writer in Christian history, and this volume includes over a hundred of his hymns, which convey a distinctive spirituality. John Wesley's spiritual experience, sometimes compared to that of Saint Augustine and Martin Luther, led him to become a great Christian leader and the founder, under God, of the Methodist tradition. This volume includes his early *Forms of Prayer*, *Scheme of Self-Examination*, classical translations of German hymns, and advice on spiritual reading included in his preface to à Kempis' *Imitation of Christ*; the account, taken from his journal, of his crucial period of spiritual experience; his rules for the early Methodist Societies, his beautiful tract *A Plain Account of Genuine Christianity*, and his meditation on the Lord's Prayer taken from a classical sermon; the Covenant Service of 1780, his description of the character of the saintly Fletcher of Madeley, and some letters of spiritual counsel including his final, celebrated letter to William Wilberforce condemning slavery. The volume ends with John Wesley's *Plain Account of Christian Perfection*, his most extended treatment of the fundamental tenet of his life and spirituality.

The Wesleys transformed the spiritual atmosphere of Britain in the eighteenth century, and they paved the way for the rise of a present-day Methodist community of almost fifty million around the world. This volume shows how their spiritual roots lay in Orthodox and Roman Catholic as well as Lutheran, Moravian, Church of England, and Puritan sources. The influence of their spirituality, although mainly encapsulated within the Methodist tradition, cannot be confined to that community. Its full potential remains to be

FOREWORD

grasped. They combined a concern for organization and inwardness, fellowship and the individual, the social and the spiritual, sacrament and evangelism, theology and practice, body and soul, life present and life to come, spiritual seriousness and spiritual gaiety, liturgy and spontaneity. The riding, the preaching, the organization, the writing, the sheer practical success of the Methodist movement tended to highlight one side of the equation. Contemporary Methodists and the Great Church Militant have much to learn from the integrity and the integralism of the Wesleys' spirituality.

INTRODUCTION

This volume of the Classics of Western Spirituality is unusual in that it features two people. The spirituality it portrays is not that of John Wesley as a separate person, nor that of Charles Wesley as an autonomous figure; it is the spirituality of the Wesleys together.

It is unlikely that there are many, if any, volumes in this series that analyze the spirituality of more than one person; certainly it is unlikely that any other volume would engage in the task of examining the spirituality of two members of the same family, not to mention that of two brothers.

Yet it is appropriate that the Wesleys should be considered together. Their brotherhood was not merely natural, it was also spiritual. They not only shared the youthful fellowship of the family environment of Epworth Rectory in Lincolnshire, but also attended the same Oxford college, Christ Church; they shared the life of the same Holy Club at Oxford; they went out to Georgia together; they shared a similar spiritual experience in 1738 after their disappointment in Georgia; their mutual aim was that of perfect love for God and man; they retained their joint love for the Church of England while leading the Methodist revival; their spirituality was similar and also complementary. It would seem as strange to consider the spirituality of Charles Wesley's hymns in isolation from the life of John Wesley as it would seem strange to analyze the spirituality of John Wesley apart from Charles Wesley and his hymns.

It would be wrong, of course, to assume that the Wesleys were carbon copies of each other. This was far from being the case. Of the two, John was the more natural leader and organizer; John's mind was more wide-ranging than that of Charles; in spite of the excellence of John's early translations of German pietist hymns, it was Charles who had the greater poetic gifts. Methodist writers such as Rattenbury have stressed the differences between the Wesleys in regard to their stance toward the Church of England and in regard to their attitude toward the crucial spiritual doctrine of perfect love.[1] In addition to these temperamental and theological divergences, it is also clear that Charles exercised his spirituality within the parameters of a happy family life with his wife and children whereas John's attempts at nuptials were little short of disastrous—his failure to marry Sophia Hopkey in Georgia triggered a series of events that led to the court case whereby he left America; later he did not marry Grace Murray, who would have shared his preaching as well as his love; finally he did marry a widow, Mrs. Vazeille, who was an unsuitable partner. Not only this, even had he married Grace Murray, they had an arrangement whereby any children they might have would be brought up at Wesley's Kingswood School leaving the parents free to travel. John's spirituality became essentially that of the traveling preacher; Charles's became that of the more sedentary spiritual leader in Bristol and later in London. However, in spite of these differences, it is remarkable how close the Wesley brothers were in their basic spirituality. Within the Methodist context, Rattenbury and others are correct to point out the minutiae that separated the Wesley brothers. When we examine the brothers within the context of Western spirituality, even when we examine them within the broader Methodist context, their dissimilarities pale into insignificance beside the basic unity of their hearts and minds.

Previous analyses of the theology and spirituality of the Wesleys have tended to concentrate on part of the work of the Wesleys so that a partial rather than an integral view of their spirituality has emerged. The reasons for this are perfectly natural. Roman Catholic writers such as Piette and Todd have emphasized the continuity of the Wesleys within the Catholic tradition;[2] Anglican writers such as Allchin and Hodges have stressed the essentially Anglican liturgical and eucharistic framework within which the Wesleys worked;[3] con-

---

[1]See J. E. Rattenbury, *The Evangelical Doctrines of Charles Wesley's Hymns* (London: Epworth, 1941); and *The Eucharistic Hymns of John and Charles Wesley* (London: Epworth, 1948).

[2]M. Piette, *John Wesley in the Evolution of Protestantism* (New York: Sheed and Ward, 1937); J. M. Todd, *John Wesley and the Catholic Church* (London: Hodder and Stoughton, 1958).

[3]H. A. Hodges and A. M. Allchin, *A Rapture of Praise* (London: Hodder and Stoughton, 1966).

INTRODUCTION

tinental writers such as Orcibal have dwelt on the influence exerted by continental mystical writers on the Wesleys;[4] a Methodist early church historian such as Outler has illuminated the importance of Eastern Fathers such as Gregory of Nyssa for the work of the Wesleys;[5] traditional Methodist writers have tended to underline the centrality of John's Aldersgate experience of May 1738, and the parallel experience of Charles Wesley, as leading to the Methodist revival and therefore to the rise of the Methodist Church. There is truth in all these insights. The Wesleys, as we shall see, were indeed influenced by the Christian tradition they inherited and took for granted; they were faithful to the liturgy, doctrines, and sacraments of the Church of England; they were influenced by the Eastern Fathers and by Roman Catholic mystical writers; the central insight of the Protestant Reformation mediated to them by the Moravians and Luther's commentaries, and experienced at Aldersgate Street, was crucial; the Methodist revival assimilated the work of many Christians and many movements through the organizing and conceptualizing genius of John Wesley. However, the Wesleys were not the sum total of the influences on them. They did not consciously synthesize various strands of thought and organization and thereby create a great movement. To suggest this would be reductionism. What rather happened was that the Wesleys inherited a Christian tradition at the beginning of the eighteenth century that contained a cluster of elements that provided the background wherein they could develop their vision of God. But what developed was *their* vision of God. This vision of God, this spirituality, transcended the influences that helped to produce it and led in turn to a radical renewal of the tradition they had inherited. In other words, the key to the Wesleys is their spirituality, their vision of God and His purpose for the life of man. The spirituality of the Wesleys helped to create what we now know as the Methodist Church—but it is not bounded by, or limited to, the Methodist Church. It is wider than that. It is a gift, so far mainly appropriated by the people called Methodists, but available in essence to all Christians.

Although our aim is to highlight the spirituality of both the Wes-

---

[4] J. Orcibal, *The Theological Originality of John Wesley and Continental Spirituality*, pp. 81–111 in *A History of the Methodist Church in Great Britain*, Vol. I (London: Epworth, 1965).

[5] A. C. Outler, *John Wesley* (New York: Oxford University Press, 1964).

ley brothers, exigencies of space dictate that we impose some sort of order and selectivity on the material. To this end, the first part of our volume will examine selected passages from the works of John Wesley to bring out the nature of his spirituality; the second part of our volume will concentrate on the hymns of Charles Wesley, which, as Bernard Manning put it, rank with the Psalms, the Book of Common Prayer, and the Canon of the Mass within Christian spirituality;[6] and the third part of our volume will examine John Wesley's main prose work on the notion of Christian Perfection, which lay at the heart of the Wesleys' spirituality.

The problem in attempting to delineate the spirituality of Protestants is alluded to by John Wesley in his life of Fletcher of Madeley, who was probably the saintliest of all the early Methodists.

> The pious members of the Church of Rome make a conscience of concealing anything from their Directors, but disclose to them all the circumstances of their lives, and all the secrets of their hearts: Whereas very few of the Protestants disclose to others, even their most intimate friends, what passes between God and their own souls; at least not of set purpose.[7]

This sentence is partly true of John Wesley himself. He has left no long account of the intimate communion of his soul with God (we are not sure whether the recent cracking of the code of his diary will remedy this), and therefore we have to make do with extracts from different works that give us glimpses of his inmost self. Neither has he left any one long spiritual commentary for the guidance of others. His *Plain Account of Christian Perfection* is a book of doctrine as well as of spirituality, and his more intimate writings, some of which we include here, are shorter in length. Nevertheless it appears that, in the passage quoted above, Wesley is tacitly acquiescing in a somewhat static view of spirituality that he is ready to question elsewhere. In order to clarify this matter, we will now look at the background of the life of John Wesley in order to place the selected passages within

---

[6]B. L. Manning, *The Hymns of Wesley and Watts* (London: Epworth, 1942), p. 14.
[7]*The Works of the Rev. John Wesley*, A.M., with the Last Corrections of the Author, ed. Thomas Jackson, London, 1829–1831, 14 vols. (henceforth cited as *Works*), vol. XI, pp. 340–41, *Life of Mr. Fletcher*. We quote from the 3rd edition.

context and in order to determine the meaning of "spirituality" within these passages and within the life of John Wesley himself. We concentrate on John Wesley for reasons of economy of space, and will pass on to Charles Wesley when we come to examine his hymns.

John Wesley was born at Epworth in 1703 into a family that could already boast two generations of ministers. His parents were both strong-minded people who were Church of England by conviction in contrast with Wesley's grandparents, who had been Dissenters by conviction. His family had a deep influence on John Wesley, and also on his brother Charles, who was born four years later in 1707. Their mother, Susanna Wesley, was a woman of very strong character who ruled the children through a benevolent despotism that involved "breaking their wills" by the time they were aged one. Nevertheless, although it is not surprising that only Charles of the ten children was able to enjoy a really happy marriage, both Susanna and Samuel Wesley had a decisive impact on the lives of their offspring. At the Epworth rectory John learned the value of prayer and Bible study, moral values and frugal living, religion in the home and instruction of children. He learned too the value of church discipline together with a model of the parish as the focal point of the world (culled from the Church of England Puritans and Richard Baxter and later exemplified in Fletcher of Madeley) along with a sense that the world could be one's parish (through the family's reading about the Danish missionaries in India, and Samuel's interest in the mission field and in Georgia). When John barely survived a fire at the rectory at the age of seven, Susanna had an intuition that he was destined for great things, and she spared no effort to aid his spiritual development. By her weekly private conferences, by her letters, by her advocacy of spiritual masters such as Pascal, by her religious instruction in the Apostles' Creed and the Ten Commandments, by her own personal example, she fueled the mind and imagination of her son. From his father, John learned to value the sacraments, to take seriously the Protestant and Roman Catholic mystics, to distrust Calvinistic particularism, to be assiduous in the work of the ministry, to value the fellowship to be found through the Church of England Societies, and, not least, to cherish inward religion. "The inward witness, son, the inward witness, that is the proof, the strongest proof of Christianity"—these were Samuel's dying words to John.[8] The elements of

---

[8]Quoted in letter to John Smith March 22, 1748, in *Works*, vol. XII, p. 100.

INTRODUCTION

Wesley's later spirituality were already there in germ in the rectory at Epworth.

Wesley spoke and wrote little about his time as a schoolboy at Charterhouse. His sojourn at Oxford University was to be more important. He entered Christ Church in 1720, and was elected to a fellowship at Lincoln College in 1726, the same year that Charles enrolled at Christ Church. Oxford was significant for Wesley in a number of ways. At the practical level it gave him a base of operations in that an Oxford fellowship enabled him to preach without having a parish. Insofar as it is well nigh impossible to be demoted from an Oxford fellowship, this meant that he could "look upon the world as his parish" without the need for incumbency in an actual parish. When he was granted the fellowship this consideration was, of course, far from his mind. In later years it would prove to be important.

Oxford enabled Wesley to train his keen intellect and to build up his formidable mind. Throughout his life, he was to retain a curiosity about many divergent subjects and in later years he would continue to investigate new areas of thought. To these he brought a logical, reasoning mind that was sharpened at Oxford by his teaching of Greek and philosophy, and above all by his (at one stage) daily leading of disputations among the undergraduates. This enabled him to pierce quickly to the heart of a complicated sequence of thoughts, and this habit would remain with him.

In the course of time two mistaken impressions have arisen about Wesley's intellectual life. One was that he was, as he described himself, a *homo unius libri*, a man of one book (the Bible), in a literal sense. The other was that he distrusted reason in favor of emotion and that his preaching was aimed at the emotions rather than the intellect. These impressions are at best half-truths and are all the more misleading because there is an element of truth in them. It is true to say that the Bible became and remained the primary source of Wesley's theology and spirituality. Yet his reading on spiritual and nonspiritual matters remained wide. Indeed Green, in an appendix to his book *The Young Mr. Wesley*, spends fourteen pages merely listing the books read by Wesley between 1725 and 1734.[9] When writing became more central to Wesley's endeavors, he covered a vast range of topics in his at-

---

[9]V. H. H. Green, *The Young Mr. Wesley* (London: Edward Arnold, 1961), Appendix I, pp. 305–19. For *homo unius libri* see *Works*, vol. V, p. iii, Preface to *Sermons*.

tempt to transmit not merely spirituality but a basic education to the needy people of the land. His horse, as it were, became his study. He rode with a slack rein and, after the early dangerous persecutions at Wednesbury and elsewhere, he rode in peace, managing to avoid the highwaymen and the potholes that beset other travelers. "History, poetry and philosophy I commonly read on horseback," he wrote in his journal in 1770, "having other employment at other times."[10] The employment during the stops in the journeying was that of leading one of the great religious movements in the history of the Church. In between times he was busy reading and writing, as well as praying. His literary output became truly staggering for one who was the main preacher and organizer of the eighteenth-century religious renewal. His edited works contain—in addition to four volumes of his journal, three volumes of his sermons, two volumes of his letters, and numerous other religious treatises—English, Latin, French, Greek, and Hebrew grammars, the revised and abridged works of numerous authors including the fifty volumes of his *Christian Library*, and volumes entitled *Compendium of Logic, History of England, Dictionary*, and *Compendium of Natural Philosophy*.[11] His occasional papers covered any number of subjects from dew on coach-glasses to popular medicine to pronunciation and gesture to slavery. Oxford gave to Wesley a breadth of intellectual interests that remained with him later and his spirituality, while centered on the Bible, comprehended the need to sustain the mind as well as the soul of man. The secret of his wide-ranging spirituality lay in the fact that he was a "Methodist," methodical in his use of time, so that interiority, preaching, reading, writing, and organizing were attended to in their due order within his overarching purpose of loving and communing with God in all that he did.

The notion that Wesley gave little weight to reason loses credence by a simple reading of any one of his treatises, even the *A Plain Account of Christian Perfection* contained in this volume. Indeed, we may sometimes wish that he had given greater bent to the more irrational and mystical part of his nature. His plain yet majestic prose proceeds inexorably with its succession of logical headings and weighed utterances. In the attention he gave to reason Wesley was in

---

[10] *Works*, vol. III, p. 393, *Journal* for March 21, 1770.

[11] See *Works*. A new *Oxford Edition of Wesley's Works* is being prepared by Dr. Frank Baker of Duke University.

fact a child of the eighteenth century. The crux lies in the use that he made of reason. His concern was not for reason and philosophy for their own sakes. He was not motivated purely by reason, nor was he interested merely in the mental faculties of his fellows. His concern was for the whole personality and he appealed to the emotions and wills of men through the mind. His concern was for biblical theology rather than philosophical theology. His concern was for faith rather than religion as a doctrinal phenomenon, either natural or revealed. As he later put it, "orthodoxy, or right opinions, is at best but a very slender part of religion, if it can be allowed to be any part of it at all."[12] His use of reason was not, then, to philosophize about religion, although he did not despise the efforts of those who, like Bishop Butler, attempted to defend the Christian tradition philosophically. Nor did he spend a great deal of time in explicating the great doctrines of the Christian tradition. He took them for granted and was willing to applaud the work of men such as Jones of Nayland who did uphold, in writing, the doctrine of the Trinity. Belief as such was, for Wesley, a secondary category. His main concern was for spirituality itself, for knowing God in the heart by faith, for practicing the presence of God, for seeking after perfect love. He "believed" the basic Christian doctrines but so, as he put it, did the devils. The point was to put those doctrines into practice in one's life and heart. For Wesley Christianity was not primarily a set of beliefs, it was an experimental way, a process, an inwardness based on orthodox doctrines and resulting in outward practice. Accordingly, his main theological concern was for those doctrines most directly concerned with experiential Christianity, namely prevenient grace, justification by faith, assurance, sanctification, and perfect love. He used his formidable powers of reason to commend experiential Christianity and those doctrines most fitted to apply it within the lives of ordinary men and women. The most notable examples of his use of reason in this way are to be found in his *An Earnest Appeal to Men of Reason and Religion* of 1743 and in the three parts of his *A Farther Appeal to Men of Reason and Religion* of 1745, but the same principle applies throughout his work and he owed his facility in logic to his training at Oxford.

It was at Oxford that Wesley immersed himself in the reading of spiritual writings. It was there too that he heard the call to a life of

---

[12]Orcibal, *Theological Originality*, p. 109.

spirituality. Paradoxically for an Oxford man, he was first influenced by the Cambridge Platonists, Smith and Cudworth, who pointed to an experience of interiority whereby the inward world of spirituality rather than the outward world became one's authentic habitat. More importantly he read Taylor, a Kempis, and William Law. In *A Plain Account of Christian Perfection* he describes how his reading of Bishop Taylor's *Rules and Exercises of Holy Living and Dying* in 1725 led to his seeking for purity of intention by dedicating all his life, thoughts, words, and actions to God. In 1726 a reading of à Kempis' *Christian's Pattern* persuaded him that he must seek after an inward religion of the heart. "I saw that 'simplicity of intention and purity of affection,' *one* design in *all* we speak or do and *one desire* ruling all our tempers, are, indeed, 'the wings of the soul,' without which she can never ascend to the mount of God."[13] A year or two later his grappling with William Law's *Christian Perfection* and *Serious Call* persuaded him of the impossibility of being "half a Christian" and of the need to devote himself wholly to God. This period of growing spiritual seriousness, from 1725–1728, coincided with his entry to the priesthood—he was ordained deacon on September 19, 1725, and priest on September 22, 1728, by Bishop Potter of Oxford.

Discussion has raged as to whether this awakening to the necessity for interiority and dedication constituted Wesley's conversion. Piette and Todd assert that it *was* effectively Wesley's conversion and they are followed by Outler who terms it "a conversion if ever there was one."[14] Much depends, of course, on what we mean by conversion and on whether we feel the need to highlight one precise moment as being determinative for Wesley's spirituality. It was clearly an important stage in his spiritual development and heralded his entry into a life of genuine spirituality. However, it was only one such stage. There were further stages to follow. The most significant point to be made about this episode in Wesley's pilgrimage is that it determined the aim of his life and spirituality. Christian Perfection, perfect love, became and remained Wesley's purpose in following the Christian way. Although the Methodist tradition did not follow him in everything, it attempted to follow him in this. His own purpose was to aim at and to achieve holiness in love, and through him the *grand depositum* of the Methodist tradition became that of scriptural

---

[13]See p. 299.
[14]Outler, *John Wesley*, p. 7.

INTRODUCTION

holiness. It is likely that the goal of perfect love would have remained Wesley's own personal spiritual end; without some of his later spiritual experiences it is unlikely that it would have become the object of the people called Methodists. In this volume we publish Wesley's main thoughts on this subject of perfect love in his *A Plain Account of Christian Perfection, as believed and taught by the Reverend Mr. John Wesley, from the year 1725 to the year 1777.*

Wesley's interest in writings on mysticism and interiority continued throughout his stay in Oxford, and indeed beyond it. His Oxford interest in mysticism extended to include non–British and non–Church of England writers, including the Roman Catholics Pascal, Scupoli, Quesnel, Fénelon, de Renty, Mme Bourignon, Mme Guyon, Tauler, the *Theologica Germanica*, and Molinos with their emphasis upon pure love and total resignation. His later contact with the Moravians made him react for a time against the mystics. As he put it in 1738, "These considerations stole upon me as I grew acquainted with the mystic writers, whose noble descriptions of union with God and internal religion made everything else appear mean, flat, and insipid. But, in truth, they made good works appear so, too; yea, and faith itself, and what not."[15] He later reacted against the Moravians themselves, who took faith and fellowship seriously but who sat loose to the requirements of the means of grace and even outward works in their zeal for inward mystical faith. The extracts in this volume from Wesley's journal for this period illustrate this stage in his development. However, the notion that Wesley suddenly repudiated the mystical influences on his development and abandoned them forever is an erroneous one, just as erroneous as the notion that because he was suspicious of the antinomian tendencies he saw in Luther and Calvin that he therefore abandoned those reformers. He assimilated the things that were helpful to him, and to the movement that grew up as a result of his work, from any and every source. The fifty volumes of his *Christian Library* of 1750–1756 contained no works by Luther and Calvin but they did include the works of five French and three Spanish Roman Catholic mystics, namely, Pascal, Brother Lawrence, Fénelon, Mme Guyon, Mme Bourignon, John of Avila, Lopez, and Molinos. In all, Wesley synthesized and abridged the work of seventeen continental experts in spirituality who were virtually unknown in the Anglo-Saxon world of the eighteenth century. It may

---

[15]See p. 102.

well be, as Orcibal suggests, that he gained help from the work of the Huguenot Poiret, whom he met in 1730 and who had already worked on Mme Bourignon, Mme Guyon, Molinos, Arndt, Nicholas, de Renty, Lopez, Fénelon and Brother Lawrence.[16] The question remains as to why he should bother, at the height of the Methodist Revival, when he had more than enough work to do, to publish unknown spiritual masters if they had not been important for him, and if he did not feel they were important for Christians in Britain. It is reasonable to suggest that mystical considerations were less important for Wesley between 1738 and 1765 when he *was* overwhelmed by the practical superintendency of the early Methodist tradition. Nevertheless, during that period he did publish selections from a number of the mystics, and by that time he had selected and assimilated some of their ideas in such a way that Cell's comment to the effect that Wesley combined the Protestant stress on faith with the Catholic stress on holiness is peculiarly appropriate.[17] The mystical writers we have mentioned played their part in Wesley's reconciliation of the seemingly opposed theological notions of justification, sanctification, and Christian perfection. These were, for Wesley, not merely doctrines but stages in the integral process of spirituality.

In addition to the stipend and ecclesiastical freedom, the logical training and the predisposition to inwardness, gifted to Wesley by Oxford, he also gained much from his leadership of the Holy Club. This group of students had formed around Charles Wesley to engage in Bible study, systematic devotions, and regular communion—and to investigate studiously, and to analyze the implications of, the works of the fourth-century monastic fathers and the liturgical practices of the early Church. After John's return to Oxford in 1729 he assumed leadership of this group. Vulgar nicknames were given to this serious-minded fellowship of people who were keen about religious practices. The one that stuck was the name "Methodist."

It is fascinating to record, in passing, how the names of famous religious traditions have come into being. Some have arisen descriptively: "Hindu" was the name given to the people who lived over the Indus in India, "Shinto" was derived from the Chinese *Shen-Tao* to signify in Japanese the "Way of the gods." Others have arisen as

---

[16]See Orcibal, *Theological Originality*, p. 111.
[17]G. C. Cell, *The Rediscovery of John Wesley* (New York: Henry Holt & Co., 1935), p. 361.

terms of abuse that later become terms of honor, such as "Christianoi," given to the Christians in Antioch; "Quakers," given to that group in 1650, and "Methodists" given to the Holy Club in Oxford.

It was in this Methodist environment of the Holy Club that Wesley learnt to be methodical not just in his study of the Bible but in the discipline of his whole life. The secret of his spirituality lay in his careful and prayerful use of time. It was his methodical habits consecrated to God that later enabled him to accomplish so much. Within the Holy Club he led a disciplined personal life, visited the prisoners in Oxford gaol, showed concern for the debtors, helped start a school, went to the relief of the poor, discovered he could live on £28 a year, and maintained a high-church stance in regard to the sacraments, the fasts of the church, confession, penance, and mortification. Together with the study of the mystics mentioned above, Wesley also more importantly entered on a serious study of the early Fathers with the help of a Patristics student named Clayton, who was a fellow-member of the Holy Club. His concern was not merely with the pre-Nicene Fathers but also with "St. Chrysostom, Basil, Jerome, Austin, and, above all, the man of a broken heart, Ephraim Syrus."[18] In other words, Wesley immersed himself not only in the Western Fathers but above all in the Eastern Fathers. His spirituality was influenced by Protestant, Catholic, and Eastern Christianity. His two heroes were Ephraim Syrus and Macarius the Egyptian, and Outler and Jaeger have shown that the *Homilies of Macarius*, extracted by Wesley for his *Christian Library*, were in fact written by a fifth-century Syrian monk who was deeply influenced by one of the greatest Eastern monks and writers on perfection, Gregory of Nyssa.[19] By returning to the early Fathers, especially Gregory of Nyssa through Macarius, Wesley was able to feast his soul with the treasures of the early Eastern Church before the medieval split between East and West had imposed a Latin captivity on the West. In the extract in our volume from Wesley's letter to Middleton immediately following *A Plain Account of Genuine Christianity*, he applauds the primitive Fathers "Clemens Romanus, Ignatius, Polycarp, Justin Martyr, Irenaeus, Origen, Clemens Alexandrinus, Cyprian; to whom I would add Macarius and Ephraim Syrus." "I exceedingly reverence them," he writes, "as well as their writings, and esteem them highly in love. I reverence them, because

---

[18]See *Address to the Clergy, Works*, vol. X, p. 484.
[19]See Outler, *John Wesley*, pp. 9–10.

they were Christians, such Christians as are above described. And I reverence their writings, because they describe true, genuine Christianity, and direct us to the strongest evidence of the Christian doctrine."[20] From this source Wesley discovered and marked that true holiness was not merely consecration of the will as à Kempis suggested, it was not merely inward quietism as Mme Guyon and Molinos (and later the Moravians) suggested, it was active, lived holiness in the Church and in the world. Wesley's reaction to the continental Catholic mystics from 1738–1765 was not matched by a similar reaction to the early Fathers, whom he continued to revere as interpreters of, rather than determiners of, scripture.

The Holy Club set Wesley's search for and study of holiness within a social context. For him spirituality, though inward, was not a solitary thing. Indeed, in *A Short History of the People Called Methodists*, he stated bluntly that "the first rise of Methodism, so called, was in November 1729, when four of us met together at Oxford."[21] He felt that fellowship was vital to Christian spirituality and that there was no such thing as a solitary Christian.

The Holy Club also set Wesley's search for holiness within a *total* social context. As he put it, "In 1730 I began visiting the prisons, assisting the poor and sick in town, and doing what other good I could by my presence or my little fortune to the bodies and souls of all men."[22] As we shall see later, in the context of the eighteenth century, he was to become an eminent social reformer and he was not slow to stress that inward holiness of the heart had necessarily to find fruit in outward works and social involvement of one sort or another. Wesley's life-style in later times remained consistent with his Holy Club ideal of living on £28 a year. In our ecological age, when the rich of the world continue to get richer and the poor poorer, Wesley may have a message for us not only in regard to inward spirituality but also in regard to outward Christian life-styles. For him spirituality was both outward and inward.

The Holy Club also set Wesley's spirituality within a liturgical context. The members of the Club agreed to communicate as often as they could, to observe the fasts of the ancient Church every Wednesday and Friday, and to attend seriously to the means of grace and to

---

[20]See p. 133.

[21]*Works*, vol. XIII, p. 273.

[22]See p. 103.

the liturgy of the Church. Although Wesley's high-churchmanship somewhat abated in later life, he retained his love for the means of grace and for the liturgy of the Church of England. In his great sermon *Means of Grace,* he was later to write, "By 'means of grace,' I understand outward signs, words, or actions, ordained of God and appointed for this end, to be the ordinary channels whereby he might convey to man, preventing, justifying, or sanctifying grace.... The chief of these means are prayer, whether in secret or with the great congregation; searching the scriptures, and receiving the Lord's Supper."[23] After 1738, John Wesley remained a high-churchman in his stress on the sacraments, especially that of the Lord's Supper. In 1740, one of the great years of the Revival, he communicated twice a week and about a hundred times during the year. He later published the sermon *The Duty of Constant Communion.*[24] He insisted that the times of the Methodist services should be kept separate from the times of parish communion services so that all the early Methodists could attend communion dispensed by a minister of the Church of England.

Throughout his life, Wesley nourished his devotion by means of the Book of Common Prayer of the Church of England. This provided the liturgical framework for his spirituality. After the American War of Independence, when it was clear that new arrangements would have to be made to speak to the new situation of the American Methodists, Wesley drew up for them a liturgy that was essentially an abridged version of the Book of Common Prayer. In a letter dated September 10, 1784, taken to America by Coke, Wesley wrote,

> And I have prepared a Liturgy little differing from that of the Church of England (I think the best constituted National Church in the world), which I advise all the travelling preachers to use on the Lord's Day in all the congregations, reading the Litany only on Wednesdays and Fridays and praying extempore on all other days. I also advise the elders to administer the Supper of the Lord on every Lord's Day.[25]

---

[23] *Works,* vol. V, pp. 187–88, Sermon XVI.

[24] *Works,* vol. VII, pp. 147–57, Sermon CI. See also J. C. Bowmer, *The Sacrament of the Lord's Supper in Early Methodism* (London: Epworth, 1951).

[25] See *Works,* vol. XIII, p. 252.

INTRODUCTION

There was no need in the America of 1784 to adhere to the Church of England as it was clear that the American Methodists were destined to become a separate body. The letter represented Wesley's convictions. The American Methodists remain to this day more liturgical than the British Methodists, and both bodies have strayed from Wesley's ideal of constant communion. It became an ideal during his Holy Club days at Oxford, and the ideal persisted throughout his ministry.

Wesley had learned much from the Holy Club, but he was not fated to remain in Oxford, nor to succeed his father at Epworth after his father's death in 1735. Instead the opportunity arose for the Holy Club to move its sphere of activities to Georgia, and Charles and John Wesley and Ingham from the club, together with Delamotte, took ship for America to missionize the Indians and the Georgian colonists. George Whitefield of the Holy Club promised to follow after ordination. To Georgia, Wesley took a piety that was real, but not yet truly effective, sacramental and liturgical principles that were admirable but somewhat high church, a desire for social involvement as part of a total spirituality, and a willingness to abandon himself fully to God and to seek after perfect love. As we look back on the development of Wesley's spirituality, we see that from 1725–1729 he had realized the necessity of devoting himself wholly to God and had begun the spiritual and mental preparation to make this possible; from 1729–1735 he had engaged in a disciplined life of liturgical, sacramental, social, and communal involvement in the Holy Club that enabled him to begin to actualize some of his aspirations after perfect love. Three of the extracts in our volume illustrate his spirituality at this period: his Oxford *Scheme of Self-Examination*, the preface and two selections from *Forms of Prayer* of 1733, and his advice on spiritual reading, adapted from the Cologne *Praemonitio ad Lectorem* of 1682, inserted in 1735 within his preface to the translation of Thomas à Kempis' *Imitation of Christ*. These are not mere period pieces, and the advice on spiritual reading illustrates his approach not just to à Kempis but to all the masters of the spiritual life.

Hitherto, Wesley had led a fairly cloistered life at Epworth, or at school, or at Oxford. The parameters within which his spirituality had developed had been well defined, and he had been able to impose his own pattern on that development under God. His decision to go to Georgia was a leap into the unknown. It would have been more understandable if he had gone to Georgia earlier, as his father had desired. It would have been more logical if he had stayed in England, or even succeeded his father at Epworth, when his mother became a widow. Instead, three weeks after that tragic event, he was away to Georgia to attempt to deepen his spirituality in new circumstances and to discover his life's work. The bare facts of his Georgian expedition are printed in the records of the colony: "Minister at Savannah; embark'd 14 Oct. 1735; arrived Feb. 1735–6; run away 3 Dec. 1737."[26] They appear to constitute a débacle. In reality they represent a period of bewilderment and spiritual seeking after the relative repose of his earlier discipline during which he was able to explore more fully his own self and the will of God for his life.

Wesley took with him to Georgia an enlightenment view of the American Indians as "noble savages." Although impressed on occasions, he generally found that they conformed more to Hobbes's view of human nature as being "nasty, brutish, and short." In fact, he spent more of his time with the colonists at Savannah. His good work there was marred by the unsuitability to the context of his high-church principles, and by the souring of his amorous entanglement with Sophia Hopkey. Yet when he finally did "run away" from Georgia to escape legal action, it had contributed much to his spiritual development. It was here that he began to condense a number of mystical works; it was here that he began the theological work on the Old and New Testaments that would bear fruit later; it was here that he experimented with some of the features of his later organization including societies, bands, lay leaders, extempore prayer and preaching, love feasts, and chapel buildings; it was here that he learned German and beautifully translated a number of German hymns.

This translation work, and his contact with the Moravians who taught him German, were crucial to Wesley's spiritual development. Through them he encountered a faith that was fearless, joyful, and inwardly felt and known. During the voyage to America on the *HMS Simmonds*, they sang during a violent storm and were not afraid to die. The Moravian Spangenberg put to Wesley the challenging questions, "Do you know Jesus Christ?" and "Does the Spirit bear witness with your spirit?" Wesley replied in the affirmative, but knew that his words were vain. In particular, the Moravians put Wesley into con-

---

[26]E. M. Coulter and A. B. Saye, eds., *A List of the Early Settlers of Georgia* (Athens, Georgia, 1949), p. 57.

tact with the German language and some of the greatest German pietist hymns. Wesley's superb translations of thirty-three of those hymns have become justly honored within Anglo-Saxon spiritual hymnody, and they were also important in his own spiritual progress. Six of his translations are included in this volume. And so, at this period in his spiritual burgeoning, Wesley was wrestling with the German and translating into fluent English verses such as these:[27]

Jesu, to thee my heart I bow;
Strange flames far from my soul remove;
Fairest among ten thousand thou,
Be thou my Lord, my Life, my Love.
                    (Zinzendorf)

O Jesu, source of calm repose,
Thy like nor man nor angel knows,
Fairest among ten thousand fair!
Even those whom death's sad fetters bound,
Whom thickest darkness compass'd round,
Find light and life, if thou appear.
                    (Freylinghausen)

Close by thy side still may I keep,
Howe'er life's various currents flow;
With steadfast eye mark every step,
And follow thee where'er thou go.
                    (Richter)

Savior, where'er thy steps I see,
Dauntless, untired I follow thee:
Oh, let thy hand support me still,
And lead me to thy holy hill.
                    (Zinzendorf)

Shall I, for fear of feeble man,
Thy Spirit's course in me restrain?

---

[27]See J. L. Nuelsen, *John Wesley and the German Hymn*, trans. T. Parry, S. H. Moore, and A. Holbrook), Hymns 2, 3, 4, 8, 10, 15, 16, 18, 23, 24, 32, (Holbrook, Calverley, 1972), pp. 111–61.

INTRODUCTION

Or, undismay'd in deed and word
Be a true witness to my Lord?
(Winckler)

Jesu, thy boundless love to me
No thought can reach, no tongue declare:
Oh, knit my thankful heart to thee,
And reign without a rival there.
Thine wholly, thine alone I am:
Be thou alone my constant flame.
(Gerhardt)

O God, of good the unfathom'd Sea,
Who would not give his heart to thee?
Who would not love thee with his might?
O Jesu, Lover of mankind,
Who would not his whole soul and mind
With all his strength to thee unite?
(Scheffler)

Be heaven even now our soul's abode,
Hid be our life with Christ in God,
Our spirit, Lord, be one with thine:
Let all our works in thee be wrought,
And fill'd with thee be all our thought,
Till in us thy full likeness shine.
(Zinzendorf)

My Savior, how shall I proclaim,
How pay the mighty debt I owe?
Let all I have, and all I am
Ceaseless to all thy glory show.
(Gerhardt)

Hence our hearts melt, our eyes o'erflow,
Our words are lost: nor will we know,
Nor will we think of aught beside
"My Lord, my Love is crucified."
(Anna Nitschmann)

INTRODUCTION

What can we offer our good Lord
(Poor nothings!) for his boundless grace?
Fain would we his great name record,
And worthily set forth his praise.
Dear Object of our growing love,
To whom our more than all we owe,
Open the Fountain from above,
And let it our full soul o'erflow.

(Spangenberg)

We do not know why Wesley chose thirty-three particular hymns to translate out of all the possibilities open to him, but it is fair to assume that he chose them both on the basis of their inherent merit as hymns and also because of their relevance to his own need. He first heard them in 1735 and finished translating them in 1737; his involvement in them was relatively brief in respect of time. Nevertheless, through the excellence of his selections and the caliber of his translations he enriched Anglo-Saxon spirituality and opened up the prospect of a new cross-fertilization between German and Anglo-Saxon piety. He realized the potential significance of hymnody as a resource for spirituality, and prepared the way for his brother Charles to make a far deeper contribution to this medium of spiritual nurture. He also spoke to his own soul. His grappling with the words of these hymns, with their notions of praise, love, faith, surrender, prayer, joy, and assurance, set him on the road to the seeking of a new inner dynamic that would creatively integrate all his other gifts. The future ingredients of his life and spirituality were already present: mysticism and inner religion, a liturgical and sacramental framework, a penchant for organization, a desire for social involvement, a seeking after perfect love. His contact with the Moravians provided the spark of an inner dynamic that was to bring out his gifts, and he became persuaded that justification by faith and living by faith were not merely doctrinal notions but could become inward realities.

The final and decisive Moravian influence was that of Peter Böhler, who guided Wesley in London between February 7 and May 4, 1738. The trauma of the flight from Georgia had heightened Wesley's desire to experience inwardly a sense of trust and confidence in God. Both he and Charles, who had also returned bewildered from Georgia, needed some resolution concerning the future direction of

INTRODUCTION

their outward lives. They needed to ascertain the will of God for them. They needed some relief from their inner and outer uncertainty. Böhler convinced Wesley that inward peace was graspable. On February 18 he said, "My brother, my brother, that philosophy of yours must be purged away." On March 4 he said, "Preach faith till you have it; and then because you have it, you will preach faith." He then produced witnesses to persuade Wesley that it was possible to experience an inner assurance of faith. Now Wesley's search for an inner trust and reliance on God was in dynamic process. His brother Charles realized this experience on May 21, 1738. On May 24, John opened his New Testament at the words of 2 Peter 1, verse four, "There are given unto us exceeding great and precious promises, even that ye should be partakers of the divine nature." The afternoon anthem at St. Paul's was "Out of the deep have I called unto Thee." In the evening he went "unwillingly" to a society in Aldersgate Street where someone was reading Luther's preface to the Epistle to the Romans. His journal summarizes succinctly and brilliantly what happened: "About a quarter before nine while he was describing the change that God works in the heart through faith in Christ, I felt my heart strangely warmed. I felt I did trust in Christ, Christ alone for my salvation; and an assurance was given me that He had taken away *my* sins, even *mine*, and saved *me* from the law of sin and death." The extracts from Wesley's *Journal* included in this volume catalog the details of the preceding events in Wesley's own words.[28]

A number of inaccurate myths have grown up in relation to the Aldersgate Street experience of John Wesley. The two main ones are that of Piette, who tends to undervalue it by comparison with Wesley's "conversion" of 1725, and that of a traditional strand within the Methodist tradition, which tends to overvalue it by denigrating what had gone before and by isolating it from a cluster of other experiences realized by Wesley in 1738–1739. The truth would appear to lie somewhere in the middle. It is difficult to underestimate the importance of the Aldersgate experience. As Wesley put it, before it he had been sometimes if not often conquered, after it he was always the conqueror. Doubts and problems would continue, but from now on he was always master of them. And it is plain matter of fact that his effectiveness as a Christian leader increased after this time out of all recognition. From being the Georgia stumbler, he eventually became the

---

[28]See pp. 105–107.

leader of the revival. On the other hand, except in this celebrated journal entry, Wesley himself did not stress the Aldersgate Street event. In the *Plain Account of Christian Perfection*, Wesley leaps straight from Georgia to his visit to the Moravians in Germany, completely omitting his experience of May 24, 1738. He does the same in his *Short History of the People Called Methodists*, wherein he traces what he calls "the three rises of Methodism" not to Aldersgate Street but to the Holy Club in November 1729, to Savannah in April 1736 "when twenty or thirty persons met at my house," and to London on May 1, 1738, "when forty or fifty of us agreed to meet together every Wednesday evening, in order to a free conversation, begun and ended with singing and prayer."[29]

In fact, the rise of Methodism as a distinctive tradition did not immediately succeed the Aldersgate experience. There is a sense in which, eighteen days later, on June 11, Wesley preached what may be construed as the opening salvo of the Methodist movement at St. Mary's Oxford in his sermon *Salvation by Faith*, which he termed "the rock and foundation of the Christian religion."[30] However, in the summer of 1738 he disappeared to Germany in order to visit the Moravian leader Zinzendorf at Herrnhut. He benefited from the opportunity to observe the organization, the Christian education, the classes and bands, the love feasts, the watch nights, and the hymn singing of the Moravians. As yet, though, he was still an observer rather than a leader. When he returned to England, he happened to read an account of the striking results of the preaching of Jonathan Edwards in Northampton New England in 1737. He was deeply impressed by the fruits of Edwards's preaching if not by his high Calvinistic theology.[31] In spite of his debt to the Moravians, he was beginning to have doubts about their quietism, and these doubts came to a head during the course of a number of disputes that arose in the Fetter Lane Society to which Wesley belonged. It seemed to Wesley that in their zeal for justification by faith the Moravians were not sufficiently emphasizing the need to attend to the means of grace and the

---

[29] *Works*, vol. XIII, p. 307.

[30] *Works*, vol. V, p. 15.

[31] See *Journal* for October 9, 1738, in *Works*, vol. I, p. 160. Wesley later extracted and published *A Faithful Narrative of the Surprising Work of God in the Conversion of Many Hundred Souls in Northampton . . . in New England*, and later still four other works by Jonathan Edwards.

obligation to engage in good works. This led him to examine again the homilies of the Church of England that expounded justification by faith.[32] He found his own view confirmed therein and he finally separated from the Fetter Lane Society. His spirituality had been deeply influenced by the Moravian stress on the inwardness of faith, but now the cord was snapped and the danger that he too would so emphasize faith as to diminish works, the means of grace, and perfect love was gone at last.

Finally, on March 29, 1739, he set out for Bristol in response to a letter from George Whitefield asking Wesley to deputize for him in Bristol while he visited America. Whitefield's preaching had begun to produce results similar to those of Jonathan Edwards. Wesley rode to Bristol in fear and trembling, realizing that for the first time he would have to preach deliberately in the open air without the benefit of a church building. On April 2, as he put it, "I submitted to be more vile, and proclaimed in the highways the glad tidings of salvation, speaking from a little eminence in a ground adjoining to the city, to about three thousand people."[33] His text was an appropriate one, "The Spirit of the Lord is upon me, because He has anointed me to preach the gospel to the poor: He has sent me to heal the brokenhearted, to preach deliverance to the captives, and recovery of sight to the blind, to set at liberty them that are bruised, to preach the acceptable year of the Lord." His preaching was successful—to Wesley's surprise and joy. The events at Bristol and his text were symbolic for the future. This marked the real beginning of the Methodist movement qua movement. It was the final episode in a sequence of spiritual events that had led Wesley from Aldersgate Street to St. Mary's Church Oxford to Germany to Jonathan Edwards to the synergism of the Anglican Homilies and finally to Bristol. From now on, John Wesley's spirituality would be inextricably bound up with that of the Methodist tradition. This is not to say that Wesley aimed to impose his own spirituality on the Methodist movement. It is doubtful whether any great religious leader has consciously founded a religious movement. Rather he was ready to respond to the call of God, and as an indirect result a great religious movement came into being. His past experiences clicked into place. He went out like Abraham,

---

[32]*Journal* for November 12, 1738, in *Works*, vol. I, p. 164.
[33]*Journal* for April 2, 1739, in *Works*, vol. I, p. 185.

INTRODUCTION

not knowing where he was going, but willing to adapt his methods to a dynamic, evolving situation. Inevitably, within this process, Wesley's own spirituality was crucial within the evolution of the movement that he was to lead.

The year 1739 represents a watershed in the development of Wesley's spirituality. Up to this time, he had been learning from others. From now on, although he continued to learn, others would be far more influenced by him. In 1725 he had heard the call to a deeper spiritual life; in 1729 he had led a band of Oxford men who together, in sheltered circumstances, sought after perfect love; in 1735 he had gone into the wilderness—almost literally in Georgia, symbolically in his soul—to ascertain God's will for the future and to do some good in the present; in 1738–1739 he discovered an inner dynamic that fused together the other elements in his interior life, and an outward role that would enable him to convey his own spirituality to others. The rest of his life was basically the story of how Wesley endeavored under God to communicate his personal spirituality to countless thousands of others.

At this point, it is appropriate to reintroduce Charles Wesley into our narrative. It would be unnecessary labor to examine minutely the development of his spirituality, which had followed the general course taken by that of his brother. Charles had studied at, and become head boy of, Westminster School, whereas John had gone to Charterhouse. Charles had been offered the opportunity of leaving his own family and becoming the heir of a relative in Ireland. He had rejected the chance, which had gone instead to a Wellesley who became a forefather of the Duke of Wellington. Charles had become a student then a lecturer at Christ Church Oxford, and the first leader of the Holy Club before the return of his brother in 1729. They had both gone out to Georgia, John to Savannah, and Charles to be secretary to Oglethorpe, the leading spirit in the new plantation. Charles quit Georgia before John in July 1736 and he arrived home without any resolution of his inner spiritual need for a personal assurance of faith and of his vocational need for a set direction for his ministry. On May 21, 1738, three days before his brother, he received an inward assurance of faith. Influenced by Luther's commentary on Galatians, he heard an inward voice asking him to arise and believe, and through the medium of interior words such as these and scripture passages such as Isaiah 40, verse 1, "Comfort ye, comfort ye, my people, says your God," he found a new inner dynamic.[34] He also found a new vocation, for he felt compelled to put his experience into the words of a hymn. Although famous, it is not one of the best of his hymns. Nor, indeed, was it the first, for Mrs. Oglethorpe mentions hymns he had written in Georgia. Yet it pointed to a latent gift for hymnody that had been uncovered by this new development in his spirituality. Like John, he was destined to preach, undergo persecution, organize, and travel in the course of his work, but the main thrust of his spirituality lay in the hymns that now began to pour from his pen. And this particular hymn, although rough-hewn, symbolizes more clearly than the related events in John's life the possibilities that were to follow. He marvels at the grace of God for him, "Where shall my wondering soul begin? How shall I all to heaven aspire?" he asks. "O how shall I the goodness tell, Father, which thou to me has showed?" he continues. He knows that the grace of God that he has found is available to all men, especially those in greatest need.

> Outcasts of men, to you I call,
> Harlots, and publicans, and thieves!
> He spreads his arms to embrace you all:
> Sinners alone his grace receive;
> No need of him the righteous have;
> He came the lost to seek and save.

"He calls you now, invites you home; Come, O my guilty brethren, come!" he cries.[35] The personalism, the adoring wonder, the immediacy, the universal invitation that were to be characteristics of the early Methodist movement are already present in this poetic composition of Charles Wesley. On this day he was writing a hymn for himself. Before long he would be writing for a wider audience.

What then was the religious stage onto which the Wesleys were about to enter with dynamic force? New towns were growing up in the north of England largely bereft of spiritual sustenance. At the be-

---

[34]See W. F. Lofthouse, *Charles Wesley,* in *A History of the Methodist Church in Britain,* vol. I (London: Epworth, 1965), pp. 115–44. See also *The Journal of the Rev. Charles Wesley,* M.A., ed. T. Jackson, vol. I (London, 1849), pp. 92–123.

[35]See Hymn 29 in the 1780 *Hymnbook;* Hymn 361 in *The Methodist Hymnbook* (London: Methodist Publishing House, 1933).

ginning of the eighteenth century, Manchester had 8,000 inhabitants; by the end of the century it would have 95,000 people within its boundaries. Churches and ministers were not present to meet the growing needs. When Fletcher later went to Madeley he found himself in an area of Shropshire where Darby of Coalbrookdale was heralding the rise of the Industrial Revolution, and where he would be able to marvel at the first iron bridge in the world. Over in Wales William Williams would write the famous hymn "Guide me, O Thou great Jehovah, Pilgrim through this barren land," as an allegory of the Christian pilgrimage but also as a prophetic vision of the beautiful Rhondda valley soon to be scarred by the outward signs of a new economic and social situation. While the psychological and social face of Britain changed, religious slumber prevailed.

The Church of England was not lacking in good or even great men as once was thought. Norman Sykes and others have portrayed the faithfulness of many ministers in different places, men who (like Samuel Wesley) labored silently and unsung.[36] The problem lay rather in the structure of the church. The Convocation had not met since 1717, nor was it destined to meet again until 1855. There was no central body to think strategically for the church. There was no structural potentiality for concerted action on any matter, not least on the question of how to utilize the Wesleys, as the medieval Church had utilized Saint Francis. The bishops spent months at the House of Lords yet lacked the power to effect meaningful change. Dioceses and parishes tended to go their separate ways and to act congregationally rather than regionally or nationally. They existed mainly in southern England away from the growing areas of population. The whole of America was hypothetically directly under the influence of the Bishop of London.

The problem lay also in the ineffectual spirituality of the church. Fine brains battled with the opponents of the church, but on the opponents' terms. Attention was focused on the heavenly city of the eighteenth-century philosophers, namely earth. Nature, creation, the Divine Reason, the existence of God, and religion provided the material for discussion at the expense of inner, experiential concerns. Archbishop Herring's visitation returns for 1743 give the impression

---

[36]See, for example, N. Sykes, *Church and State in England in the Eighteenth Century*, Historical Association Pamphlet 78 (Cambridge, 1934).

of a band of not unworthy ministers attempting to fulfill their work according to the standards of their day.[37] The trouble was that the standards of 1743 were not noted for inwardness or spirituality. Into this situation rode the Wesleys, inwardly equipped, and outwardly ready in the case of John, to ride a quarter of a million miles to preach the unsearchable riches of Christ. They came not just as evangelists, although they were certainly that, but also as conveyors of an integral spirituality. Their evangelism was part of their spirituality.

From 1739 onward, it is impossible to analyze the spirituality of the Wesleys without examining their role in the Methodist Revival. In preference to giving a history of the early Methodist movement, I intend to interpret their spirituality by reference to the other groups within the eighteenth-century renewal. Earlier Methodists tended to assume that the Methodist Revival began at Aldersgate Street and that the whole movement was led by John Wesley. We have seen that the first claim is inaccurate, and the same is true of the second. We can understand better the achievement and spirituality of the Wesleys by analyzing their place within the whole spectrum of the revival.

In fact there were five main streams within the revival, and also five somewhat differing interpretations of spirituality. All of them agreed on the basic question of justification by faith, but they differed in other ways. The first group was that led by the Wesleys themselves, and we will examine the spirituality of this group as we briefly investigate the others. The towering stature of the Wesleys has tended to obscure the fact of the four other separate, if related, groups, which contributed by their divergence to the continuing evolution of the Wesleys' spirituality. The hymns, journals, letters, treatises, sermons and tracts that from now on encapsulated the spirituality of the Wesleys were not written in a vacuum. They emerged as catalysts and responses within a dynamic situation within which the Wesleys were the dominant but not the only factor.

The first of the other four groups within the revival was the Moravians themselves. We have noted their positive influence on the Wesleys from 1735–1738, and from 1739 onward they continued to be an influence, but in a more negative fashion. They did not immediately decline after the defection of the Wesleys but continued as a vig-

---

[37]S. L. Ollard and P. C. Walker, *Archbishop Herring's Visitation Returns*, vol. I, 1743, p. XVIIII.

orous group. Indeed, after the Wesleys had left the Fetter Lane Society, Moravian influence in England increased rather than the reverse, and for the next fifteen years their influence spread in different parts of the land. One of Wesley's most famous early lay preachers, John Cennick, was ordained by Böhler in September 1749 and it was by no means clear to anyone alive in 1750 that the future lay with the Wesleys rather than with the Moravians.

The Moravians' theology tended toward quietism—being quiet before God, and leaving everything to God. They also had the habit of referring in a somewhat sentimental way to the intimate details of Christ's death on the cross. The Wesleys reacted, in their spirituality, to all these facets of the Moravian tradition. They interpreted justification by faith, which they had learned experientially from the Moravians, through the medium of the Church of England homilies, liturgy, and sacraments. They acknowledged the primacy of God's grace, but insisted that man must respond to the prevenient grace of God in the process of leaving all to God. They stressed the means of grace and active involvement in the world over against the quietism of the Moravians. John Wesley had already modified the sentimentality of Moravian descriptions of the death of Christ in his translations of their hymns, for example by reducing the nineteen verses of Zinzendorf's "Jesu, to Thee my heart I bow" to six, and he was a constant influence for good in insisting on the poetic propriety of Charles Wesley's hymns, even to the extent of criticizing the "sentimentality" of one of Charles's greatest hymns, "Jesu, Lover of my soul, Let me to Thy bosom fly." The spirituality of Charles Wesley's hymns was influenced positively and negatively by the Moravians. This is brought out in the preface and selection of hymns from the 1780 hymnbook that we use in this volume. As John puts it in the preface, "Here are, allow me to say, both the purity, the strength, and the elegance of the English language; and, at the same time, the utmost simplicity and plainness, suited to every capacity." However, "That which is of infinitely more moment than the spirit of poetry is the spirit of piety," and John commends the hymnbook as a means of quickening the spirit of devotion, of confirming faith, of enlivening hope, and of kindling and increasing love to God and man.[38] It has amply fulfilled this task during the intervening years. It has done this by including the Moravian assurance of faith and the Moravian pas-

---

[38]See pp. 176–177.

sion within its integral spirituality, while avoiding the Moravian sentimentality and infelicity of language.

In 1745 Charles Wesley's *Hymns on the Lord's Supper* was first published with a preface extracted by John Wesley from Dean Brevint's *Christian Sacrament and Sacrifice*. We include some of the hymns in this volume, and they too were occasioned partly by the Wesleys' reaction against Moravian quietism. During the same period, Charles Wesley also wrote a number of hymns on the great festivals of the Church, including the celebrated "Hark! the Herald-Angels Sing" and "Christ the Lord Is Risen Today." This corpus of hymns assumed the background of the liturgical year and sacramental practice of the Church of England and was not included in the 1780 hymnbook, which stressed the distinctive spirituality of the Methodist movement. We include in this volume a number of Charles Wesley's hymns from the 1876 supplement to the 1780 hymnbook, including some on the great festivals of the Church. We do this to illustrate the development whereby, after the Wesleys' attempt to keep the Methodist movement within the Church of England had posthumously failed, the various Methodist churches felt constrained to include, in their hymnbooks, hymns on the sacraments and festivals that had been written originally to speak to the Church of England context. In general, the later Methodists paid less attention to the sacramental hymns than did the Anglicans, and the Church of England paid less attention to the hymns in the 1780 book than did the Methodists. The Wesleys themselves combined a mutual stress on sacramental and evangelical spirituality. They contributed toward a sacramental revival within the Church of England that was later commented on by the High Anglicans, as well as to the evangelical revival in all the churches. We will glance briefly at some of the aspects of the sacramental spirituality of Charles Wesley's hymns, which were in themselves a partial reaction to the Moravian quietism.

The first part of *Hymns on the Lord's Supper* consists of twenty-seven hymns (of which we selected three) that look at the Eucharist as a memorial of the sufferings and death of Christ; the second part consists of sixty-five hymns (of which we selected thirteen) that look at it as a sign and means of grace; the third part consists of twenty-three hymns (of which we selected three) that look at it as a pledge of heaven; the fourth part consists of twelve hymns (of which we selected two) that look at it as a sacrifice; the fifth part consists of thirty hymns (of which we selected two) that look at it as involving a sacrifice of our persons; and the final part, which consists of nine hymns, concentrates on the postcommunion period. The final hymn of Wesley's (our second selection from part six) is an extraordinary composition, extending to twenty-two verses [97].[39] In it Charles looks back to the golden age of the early Church during which, he suggests, communion was partaken every day.

> In holy fellowship they lived,
> Nor would from the commandment move
> But every joyful day received
> The tokens of expiring love.

He goes on to suggest that the beauty of the lives of the early Christians was influenced by their eucharistic practice.

> Throughout their spotless lives was seen
> The virtue of this heavenly food;
> Superior to the sons of men,
> They soared aloft and walked with God.

The sacramental food also sustained them in death.

> Strong in the strength herewith received,
> And mindful of the Crucified,
> His confessors for him they lived,
> For him his faithful martyrs died.

What then has happened, he mourns, to the Church of the eighteenth century?

> Why is the faithful seed decreased,
> The life of God extinct and dead?
> The daily sacrifice is ceased,
> And charity to heaven is fled.

He longs for the return of sacramental seriousness, not merely for the sake of the "faithful seed" but also for its cosmic significance for the world.

---

[39] See Hymn 97. Hymn numbers are henceforth indicated in square brackets.

Return and with thy servants sit,
Lord of the sacramental feast;
And satiate us with heavenly meat,
And make the *world* thy happy guest.

The sacrament is an anticipation not only of heaven but also of the millennium on earth.

Erect thy tabernacle here,
The *New Jerusalem* send down,
Thy standard in the heavens display,
And bring the joy which ne'er shall end.

This is a remarkable example in a series of impressive hymns of eucharistic devotion. They cross ecclesiastical boundaries, and as the Roman Catholic layman Todd writes, "the great majority of Charles's hymns on the Eucharist could be sung in a Catholic church."[40]

The predominant note sounded by Charles is that of the joyful presence of the Lord among his people at his own supper.

We need not now go up to heaven,
To bring the long-sought Savior down;
Thou are to all already given,
Thou dost even now thy banquet crown:
To every faithful soul appear,
And show thy real presence here. [92]

The words "real presence" are not used in any polemical sense. It was a plain statement of eucharistic fact that the Lord's Supper was a means of grace whereby one could know the presence of the risen Christ. On occasion the stress is on the Holy Spirit's bringing Christ's presence to the congregation.

Come, thou Witness of his dying,
Come, Remembrancer Divine,
Let us feel thy power applying
Christ to every soul and mine. [74]

---

[40]Todd, *John Wesley and the Catholic Church*, p. 148.

INTRODUCTION

On occasion the emphasis is on the Spirit's presence in the elements.

> Come, Holy Ghost, thine influence shed,
> And realize the sign;
> Thy life infuse into the bread,
> Thy power into the wine. [85]

It is not so much a matter of theology, it is a question of spirituality.

The same is true of Charles's references to the sacrifice of Christ in the Eucharist. The philosophical or theological nature of the sacrifice is not his concern; he is joyfully aware that Christ has died sacrificially for all men and that in the Lord's Supper this is personally and poignantly obvious.

> With solemn faith we offer up,
> And spread before thy glorious eyes
> That only ground of all our hope,
> That precious bleeding Sacrifice,
> Which brings thy grace on sinners down,
> And perfects all our souls in one. [93]

In response to the sacrifice of Christ, the Christian sacrifices himself to God in the Eucharist.

> Our souls and bodies we resign,
> With joy we render thee
> Our all, no longer ours, but thine
> Through all eternity. [58]

There is a sense too in which the corporate sacrifice of the Church is united to Christ's own sacrifice and offered up by him to God.

> With him, the Cornerstone,
> The living stones conjoin;
> Christ and his church are one
> One body and one vine;
> For us he uses all his powers,
> And all he has, or is, is ours. [94]

31

INTRODUCTION

Insofar as the Lord's Supper necessarily centers on the death of Christ, there is an overlap between preaching and sacrament in Charles' spirituality. Although not uninterested in doctrines of the atonement, his main concern is with the reality of the experience that Christ has died for our sins. This could be known personally by means of preaching, or by means of the sacrament. Christ's death was part of God's whole design for man, which included Christ's incarnation, life, resurrection, ascension, and kingship as well as his death. It resulted in man's sanctification and union with God in perfect love, as well as in man's justification. In a nonsacramental hymn, written a year after his spiritual experience of May 21, 1738, Wesley summed up the ineffable mystery of the death of Christ.

> 'Tis mystery all! The Immortal dies:
> Who can explore his strange design?
> In vain the firstborn seraph tries
> To sound the depths of love divine!
> 'Tis mercy all! let earth adore,
> Let angel-minds enquire no more. [18]

The same adoring wonder shines forth in a number of his hymns on the Eucharist as a memorial.

> Endless scenes of wonder rise
> With that mysterious tree,
> Crucified before our eyes
> Where we our Maker see:
> Jesus, Lord, what hast thou done?
> Publish we the death divine,
> Stop, and gaze, and fall, and own
> Was never love like thine! [75]

Participation in the Eucharist as a means of grace that mediated the death of Christ was a meaningful resource for triumphant living on earth.

> Jesu, we follow thee,
> In all thy footsteps tread,
> And pant for full conformity
> To our exalted Head. [95]

INTRODUCTION

Faithful use of the Lord's Supper was also an earnest of heaven.

> To heaven the mystic banquet leads;
> Let us to heaven ascend,
> And bear this joy upon our heads
> Till it in glory end. [90]

In Charles Wesley's sacramental hymns we find a salutary corrective to the stillness of the Moravians; we also find a spiritual resource for the whole Church in our ecumenical age. In them he managed to combine an evangelical passion with a sacramental stress, and in so doing he held together elements that have so often, in the history of the Church, been put asunder.

The same applies to his hymns on the great festivals of the Church that are to be found in this volume. They follow the liturgical year, they outline God's plan of salvation in Christ, but they make those great events personal. Christ's birth, "Our God contracted to a span, Incomprehensibly made man" [107]; Christ's death, "Would Jesus have the sinner die? Why hangs he then on yonder tree?" [5]; Christ's resurrection, "Love's redeeming work is done, Fought the fight, the battle won" [111]; Christ's ascension, "Him though highest heaven receives, Still he loves the earth he leaves" [112]; Christ's return, "Lo! he comes with clouds descending, Once for favored sinners slain" [101]; Pentecost, "Granted is the Savior's prayer, Sent the gracious Comforter" [116]—all these become spiritual events in the life of the singer as well as points on a liturgical calendar. At the same time, liturgical and sacramental integrity is safeguarded.

The second alternative group that comprised the Methodist Revival (after the Moravians) was the Calvinistic Methodists. They were loosely organized around George Whitefield and the Countess of Huntingdon. They became strong in Wales, where John Wesley rarely went. Indeed, before Aldersgate Street, and before the Wesleys were even on the scene, a Welshman, Griffith Jones, had been converted, preached in the open air, conceived a circuit system, and been persecuted for his zeal. Although loosely attached to the Church of England, the Calvinistic Methodists, like John Wesley, were wont to ignore parish boundaries in the interests of preaching the Gospel to those who needed it most. Like him, they preached in the open air, employed lay preachers, and in other ways were in danger of infringing the strict letter of the canon law of the Church of England. For this reason, both groups were opposed by the regular evangelical clergy of that church.

George Whitefield was almost certainly a greater preacher than John Wesley.[41] He may well have been one of the greatest preachers of all time. However, Wesley called his work "a rope of sand." The reason was that Whitefield was not an organizer. Wesley, on the other hand, was probably one of the most gifted organizers the Church has known. He not only preached, he organized those who responded to his preaching so that they in turn could deepen their own spirituality and pass it on to others. This did not happen according to a preconceived plan. John Wesley applied what he had learned from his father, from the Church of England Societies, from the Holy Club, from Georgia, from the Moravians, to the situation of the Methodist Revival as it developed. Looking back in 1787 he wrote that he and Charles had had no plan at all.

> They only went hither and thither, wherever they had a prospect of saving souls. But when more and more asked, "What must I do to be saved?" they were desired to meet all together. Twelve came the first Thursday night; forty the next, soon after, a hundred. And they continued to increase till, three or four and twenty years ago, the London Society amounted to about 2,800.[42]

By means of prayerful improvisation, Wesley built up a strongly organized Methodist movement, a kind of missionary society, within the Church of England. The organization was provided by the situation rather than imposed upon it. His aim was "not to form any new sect; but to reform the nation, particularly the Church; and to spread Scriptural holiness over the land."[43] This was the mission, but Wesley knew, like Loyola, that mission must be organized, and organization has remained a strong point of the Methodists ever since. Wesley's organization was based on the local society, and wherever he went he formed societies. Within the early societies, band meet-

---

[41]See, for example, J. C. Pollock, *George Whitefield and the Great Awakening* (London: Hodder and Stoughton, 1973).

[42]See *Works*, vol. VII, p. 207, Sermon CVII, *On God's Vineyard*.

[43]See *Works*, vol. VIII, p. 299, *The Large Minutes*.

ings sprang up for more intense fellowship. However, in 1742 the Bristol Methodists met together to discuss the financing of the New Room. A certain Captain Foy offered to visit a class of eleven members to collect one penny a week from them, and others offered to follow his example. Wesley's fertile brain intuited that the "class" could become a medium of spirituality rather than of pure finance, and henceforth he divided the societies into class meetings for fellowship. He was influenced, of course, by his experiences at Epworth, at the Church of England Societies, at the Holy Club, in Georgia, and among the Moravians, but he adapted his spirituality to the new Christians who were flocking into the movement. He saw that Christian fellowship, *koinonia*, was not inimicable to organization, indeed it was intrinsic to the Christian life. The *koinonia* of the early Methodists was immortalized in some of Charles Wesley's hymns.

> He bids us build each other up;
> And, gathered into one,
> To our high calling's glorious hope
> We hand in hand go on.
>
> We all partake the joy of one,
> The common peace we feel,
> A peace to sensual minds unknown,
> A joy unspeakable.
>
> And if our fellowship below
> In Jesus be so sweet,
> What heights of rapture shall we know,
> When round his throne we meet. [98]

The Methodist class meeting became the quintessence of the intimate Christian fellowship group, which has become so important in the more recent history of the Church. An early description of the early Methodist societies and classes is given in the extract in our volume entitled *The Nature, Design, and General Rules of the United Societies, in London, Bristol, Kingswood, Newcastle-Upon-Tyne, &c.* In reading this, we see that Wesley commends an ascetic as well as a joyful spirituality. The society was "a company of men having the form and seeking the power of godliness, united in order to pray together, to receive the word of exhortation, and to watch over one another in love, that they may help each other to work out their salvation."[44] Salvation, however, was not just an inward experience. It must evidence itself in fruits. These fruits included not just faithful attendance on the means of grace, but also a negative abstention from evil and a positive attachment to good. The Methodist societies and classes, in spite of their successful spread, were no soft options. The ultimate aim was scriptural holiness, perfect love, and this involved conforming one's whole life to the will of God. In other words, the societies and classes were a social contextualization of Wesley's own spirituality.

Leadership was needed for the societies and classes. At first Wesley was loathe to accept laymen as preachers. His own mother eventually persuaded him in the case of Thomas Maxfield. "It is the Lord," she said, "let Him do what seems [to] Him good."[45] Laymen assumed increasing importance in the growing movement as preachers, society stewards, class leaders, and so on, and they have remained important in Methodism ever since.

The societies were never meant to be independent from one another. They were from the first united or connectional societies. Before long, the idea of the "round" or "circuit" developed. Traveling lay preachers were put in charge of a number of societies organized into circuits, and they in turn were organized by Wesley's Annual Conference under his own supervision. Thus there arose a remarkable system of connected caring. At grass roots Methodists were joined in classes, classes were joined in societies, societies were joined in circuits, and circuits were joined together under the conference superintended by John and Charles Wesley with the help of faithful laymen. The point is that this connectional system was not merely a stroke of administrative genius, it was a system of connected spirituality. The organization per se was not the important factor; what mattered was the spirituality that was channeled through the system.

This same system of annual conferences, circuit riders, and local societies, when transplanted across the Atlantic, was to be even more

---

[44]See p. 108. See *Journal* for April 25, 1742, for his first appointment of Class Leaders, in *Works*, vol. 1, p. 364.

[45]In the *Minutes* of 1746 Wesley later described the lay preachers, in a striking phrase, as "extraordinary messengers, designed of God to provoke the others to jealousy." See publications of Wesley Historical Society, no. I, p. 34, 1896.

successful in the American west than in Britain. It resulted in the extraordinary growth of American Methodism so that by 1855, from a standing start in 1771, it was the largest Protestant body in the United States, with a million and a half members. In the process of adaptation the original spirituality of the Wesleys became modified as well. Nevertheless the notion of the necessity and usefulness of organization, and the notion that spirituality must be shared both intimately and widely, remained a legacy of the Wesleys. In this they differed from Whitefield and the Calvinistic Methodists.

They differed also in regard to doctrine. The theology of the Wesleys was Arminian, that of the other group was Calvinistic. This doctrinal divergence amounted also to a divergence of spirituality. There are, of course, different brands of Calvinism, as indeed there are different brands of Arminianism. As John Wesley wrote in the Minutes of Conference of 1745, "We stand on the very edge of Calvinism," and he shared the Calvinistic stress on the grace of God and justification by faith.[46] His Arminianism was not quite that of Arminius himself, nor that of the seventeenth-century Laudians. Likewise the moderate Calvinists often looked on the Wesleyans more in sorrow than in anger. Yet there were deep, underlying differences that sometimes became acute. These emerged obtrusively in the Calvinistic Controversy that ensued in the 1770s after the death of Whitefield. They emerged less destructively, but also more importantly, right at the beginning of the Methodist Revival. Again it was Charles Wesley's hymns, as well as John's more labored prose, that responded to the situation in *Hymns on God's Everlasting Love* of 1741. These hymns put into poetry what John was to put into prose and what both the brothers were to speak with their mouths and act out in their spirituality. The Wesleys stressed that, through the prevenient grace of God, man has free will. No man, they claimed, is predestined to damnation. The "heathen," they asserted, can be saved if they follow the light they have. God does not force our wills, was their conviction. Yet God's grace, though boundless, is not cheap; he requires holiness as well as faith. But the perfect love that he requires of us stems from the fact that the ground of his being is love, and that love is available to all, whether beggar or prostitute, worthy or not. Charles's hymns conveyed these prosaic truths in poetic form. What

---

[46]*Minutes* of 1745, Question 23, "Wherein may we come to the very edge of Calvinism?" in *Works*, vol. VIII, p. 285.

he had found, *all* could find. The Wesleys combined a deep personalism with an Arminian longing that the whole world might find the grace of God. "For all, for all, my Savior died," Charles wrote. Both the "my" and the "all" were of paramount importance. In ringing verses, Charles pressed his convictions home.

> O let me kiss thy bleeding feet,
> And bathe and wash them with my tears;
> The story of thy love repeat
> In *every* drooping sinner's ears,
> That *all* may hear the quickening sound:
> If I, even I, have mercy found! [5]

Many of the verses of these hymns have a haunting, even an imploring appeal to the emotions through the minds of men. Their urgency speaks to us even now.

> O let thy love my heart constrain,
> Thy love for *every* sinner free,
> That *every* fallen soul of man
> May taste the grace that found out me;
> That *all* mankind, with me, may prove
> Thy sovereign, everlasting love. [5]

The fact that the underlined words are torpedoes aimed at the Calvinist position is secondary to the appealing spirituality built into the phrases. In these verses, the Wesleys' Arminian spirituality took wings.

> O for a trumpet voice
> On *all* the world to call!
> To bid their hearts rejoice
> In him who died for *all*;
> For *all* my Lord was crucified,
> For *all*, for *all* my Savior died. [6]

And so the appeal of God's love in Christ for all men rang out in a poetry and a music that was sung and experienced and acted on.

INTRODUCTION

'Tis Love! 'tis Love! Thou diedst for me!
I hear thy whisper in my heart;
The morning breaks, the shadows flee,
Pure, *universal* Love thou art;
To me, to *all*, thy mercies move:
Thy nature and Thy name is Love. [14]

Countless thousands responded to the implicit appeal of the message contained in these rapturous hymns.

Would Jesus have the sinner die?
Why hangs he then on yonder tree?
What means that strange expiring cry?
(Sinners he prays for you and me)
"Forgive them, Father, O forgive
They know not that by me they live!" [5]

Most of these verses were written at a fair speed in the midst of a busy, traveling, preaching ministry. They were written from the heart. The phrases rolled on, "For *all* thou hast in Christ prepared sufficient, sovereign, saving grace,"

Father, whose *everlasting love*
Thy only Son for sinners gave,
Whose grace to *all* did *freely* move,
And sent him down a *world to save.* [121]

The Calvinists generally disagreed. They felt that the Wesleys' spirituality set all on man, on man's will, on man's choosing, on man's taking pains, on man's being a good husband of God's grace, whereas the point was to emphasize God's grace, God's will, God's choosing, God's distinguishing love. It is easy to overstress but also to understress the differences between the two groups. The Wesleyan Revival was unusual in that it was Arminian in approach. Other mid-century Protestant renewals have usually been Calvinistic in tone ranging from Calvin himself in the sixteenth century, through the Puritans of the seventeenth century, the non-Wesleyans of the eighteenth century, the 1858 movement of the nineteenth century, to the Barthians of the twentieth century. The Wesleys were both evangelical and Arminian. In this, as in other ways, they were catholic in their spirituality.

The third group in the eighteenth-century revival (after the Moravians and the Calvinistic Methodists) was the half-regular Evangelical clergy. Like the other groups, they stressed justification by faith. In contrast with Wesley they remained in a parish and worked from there. Men such as Thomson, Bennett, Grimshaw of Hawarth, Venn of Huddersfield, Berridge of Everton, and Fletcher of Madeley had parishes where they preached, and visited, and addressed the usual parish meetings. But they were also ready to use the parish as a base for outside preaching, open-air preaching, building meeting houses, supporting lay preachers, joining in circuits, and attending Wesley's conferences. The regular Evangelicals therefore accused them of breaking church order, but at the same time the half-regulars were bound to a parish and not free to preach where they wished. Some of them were moderate Calvinists. Fletcher of Madeley was not. He was the most authentic example of the Wesleyan spirituality in action. He was the archetypal Wesleyan "saint." We include an extract from John Wesley's *Life of Fletcher* in this volume, and will pause for a while to examine him, both for the sake of his Arminian spirituality and as an example of the half-regulars.[47]

Here was a saint. Of him, John Wesley commented, "So unblameable a character in every respect I have not found either in Europe or America; and I scarce expect to find another such on this side of eternity."[48] Friends and opponents, parishioners and acquaintances, agreed together concerning his saintliness. Tradition has it that testimony is available from an unlikely quarter. John Fletcher's brother-in-law, Monsieur de Bottens, was an intimate friend of Voltaire. The persistent story, first printed by Abbey and Overton in *The English Church in the Eighteenth Century*, tells how Voltaire was asked if he knew anyone whose life corresponded with that of Christ in the Gospels.[49] Voltaire replied that he did know of such a person. And he quoted John Fletcher, Vicar of Madeley.

Here too was the man asked by Wesley, with the agreement and

---

[47]Fletcher's *Works* were edited in London by Joseph Benson in 1806–1808. See G. Lawton, *Shropshire Saint* (London: Epworth, 1960).

[48]*Works*, vol. XI, p. 365, *Life of Fletcher*.

[49]C. J. Abbey and J. H. Overton, *The English Church in the Eighteenth Century* (London: Longmans Green & Co., 1887), p. 343.

acclaim of the early Methodist preachers, to succeed him as the leader of the Arminian Methodists. Fletcher never did succeed Wesley. Wesley lived; Fletcher died. Fletcher's health got worse in the 1770s; Wesley's health recovered during the 1770s, and he survived to lead on. Fletcher was designated as, but did not become, Wesley's successor. However, he *did* become Wesley's penman. It was Fletcher who took up the pen to defend Wesley during the Calvinistic Controversy. It was Fletcher who put Wesley's thought into a system, and he was the first systematic theologian of the Wesleyan movement. His early theological fame did not survive, his reputation for saintliness did.

There is a certain romance in Fletcher's spirituality. John Fletcher of Madeley was really Jean Guillaume de la Fléchère of Nyon in Switzerland. In a Swiss valley he grew up. In a Swiss university he was educated. Like Saint Francis, he almost became a soldier. By the margin of a maidservant's clumsiness, he was kept in Europe, he was kept out of the army, and his life was saved. And so, from the Swiss mountains, de la Fléchère improbably made his way to Britain to make a significant contribution to the Methodist movement.

In Fletcher, there was not the romance of constant travel, as with Wesley. He could not claim "the world is my parish," as did John Wesley. Here is the more subtle piety of one who could claim that the parish was his world. For Fletcher knew that God had given him Madeley, and that at a time when it was becoming a center of the early Industrial Revolution. In 1759 Nathaniel Gilbert had asked Fletcher to go with him to the West Indies to begin preaching the Gospel there. If he had agreed, he would have been one of the early Protestant missionaries. But he refused, and ended up in Madeley where he exercised his spirituality, like the Curé D'Ars, in the care of souls. His main diversion, while at Madeley, was to travel periodically to Trevecka in Wales where he became the first Visitor, or president, of one of the earliest theological colleges. Even this ended with the onset of the later Calvinistic Controversy, and he was free to serve and love the people of Madeley alone. Although an Arminian Methodist like Wesley, he was bound spiritually to *all* the people of a *particular* parish. His spirituality was circumscribed but enriched by Madeley.

However, although not irregular in regard to certain facets of church order, as was Wesley, Fletcher was not completely regular in his churchmanship. He was a half-regular. He was willing to build preaching houses in his parish. He was willing to preach in the open air and outside his parish. He used Madeley as the center of a sort of circuit, and he used other Methodist practices such as class and band meetings. He played a significant part in Wesley's conferences of 1777, 1781, and 1784, and supported Wesley and the Methodist preachers in other ways.

For this reason, Fletcher and the half-regulars, as well as the Moravians, the Calvinistic Methodists, and the Arminian Methodists, incurred the displeasure of the group of regular Evangelical clergy that formed after 1746 around Samuel Walker of Truro.[50] This group represented the fifth and final stream within the revival. Walker's group differed from the Wesleys in regard to both doctrine and church order. The doctrinal disagreement illustrated a difference of opinion concerning spirituality, and the discussion in regard to church order illustrated some of the reasons why the Wesleyan movement, although designed as a movement of mission within the Church of England, eventually became the separate Methodist Church.

The two points of doctrine and spirituality that lay at the center of the discussion between Walker and the Wesleys were those of Assurance and Christian Perfection. As far as Walker was concerned, the notion of Assurance formed an Achilles Heel within the Wesleyan position. It was a matter of temperament rather than faith. An assurance of faith, spiritually experienced, was not essential to genuine Christianity. Although not insisting that it was essential, the Wesleys stressed that Assurance, the witness of God's Spirit with our spirit that we are His children, was not only possible but desirable for Christian spirituality. Equally, Walker cast doubts on the Wesleyan emphasis on Christian Perfection. He felt that it was not possible of attainment in this life, and that it was unwise to propose perfect love as an ideal for this life. It was obtainable only in heaven. As far as Wesley was concerned, Christian Perfection, or perfect love, was at the center of his spirituality. His purpose was to aim for perfect love in his own life, and to "spread scriptural holiness through the land." It was not an optional extra added to faith, it was a deeper achievement within the life of faith, and a necessary consequence of true faith. His most comprehensive statement concerning Christian Per-

---

[50]Walker arrived in Truro and Hervey published his *Meditations* in 1746; by 1748 Romaine was in London, and by 1753 Adam had begun his friendship with Walker. Hervey through his writings, Romaine in the capital city, Adam as lieutenant to Walker, and above all Walker himself as leader were important in the beginnings of the regular Evangelical movement.

fection is included in this volume in *A Plain Account of Christian Perfection.*

Rather than analyzing the exchanges between the Walker group and the Wesley group concerning Assurance and Christian Perfection, we will now briefly use the context of that discussion to analyze the overall progression within the Wesleys' spirituality as it became actualized within the Arminian Methodist movement. As we have seen, it was developed within the parameters of the Church of England liturgy and sacraments, and within the framework of an Arminian theology that stressed that this spirituality was potentially available for all men. Recent thinking on the Wesleys has emphasized the fact that they had a genuine theology centered on the connected doctrines of original sin, prevenient grace, repentance, justification by faith, assurance, sanctification, perfect love, and glorification.[51] This is true, and it is correct that their divergence from Walker was a doctrinal disagreement about Assurance and Christian Perfection, and that their dispute with the Calvinists was a theological disharmony concerning free will, predestination, the imputed righteousness of Christ, and the role of works and the law in salvation. Without disputing the claim that the Wesleys together with Fletcher did have a worked-out theological system, it is our contention that this system was the handmaid of a distinctive spirituality. The theology and the spirituality went together, and the theology was meaningful not so much in itself but according as it contributed to the deepening of Christian experience and practice. Again, Charles Wesley's hymns exemplify the progression within this spirituality.

Spirituality as the Wesleys understood it begins with the stirrings of "conscience," which are activated by the prevenient grace of God. This conscience, this free will, this embryonic spirituality, is not a natural gift of man; it is triggered by the prevenient grace of God. Nevertheless, because the prevenient grace of God operates in all men, all men have this embryonic spirituality, including the Jews and those outside the Judaeo-Christian world. The Jewish dispensation vouchsafed to Moses is lower than the Christian dispensation but higher than the heathen dispensation. Salvation in the lower dispensations belongs to anyone who in God's account sincerely and uprightly follows the light of his dispensation, albeit through the merits

---

[51]See Outler, *John Wesley,* p. 28: "That Wesley should have become the patron saint of the theological indifferentism is mildly outrageous."

of the unknown Christ. Spirituality is present therefore at a lower level in the non-Christian dispensations. This notion was, of course, contrary to Calvinistic beliefs.

However, the main concern of the Wesleys was not with non-Christian religion, nor with a mediocre form of Christian faith. They agreed that it was possible to have a faith that remained at the level of that of a servant but, as John Wesley put it, his aim was "to promote, so far as I am able, vital, practical religion; and by the grace of God to beget, preserve, and increase the life of God in the souls of men."[52] This was true spirituality; it was the faith of a son. It combined inward faith with outward works, individual interiority with communal fellowship, the grace of God with the response of men, spiritual experience with social involvement, ascetic intent with a purpose to actively love all men. These characteristics of spirituality have often been held separately, or even severally; rarely have they been held integrally.

Like the other groups in the overall Methodist movement, the Wesleys recognized the centrality of justification by faith, which involved basically "pardon, the forgiveness of sins." Their originality lay in linking justification with a more positive spiritual sensation that they described in terms of spiritual birth, or new birth. Faith was not merely a passive acceptance of what God has done for us in Christ, it was also a "spiritual sensation." The Wesleys were now passing beyond the realms of doctrinal formulation into the area of spiritual experience. This inwardness was not amenable to the rationalism of the Enlightenment. It was not even amenable to the empiricism with which they sympathized, for even that was too limited in its concept of experience. The new birth was an entry (analogous to natural birth) into a new, spiritual environment wherein our hitherto embryonic spiritual senses could be quickened by the Holy Spirit. The importance of this can be illustrated by their emphasis on "feelings." Feeling was for them no mere emotional state, but analogous to the sense of *touch*. It was not a physical or human attribute but a spiritual attribute, comparable perhaps to our outward feelings yet an inward not an outward sensation. They were pointing to an inner, invisible realm that cannot be seen but whose internal reality, when activated by faith, is more certain than so-called rational or empirical evidences. As Wesley wrote, in *A Plain Account of Genuine Christianity*

---

[52] *Works*, vol. XIII, p. 197, letter to Samuel Walker dated September 3, 1756.

INTRODUCTION

(included in our volume), faith "gives a more extensive knowledge of things invisible, showing what eye had not seen, nor ear heard, neither could it before enter into our heart to conceive. And all these it shows in the clearest light, with the fullest certainty and evidence."[53] What Christianity promised doctrinally it accomplished inwardly: "It is holiness and happiness, the image of God impressed on a created spirit; a fountain of peace and love springing up into everlasting life."[54]

According to the Wesleys, not only justification but this new spirituality was open to all. It was not the prerogative of spiritual masters, or monastic inhabitants, or priests, or even long-established Christians. It was the potential birthright of every human being. Through the preventing grace of God, each person was equipped with an embryonic spirituality; through the justifying grace of God, each person could receive forgiveness, and have activated "faculties suited to things invisible." As Charles Wesley put it,

> Come, sinners, to the gospel feast,
> Let every soul be Jesu's guest;
> Ye need not one be left behind,
> For God hath bidden all mankind.
>
> Sent by my Lord, on you I call,
> The invitation is to *all:*
> Come, all the world: come, sinner, thou!
> All things in Christ are ready now. [2]

The invitation to forgiveness and pilgrimage, when accepted, sparks a person's latent spirituality.

> To him that in thy name believes
> Eternal life with thee is given
> Into himself he all receives,
> Pardon, and holiness, and heaven.
>
> The things unknown to feeble sense,
> Unseen by reason's glimmering ray,

---

[53]See p. 128.
[54]See p. 129.

INTRODUCTION

> With strong, commanding evidence,
> Their heavenly origin display.
>
> Faith lends its realizing light,
> The clouds disperse, the shadows fly;
> The Invisible appears in sight,
> And God is seen by mortal eye. [11]

These lines were written not primarily for kings or landed owners, but for miners and workers in the Londons, Bristols, and Newcastles of the eighteenth century—for men mostly new to the Church and the Christian tradition.

The teaching of the Wesleys on justification and the new birth led naturally to their teaching on Assurance. Walker of Truro, in objecting to this, was objecting to the spirituality that lay behind it. The implication of the Wesleys' teaching was not only that one's spiritual senses could be activated but that one could know that this was the case, one could have the witness of God's Spirit with one's own spirit that one was a child of God, that one was "on the way." This inward assurance was not essential, but plainly it was desirable in the life of spirituality. Again Charles Wesley expresses this beautifully in verse.

> We by his Spirit prove
> And know the things of God,
> The things which freely of his love
> He hath on us bestowed;
> His Spirit to us he gave,
> And dwells in us, we know;
> The witness in ourselves we have,
> And all its fruits we show. [12]

According to Walker, it was arrogance; according to Bishop Butler, "the pretending to extraordinary revelations and gifts of the Holy Ghost is a horrid thing." Wesley retorted that it was not extraordinary at all but "what every Christian may receive and ought to expect and pray for."[55] It was not an assurance about oneself, but an assur-

---

[55] *Works*, vol. XIII, p. 500, *Conversation with the Bishop of Bristol*. J. S. Lawton in *Miracles and Revelation* (London: Lutterworth, 1959, pp. 107–11) argues that Wesley

ance about God conveyed by God. It was not a permanent state but an assurance about one's present situation. As such, it was a joyful experience. And some of Charles Wesley's most infectious verses were written to rehearse this experience.

My God, I am thine;
What a comfort divine,
What a blessing to know that my Jesus is mine!
In the heavenly Lamb
Thrice happy I am,
And my heart it doth dance at the sound of his name. [20]

My God! I know, I feel thee mine,
And will not quit my claim,
Till all I have is lost in thine,
And all renewed I am. [45]

According to John Wesley, the ante-Nicene Fathers, such as Clement of Rome, Ignatius, Polycarp, and Origen, had both taught and known assurance of faith, and it had been a possession of true Christians in the Church down the ages.

For the Wesleys, the crux of spirituality lay not in justification and spiritual birth, whether accompanied by assurance or not; it lay rather in Christian Perfection or perfect love. According to them, spirituality involved an ongoing process of sanctification, the aim of which was to love God with all one's heart, mind, soul, and strength, and to love one's neighbor as oneself. They knew that the high peaks of spiritual experience were not usually possible on a continuing basis. For many people there were times of spiritual conflict, dullness, and backsliding, and recovery from them. Times of inner dryness were liable to supervene. As Charles put it,

Jesus, the all-restoring Word,
My fallen spirit's hope,
After thy lovely likeness, Lord,
Ah, when shall I wake up? [104]

---

pointed Apologetics in a new direction, away from miracles in the external world toward the miracles of inward spirituality wrought by God.

INTRODUCTION

The theoretical backing for the spirituality of sanctification rested in their notion of the differing nature of justification and the new birth, even though they might be, in spiritual experience, inseparable from each other. John Wesley wrote that

> justification implies only a relative, the new birth a real, change. God in justifying us does something for us; in begetting us again, He does the work in us. . . . The one restores us to the favor, the other to the image, of God. The one is the taking away of the guilt, the other the taking away the power, of sin: so that, although they are joined together in point of time, yet are they of wholly distinct natures.[56]

The other groups in the revival, to a greater or lesser extent, emphasized the role of justification and faith in spirituality; the Wesleys laid the greater stress on sanctification, holiness, love, and Christian Perfection. In a sense the other groups were being faithful to the classical theology and spirituality of the Reformation, which had stressed the fact of man's sin and the centrality of the death of Christ in redeeming man from sin. The Wesleys stressed man's sin and Christ's death, but as part of a greater whole. The glorious mystery of Christ included not only His death, but also His birth, life, resurrection, ascension, and glorification. The glorious mystery of the Christian life included not only forgiveness for sin, but also sharing the divine nature, dwelling in God, entering into unity with the divine, living in union with God, attaining perfect love for God and man, and entering into Christ's glorification. In other words, there is a return to the notion of the early Church, and especially the Eastern Fathers, that God became man so that man might become divine. Again Charles Wesley's hymns clothe the ideas in words:

> Heavenly Father, Life divine,
> Change my nature into thine!
> Move and spread throughout my soul,
> Actuate and fill the whole!
> Be it I no longer now
> Living in the flesh, but thou. [50]

---

[56] *Works*, vol. V, pp. 223–33, *Sermon* XIX, *The Great Privilege of Those That Are Born of God.*

INTRODUCTION

Thy nature, gracious Lord, impart!
Come quickly from above,
Write thy new name upon my heart,
Thy new, best name of love. [42]

I shall fully be restored
To the image of my Lord
Witnessing to all mankind,
Jesu's is a *perfect* mind. [43]

This vision of a spirituality of perfect love and being restored to the image of God occurs also outside the hymns that deal with Christian Perfection. It is the purpose of Christ's incarnation.

He deigns in flesh to appear,
Widest extremes to join;
To bring our vileness near,
And make us all divine:
And we the life of God shall know,
For God is manifest below. [107]

Or, as a verse of "Hark the Herald Angels Sing" puts it,

Adam's likeness now efface,
Stamp thine image in its place:
Second Adam from above,
Reinstate us in thy love. [105]

Perfect love is the end purpose of all Christ's work on earth. It is the purpose for which man was created. Man can know it on earth. It will be consummated in heaven. As Charles Wesley's great ascension hymn states (in another little-known verse):

There we shall with thee remain,
Partners of thy endless reign;
There thy face unclouded see,
Find our heaven of heavens in thee. [112]

The Wesleys' spirituality of Christian Perfection contained a cluster of interlocking ideas. Perfect love was at the center, purity of heart was important, the possibility of obtaining a character free from known sin was there, purity of intention was central, the fruits of the Spirit were paramount, the possibility of an inner experience of perfect love was present, and above all lived a conviction that there were no limits to what God could do with a human life if it was fully given into His hands. Although John and Charles Wesley were not fully at one in their notion of perfect love—Charles had a more exalted view of it whereas John was more inclined to stress it as a present possibility—they were agreed in essentials. For them, perfect love was the fulfillment of faith. It amounted to holiness. It, like faith, was the product of God's grace, which was not given all at once but from moment to moment. Yet it was real holiness within the life of the Christian. As John Wesley asserted, "The imagination that faith *supersedes* holiness is the very marrow of antinomianism."[57] Perfect love was both inward and outward holiness. It was possible for all men. It was the point of human life. In *Meditation on the Lord's Prayer,* extracted from one of John Wesley's sermons and included in this volume, he longs for the time when "all the inhabitants of the earth, even the whole race of mankind, may do the will of their Father which is in heaven, as *willingly* as the holy angels; that these may do it *continually,* even as they, without any interruption of their willing service, yea, and that they may do it *perfectly.*"[58] In this sense, Christian perfection was utter surrender and resignation to the will of God.

However, perfect love normally took a long time to be manifested in the spirituality of a Christian. Indeed Walker, and Wesley's other opponents, denied that it was possible at all in this life. It normally presupposed a long process of sanctification. It presupposed inward prayer, faithful attendance on the means of grace, social involvement, and *koinonia.* It presupposed not only spiritual conflict but spiritual striving. In the 1780 *Hymnbook* there are seven sections for believers. The first is "for believers rejoicing," and certainly joy was a primary characteristic of the Wesleys' spirituality.

With calmly reverential joy,
O let us all our lives employ
In setting forth thy love:

---

[57] *Works,* vol. VII, p. 317, *Sermon CXX, The Wedding Garment.*
[58] See p. 116.

And raise in death our triumph higher,
And sing with all the heavenly choir,
That endless song above. [19]

Spirituality, however, was not all joy. The second section is "for believers fighting."

Soldiers of Christ, arise,
And put your armor on,
Strong in the strength which God supplies
Through his eternal Son;
Strong in the Lord of hosts,
And in his mighty power,
Who in the strength of Jesus trusts
Is more than conqueror. [30]

Alongside fighting, there was the inward joy and labor of praying, and the third section is "for believers praying."

Jesus, my strength, my hope,
On thee I cast my care,
With humble confidence look up,
And know thou hear'st my prayer.
Give me on thee to wait,
Till I can all things do,
On thee, almighty to create,
Almighty to renew. [31]

Spirituality also involved watching, and the fourth section is "for believers watching."

Be it my only wisdom here
To serve the Lord with filial fear,
With loving gratitude;
Superior sense may I display,
By shunning every evil way,
And walking in the good. [33]

Watching, however, was not to be substituted for working, and the fifth section is "for believers working."

INTRODUCTION

> Forth in thy name, O Lord, I go,
> My daily labor to pursue,
> Thee, only thee, resolved to know,
> In all I think, or speak, or do. [35]

Spirituality also involved suffering, and the sixth section is "for believers suffering."

> Who suffer with our Master here,
> We shall before his face appear,
> And by his side sit down;
> To patient faith the prize is sure,
> And all that to the end endure
> The cross, shall wear the crown. [40]

> Thee, Jesus, full of truth and grace,
> Thee, Savior, we adore,
> Thee in affliction's furnace praise,
> And magnify thy power. [39]

This part of the hymnbook ends with a section on "believers seeking for full redemption," in other words for Christian Perfection, and thus the point is made that Christian Perfection is normally the culmination of a long process of giving one's whole self and one's whole possibilities to God.

> Let us, to perfect love restored,
> Thy image here retrieve,
> And in the presence of our Lord
> The life of angels live. [41]

> Give me a new, a perfect heart,
> From doubt, and fear, and sorrow free;
> The mind which was in Christ impart,
> And let my spirit cleave to thee. [51 variant]

> Refining fire, go through my heart,
> Illuminate my soul;
> Scatter thy life through every part,
> And sanctify the whole. [45]

INTRODUCTION

Savior from sin, I wait to prove
That Jesus is thy healing name;
To lose, when perfected in love,
Whate'er I have, or can, or am:
I stay me on thy faithful word,
"The servant shall be as his Lord." [47]

It is important to remember that the hymns we have quoted, and
the many more we have included in this volume, were not primarily
private devotional pieces. They were written to be sung. In practice,
many Methodists and others down the years have cherished these
hymns as devotional aids and as food for the individual soul. However, their main function was as hymns. They were sung in the societies and classes and eventually in other Christian circles. The
result was that hymn singing as such became an increasingly important vehicle for communal worship and for spirituality. At the same
time, the fact that the hymns were often sung tended to commend the
spirituality contained in them to those who did the singing. The poet
Southey remarked that "perhaps no poems have ever been so devout-
ly committed to memory as these.... The manner in which they
were sung tended to impress them strongly on the mind: The tune
was made wholly subservient to the words, not the words to the
tune."[59]

However, in spite of the importance of hymns and fellowship in
the Wesleys' spirituality of perfect love, in spite of their emphasis on
social involvement, which we will analyze shortly, in spite of their
Arminian stress that God's love can utterly transform *all* men, there
remains their insistence on the personal nature of the spirituality of
Christian Perfection. It was not merely "the loving God with all our
heart, mind, soul, and strength," but a personal awareness that this
is the case. It was the conscious conviction, in a present experience,
of the reality of one's utter love for God and man in response to God's
own love. It was a luminous experiential self-awareness of the fact of
perfect love in one's own life. John Wesley writes:

> If a man be deeply and fully convinced, after justification, of
> inbred sin; if he then experience a gradual mortification of

---

[59]R. Southey, *Life of Wesley*, vol. II, new ed. (London, 1925), p. 97.

sin, and afterwards an entire renewal in the image of God;
if to this change, immensely greater than that wrought when
he was justified, be added a clear, direct witness of the renewal; I judge it as impossible this man should be deceived
herein, as that God should lie.[60]

Christian Perfection implied that all one's thoughts, words, and deeds
were governed by pure love, but it did not imply perfection in knowledge or freedom from infirmities or freedom from temptation. Nor
did it imply an inability to grow further in grace, nor an inability to
fall from grace. It was not perfection in the Latin sense of "faultless,"
nor was it an absolute state; it was part of a dynamic, ongoing process
that would end in glorification with Christ. The present experience
of Christian perfection in regard to one's conscious will and premed-
itated actions was not a future guarantee, nor a leap into a fresh state
of grace, but a spiritual experience of conformity with Christ in perfect love.

The Wesleys' differences with Walker and his group extended
beyond doctrinal disagreements concerning Assurance and perfect
love. Walker highlighted the question of Wesley's relationship to the
Church of England. His friend, Adam of Winteringham, asserted
roundly to Walker in 1756 that "Methodism as to its external form is
such a deviation from the rule and constitution of the Church of England that all attempts to render them consistent must be in vain."[61]
Walker was crystal clear in his own mind about Wesley's lay preachers and he stated plainly that their permission or appointment was in
fact a partial separation from the Church of England, the essence of
which, considered as such, consisted in her orders and laws, rather
than in her doctrines and worship, which constituted her a Church
of Christ. Wesley replied that he was loyal to the Church of England,
that the preachers were not ordained, and that his people went to the
parish churches for communion. He also partly admitted Walker's
points. "We have," he said, "out of necessity, not choice, slowly and
warily varied (from the Church) in some points of discipline, by

---

[60]See p. 335.

[61]See Edwin Sidney, *The Life, Ministry and Selections from the Remains of the Rev.
Samuel Walker, B.A., formerly of Truro, Cornwall* (London: Baldwin and Cradock, 1835),
pp. 220, 222, 280–82.

preaching in the field, by extempore prayer, by employing lay preachers, by forming and regulating societies, and by holding yearly conferences. But we did none of these things until we were convinced we could no longer omit them but at peril of our souls."[62] To preach the Gospel was ultimately more important within the Wesleys' spirituality than to obey the minutiae of church rules when those rules hindered the Gospel's being preached. A strong but flexible central body would probably have kept the Wesleyan movement within the Church of England, as Saint Francis had been kept within the confines of the medieval Church. Such a body was not present. The Wesleys asserted, "We look upon ourselves, not as the authors or ringleaders of a particular sect or party—it is the farthest thing from our thoughts—but as messengers of God, to those who are Christians in name but heathens in heart and life, to call them back to that from which they are fallen, to real, genuine Christianity."[63] From the standpoint of his Oxford ordination and Lincoln fellowship Wesley could look on the whole world as his parish[64] and mobilize his traveling preachers as itinerant purveyors of his vision of spirituality. The Wesleys were sincere in their desire and steadfast in their intent to keep their movement within the Church of England—Charles even more so than John—but Walker pinpointed the dilemma, and the preachers themselves began to become restless in later times. The very success of the Wesleys exacerbated the possibilities of tension as the movement spread not merely into the new urban centers where there was a minimal ecclesiastical presence but into other areas as well.

One must realize that it was not just the outward signs of potential separation that were important—notably the Deed of Declaration of 1784 giving the Legal Hundred (i.e., the conference) authority to succeed Wesley after his death, his ordaining on September 20, 1784, of Whatcoat and Vasey as presbyters and Coke as superintendent for the postrevolutionary American Methodist Church bereft of the sacraments, and the licensing of Methodist chapels in 1787. The crux of the matter lay in Wesley's spirituality itself, which centered on the

---

[62]See Wesley's letters to Walker, *Works*, vol. XIII, pp. 193–207, especially p. 195.

[63]*Works*, vol. XIII, pp. 227–28, *Reasons Against a Separation from the Church of England*.

[64]Quoted in letter to Hervey, March 20, 1739. See Outler, *John Wesley*, p. 72.

grace of God. It was God's preventing grace that enabled one's conscience to search for forgiveness and wholeness; it was God's saving
grace that enabled one to receive justification by faith and activation
of one's embryonic spiritual faculties; it was God's sanctifying grace
that enabled one to grow in love and the fruits of the Spirit; it was
God's cooperating grace that enabled one to respond to the limits of
perfect love; it was God's sacramental grace that used the sacraments
and other outward and visible signs as responsive means. To be sure,
man's response was vital, but it was a *response*. It was a response that
all men could make if they would. Insofar as institutions stifled the
possibility of man's response, to that extent they stifled the grace of
God and supporting institutions must be allowed to supplement their
deficiency. What arose as a supplemental movement, a missionary society within the Church of England, to deepen that Church's largely
dormant spirituality and to convey the grace of God not just to those
who needed it but to those who needed it most—this Methodist movement was destined, after the Wesleys' deaths, to develop into separate
churches. Perhaps it is no accident that in recent ecumenical times
Methodist Churches have often been "Bridge Churches." They have
developed their own structures and attempted to keep in trust what
they inherited from the Wesleys and others, but they have maintained
a healthy awareness of the basics that unite them with others. Those
basics center on spirituality. For the Wesleys, spirituality lay at the
heart of everyday Christianity. "Is your heart right, as my heart is
with your heart?" asked Wesley of others in his sermon *Catholic Spirit*;[65] "If it be, give me your hand," he replied. His dying words were
"the best of all is God is with us." In *A Plain Account of Genuine Christianity* he says of the genuine Christian, "Forgive his particularities
of opinion and (what you think) superstitious modes of worship.
These are circumstances but of small concern and do not enter into
the essence of his character. Cover them with a veil of love and look
at his substance: his tempers, his holiness, his happiness." "This," he
writes, "is the plain, naked portraiture of a Christian."[66]

Lest we leave the simplistic impression that the spirituality of the
Wesleys is primarily an individual interiority, let us return briefly to
the more social side of their concern. John Wesley was, in the context
of his day, a great social reformer. The springs of his love for his fel-

---

[65] *Works*, vol. V, pp. 492–504, *Sermon* XXXIX.
[66] See p. 125.

lowmen reveal themselves in a beautiful passage from *A Plain Account of Genuine Christianity.* This love, he writes,

> soars above all these scanty bounds, embracing neighbors and strangers, friends and enemies; yea, not only the good and gentle but also the froward, the evil and unthankful. For he loves every soul that God has made, every child of man, of whatever place or nation. And yet this universal benevolence does in nowise interfere with a peculiar regard for his relations, friends, and benefactors, a fervent love for his country and the most endeared affection to all men of integrity, of clear and generous virtue.[67]

John (in contrast with Charles) was not successful in his marriage. With this exception his commitments matched his words. He and Charles were faithful to each other throughout their long lives, and he was loyal to his friends and relatives. He had a strong but not blind commitment to his church and country. His universal love had a firm local base. He supported his king, even during the American War of Independence, despite the embarrassment of the American preachers. He despised the frivolity of the rich yet was not opposed to the class structure. There is a small element of truth in the famous claim that Wesley saved England from revolution.[68] This was not so much because he opposed the French Revolution, which came at the end of his life, or because he was aware of the deeper implications of the Industrial Revolution that was evolving around him, but because his work constituted in itself a social leaven. His motto, "go to those who need you most,"[69] took him into areas of need, and his constant travel from Cornwall to Scotland via Bristol, London, Newcastle, and the industrial regions of the north brought him into contact with the new and rootless artisan-type class, which had the most obvious basic insecurities. His approach to them was not sociological (Durkheim would come a hundred years later) but one of involvement and concern for all aspects of their lives.

---

[67]See p. 122.

[68]Dr. Whitehead's oration at Wesley's funeral service stressed the leavening influence of Methodism in a politically restive situation.

[69]Included in the *Minutes* of 1745 as an injunction to the preaching Assistants, this provided Wesley's own motivation.

INTRODUCTION

John Wesley was not afraid to speak prophetically about social evils. In 1767 he wrote *Word to a Smuggler*[70] to combat the evils of smuggling when to do so, especially in Cornwall, was rather like challenging the Mafia in modern times. In his *Word to a Freeholder*,[71] attacking bribery and corruption in politics, he advised voters to vote incorruptibly as though each election depended on them. In his *Thoughts on Slavery*[72] of 1774 he was the first leading Britisher to attack that institution, and he persuaded the American conference of 1780 to declare it as being against the laws of God. One of the last acts of his life was to write to Wilberforce in 1791 the letter included in this volume encouraging Wilberforce to persevere "in the name of God and in the power of his might, till even American slavery (the vilest that ever saw the sun) shall vanish away."[73]

Wesley continued the work, begun in the Holy Club, of helping debtors and prisoners, and alleviating poverty. In addition to writing numerous religious articles, he also produced a lot of cheap literature on general subjects for the poorer populace; he founded schools in places such as London, Bristol, and Newcastle; he encouraged the Sunday School movement, stimulated by the work of Hannah Ball, Robert Raikes, and Fletcher of Madeley, as a medium of popular education. He ranks as a notable educator.

In short, his spirituality had a strong social component built into it. For himself and others, spirituality could never be a purely inward thing. It applied to the whole of life. "Christianity is essentially a social religion," he wrote, "and to turn it into a solitary religion is indeed to destroy it."[74] Accordingly, he advised his people in regard to stewardship, self-denial, conversation, use of time, temperance, the conduct of business, the choice of a career, courtesy, reading habits, the use of money, leisure, joy in daily living, and practical ways of helping others.[75] However, he was aware that social involvement must remain part of an integral spirituality and not become an end in itself. He foresaw the dilemma of the Protestant Ethic, "wherever true Christianity spreads, it must cause diligence and frugality, which

---

[70] *Works*, vol. XI, pp. 174–78.

[71] *Works*, vol. XI, pp. 196–98.

[72] *Works*, vol. XI, pp. 59–79.

[73] See p. 171.

[74] *Works*, vol. V, p. 296, *Sermon on the Mount IV.*

[75] See P. S. Watson, *The Message of the Wesleys*, pp. 175–94 (London: Epworth, 1964).

in the natural course of things must beget riches."[76] The danger then was that riches would replace God as a motivating principle. His advice was to gain all one could, save all one could, and give all one could. The social and material life of man was part and parcel of the central search for perfect love. As he put it, serious Christians "not only abstained from all appearance of evil, were zealous in good works in every kind, and attended all the ordinances of God, but likewise used all diligence to attain the whole mind that was in Christ, and labored to walk in every point as their beloved Master."[77] For Wesley spirituality was holistic. It was based on the utter dedication of the total life to God. This central aim was summed up in the Covenant Service adapted by Wesley from the service of Richard Alleine, the Puritan.[78] This has developed into one of the finest devotional services in the Christian Church, and we include Wesley's 1780 service and a more modern Methodist adaptation of it in this volume in the hope that those unacquainted with it will begin to use it as a devotional treasure of the "Great Church." The words of the adapted covenant, usually held now at the beginning of the year, can hardly fail to move the heart, and they sum up Wesley's conviction that spirituality is the surrender of every part of a person's whole life to God.

> I am no longer my own, but yours. Put me to what you will, rank me with whom you will; put me to doing, put me to suffering; let me be exalted for you or brought low for you; let me be full, let me be empty; let me have all things, let me have nothing; I freely and heartily yield all things to your pleasure and disposal. And now, O glorious and blessed God, Father, Son, and Holy Spirit, you are mine, and I am yours. So be it. And the Covenant which I have made on earth, let it be ratified in heaven.[79]

At John Wesley's funeral service in 1791 the presiding minister read the familiar words "forasmuch as it has pleased Almighty God to take unto Himself the soul of our dear," and at that point he

---

[76] *Works*, vol. VII, p. 290, *Sermon CXVI, Causes of the Inefficacy of Christianity.*

[77] *Works*, vol. VII, p. 28, *Sermon LXXXIX, The More Excellent Way.*

[78] See D. Tripp, *The Renewal of the Covenant in the Methodist Tradition* (London: Epworth, 1969).

[79] See p. 387.

paused and added the words "father here departed."[80] Much has happened since Wesley's death as the "father in God" of the Arminian Methodists. The American Methodists had already begun to follow their divergent way. Wesley and Fletcher of Madeley had written against the American Revolution, and Fletcher had been offered preferment for his efforts, to which he had typically replied that he did not want promotion but "more grace." Wesley's stature, and Fletcher's saintliness, survived their opposition to American independence. However, it was in the nature of things that at the Baltimore Christmas Conference of 1784 the American Methodist Episcopal Church was set up with Asbury and Coke as its first bishops. Asbury became the American Wesley as far as travel was concerned. When he had been sent out by Wesley in 1771 there had been no Methodist Church—only six evangelists and a thousand adherents. When he died in 1816 there was a fine church, 695 preachers and 214,000 members. He adapted Wesley's methods to the American frontier and became the "prophet of the long road," eventually dying in another's house trying to take a missionary collection.[81] By 1810, one American in thirty-nine was a Methodist; in 1860, a third of all American Protestants were Methodists. The American Methodists inherited the Wesleys' spirituality as far as the Arminian doctrines—fellowship, evangelism, and organization—were concerned. Less evident was the Wesleys' concern for the sacraments, spiritual writers, the early Church, inwardness, and the "ladder of sanctification." One strand in American Methodism pursued the path of "holiness" interpreted as a second blessing experience that elevated one into a superior state of grace.[82] The Pentecostals and Charismatics were later to adapt this in different ways. Insofar as Wesley had talked about the possibility of Assurance and Christian Perfection as conscious experiences, they could find echoes in their spirituality of his own. The difference was that he thought of these experiences as part of a dynamic, ongoing, developing spirituality wherein these experiences were not ends in themselves but signposts on the way to perfect love consisting of outward and inward holiness. Other strands within American Method-

---

[80]See M. Edwards, *John Wesley*, in *A History of the Methodist Church in Great Britain*, p. 77.

[81]See H. Asbury, *A Methodist Saint: The Life of Bishop Asbury* (New York: A. A. Knopf, 1927).

[82]See J. L. Peters, *Christian Perfection and American Methodism* (New York: Abingdon, 1956).

ism concerned themselves with social involvement, either in particular concerns such as slavery, race, and ethnicity, or in a conviction that social involvement in general was the key to effective spirituality. The Wesleys had stressed social concern but within the context of a wider spirituality.

Of the five groups within the Methodist Revival in Britain, the Moravians and the half-regulars were no longer thriving forces at Wesley's death. The Calvinistic Methodists continued, although hampered by their loose organization. The future lay with the Evangelical regular clergy, who remained within the Church of England, and the Methodists, who developed into a separate church. By 1833, there were 300,000 British Methodists. During the nineteenth century three main groups arose among their number: the Wesleyan Methodists, who stressed the authority of the conference hierarchy; the Primitive Methodists, who worked less formally and more democratically, and were also active among the working class miners of the north and agricultural laborers of the south; and a number of smaller groups, stressing spontaneous evangelism and the role of laymen, who became the United Methodists. These three bodies united in 1932 to form the British Methodist Church. The British Methodists inherited, along with the American Methodists, the spirituality of the Wesleys. John Wesley's *Sermons* and *Notes on the New Testament* became the "canon" of the British Methodists. However, more important than John's prose works, which outlined Methodist doctrinal orthodoxy, were the Wesleys' works of spirituality and especially Charles Wesley's hymns. As Bett describes it, "Those hymns were our devotional and experimental standard. They expressed and safeguarded the norm of Methodist experience, and helped to re-create it from generation to generation, because they were in constant use both in public worship and private devotion."[83] Those hymns had an importance transcending Methodism and rank, after the Bible, as one of the most significant religious influences on Anglo-Saxon Christianity.

Another development, less spectacular than those in Britain and America yet even more exciting, was that on the mission field. Thomas Coke, co-leader with Asbury of the American Methodists, was a symbol of the missionary thrust built into Methodism. He was not content to stay in America and make it his parish, like Asbury; he literally looked on the world as his parish, and he died on May 3, 1814,

---

[83]H. Bett, *The Spirit of Methodism* (London: Epworth, 1937), pp. 241–42.

on shipboard in the Indian Ocean on his way as a missionary to Ceylon.[84] There are now Methodist Churches, or United Churches including ex-Methodists, in Africa, Asia, Europe, South America, and Australasia. The World Methodist Council, formed in 1881, links together Methodist groups working in about a hundred lands and serving a roll of about 45 million people, the largest concentration being the fourteen million members of the American United Methodist Church formed in 1968 after an earlier union in 1939.

Present-day Methodists can move in four different directions. In the first place, they can remain more or less the same; second, they can look forward to establishing closer links within world Methodism and think in terms of a world Methodist community; third, they can seek unity with other Christians within particular national boundaries, and this has happened with the founding of united churches in countries such as Canada, Sri Lanka, India, and Australasia; and, finally, they can work for the global unity of the whole church through the medium of the World Council of Churches. These four aims are not necessarily mutually incompatible. But whatever happens, whether Methodists remain in separate churches or unite in wider churches, they hold in trust certain key deposits inherited from the Wesleys. And they are basically deposits centering on spirituality. These deposits include: Charles Wesley's hymns, the Covenant Service, faith as living reality rather than belief per se, perfect love, mission based on the conviction that "for all, for all, my Savior died," the importance of laymen, fellowship as *koinonia*, the spiritual importance of organization, a creative tolerance based on the notion that true religion is inward and social rather than merely doctrinal, and a pragmatic openness to developing situations. These are held in trust, and offered by Methodists to the Coming Great Church.

However, the influence of the spirituality of the Wesleys cannot be confined within the Methodist tradition. As we have suggested, certain elements of their spirituality have been influential in other traditions. Their eucharistic hymns and notions were available for the nineteenth-century Oxford Movement's return to eucharistic seriousness, and they helped to increase sacramental observance in the lax eighteenth-century Church. Their view that Assurance and Christian Perfection could be realizable spiritual experiences (albeit in a

---

[84]C. J. Davey, *The March of Methodism* (London: Epworth, 1951), p. 20.

dynamic continuum) fed into the nineteenth-century holiness movements, and the twentieth-century Pentecostal and Charismatic movements. Their concern for social involvement has not gone unnoticed in the Social Gospel movement. Charles Wesley's hymns and John Wesley's translations of the German hymns have fed into the spirituality of the whole Church.

The uniqueness of the Wesleys' spirituality was such that some elements in it have been largely neglected or unnoticed by most Christian groups. Above all, they were unique for the integral nature of their spirituality. They were able to hold together what most Christian groups, even today, tend to keep apart. In their prayer life, they combined liturgical prayer, extempore prayer, silent prayer, sung prayer, prayers of their own composition, prayers arising out of Bible study, and prayer stimulated by study of the spiritual classics. Symbolical of this is the patch worn away on the wall of Fletcher of Madeley's study against which he used to kneel to offer his prayers—read, extempore, or silent. The Wesleys, like their friend Fletcher, not only prayed long and hard daily, they also used a variety of prayer forms. John Wesley in particular would have been thrilled by the Classics of Western Spirituality because it represents, in a major way, what he was attempting to do in his own day, namely to make available to all Christians Western spiritual writings not merely as academic treatises but as aids to prayer and spirituality.

Spirituality for the Wesleys was not confined to the prayer life of the individual. Fellowship with others was needed for its true expression. Although they built up a unique system that connected individual Christians with thousands of others through their societies, classes, circuits, and conferences, the crux of their organization was the intimate fellowship, the *koinonia*, of the class meeting. However, the fellowship group was itself part of a greater whole, the society, which in turn depended on the sacramental life and liturgy of the worshiping church. Preaching and sacrament, extempore prayer and communal liturgical prayer, were linked. They were different sides of the same coin.

The Wesleys did not confine spirituality to life in the Church, whether communal or individual. It had to do with the whole of life, and the whole of life included secular pursuits and wider society. Love for God and love for man were linked. Arminian concern for all men included their material as well as their spiritual needs. Discipleship for the individual included his or her working life, family life, and leisure life, as well as church life. Social concern was therefore part of spirituality.

Spirituality was, in fact, both inward and outward. Inwardly, it involved the awakening of a person's spiritual faculties, prefigured in baptism, accomplished at justification and the new birth, deepened by sanctification, strengthened by advances along a ladder of inward holiness leading toward pure love, punctuated by spiritual experiences of Assurance and Christian Perfection, issuing in internal purity and goodness, and leading to the blessedness of glorification with Christ. Inward spirituality was a growing inner union with God in Christ, Whose nature was love. Outwardly, spirituality involved a growing love for one's fellowmen. Inward holiness and outward fruits went together. Outward spirituality involved not only helping others, and going to those who needed one most; it also involved adopting a frugal and wholesome life-style that would enable this more readily to happen.

Modern findings have raised question marks about some of the minutiae of the Wesleys' spirituality. Psychology has opened up the reality of our unconscious thoughts as well as the "known sins" of our conscious minds; sociology has opened up the influence of social structures as well as the influence individuals may have on society; our modern world of computers, cosmonauts, and communists has added technological revolution to the industrial revolution of the Wesleys' time. Nevertheless the general principles of their integral spirituality are as valid as ever, perhaps even more so in our age of ecological as well as inward need.

It is not so much that their spirituality has been tried and found wanting. Certain elements of it have been tried and have borne fruit especially through the medium of the Methodist tradition. Even so, in its wholeness the spirituality of the Wesleys has never been fully tried.

It is our hope that through this book the whole Church will be led again to look at the spirituality of the Wesleys and to so reinterpret it that its principles may be actualized in our present global situation.

BRIEF NOTES
on
SPECIFIC EXTRACTS

SECTION I: SELECTED WRITINGS FROM JOHN WESLEY

[1] Preface and Extracts from *A Collection of Forms of Prayer for Every Day in the Week*

Reputed to be Wesley's first published work in 1733, it went through nine known editions by 1748. The prayers reflect Wesley's spirituality when aged thirty, as well as the ethos of the Holy Club and the needs of his Oxford pupils (for whom they were composed). He used scripture quotations, collects, and adaptations from books of devotion by Hickes and Sphinkes, as well as his own ideas. He aimed to cover weekly the whole range of Christian faith and practice. F. C. Gill's revised edition, *John Wesley's Prayers,* was published by Epworth, London, as recently as 1951. The Preface is from the sixth edition of 1775.

[2] *A Scheme of Self-Examination Used by the First Methodists in Oxford*

A fragment attributed to Wesley and infrequently published since. It reflects Wesley's central concern, to love God wholeheartedly, and one's neighbor as oneself. Reflects the "methodical" spirituality of the Oxford Methodists but not their daily and weekly rounds of private and group devotions.

BRIEF NOTES

[3] *Advice on Spiritual Reading*

Part of the Preface to Wesley's correction of Thomas à Kempis' *Treatise of the Imitation of Christ* published in 1735. He adapts from the *Praemonitio ad Lectorum* prefixed to the Cologne edition of 1682. Wesley is important as an editor and publisher as well as in his own capacity as a writer. He extracted from and creatively abridged countless spiritual and other classics. His advice on spiritual reading is universally applicable (not just to à Kempis). At least three editions are known of this full (319 page) version of the *Imitation of Christ*. The shorter 1741 extract was widely printed.

[4] *Translations of German Hymns*

In all, Wesley translated thirty-three German hymns: one each by Arnold, Bohmer, Deszler, Dober, Gmelin, Gotter, Ernst Lange, Joachim Lange, Rothe, Spangenberg, and Winckler; two by Freylinghausen, Richter, and Tersteegen; four by Gerhardt and Scheffler; and eight by Zinzendorf. Of these, Maria Bohmer, Anna Dober, Spangenberg, and Zinzendorf were Moravians, the rest Lutheran Pietists. Wesley had access to the Moravian Hymn Book, which in its 1735 edition had 991 hymns, and to the Freylinghausen Hymn Book, which contained 1,581 hymns. Although his thirty-three hymns were published in collections from 1737–1742 it is reasonably certain that all the translations were made in Georgia.

Wesley's translations reproduced the power of the originals in excellent English. Most of them appear in the collections of hymns that were of particular importance in the early Methodist movement, namely those of 1737, 1738, 1739, 1740, 1741, 1742, 1753, 1765, 1780, and 1785. Twenty-two of Wesley's thirty-three translations are still to be found in forty-nine of the best-known hymn books of the main churches in Britain and North America. They have been of deep spiritual influence in their own right as well as being a contribution to Wesley's development. The three numbers at the head of the six translations we use are our own, that of the 1876 *Hymnbook*, and that of the 1933 *Hymnbook*.

[5] Extracts from John Wesley's journal from January 8 to May 24, 1738

From 1725 Wesley got into the habit of noting down the experiences and events of his life. The code of his diaries has recently been broken, and eventually we will receive the fruits of this breakthrough. However, from time to time Wesley himself compiled and published *Extracts of the Journal,* and twenty-one of these extracts together made up the complete *Journal* that we have now. They are highly informative about the Methodist movement and the Britain of the eighteenth century; they are less so in relation to Wesley's own interior life. One particular passage that we quote has, nevertheless, achieved virtual parity with such famous accounts of spiritual experience as that of Saint Augustine in the Milan garden. We include not only the Aldersgate experience, but key passages covering the vital period of 1738, which were first published in 1740. All the passages are from the published *Journal* except the six paragraphs beginning "1. For many years . . ." and ending "6. yea, and faith itself, and what not," which are taken from J. Whitehead, *The Life of the Rev. John Wesley, M.A.,* vol. II, pp. 54–56, 1793–1796. In spite of the *Journal's* reticence about the interiority of Wesley's spirituality, it has been reprinted many times and is acknowledged to be a classic. Our text is a collation of Curnock's standard edition and the fifth edition of 1775.

[6] *The Nature, Design, and General Rules of the United Societies in London, Bristol, Kingswood, Newcastle-Upon-Tyne, etc.*
    It first appeared in 1743, and by 1794 had gone through twenty-three editions. It summarizes succinctly the ascetic spirituality and the organizational principles that motivated the early Methodist movement.

[7] *A Meditation on the Lord's Prayer.* An extract from Wesley's sermon entitled *Sermon on the Mount VI*
    Our extract contains the main part of this sermon, which was first published in 1748. It became one of the forty-four *Sermons on Several Occasions,* which, together with Wesley's *Notes on the New Testament,* constituted the standard doctrines of the Methodist Connection according to the Trust-Deeds of Methodist Churches. These forty-four discourses were published in four volumes in 1746, 1748, 1750 and 1760, and have gone through innumerable editions from that time until the present day. It is interesting to note that three of these sermons have texts from the Old Testament, and twenty-one from the Gospels, leaving twenty sermons on texts from the rest of the

New Testament. This was one of thirteen sermons on the sermon on the mount. Although Wesley's sermons have become classics in their own right, this one relates more obviously to his spirituality.

[8] *A Plain Account of Genuine Christianity*

First printed as a separate pamphlet in Dublin in 1753, this extract had already appeared as part of *A Letter to the Reverend Doctor Conyers Middleton, Occasioned by His Late Free Enquiry* published in 1749.

Middleton (1683–1750) was essentially a Cambridge deist who published in 1749 *A Free Inquiry into the Miraculous Powers which Are Supposed to Have Subsisted in the Christian Church from the Earliest Ages through Several Successive Centuries: By Which It Is Shown that We Have No Sufficient Reason to Believe, Upon the Authority of the Primitive Fathers, that Any Such Powers Were Continued to the Church After the Days of the Apostles.* In his letter of reply, Wesley spent sixty pages in an inexpert academic riposte defending the Fathers against Middleton, but then he changed the ground of argument by depicting his vision of genuine Christianity, the point being that the genuine Christian life is in itself a miracle reflecting the supernatural power of God and his Spirit, which has been and remains with the Church down the ages. The latter part of the letter became a separate tract, *A Plain Account of Genuine Christianity*, which gives Wesley's portrait of the ideal Christian, and as such it was widely circulated and became very well known. It is probably the most beautiful example of Wesley's tracts on spirituality. Our text is a collation of the first, third, and sixth editions (1753, 1761, and 1779). Section III, 11ff, was not part of *A Plain Account of Genuine Christianity*, but was the conclusion of Wesley's letter to Middleton.

[9] *Directions for Renewing Our Covenant with God*

Our text is Wesley's Covenant Service of 1780, which is based on the *Vindiciae Pietatis* of the Puritan Richard Alleine, which Wesley had abridged for his *Christian Library* in 1755. On December 25, 1747, Wesley had urged the Methodists to renew their covenant with God, and his first service was held in the French Church at Spitalfields on August 11, 1755. The 1780 service was used for almost a century in that form but has since been revised to enable greater participation and is now one of the finest liturgical services within the whole Christian Church. The Covenant Service is often held at the beginning of the year but can be held at any time. From 1755 it has become a classical part of Methodist spirituality and increasingly is being integrated into the life of other churches. It epitomizes the complete giving to God of the whole self that was the essence of Wesley's own spirituality.

[10] Extract from *A Short Account of the Life and Death of the Reverend John Fletcher*

First published in 1786, this extract sums up the character of Fletcher of Madeley and is based largely on texts supplied by Fletcher's widow and brother. Wesley never vaunted his own spiritual prowess and was strangely quiet about his own achievements. In this piece he describes a colleague and friend who did begin to meet Wesley's requirements for an ideal Christian. Although the two were very different, we see in Fletcher something of Wesley himself. Fletcher was recognized as one of the saints of the early Methodists, and although his own writings later declined in popularity the reputation of his saintly spirituality remains.

[11] *Eleven Letters of Spiritual Counsel, July 25, 1767 to February 24, 1791*

Telford's edition of Wesley's *Letters* (8 vols [London: Epworth, 1931]) contains 2,670 epistles written to a variety of people on a variety of subjects. They focus mainly on the pastoral, administrative, theological, and devotional matters thrown up by the Methodist Revival, and these concerns are sometimes mingled in the same letter. Some of them have become famous in their own right, not least the final one, written at the end of Wesley's life, to encourage Wilberforce in his fight against slavery, a long-standing concern of Wesley's. The other ten, all written to women, reveal Wesley's skill as a spiritual counsellor. The title at the head of each letter is my own.

SECTION II: CHARLES WESLEY'S HYMNS

[1] Selections from the 1780 *Hymnbook*

We include the preface and 72 hymns from this most famous of all of the Wesleys' hymn books. The first number at the top of each hymn is our own; the second is the number that appears in the 1780 *Hymnbook;* the third is the number (if any) that appears in the latest

(1933) hymn book. Daggers beside particular verses indicate that these verses were present in the 1780 book but are absent in the 1933 book. In all cases the whole of the original hymn is inserted. This has caused problems in regard to expressions that are regarded as infelicitous in the present age such as "worm" describing a person or "bowels" indicating compassion. I have preferred to keep the whole hymn as it was, and if necessary to leave out hymns, fragments of which have become famous, rather than to tamper with the verses or wording. I have however altered some of the titles of the sections in the *Hymnbook* to aid understanding. "Exhorting, and beseeching to return to God" becomes "Adoration and return to God"; "For mourners brought to the birth" and "recovered" becomes "Praying for Light and Assurance"; "For believers seeking for full redemption" becomes "For believers seeking perfect love"; and "For believers brought to the birth and saved" becomes "For mature believers." At the bottom of each hymn is an indication of the collection wherein it first appeared.

Charles Wesley's hymns were not only written in beautifully fashioned English, they also had a structure giving internal direction to their spirituality. To take but one example, "Sons of God, triumphant rise," number 96. The first verse of this postcommunion hymn encourages us to rejoice in exaltation after the wonder of the communion service; the last line of the second verse announces the main theme, "pardon, grace and glory ours"; verses 3 and 4 expand on the theme of "pardon"; verses 5 and 6 expand upon the theme of "grace"; and verses 7 and 8 expand upon the theme of "glory." A basic structure appears in virtually all Charles Wesley's hymns.

They are also remarkable in their ability to quote or interpret scripture. The index to the 1780 *Hymnbook* indicates that only Ezra, Obadiah, Nahum, and Zephaniah of the Old Testament, and III John of the New Testament, are not illustrated in the hymns. By the side of the first hymn in our selection we insert the scripture references alluded to within its verses. This instinctive use of scripture is typical of all the hymns.

The hymns have become classics for other reasons as well. They illustrate not only scripture but the main Christian doctrines in a creative way. They do not rest content with objective description but are experiential as well. They are also mystical in that they deal with an external world that transcends doctrine, history, and experience. Indeed, the 1780 *Hymnbook* is essentially a book of spirituality. The hymns were sung spirituality, and could be used for private spirituality. In them, Wesley traces the progression in spirituality of those whom he calls, in the preface, "real Christians." He begins with hymns of adoration that are also exhortations to encourage commitment to God. He then points out why people should become committed to God under headings such as the pleasantness of religion, the goodness of God, the fact of death, the blessing that ensues, and the inwardness of religion. He continues with hymns that are prayers for light and assurance, and that actively seek commitment. When commitment is reached, he follows with hymns for Christians rejoicing, fighting, praying, watching, working, suffering, seeking for perfect love, achieving spiritual maturity, and interceding for the world. He ends with corporate hymns for the church or groups of Christians meeting, praying, and parting.

By 1812, the 1780 *Hymnbook* had already gone through twenty-four editions. It was supplemented in 1830 and 1876, and twentieth-century hymn books have been more inclined to rearrange the hymns under different headings. Many of these hymns remain the crowning glory of Christian hymnody, as well as classics of Western spirituality.

Our text is a collation of the main editions of Wesley's lifetime.

[2] Selection of Charles Wesley's Hymns from *Hymns of the Lord's Supper*

These were first published in 1745 and there was little change throughout the nine editions of Wesley's lifetime from the first. They were preceded by an extract from Dr. Daniel Brevint's *The Christian Sacrament and Sacrifice*, which provided the basic headings under which the hymns are grouped. They were the most widely used of all the particular collections, although of course less so than the great general collections. They appeared during the same period (1744–1745) as other famous particular collections of hymns for Easter, Ascension, Whitsun, and Trinity Sunday. The first number at the top of each hymn is our own; the second is the number that appears in the 1745 *Hymns of the Lord's Supper;* the third is the number (if any) that appears in the latest (1933) hymn book.

[3] Selections of Other Hymns by Charles Wesley from the 1876 Supplement

The editors of the 1830 and 1876 hymn books included some

hymns in the canon of the 1780 *Hymnbook* that had not been inserted therein by the Wesleys, and they added a supplement to the resulting canon. We include some of the hymns added to the 1780 canon by the 1876 hymn book, and some from the supplement of the 1876 book. The first number at the top of each hymn is our own; the second is the number that appears in the 1876 hymn book; the third is the number (if any) that appears in the latest (1933) hymn book. Any of the second numbers lower than 539 are additions, marked in the 1876 book by an asterisk, to the canon of the 1780 *Hymnbook*. Some of the hymns in this section are equally classics with the hymns that appear in the other two sections. This applies not just to the hymns for great festivals, which were deliberately excluded from the 1780 *Hymnbook*, but to other hymns concerning which the Methodist tradition was willing, as it were, to overrule the Wesleys' choice. Again we quote the whole of the original hymn and mark by a dagger the verses left out by the 1876 book.

SECTION III: A PLAIN ACCOUNT OF CHRISTIAN PERFECTION

Our text is based on a collation of the second edition of 1766 with the sixth edition of 1789. This text has gone through at least thirty-seven known editions. It provides a partial spiritual autobiography of John Wesley. It includes portions of his other works on Christian Perfection, including *The Character of a Methodist*, which we would have included in this volume if it were not already substantially present in *A Plain Account of Christian Perfection*. This work is one of Wesley's longer pieces. Because of the intense business of his life he specialized in shorter pieces. It summarizes his reflections on his most distinctive contribution to Western spirituality and on what he called the "Grand Depositum" of the people called Methodists. It also summarizes some of the main phases in early Methodist history as well as in John Wesley's own pilgrimage. Like many of Wesley's works it was written in haste rather than leisure and is mildly polemical in that he is responding to the charge that he had changed his teaching on Christian Perfection during the course of the revival. He claims that this central vision has been his from 1725 throughout his whole life and that he had not substantially changed it at all. He maintains that perfection is the whole point and purpose of the Christian life.

BRIEF NOTES

Appendix

Wesley's beautiful Covenant Service has been adapted and renewed by the Methodist tradition during the last two hundred years. We include a recent version of the Covenant Service that can be used contemporaneously by Christian individuals or groups to renew their own spiritual life. *A Service for Such as Would Make or Renew Their Covenant with God* was edited by George B. Robson and published by the Conference Office of the Wesleyan Methodist Church, 25–35 City Road, London, E.C.1., before the union of the British Methodist Church in 1933. It transcends denominations. It is our hope that all who take this book will read it both carefully and prayerfully.

General Editorial Policy

Direct quotations and paraphrases of scripture are underlined to indicate Wesley's reliance on scripture and his interweaving of texts. His archaic verb forms, spelling, and punctuation are generally modernized, although most of his italics and some of his unusual capitalizations are kept to indicate his emphases. On one or two occasions archaic words incomprehensible to the modern reader are changed into modern synonyms.

SELECTED WRITINGS
of
JOHN WESLEY

[1]

JOHN WESLEY'S SPIRITUALITY: A COLLECTION OF FORMS OF PRAYER FOR EVERY DAY IN THE WEEK
(first printed in 1733)

PREFACE

The intention of the collector of these prayers was, First, to have forms of prayer for every day in the week, each of which contained something of deprecation, petition, thanksgiving, and intercession. Secondly, to have such forms for those days which the Christian Church has ever judged peculiarly proper for religious rejoicing, as contained little of deprecation, but were explicit and large in acts of love and thanksgiving. Thirdly, to have such for those days which from the age of the Apostles have been set apart for religious mourning, as contained little of thanksgiving, but were full and express in acts of contrition and humiliation. Fourthly, to have intercessions every day for all those whom our own Church directs us to remember in our prayers. And, Fifthly, to comprise in the course of petitions for the week the whole scheme of our Christian duty.

Whoever follows the direction of our excellent Church, in the interpretation of the Holy Scriptures, by keeping close to that sense of them which the Catholic Fathers and ancient Bishops have delivered to succeeding generations, will easily see that the whole system of Christian duty is reducible to these five heads:

First: The renouncing ourselves. *If any man will come after me, let him renounce himself, and follow me.* (Matthew 16:24) This implies (1) a thorough conviction that we are not our own; that we are not the proprietors of ourselves, or anything we enjoy; that we have no right to dispose of our goods, bodies, souls, or any of the actions or passions of them; (2) a solemn resolution to act suitably to this conviction: not to live to ourselves; not to pursue our own desires; not to please ourselves; nor to suffer our own will to be any principle of action to us.

Secondly: Such a renunciation of ourselves naturally leads to the devoting of ourselves to God. As this implies (1) a thorough conviction that we are God's; that He is the proprietor of all we are, and all we have; and that not only by right of creation, but of purchase; for He died for all, and therefore *died for all, that they which live should not henceforth live unto themselves, but unto Him that died for them;* (2) a solemn resolution to act suitably to this conviction: to live unto God; to render unto God the things which are God's, even all we are, and all we have; to glorify Him in our bodies, and in our spirits, with all the powers and all the strength of each; and to make his will our sole principle of action.

Thirdly: Self-denial is the immediate consequence of this. For whosoever has determined to live no longer to the desires of men, but to the Will of God, will soon find that he cannot be true to his purpose without denying himself, and taking up his cross daily. He will daily feel some desire which this one principle of action, the will of God, does not require him to indulge. In this, therefore, he must either deny himself, or so far deny the faith. He will daily meet with some means of drawing nearer to God, which are unpleasing to flesh and blood. In this, therefore, he must either take up his cross, or so far renounce his Master.

Fourthly: By a constant exercise of self-denial, the true follower of Christ continually advances in mortification. He is more and more dead to the world, and the things of the world, till at length he can say, with that perfect disciple of his Lord (Marquis de Renty), "I desire nothing but God," or, with Saint Paul, *I am crucified unto the world; I am dead with Christ; I live not, but Christ liveth in me.*

Fifthly: Christ liveth in me. This is the fulfilling of the law, the last stage of Christian holiness: This maketh the man of God perfect. He that being dead to the world is alive to God; the desire of whose soul is unto his name; who has given Him his whole heart; who delights in Him, and in nothing else but what tends to Him; who, for his sake, burns with love to all mankind; who neither thinks, speaks, nor acts, but to fulfill his will, is on the last round of the ladder to heaven: Grace hath had its full work upon his soul: The next step he takes is into glory.

May the God of glory give unto us who have not already attained this, neither are already perfect, to do this one thing; *forgetting those things which are behind, and reaching forth unto those things which are be-*

fore, to press toward the mark for the prize of our high calling in Christ Jesus!

May He so enlighten our eyes that *we may reckon all things but loss for the excellency of the knowledge of Christ Jesus our Lord;* and so stablish our hearts that we may rejoice to suffer the loss of all things, and count them but dung, that we may win Christ!

SUNDAY EVENING

General Questions which a serious Christian may propose to himself before he begins his Evening Devotions

1. With what degree of attention and fervor did I use my morning prayers, public or private?
2. Have I done anything without a present, or at least a previous, perception of its direct or remote tendency to the glory of God?
3. Did I in the morning consider what particular virtue I was to exercise, and what business I had to do, in the day?
4. Have I been zealous to undertake, and active in doing, what good I could?
5. Have I interested myself any further in the affairs of others than charity required?
6. Have I, before I visited or was visited, considered how I might thereby give or receive improvement?
7. Have I mentioned any failing or fault of any man, when it was not necessary for the good of another?
8. Have I unnecessarily grieved anyone by word or deed?
9. Have I before or in every action considered how it might be a means of improving in the virtue of the day?

Particular Questions relative to the Love of God

1. Have I set apart some of this day to think upon his perfections and mercies?
2. Have I labored to make this day a day of heavenly rest, sacred to divine love?
3. Have I employed those parts of it in works of necessity and mercy which were not employed in prayer, reading, and meditation?

JOHN WESLEY

O My Father, my God, I am in your hand; and may I rejoice above all things in being so. Do with me what seems good in your sight; only let me love you with all my mind, soul, and strength.

I magnify you for granting me to be born in your Church, and of religious parents; for washing me in your baptism, and instructing me in your doctrine of truth and holiness; for sustaining me by your gracious providence, and guiding me by your blessed Spirit; for admitting me, with the rest of my Christian brethren, to wait on you at your public worship; and for so often feeding my soul with your most precious body and blood, those pledges of love and sure conveyances of strength and comfort. Oh, be gracious unto all of us, whom you have this day (or at any time) admitted to your holy table. Strengthen our hearts in your ways against all our temptations, and make us *more than conquerors* in your love.

O my Father, my God, deliver me, I beseech you, from all violent passions: I know how greatly obstructive these are of both the knowledge and the love of you. Oh, let none of them find a way into my heart, but let me ever possess my soul in meekness. O my God, I desire to fear them more than death; let me not serve these cruel tyrants, but do you reign in my breast; let me be ever your servant, and love you with all my heart.

Deliver me, O God, from too intense an application to even necessary business. I know how this dissipates my thoughts from the one end of all my business, and impairs that lively perception I would ever retain of your standing at my right hand. I know the narrowness of my heart, and that an eager attention to earthly things leaves it no room for the things of heaven. Oh, teach me to go through all my employments with so truly disengaged a heart that I may still see you in all things, and see you therein as continually looking upon me, and searching my reins; and that I may never impair that liberty of spirit which is necessary for the love of you.

Deliver me, O God, from a slothful mind, from all lukewarmness, and all dejection of spirit. I know these cannot but deaden my love to you; mercifully free my heart from them, and give me a lively, zealous, active, and cheerful spirit, that I may vigorously perform whatever you command, thankfully suffer whatever you choose for me, and be ever ardent to obey in all things your holy love.

Deliver me, O God, from all idolatrous love of any creature. I know infinite numbers have been lost to you by loving those creatures for their own sake, which you permit, nay, even command, to love subordinately to you. Preserve me, I beseech you, from all such blind affection; be a guard to all my desires, that they fix on no creature any farther than the love of it tends to build me up in the love of you. You require me to love you with all my heart: Undertake for me, I beseech you, and be my security, that I may never open my heart to anything but out of love to you.

Above all, deliver me, O my God, from all idolatrous self-love. I know, O God (blessed be your infinite mercy for giving me this knowledge) that this is the root of all evil. I know you made me not to do my own will but yours. I know the very corruption of the devil is the having of a will contrary to yours. Oh, be my helper against this most dangerous of all idols, that I may both discern all its subtleties and withstand all its force. O you who have commanded me to renounce myself, give me strength, and I will obey your command. My choice and desire is to love myself, as all other creatures, in and for you. Oh let your almighty arm so stablish, strengthen, and settle me that you may ever be the ground and pillar of all my love.

By this love of you, my God, may my soul be fixed against its natural inconstancy; by this may it be reduced to an entire indifference as to all things else, and simply desire what is pleasing in your sight. May this holy flame ever warm my breast, that I may serve you with all my might; and let it consume in my heart all selfish desires, that I may in all things regard not myself but you.

O my God, let your glorious name be duly honored and loved by all the creatures you have made. Let your infinite goodness and greatness be ever adored by all angels and men. May your Church, the Catholic seminary of divine love, be protected from all the powers of darkness. Oh, vouchsafe to all who call themselves by your name one short glimpse of your goodness. May they once taste and see how gracious you are, that all things else may be tasteless to them; that their desires may be always flying up toward you, that they may render to you love, and praise, and obedience, pure and cheerful, constant and zealous, universal and uniform, like that the holy angels render to you in heaven.

Send forth your blessed Spirit into the midst of these sinful nations, and make us a holy people: Stir up the heart of our Sovereign, of the Royal Family, of the Clergy, the Nobility, and of all whom you have set over us, that they may be happy instruments in your hand of promoting this good work. Be gracious to the Universities, to the Gentry and Commons of this land: And comfort all that are in afflic-

81

tion; let the trial of their faith work patience in them, and perfect them in hope and love.

Bless my father, &c., my friends and relations, and all that belong to this family; all that have been instrumental to my good, by their assistance, advice, example, or writing; and all that do not pray for themselves.

Change the hearts of my enemies, and give me grace to forgive them, even as you for Christ's sake forgive us.

O Shepherd of Israel, vouchsafe to receive me this night and ever into your protection; accept my poor services, and pardon the sinfulness of these and all my holy duties. Oh, let it be your good pleasure shortly to put a period to sin and misery, to infirmity and death, to complete the number of your elect, and to hasten your kingdom; that we, and all that wait for your salvation, may eternally love and praise you, O God the Father, God the Son, and God the Holy Ghost, throughout all ages, world without end. Our Father, &c.

MONDAY MORNING

General Questions, which may be used every Morning.

Did I think of God first and last?

Have I examined myself how I behaved since last night's retirement?

Am I resolved to do all the good I can this day, and to be diligent in the business of my calling?

O God, who are the giver of all good gifts, I your unworthy servant entirely desire to praise your name for all the expressions of your bounty toward me. Blessed be your love for giving your Son to die for our sins, for the means of grace, and for the hope of glory. Blessed be your love for all the temporal benefits which you have with a liberal hand poured out upon me; for my health and strength, food and raiment, and all other necessaries with which you have provided your sinful servant. I also bless you that, after all my refusals of your grace, you still have patience with me, have preserved me this night, and given me yet another day to renew and perfect my repentance. Pardon, good Lord, all my former sins, and make me every day more zealous and diligent to improve every opportunity of building up my soul in your faith, and love, and obedience. Make yourself always present to my mind, and let your love fill and rule my soul, in all those places, and companies, and employments to which you call me this day. In all my passage through this world, suffer not my heart to be set upon it; but always fix my single eye and my undivided affections on *the prize of my high calling.* This one thing let me do; let me so press toward this as to make all things else minister unto it; and be careful so to use them as thereby to fit my soul for that pure bliss which you have prepared for those that love you.

O you who are good and do good, who extend your loving-kindness to all mankind, the work of your hands, your image, capable of knowing and loving you eternally: Suffer me to exclude none, O Lord, from my charity, who are the objects of your mercy; but let me treat all my neighbors with that tender love which is due to your servants and to your children. You have required this mark of my love to you: Oh, let no temptation expose me to ingratitude, or make me forfeit your loving-kindness, which is better than life itself. But grant that I may assist all my brethren with my prayers, where I cannot reach them with actual services. Make me zealous to embrace all occasions that may administer to their happiness, by assisting the needy, protecting the oppressed, instructing the ignorant, confirming the wavering, exhorting the good, and reproving the wicked. Let me look upon the failings of my neighbor as if they were my own; that I may be grieved for them, that I may never reveal them but when charity requires, and then with tenderness and compassion. Let your love to me, O blessed Savior, be the pattern of my love to him. You thought nothing too dear to part with, to rescue me from eternal misery: Oh, let me think nothing too dear to part with to set forward the everlasting good of my fellow Christians. They are members of your body; therefore I will cherish them. You have redeemed them with an inestimable price; assisted by your Holy Spirit, therefore, I will endeavor to recover them from a state of destruction; that thus adorning your holy Gospel, by doing good according to my power, I may at last be received into the endearments of your eternal love, and sing everlasting praise unto the Lamb that was slain and sits on the throne forever.

Extend, I humbly beseech thee, your mercy to all men, and let them become your faithful servants. Let all Christians live up to the holy religion they profess; especially these sinful nations. Be entreated for us, good Lord; be glorified by our reformation, and not by our destruction. *Turn us, and so shall we be turned:* Oh, be favorable to your people; give us grace to put a period to our provocations, and do put a period to our punishment. Defend our Church from schism, heresy, and sacrilege, and the King from all treasons and conspiracies. Bless all Bishops, Priests, and Deacons, with apostolical graces, exemplary lives, and sound doctrine. Grant to the Council wisdom from above, to all Magistrates integrity and zeal, to the Universities quietness and industry, and to the Gentry and Commons pious and peaceable and loyal hearts.

Preserve my parents, my brothers and sisters, my friends and relations, and all mankind, in their souls and bodies. Forgive my enemies, and in your due time make them kindly affected toward me. Have mercy on all who are *afflicted in mind, body, or estate; give them patience under their sufferings, and a happy issue out of all their afflictions.* O grant that we, with those who are already dead in your faith and fear, may together partake of a joyful resurrection, through him who lives and reigns with you and the Holy Ghost, one God, world without end.

[2]

A SCHEME OF SELF-EXAMINATION
Used by the First Methodists in Oxford

Sunday—Love of God and Simplicity:
Means of which are, Prayer and Meditation

1. Have I been simple and recollected in everything I said or did? Have I (a) been simple in everything, that is, looked upon God, my Good, my Pattern, my one Desire, my Disposer, Parent of Good; acted wholly for him; bounded my views with the present action or hour? (b) Recollected? that is, has this simple view been distinct and uninterrupted? Have I, in order to keep it so, used the signs agreed upon with my friends, wherever I was? Have I done anything without a previous perception of its being the will of God? or without a perception of its being an exercise or a means of the virtue of the day? Have I said anything without it?

2. Have I prayed with fervor? at going in and out of church? in the church? morning and evening in private? Monday, Wednesday, and Friday, with my friends, at rising? before lying down? on Saturday noon? all the time I am engaged in exterior work in private? before I go into the place of public or private prayer, for help therein? Have I, wherever I was, gone to church morning and evening, unless for necessary mercy? and spent from one hour to three in private? Have I, in private prayer, frequently stopped short and observed what fervor? Have I repeated it over and over, till I adverted to every word? Have I at the beginning of every prayer or paragraph owned I cannot pray? Have I paused before I concluded in his name, and adverted to my Savior now interceding for me at the right hand of God, and offering up these prayers?

3. Have I duly used ejaculations? that is, have I every hour prayed for humility, faith, hope, love, and the particular virtue of the day? considered with whom I was the last hour, what I did, and how? with regard to recollection, love of man, humility, self-denial, resig-

nation, and thankfulness? considered the next hour in the same respects, offered up all I do to my Redeemer, begged his assistance in
every particular, and commended my soul to his keeping? Have I
done this deliberately, not in haste, seriously, not doing anything else
the while, and fervently as I could?

4. Have I duly prayed for the virtue of the day? that is, have I
prayed for it at going out and coming in? deliberately, seriously, fervently?

5. Have I used a Collect at nine, twelve, and three? and grace before and after eating? aloud at my own room? deliberately, seriously,
fervently?

6. Have I duly meditated? every day, unless for necessary mercy,
(a) From six, &c., to prayers? (b) From four to five? What was particular in the providence of this day? How ought the virtue of the day
to have been exerted upon it? How did it fall short? (Here faults.)
(c) On Sunday, from six to seven, with Kempis? from three to four
on redemption, or God's attributes? Wednesday and Friday, from
twelve to one, on the Passion? after ending a book, on what I had
marked in it?

Monday—Love of Man

1. Have I been zealous to do, and active in doing, good? that is,
Have I embraced every probable opportunity of doing good, and preventing, removing, or lessening evil? Have I pursued it with my
might? Have I thought anything too dear to part with, to serve my
neighbor? Have I spent an hour at least every day in speaking to
someone or other? Have I given anyone up till he expressly renounced me? Have I, before I spoke to any, learned, as far as I could,
his temper, way of thinking, past life, and peculiar hindrances, internal and external? fixed the point to be aimed at? then the means to
it? Have I in speaking proposed the motives, then the difficulties,
then balanced them, then exhorted him to consider both calmly and
deeply, and to pray earnestly for help? Have I in speaking to a stranger explained what religion is not? (not negative, not external;) and
what it is? (a recovery of the image of God;) searched at what step in
it he stops, and what makes him stop there? exhorted and directed
him? Have I persuaded all I could to attend public prayers, sermons,
and sacraments, and in general to obey the laws of the Church Catholic, the Church of England, the State, the University, and their re-

spective Colleges? Have I, when taxed with any act of obedience, avowed it, and turned the attack with sweetness and firmness? Have I disputed upon any practical point, unless it was to be practiced just then? Have I in disputing, (i.) Desired him to define the terms of the question; to limit it; what he grants, what denies? (ii.) Delayed speaking my opinion? let him explain and prove his? then insinuated and pressed objections? Have I after every visit asked him who went with me, "Did I say anything wrong?" Have I when anyone asked advice directed and exhorted him with all my power?

2. Have I rejoiced with and for my neighbor in virtue or pleasure? grieved with him in pain, for him in sin?

3. Have I received his infirmities with pity, not anger?

4. Have I thought or spoke unkindly of or to him? Have I revealed any evil of anyone, unless it was necessary to some particular good I had in view? Have I then done it with all the tenderness of phrase and manner consistent with that end? Have I anyway appeared to approve them that did otherwise?

5. Has goodwill been, and appeared to be, the spring of all my actions toward others?

6. Have I duly used intercession? Before, after, speaking to any? For my friends on Sunday? For my pupils on Monday? For those who have particularly desired it, on Wednesday and Friday? For the family in which I am, every day?

[3]

ADVICE ON SPIRITUAL READING.
PART OF THE PREFACE
TO JOHN WESLEY'S ABRIDGMENT
OF THOMAS À KEMPIS' TREATISE OF
THE IMITATION OF CHRIST.
1735

---

1. It is to these alone who, knowing they have not yet attained, neither are already perfect, mind this one thing, and, pressing toward the mark, despise no assistance which is offered them, that the following advices are proposed, concerning the manner of reading this (or any other religious) treatise.

2. First: Assign some stated time every day for this employment; and observe it, so far as you possibly can, inviolably. But if necessary business, which you could not foresee or defer, should sometimes rob you of your hour of retirement, take the next to it; or, if you cannot have that, at least the nearest you can.

3. Secondly: Prepare yourself for reading, by purity of intention, singly aiming at the good of your soul, and by fervent prayer to God, that he would enable you to see his will, and give you a firm resolution to perform it. An excellent form of prayer for this very purpose you have in the second or third book of this treatise.

4. Thirdly: Be sure to read, not cursorily or hastily, but leisurely, seriously, and with great attention; with proper pauses and intervals, and that you may allow time for the enlightenings of the divine grace. To this end, recollect, every now and then, what you have read, and consider how to reduce it to practice. Further, let your reading be continued and regular, not rambling and desultory. To taste of many things, without fixing upon any, shows a vitiated palate, and feeds the disease which makes it pleasing. Whatsoever book you begin, read, therefore, through in order: Not but that it will be of great service to read those passages over and over that more nearly concern your-

self, and more closely affect your inclinations or practice; especially if you press them home to your soul, by adding a particular examination of yourself upon each head.

5. Fourthly: Labor to work yourself up into a temper correspondent with what you read; for that reading is useless which only enlightens the understanding, without warming the affections. And therefore intersperse, here and there, earnest aspirations to God, for his heat as well as his light. Select also any remarkable sayings or advices, and treasure them up in your memory; and these you may either draw forth in time of need, as arrows from a quiver, against temptation (more especially against the solicitations to that sin which most easily besets you) or make use of as incitements to any virtue, to humility, patience, or the love of God.

6. Conclude all with a short ejaculation to God, that he, without whom *neither is he that planteth anything, nor he that watereth*, would so bless the good seed sown in your heart, that it may bring forth fruit unto life eternal.

[4]

JOHN WESLEY'S TRANSLATIONS
OF SOME GERMAN HYMNS

1. (344) ((433))

1. THOU hidden love of God, whose height,
        Whose depth unfathom'd no man knows,
    I see from far thy beauteous light,
        Inly I sigh for thy repose.
    My heart is pain'd, nor can it be
    At rest, till it finds rest in thee.

2. Thy secret voice invites me still
        The sweetness of thy yoke to prove;
    And fain I would: but though my will
        Be fix'd, yet wide my passions rove.
    Yet hindrances strew all the way;
    I aim at thee, yet from thee stray.

3. 'Tis mercy all, that thou hast brought
        My mind to seek her peace in thee;
    Yet while I seek, but find thee not,
        No peace my wandering soul shall see.
    Oh, when shall all my wanderings end,
    And all my steps to thee-ward tend?

4. Is there a thing beneath the sun
        That strives with thee my heart to share?
    Ah, tear it thence, and reign alone,
        The Lord of every motion there:
    Then shall my heart from earth be free,
    When it has found repose in thee.

5. Oh, hide this SELF from me, that I
      No more, but CHRIST in me may live!
   My vile affections crucify,
      Nor let one darling lust survive.
   In all things nothing may I see,
   Nothing desire or seek but thee!

6. O LOVE, thy sovereign aid impart,
      To save me from low-thoughted care:
   Chase this self-will through all my heart,
      Through all its latent mazes there.
   Make me Thy duteous child, that I
   Ceaseless may, "Abba, Father," cry.

7. Ah no! ne'er will I backward turn:
      Thine wholly, thine alone I am!
   Thrice happy he who views with scorn
      Earth's toys, for thee his constant flame.
   Oh, help, that I may never move
   From the blest footsteps of thy love!

8. Each moment draw from earth away
      My heart, that lowly waits thy call:
   Speak to my inmost soul, and say,
      "I am thy Love, thy God, thy All!"
   To feel thy power, to hear thy voice,
   To taste thy love is all my choice!

                                   Gerhard Tersteegen
                                   1697–1769

2. (831) ((507))

1. COMMIT thou all thy griefs
      And ways into his hands;
      To his sure truth and tender care,
      Who earth and heaven commands.
2. Who points the clouds their course,
      Whom winds and seas obey;
      He shall direct thy wandering feet,
      He shall prepare thy way.

91

3. Thou on the Lord rely,
   So safe shalt thou go on;
   Fix on his work thy steadfast eye,
   So shall thy work be done.
4. No profit canst thou gain
   By self-consuming care:
   To him commend thy cause, his ear
   Attends the softest prayer.

5. Thy everlasting truth,
   Father, thy ceaseless love
   Sees all thy children's wants, and knows
   What best for each will prove.
6. And whatso'er thou will'st,
   Thou dost, O King of kings;
   What thy unerring wisdom chose
   Thy power to being brings.

7. Thou everywhere hast way,
   And all things serve thy might;
   Thy every act pure blessing is,
   Thy path unsullied light.
8. When Thou arisest, Lord,
   What shall Thy work withstand?
   When all thy children want Thou giv'st,
   Who, who shall stay thy hand?

9. Give to the winds thy fears,
   Hope, and be undismay'd;
   God hears thy sighs, and counts thy tears,
   God shall lift up thy head.
10. Through waves and clouds and storms
    He gently clears thy way;
    Wait thou His time, so shall this night
    Soon end in joyous day.

11. Still heavy is thy heart?
    Still sink thy spirits down?
    Cast off the weight, let fear depart,
    And every care be gone.

12. What though thou rulest not?
    Yet heaven and earth and hell
    Proclaim, God sitteth on the throne
    And ruleth all things well!

13. Leave to his sovereign sway
    To choose and to command;
    So shalt thou wondering own, his way
    How wise, how strong his hand.

14. Far, far above thy thought
    His counsel shall appear,
    When fully he the work hath wrought
    That caused thy needless fear.

15. Thou seest our weakness, Lord,
    Our hearts are known to Thee;
    Oh, lift thou up the sinking hand,
    Confirm the feeble knee!

16. Let us in life, in death,
    Thy steadfast truth declare,
    And publish with our latest breath
    Thy love and guardian care!

                                        Paulus Gerhardt
                                        1607–1676

3. (431) ((573))

1. JESU, thy light again I view,
       Again thy mercy's beams I see,
   And all within me wakes, anew
       To pant for thy immensity:
   Again my thoughts to thee aspire
   In fervent flames of strong desire.

2. But, Oh! what offering shall I give
       To thee, the Lord of earth and skies?
   My spirit, soul, and flesh receive
       A holy, living sacrifice.
   Small as it is, 'tis all my store:
   More shouldst thou have, if I had more.

3.   Now then, my God, thou hast my soul;
     No longer mine, but thine I am:
  Guard thou thy own: possess it whole,
     Cheer it by hope, with love inflame.
  Thou hast my spirit; there display
  Thy glory to the perfect day.

4.   Thou hast my flesh; thy hallow'd shrine,
     Devoted solely to Thy will:
  Here let thy light forever shine,
     This house still let thy presence fill:
  O Source of Life, live, dwell, and move
  In me, till all my life be love.

5.   Oh, never in these veils of shame,
     Sad fruits of sin, my glorying be!
  Clothe with salvation through thy name
     My soul, and may I put on Thee!
  Be living faith my costly dress,
  And my best robe thy righteousness!

6.   Send down thy likeness from above,
     And let this my adorning be:
  Clothe me with wisdom, patience, love,
     With lowliness and purity,
  Than gold and pearls more precious far,
  And brighter than the morning star.

7.   Lord, arm me with thy Spirit's might,
     Since I am call'd by thy great name:
  In thee my wandering thoughts unite,
     Of all my works be thou the aim.
  Thy love attend me all my days,
  And my sole business be thy praise!

Joachim Lange
1670–1744

SELECTED WRITINGS

4. (494) ((683))

1. LO, God is here! Let us adore,
    And own how dreadful is this place!
Let all within us feel his power,
    And silent bow before his face.
Who know his power, his grace who prove,
Serve him with awe, with reverence love.

2. Lo, God is here! him day and night
    The' united choirs of angels sing:
To him enthroned above all height
    Heaven's hosts their noblest praises bring:
Disdain not, Lord, our meaner song,
Who praise thee with a stammering tongue.

3. Gladly the toys of earth we leave,
    Wealth, pleasure, fame, for thee alone:
To thee our will, soul, flesh we give;
    O take, O seal them for thy own!
Thou art the God; thou art the Lord:
Be thou by all thy works adored!

4. Being of beings, may our praise
    Thy courts with grateful fragrance fill;
Still may we stand before thy face,
    Still hear and do thy sovereign will.
To thee may all our thoughts arise,
Ceaseless, accepted sacrifice!

5. In thee we move. All things of thee
    Are full, thou Source and Life of all!
Thou vast, unfathomable Sea!
    Fall prostrate, lost in wonder, fall,
Ye sons of men; for God is man!
All may we lose, so Thee we gain!

6. As flowers their opening leaves display,
    And glad drink in the solar fire,
So may we catch thy every ray,

JOHN WESLEY

So may thy influence us inspire:
Thou Beam of the Eternal Beam,
Thou purging Fire, thou quickening Flame!

Gerhard Tersteegen
1697–1769

5. (210) ((445))

1. THEE will I love, my strength, my tower;
   Thee will I love, my joy, my crown;
   Thee will I love with all my power,
   In all my works, and thee alone!
   Thee will I love, till the pure fire
   Fill my whole soul with chaste desire.

2. Ah! why did I so late thee know,
   Thee, lovelier than the sons of men!
   Ah! why did I no sooner go
   To thee, the only ease in pain!
   Ashamed I sigh, and inly mourn
   That I so late to thee did turn.

3. In darkness willingly I stray'd;
   I sought thee, yet from thee I roved:
   For wide my wandering thoughts were spread,
   Thy creatures more than thee I loved.
   And now, if more at length I see,
   'Tis through thy light, and comes from thee.

4. I thank thee, Uncreated Sun,
   That thy bright beams on me have shined;
   I thank thee, who hast overthrown
   My foes, and heal'd my wounded mind;
   I thank thee, whose enlivening voice
   Bids my freed heart in thee rejoice.

5. Uphold me, in the doubtful race,
   Nor suffer me again to stray;
   Strengthen my feet, with steady pace

Still to press forward in thy way;
My soul and flesh, O Lord of Might,
Fill, satiate with thy heavenly light.

6. Give to my eyes refreshing tears;
        Give to my heart chaste, hallow'd fires;
    Give to my soul, with filial fears,
        The love that all heaven's host inspires:
    "That all my powers, with all their might
    In thy sole glory may unite."

7. Thee will I love, my joy, my crown!
        Thee will I love, my Lord, my God!
    Thee will I love, beneath thy frown
        Or smile, thy sceptre or thy rod.
    What though my flesh and heart decay?
    Thee shall I love in endless day!

Johann Scheffler
1624 –1677

6. (189) ((375))

1. NOW I have found the ground, wherein
        Sure my soul's anchor may remain—
    The wounds of Jesus, for my sin
        Before the world's foundation slain:
    Whose mercy shall unshaken stay,
    When heaven and earth are fled away.

2. Father, thy everlasting grace
        Our scanty thought surpasses far:
    Thy heart still melts with tenderness,
        Thy arms of love still open are
    Returning sinners to receive,
    That mercy they may taste, and live.

3. O Love, thou bottomless abyss!
        My sins are swallow'd up in thee:
    Cover'd is my unrighteousness,

Nor spot of guilt remains in me,
While Jesu's blood, through earth and skies,
Mercy, free, boundless mercy, cries!

4. With faith I plunge me in this sea;
       Here is my hope, my joy, my rest:
   Hither, when hell assails, I flee,
       I look into my Savior's breast!
   Away, sad doubt, and anxious fear!
   Mercy is all that's written there.

5. Though waves and storms go o'er my head,
       Though strength, and health, and friends be gone,
   Though joys be wither'd all, and dead,
       Though every comfort be withdrawn,
   On this my steadfast soul relies,
   Father, thy mercy never dies.

6. Fix'd on this ground will I remain,
       Though my heart fail, and flesh decay:
   This anchor shall my soul sustain,
       When earth's foundations melt away;
   Mercy's full power I then shall prove,
   Loved with an everlasting love.

Johann Andreas Rothe
1688–1758

[5]

EXTRACTS FROM JOHN WESLEY'S JOURNAL
8th January to 24th May
1738

SUNDAY 8 January 1738: In the fullness of my heart, I wrote the following words:

By the most infallible of proofs, inward feeling, I am convinced:

1. Of unbelief—having no such faith in Christ as will prevent my heart from being troubled, which it could not be if I believed in God and rightly believed also in [Christ];

2. Of pride throughout my life past, inasmuch as I thought I had what I find I have not;

3. Of gross irrecollection, inasmuch as in a storm I cry to God every moment; in a calm, not;

4. Of levity and luxuriancy of spirit, recurring whenever the pressure is taken off; and appearing by my speaking words not tending to edify; but most by my manner of speaking of my enemies.

Lord, save, or I perish! Save me:

1. By such a faith as implies peace in life and in death;

2. By such humility as may fill my heart from this hour forever, with a piercing, uninterrupted sense, *nihil est quod hactenus feci*; (I have done nothing hitherto) having evidently built without a foundation;

3. By such a recollection as may cry to thee every moment, especially when all is calm. Give me faith, or I die; give me a lowly spirit: otherwise, *mihi non sit suave vivere*; (Let life be a burden to me).

4. By steadiness, seriousness, σεμνότης, sobriety of spirit; avoiding, as fire, every word that tends not to edifying, and never speaking of any who oppose me; or sin against God, without all my own sins set in array before my face.

TUESDAY 24: We spoke with two ships, outward-bound, from whom we had the welcome news of our wanting but one hundred and sixty leagues of the Land's End. My mind was now full of thought, part of which I wrote down as follows:

I went to America to convert the Indians but, oh, who shall convert me? Who, what, is he that will deliver me from this evil heart of unbelief? I have a fair summer religion. I can talk well, nay, and believe myself, while no danger is near. But let death look me in the face, and my spirit is troubled. Nor can I say, *to die is gain.*

I have a sin of fear, that when I've spun
My last thread, I shall perish on the shore!

I think, verily, if the Gospel be true, I am safe, for I not only have given and do give all my goods to feed the poor; I not only give my body to be burned, drowned, or whatever God shall appoint for me; but I follow after charity (though not as I ought, yet as I can) if haply I may attain it. I *now* believe the Gospel is true. *I show my faith by my works* by staking my all upon it. I would do so again and again a thousand times, if the choice were still to make. Whoever sees me, sees I would be a Christian. Therefore *are my ways not like other men's ways?* Therefore, I have been, I am, I am content to be, a *by-word, a proverb of reproach.* But in a storm I think, "What if the Gospel be not true? Then thou art of all men most foolish. For what have you given up your goods, your ease, your friends, your reputation, your country, your life? For what are you wandering over the face of the earth— a dream, a cunningly devised fable? Oh, who will deliver me from this fear of death? What shall I do? Where shall I fly from it? Should I fight against it by thinking or by not thinking of it?" A wise man advised me some time since, "Be still and go on." Perhaps this is best, to look upon it as my cross; when it comes, to let it humble me and quicken all my good resolutions, especially that of praying without ceasing, and at other times to take no thought about it, but quietly go on in the work of the Lord.

1. For many years I have been tossed by various winds of doctrine. I asked long ago, "What must I do to be saved"? The scripture answered, "Keep the commandments, believe, hope, love; follow after these tempers till you have fully attained (that is, till death) by all those outward works and means which God has appointed, by walking as Christ walked."

2. I was early warned against laying, as the papists do, too much

stress on outward works—or on a faith without works; which, as it does not include, so it will never lead to, true hope or charity. Nor am I sensible that to this hour I have laid too much stress on either; having from the very beginning valued both faith and the means of grace and good works, not on their own account, but as believing that God, who had appointed them, would by them bring me in due time to the mind that was in Christ.

3. But before God's time was come, I fell among some Lutheran and Calvinist authors, whose confused and indigested accounts magnified faith to such an amazing size that it quite hid all the rest of the commandments. I did not then see that this was the natural effect of their overgrown fear of popery, being so terrified with the cry of merit and good works that they plunged at once into the other extreme. In this labyrinth I was utterly lost, not being able to find out what the error was, nor yet to reconcile this uncouth hypothesis either with scripture or common sense.

4. The English writers, such as Bishop Beveridge, Bishop Taylor, and Mr. Nelson, a little relieved me from these well-meaning, wrong-headed Germans. Their accounts of Christianity I could easily see to be, in the main, consistent both with reason and scripture. Only when they interpreted scripture in different ways I was often much at a loss. And again, there was one thing much insisted on in scripture—the unity of the Church—which none of them, I thought, clearly explained or strongly inculcated.

5. But it was not long before Providence brought me to those who showed me a sure rule of interpreting scripture, viz: *Consensus veterum: quod ab omnibus, quod ubique, quod semper creditum* (The consensus of antiquity: that which has been believed by everyone, everywhere and always). At the same time they sufficiently insisted upon a due regard to the one Church at all times and in all places.

Nor was it long before I bent the bow too far the other way:

1. By making antiquity a coordinate rather than subordinate rule with scripture.

2. By admitting several doubtful writings as undoubted evidences of antiquity.

3. By extending antiquity too far, even to the middle or end of the fourth century.

4. By believing more practices to have been universal in the ancient Church than ever were so.

5. By not considering that the decrees of one provincial synod could bind only that province; and that the decrees of a general synod [bound] only those provinces whose representatives met therein.

6. By not considering that the most of those decrees were adapted to particular times and occasions; and consequently, when these occasions ceased, must cease to bind even those provinces.

These considerations insensibly stole upon me as I grew acquainted with the mystic writers, whose noble descriptions of union with God and internal religion made everything else appear mean, flat and insipid. But, in truth, they made good works appear so, too; yea, and faith itself, and what not?

What occurred on WEDNESDAY 24th (May), I think best to relate at large, after premising what may make it the better understood. Let him that cannot receive it ask the Father of lights that he would give more light both to him and me.

1. I believe, till I was about ten years old, I had not sinned away that washing of the Holy Ghost which was given me in baptism, having been strictly educated and carefully taught that I could only be saved by universal obedience, by keeping all the commandments of God—in the meaning of which I was diligently instructed. And those instructions, so far as they respected outward duties and sins, I gladly received and often thought of. But all that was said to me of inward obedience or holiness I neither understood nor remembered. So that I was indeed as ignorant of the true meaning of the law as I was of the Gospel of Christ.

2. The next six or seven years were spent at school, where, outward restraints being removed, I was much more negligent than before, even of outward duties, and almost continually guilty of outward sins which I knew to be such, though they were not scandalous in the eye of the world. However, I still read the scriptures and said my prayers, morning and evening. And what I now hoped to be saved by was (1) not being so bad as other people; (2) having still a kindness for religion; and (3) reading the Bible, going to church and saying my prayers.

3. Being removed to the university for five years, I still said my prayers both in public and in private, and read with the scriptures several other books of religion, especially comments on the New Testament. Yet I had not all this while so much as a notion of inward holiness; nay, went on habitually, and for the most part very content-

edly, in some or other known sin—indeed, with some intermissions and short struggles, especially before and after the Holy Communion, which I was obliged to receive thrice a year. I cannot well tell what I hoped to be saved by now, when I was continually sinning against that little light I had, unless by those transient fits of what many divines taught me to call "repentance."

4. When I was about twenty-two, my father pressed me to enter into Holy Orders. At the same time, the providence of God directing me to Kempis's *Christian Pattern*, I began to see that true religion was seated in the heart and that God's law extended to all our thoughts as well as words and actions. I was, however, very angry at Kempis for being *too strict*, though I read him only in Dean Stanhope's translation. Yet I had frequently much sensible comfort in reading him, such as I was an utter stranger to before. Meeting likewise with a religious friend, which I never had till now, I began to alter the whole form of my conversation, and to set in earnest upon "a new life." I set apart an hour or two a day for religious retirement. I communicated every week. I watched against all sin, whether in word or deed. I began to aim at, and pray for, inward holiness. So that now, *doing so much and living so good a life*, I doubted not but I was a good Christian.

5. Removing soon after to another college, I executed a resolution which I was before convinced was of the utmost importance—shaking off at once all my trifling acquaintance. I began to see more and more the value of time. I applied myself closer to study. I watched more carefully against actual sins; I advised others to be religious, according to that scheme of religion by which I modeled my own life. But meeting now with Mr. Law's *Christian Perfection* and *Serious Call* (although I was much offended at many parts of both, yet) they convinced me more than ever of the exceeding height and breadth and depth of the law of God. The light flowed in so mightily upon my soul that everything appeared in a new view. I cried to God for help and resolved not to prolong the time of obeying him, as I had never done before. And by my continued *endeavor to keep his whole law*, inward and outward, *to the utmost of my power*, I was persuaded that I should be accepted of him and that I was even then in a state of salvation.

6. In 1730 I began visiting the prisons, assisting the poor and sick in town, and doing what other good I could by my presence or my little fortune to the bodies and souls of all men. To this end I abridged

myself of all superfluities, and many that are called necessaries of life. I soon became a *by-word* for so doing, and I rejoiced that *my name was cast out as evil.* The next spring I began observing the Wednesday and Friday fasts commonly observed in the ancient Church, tasting no food till three in the afternoon. And now I knew not how to go any further. I diligently strove against all sin. I omitted no sort of self-denial which I thought lawful. I carefully used, both in public and private, all the means of grace at all opportunities. I omitted no occasion of doing good. I for that reason suffered evil. And all this I knew to be nothing unless as it was directed toward inward holiness. Accordingly this, the image of God, was what I aimed at in all, by doing his will, not my own. Yet when, after continuing some years in this course, I apprehended myself to be near death, I could not find that all this gave me any comfort or any assurance of acceptance with God. At this I was then not a little surprised, not imagining I had been all this time building on the sand, nor considering that *other foundation can no man lay than that which is laid by God, even Christ Jesus.*

7. Soon after, a contemplative man convinced me still more than I was convinced before that outward works are nothing, being alone; and in several conversations instructed me how to pursue inward holiness, or a union of the soul with God. But even of his instructions (though I then received them as the words of God) I cannot but now observe (a) that he spoke so incautiously against *trusting* in *outward works* that he discouraged me from *doing* them at all; (b) that he recommended (as it were, to supply what was wanting in them) *mental prayer* and the like exercises, as the most effectual means of purifying the soul and uniting it with God. Now these were, in truth, as much *my own works* as visiting the sick or clothing the naked; and the "union with God" thus pursued was as really *my own righteousness* as any I had before pursued under another name.

8. In this *refined* way of trusting to my own works and my own righteousness (so zealously inculcated by the mystic writers), I dragged on heavily, finding no comfort or help therein till the time of my leaving England. On shipboard, however, I was again active in outward works, where it pleased God of his free mercy to give me twenty-six of the Moravian brethren for companions, who endeavored to show me a more excellent way. But I understood it not at first. I was too learned and too wise, so that it seemed foolishness unto me. And I continued preaching and following after, and trusting in that righteousness whereby no flesh can be justified.

9. All the time I was at Savannah I was thus beating the air. Being ignorant of the righteousness of Christ, which, by a living faith in him, bringeth salvation *to every one that believeth*. I sought to establish my own righteousness, and so labored in the fire all my days. I was now properly *under the law*. I knew that *the law* of God was *spiritual; I consented to it that it was good.* Yea, *I delighted in it after the inner man.* Yet was I *carnal, sold under sin.* Every day was I constrained to cry out, *What I do, I allow not: for what I would, I do not; but what I hate, that I do. To will is indeed present with me; but how to perform that which is good, I find not. For the good which I would, I do not, but the evil which I would not, that I do. I find a law that when I would do good, evil is present with me, even the law in my members, warring against the law of my mind and still bringing me into captivity to the law of sin.*

10. In this state I was indeed fighting continually, but not conquering. Before, I had willingly served sin; now it was unwillingly, but still I served it. I fell and rose and fell again. Sometimes I was overcome and in heaviness: sometimes I overcame and was in joy. For as in the former state I had some foretastes of the terrors of the law, so had I in this of the comforts of the Gospel. During this whole struggle between nature and grace which had now continued above ten years, I had many remarkable returns to prayer, especially when I was in trouble. I had many sensible comforts, which are indeed no other than short anticipations of the life of faith. But I was still *under the law*, not *under grace* (the state most who are called Christians are content to live and die in), for I was only *striving with*, not *freed from*, *sin*. Neither had I *the witness of the Spirit with my spirit*, and indeed could not, for I *sought it not by faith, but as it were by the works of the law*.

11. In my return to England, January 1738, being in imminent danger of death and very uneasy on that account, I was strongly convinced that the cause of that uneasiness was unbelief and that the gaining a true, living faith was the one thing needful for me. But still I fixed not this faith on its right object: I meant only faith in God, not faith in or through Christ. Again, I knew not that I was *wholly void of this faith* but only thought *I had not enough* of it. So that when Peter Böhler, whom God prepared for me as soon as I came to London, affirmed of true faith in Christ (which is but one) that it had those two fruits inseparably attending it, "dominion over sin, and constant peace from a sense of forgiveness," I was quite amazed and looked upon it as a new Gospel. If this was so, it was clear I had not

faith. But I was not willing to be convinced of this. Therefore I disputed with all my might and labored to prove that faith might be where these were not, especially where the sense of forgiveness was not; for all the scriptures relating to this I had been long since taught to construe away and to call all Presbyterians who spoke otherwise. Besides, I well saw no one could, in the nature of things, have such a sense of forgiveness and not *feel* it. But I felt it not. If, then, there was no faith without this, all my pretensions to faith dropped at once.

12. When I met Peter Böhler again, he consented to put the dispute upon the issue which I desired, namely, scripture and experience. I first consulted the scripture. But when I set aside the glosses of men and simply considered the words of God, comparing them together, endeavoring to illustrate the obscure by the plainer passages, I found they all made against me and was forced to retreat to my last hold, "that experience would never agree with the *literal interpretation* of those scriptures. Nor could I therefore allow it to be true, till I found some living witnesses of it." He replied he could show me such at any time; if I desired it, the next day. And, accordingly, the next day he came again with three others, all of whom testified of their own personal experience that a true living faith in Christ is inseparable from a sense of pardon for all past, and freedom from all present, sins. They added with one mouth that this faith was the gift, the free gift of God, and that he would surely bestow it upon every soul who earnestly and perseveringly sought it. I was not thoroughly convinced and, by the grace of God, I resolved to seek it unto the end, first, by absolutely renouncing all dependence, in whole or in part, upon *my own* works or righteousness—on which I had really grounded my hope of salvation, though I knew it not, from my youth up; second, by adding to "the constant use of all the 'other' means of grace," continual prayer for this very thing—justifying, saving faith, a full reliance on the blood of Christ shed for *me*, a trust in him, as *my* Christ, as *my* sole justification, sanctification, and redemption.

13. I continued thus to seek it (though with strange indifference, dullness and coldness and unusually frequent relapses into sin) till Wednesday, May 24. I think it was about five this morning, that I opened my Testament on those words, τὰ μέγιστα ἡμῖν καὶ τίμια ἐπαγγέλματα δεδώρηται, ἵνα [διὰ τούτων] γένησθε θείας κοινωνοὶ φύσεως, *There are given unto us exceeding great and precious promises, even that you should be partakers of the divine nature* (2 Pet. 1:4). Just as I went out, I opened it again on those words, *You are not far*

from the kingdom of God. In the afternoon I was asked to go to St. Paul's. The anthem was *Out of the deep have I called unto you, O Lord: Lord, hear my voice. O let your ears consider well the voice of my complaint. If you, Lord, will be extreme to mark what is done amiss, O Lord, who may abide it? For there is mercy with you; therefore shall you be feared. O Israel, trust in the Lord, for with the Lord there is mercy and with him is plenteous redemption. And he shall redeem Israel from all his sins.*

14. In the evening, I went very unwillingly to a society in Aldersgate Street, where one was reading Luther's Preface to the Epistle to the Romans. About a quarter before nine, while he was describing the change which God works in the heart through faith in Christ, I felt my heart strangely warmed. I felt I did trust in Christ, Christ alone for salvation; and an assurance was given me that he had taken away *my* sins, even *mine*, and saved *me* from the law of sin and death.

15. I began to pray with all my might for those who had in a more especial manner despitefully used me and persecuted me. I then testified openly to all there what I now first felt in my heart. But it was not long before the enemy suggested, "This cannot be faith, for where is your joy?" Then was I taught that "peace and victory over sin are essential to faith in the Captain of our salvation but that, as to the transports of joy—that usually attend the beginning of it especially in those who have mourned deeply—God sometimes giveth, sometimes withholdest them, according to the counsels of his own will."

16. After my return home, I was much buffeted with temptations, but cried out and they fled away. They returned again and again. I as often lifted up my eyes and he *sent me help from his holy place.* And herein I found [in what] the difference between this and my former state chiefly consisted. I was striving, yea, fighting with all my might under the law, as well as under grace. But then I was sometimes, if not often, conquered; now, I was always conqueror.

THE
NATURE, DESIGN,
AND GENERAL RULES
OF THE
UNITED SOCIETIES,

in London, Bristol, Kingswood,
Newcastle-upon-Tyne, &c.,
1743

---

1. In the latter end of the year 1739, eight or ten persons came to me in London, who appeared to be deeply convinced of sin, and earnestly groaning for redemption. They desired (as did two or three more the next day) that I would spend some time with them in prayer, and advise them how to flee from the wrath to come; which they saw continually hanging over their heads. That we might have more time for this great work, I appointed a day when they might all come together, which from thenceforward they did every week, namely, on Thursday, in the evening. To these, and as many more as desired to join with them, (for their number increased daily,) I gave those advices, from time to time, which I judged most needful for them; and we always concluded our meeting with prayer suited to their several necessities.

2. This was the rise of the United Society, first in London, and then in other places. Such a society is no other than "a company of men having the form and seeking the power of godliness, united in order to pray together, to receive the word of exhortation, and to watch over one another in love, that they may help each other to work out their salvation."

3. That it may the more easily be discerned, whether they are indeed working out their own salvation, each society is divided into smaller companies, called *classes*, according to their respective places

of abode. There are about twelve persons in every class; one of whom is styled *the Leader.* It is his business, (a) To see each person in his class once a week at least, in order to inquire how their souls prosper; to advise, reprove, comfort, or exhort, as occasion may require; to receive what they are willing to give toward the relief of the poor. (b) To meet the minister and the Stewards of the society once a week; in order to inform the Minister of any that are sick, or of any that walk disorderly, and will not be reproved; to pay to the Stewards what they have received of their several classes in the week preceding; and to show their account of what each person has contributed.

4. There is one only condition previously required in those who desire admission into these societies—a desire *to flee from the wrath to come, to be saved from their sins:* But, wherever this is really fixed in the soul, it will be shown by its fruits. It is therefore expected of all who continue therein that they should continue to evidence their desire of salvation,

First, by doing no harm, by avoiding evil in every kind; especially that which is most generally practiced: Such is, the taking the name of God in vain; the profaning the day of the Lord, either by doing ordinary work thereon or by buying or selling; drunkenness, buying or selling spirituous liquors, or drinking them, unless in cases of extreme necessity; fighting, quarreling, brawling; brother going to law with brother; returning evil for evil, or railing for railing; the using many words in buying or selling; the buying or selling uncustomed goods; the giving or taking things on usury, that is unlawful interest; uncharitable or unprofitable conversation, particularly speaking evil of Magistrates or of Ministers; doing to others as we would not they should do unto us; doing what we know is not for the glory of God, as the "putting on of gold or costly apparel"; the taking such diversions as cannot be used in the name of the Lord Jesus; the singing those songs, or reading those books, which do not tend to the knowledge or love of God; softness, and needless self-indulgence; laying up treasures upon earth; borrowing without a probability of paying; or taking up goods without a probability of paying for them.

5. It is expected of all who continue in these societies that they should continue to evidence their desire of salvation,

Secondly, by doing good, by being, in every kind, merciful after their power; as they have opportunity, doing good of every possible sort, and as far as is possible, to all men; to their bodies, of the ability which God giveth, by giving food to the hungry, by clothing the naked, by visiting or helping them that are sick, or in prison; to their souls, by instructing, reproving, or exhorting all they have any intercourse with; trampling under foot that enthusiastic doctrine of devils, that "we are not to do good unless our heart be free to it": By doing good especially to them that are of the household of faith, or groaning so to be; employing them preferably to others, buying one of another; helping each other in business; and so much the more, because the world will love its own, and them only: By all possible diligence and frugality, that the gospel be not blamed: By running with patience the race that is set before them, *denying themselves, and taking up their cross daily;* submitting to bear the reproach of Christ, to be as the filth and offscouring of the world; and looking that men should *say all manner of evil of them falsely for the Lord's sake.*

6. It is expected of all who desire to continue in these societies that they should continue to evidence their desire of salvation,

Thirdly, by attending upon all the ordinances of God. Such are, the public worship of God; the ministry of the word, either read or expounded; the supper of the Lord; family and private prayer; searching the scriptures; and fasting, or abstinence.

7. These are the General Rules of our societies; all which we are taught of God to observe, even in his written word, the only rule, and the sufficient rule, both of our faith and practice. And all these, we know, his Spirit writes on every truly awakened heart. If there be any among us who observe them not, who habitually break any of them, let it be made known unto them who watch over that soul as they that must give an account. We will admonish him of the error of his ways; we will bear with him for a season: But then if he repent not, he hath no more place among us. We have delivered our own souls.

[7]

A MEDITATION ON THE LORD'S PRAYER. AN EXTRACT FROM WESLEY'S SERMON ON THE MOUNT VI
(first published 1748)

1. After having taught the true nature and ends of prayer, our Lord subjoins an example of it; even that divine form of prayer which seems in this place to be proposed by way of pattern chiefly, as the model and standard of all our prayers: *After this manner therefore pray yet.* Whereas, elsewhere he enjoins the use of these very words: *He said unto them, When you pray, say*— (Luke 11:2).

2. We may observe, in general, concerning this divine prayer, First, that it contains all we can reasonably or innocently pray for. There is nothing which we have need to ask of God, nothing which we can ask without offending him, which is not included, either directly or indirectly, in this comprehensive form. Secondly, that it contains all we can reasonably or innocently desire; whatever is for the glory of God, whatever is needful or profitable, not only for ourselves, but for every creature in heaven and earth. And, indeed, our prayers are the proper test of our desires; nothing being fit to have a place in our desires which is not fit to have a place in our prayers: What we may not pray for, neither should we desire. Thirdly, that it contains all our duty to God and man; whatsoever things are pure and holy, whatsoever God requires of the children of men, whatsoever is acceptable in his sight, whatsoever it is whereby we may profit our neighbor, being expressed or implied therein.

3. It consists of three parts—the preface, the petitions, and the doxology, or conclusion. The preface, *Our Father who are in heaven,* lays a general foundation for prayer; comprising what we must first know of God before we can pray in confidence of being heard. It likewise points out to us all those tempers with which we are to approach

111

to God, which are most essentially requisite, if we desire either our prayers or our lives should find acceptance with him.

4. *Our Father:* If he is a Father, then he is good, then he is loving, to his children. And here is the first and great reason for prayer. God is willing to bless; let us ask for a blessing. *Our Father:* our Creator; the Author of our being; he who raised us from the dust of the earth; who breathed into us the breath of life, and we became living souls. But if he made us, let us ask, and he will not withhold any good thing from the work of his own hands. *Our Father:* our Preserver; who, day by day, sustains the life he has given; of whose continuing love we now and every moment receive life and breath and all things. So much the more boldly let us come to him, and we shall *obtain mercy, and find grace to help in time of need.* Above all, the Father of our Lord Jesus Christ, and of all that believe in him; who justifies us *freely by his grace, through the redemption that is in Jesus;* who has *blotted out all our sins, and healed all our infirmities;* who has received us for his own children, by adoption and grace; and, *because* we *are sons, has sent forth the Spirit of his Son into* our *hearts, crying, Abba, Father;* who *has begotten us again of incorruptible seed,* and *created us anew in Christ Jesus.* Therefore we know that he hears us always; therefore we pray to him without ceasing. We pray, because we love; and *we love him because he first loved us.*

5. *Our Father:* Not *mine* only who now cry unto him, but *ours* in the most extensive sense. The God and *Father of the spirits of all flesh;* the Father of angels and men: So the very Heathens acknowledge him to be, Πατὴρ ἀνδρῶν τε θεῶν τε. The Father of the universe, of all the families both in heaven and earth. Therefore with him there is no respect of persons. He loves all that he has made. *He is loving unto every man, and his mercy is over all his works.* And the Lord's delight is in them that fear him, and put their trust in his mercy; in them that trust in him through the Son of his love, knowing they are *accepted in the Beloved.* But *if God so loved us, we ought also to love one another;* yea, all mankind; seeing *God so loved the world that he gave his only begotten Son,* even to die the death, that they *might not perish, but have everlasting life.*

6. *Who are in heaven:* High and lifted up, God over all, blessed forever: Who, sitting on the circle of the heavens, beholds all things both in heaven and earth; whose eye pervades the whole sphere of created being; yea, and of uncreated night; unto whom *are known all his works,* and all the works of every creature, not only *from the begin-*

ning of the world (a poor, low, weak translation) but ἀπ' αἰωνος, from all *eternity*, from everlasting to everlasting; who constrains the host of heaven, as well as the children of men, to cry out with wonder and amazement, Oh, the depth! *the depth of the riches, both of the wisdom and of the knowledge of God! Who are in heaven:* The Lord and Ruler of all, superintending and disposing all things; who are the King of kings, and Lord of lords, the blessed and only Potentate; who are strong and girded about with power, doing whatsoever pleases you; the Almighty; for whensoever you will, to do is present with you. *In heaven:* Eminently there. Heaven is your throne, *the place where your honor* particularly *dwells.* But not there alone; for you fill heaven and earth, the whole expanse of space. *Heaven and earth are full of your glory. Glory be to you, O Lord most high!*

Therefore should we *serve the Lord with fear, and rejoice unto him with reverence.* Therefore should we think, speak, and act, as continually under the eye, in the immediate presence, of the Lord, the King.

7. *Hallowed be your name.* This is the first of the six petitions, whereof the prayer itself is composed. The name of God is God himself, the nature of God so far as it can be discovered to man. It means therefore, together with his existence, all his attributes or perfections: his Eternity, particularly signified by his great and incommunicable name, JEHOVAH, as the Apostle John translates it: Τὸ Α καὶ τὸ Ω, ἀρχὴ καὶ τέλος, ὁ ὢν καὶ ὁ ἦν καὶ ὁ ἐρχόμενος—*The Alpha and Omega, the beginning and the end; he which is, and which was, and which is to come;* his Fulness of Being, denoted by his other great name, *I AM THAT I AM!* —his omnipresence;—his omnipotence; who is indeed the only Agent in the material world; all matter being essentially dull and inactive, and moving only as it is moved by the finger of God; and he is the spring of action in every creature, visible and invisible, which could neither act nor exist without the continual influx and agency of his almighty power; —his wisdom, clearly deduced from the things that are seen, from the goodly order of the universe; —his Trinity in Unity, and Unity in Trinity, discovered to us in the very first line of his written word; —literally, *the Gods created,* a plural noun joined with a verb of the singular number; as well as in every part of his subsequent revelations, given by the mouth of all of his holy Prophets and Apostles; —his essential purity and holiness; — and, above all, his love, which is the very brightness of his glory.

In praying that God, or his name, may be hallowed or glorified, we pray that he may be known, such as he is, by all that are capable thereof, by all intelligent beings, and with affections suitable to that knowledge; that he may be duly honored, and feared, and loved, by all in heaven above and in the earth beneath; by all angels and men, whom for that end he has made capable of knowing and loving him to eternity.

8. *Your kingdom come.* This has a close connection with the preceding petition. In order that the name of God might be hallowed, we pray that his kingdom, the kingdom of Christ, may come. This kingdom then comes to a particular person, when he *repents and believes the Gospel;* when he is taught of God, not only to know himself, but to know Jesus Christ and him crucified. As *this is life eternal, to know the only true God, and Jesus Christ whom he hath sent;* so it is the kingdom of God begun below, set up in the believer's heart; *the Lord God Omnipotent* then *reigns,* when he is known through Christ Jesus. He takes unto himself his mighty power, that he may subdue all things unto himself. He goes on in the soul conquering and to conquer, till he has put all things under his feet, till *every thought is brought into captivity to the obedience of Christ.*

When therefore God shall *give his Son the Heathen for his inheritance, and the uttermost parts of the earth for his possession;* when *all kingdoms shall bow before him, and all nations shall do him service;* when *the mountain of the Lord's house,* the Church of Christ, *shall be established in the top of the mountains;* when *the fulness of the Gentiles shall come in, and all Israel shall be saved;* then shall it be seen that *the Lord is King, and has put on glorious apparel,* appearing to every soul of man as King of kings and Lord of lords. And it is meet for all those who love his appearing to pray that he would hasten the time; that this his kingdom, the kingdom of grace, may come quickly, and swallow up all the kingdoms of the earth; that all mankind, receiving him for their King, truly believing in his name, may be filled with righteousness, and peace, and joy, with holiness and happiness, till they are removed hence into his heavenly kingdom, there to reign with him forever and ever.

For this also we pray in those words, *Your kingdom come:* We pray for the coming of his everlasting kingdom, the kingdom of glory in heaven, which is the continuation and perfection of the kingdom of grace on earth. Consequently this, as well as the preceding petition, is offered up for the whole intelligent creation, who are all interested in this grand event, the final renovation of all things, by God's putting an end to misery and sin, to infirmity and death, taking all things into his own hands, and setting up the kingdom which endures throughout all ages.

Exactly answerable to all this are those awful words in the prayer at the burial of the dead: "Beseeching you; that it may please you of your gracious goodness, shortly to accomplish the number of your elect, and to hasten your kingdom: That we, with all those that are departed in the true faith of your holy name, may have our perfect consummation and bliss, both in body and soul, in your everlasting glory."

9. *Your will be done in earth, as it is in heaven.* This is the necessary and immediate consequence wherever the kingdom of God is come; wherever God dwells in the soul by faith, and Christ reigns in the heart by love.

It is probable, many, perhaps the generality of men, at the first view of these words, are apt to imagine they are only an expression of, or petition for, resignation; for a readiness to suffer the will of God, whatsoever it be, concerning us. And this is unquestionably a divine and excellent temper, a most precious gift of God. But this is not what we pray for in this petition; at least, not in the chief and primary sense of it. We pray, not so much for a passive, as for an active, conformity to the will of God, in saying, *Your will be done in earth, as it is in heaven.*

How is it done by the angels of God in heaven, those who now circle in his throne rejoicing? They do it *willingly;* they love his commandments, and gladly hearken to his words. It is their meat and drink to do his will; it is their highest glory and joy. They do it *continually;* there is no interruption in their willing service. They rest not day or night, but employ every hour (speaking after the manner of men; otherwise our measures of duration, days, and nights, and hours, have no place in eternity) in fulfilling his commands, in executing his designs, in performing the counsel of his will. And they do it *perfectly.* No sin, no defect belongs to angelic minds. It is true, *the stars are not pure in his sight,* even the morning-stars that sing together before him. *In his sight,* that is, in comparison of him, the very angels are not pure. But this does not imply that they are not pure in *themselves.* Doubtless they are; they are without spot and blameless. They are altogether devoted to his will, and perfectly obedient in all things.

If we view this in another light, we may observe the angels of

God in heaven do *all* the will of God. And they do nothing else, nothing but what they are absolutely assured is his will. Again, they do all the will of God *as* willed; in the manner which pleases him, and no other. Yea, and they do this only *because* it is his will; for this end, and no other reason.

10. When therefore we pray that the will of God may *be done in earth as it is in heaven,* the meaning is that all the inhabitants of the earth, even the whole race of mankind, may do the will of their Father which is in heaven, as *willingly* as the holy angels; that these may do it *continually,* even as they, without any interruption of their willing service; yea and that they may do it *perfectly,* that "the God of peace, through the blood of the everlasting covenant, may make them perfect in every good work to do his will, and work in them" all "which is well-pleasing in his sight."

In other words, we pray that we and all mankind may do the whole will of God in all things; and nothing else, not the least thing but what is the holy and acceptable will of God: We pray that we may do the whole will of God as he wills, in the manner that pleases him: And, lastly, that we may do it *because* it is his will; that this may be the sole reason and ground, the whole and only motive, of whatsoever we think, or whatsoever we speak or do.

11. *Give us this day our daily bread.* In the three former petitions we have been praying for all mankind. We come now more particularly to desire a supply for our own wants. Not that we are directed, even here, to confine our prayer altogether to ourselves; but this, and each of the following petitions, may be used for the whole Church of Christ upon earth.

By "bread" we may understand all things needful, whether for our souls or bodies: τὰ πρὸς ζωῆν καὶ εὐσέβειαν—the things pertaining to life and godliness: We understand not barely the outward bread, what our Lord terms *the meat which perisheth;* but much more the spiritual bread, the grace of God, the food *which endures unto everlasting life.* It was the judgment of many of the ancient Fathers that we are here to understand the sacramental bread also; daily received in the beginning by the whole Church of Christ, and highly esteemed, till the love of many waxed cold, as the grand channel whereby the grace of his Spirit was conveyed to the souls of all the children of God.

Our daily bread. The word we render *daily* has been differently explained by different commentators. But the most plain and natural sense of it seems to be this, which is retained in almost all translations, as well ancient as modern: what is sufficient for this day, and so for each day as it succeeds.

12. *Give us:* For we claim nothing of right, but only of free mercy. We deserve not the air we breathe, the earth that bears, or the sun that shines upon us. All our desert, we own, is hell: But God loves us freely; therefore, we ask him to give what we can no more procure for ourselves, than we can merit it at his hands.

Not that either the goodness or the power of God is a reason for us to stand idle. It is his will that we should use all diligence in all things, that we should employ our utmost endeavors, as much as if our success were the natural effect of our own wisdom and strength: And then, as though we had done nothing, we are to depend on Him, the giver of every good and perfect gift.

This day: For we are to take no thought for the morrow. For this very end has our wise Creator divided life into these little portions of time, so clearly separated from each other that we might look on every day as a fresh gift of God, another life, which we may devote to his glory; and that every evening may be as the close of life, beyond which we are to see nothing but eternity.

13. *And forgive us our trespasses, as we forgive them that trespass against us.* As nothing but sin can hinder the bounty of God from flowing forth upon every creature, so this petition naturally follows the former; that, all hindrances being removed, we may the more clearly trust in the God of love for every manner of thing which is good.

Our trespasses: The word properly signifies *our debts.* Thus our sins are frequently represented in scripture; every sin laying us under a fresh debt to God, to whom we already owe, as it were, ten thousand talents. What, then, can we answer when he shall say, *Pay me that you owe?* We are utterly insolvent; we have nothing to pay; we have wasted all our substance. Therefore, if he deal with us according to the rigor of his law, if he exact what he justly may, he must command us to be *bound hand and foot, and delivered over to the tormentors.*

Indeed we are already bound hand and foot by the chains of our own sins. These, considered with regard to ourselves, are chains of iron and fetters of brass. They are wounds wherewith the world, the flesh, and the devil have gashed and mangled us all over. They are diseases that drink up our blood and spirits, that bring us down to the chambers of the grave. But, considered as they are here, with regard to God, they are debts immense and numberless. Well, therefore, seeing we have nothing to pay, may we cry unto Him, that he would frankly forgive us all!

The word translated *forgive* implies either to forgive a debt, or to unloose a chain. And, if we attain the former, the latter follows of course: If our debts are forgiven, the chains fall off our hands. As soon as ever, through the free grace of God in Christ, we *receive forgiveness of sins*, we receive likewise *a lot among those which are sanctified, by faith which is in him.* Sin has lost its power: It has no dominion over those who are under grace, that is, in favor with God. As *there is now no condemnation to them that are in Christ Jesus,* so they are freed from sin as well as from guilt. *The righteousness of the law is fulfilled in* them, and they *walk not after the flesh but after the Spirit.*

14. *As we forgive them that trespass against us.* In these words our Lord clearly declares both on what condition, and in what degree or manner, we may look to be forgiven of God. All our trespasses and sins are forgiven us, *if* we forgive, and *as* we forgive, others. This is a point of the utmost importance. And our blessed Lord is so jealous lest at any time we should let it slip out of our thoughts that he not only inserts it in the body of his prayer, but presently after repeats it twice over. *If,* says he, *you forgive men their trespasses, your heavenly Father will also forgive you: But if you forgive not men their trespasses, neither will your Father forgive your trespasses* (verses 14, 15). Secondly, God forgives us *as* we forgive others. So that if any malice or bitterness, if any taint of unkindness or anger remains, if we do not clearly, fully, and from the heart forgive all men their trespasses, we so far cut short the forgiveness of our own: God cannot clearly and fully forgive us: He may show us some degree of mercy; but we will not suffer him to blot out all our sins, and forgive all our iniquities.

In the meantime, while we do not from our hearts forgive our neighbor his trespasses, what manner of prayer are we offering to God whenever we utter these words? We are indeed setting God at open defiance; we are daring him to do his worst. *Forgive us our trespasses, as we forgive them that trespass against us.* That is, in plain terms, "Do not forgive us at all: We desire no favor at your hands. We pray that you will keep our sins in remembrance, and that your wrath may abide upon us." But can you seriously offer such a prayer to God?

And has he not yet cast you quick into hell? Oh, tempt him no longer! Now, even now, by his grace, forgive as you would be forgiven! Now have compassion on your fellow-servant, as God has had, and will have, pity on you!

15. *And lead us not into temptation, but deliver us from evil.—And lead us not into temptation.* The word translated *temptation* means trial of any kind. And so the English word temptation was formerly taken in an indifferent sense, although now it is usually understood of solicitation to sin. Saint James uses the word in both these senses; first, in its general, then in its restrained, acceptation. He takes it in the former sense when he says, *Blessed is the man that endures temptation: For when he is tried,* or approved of God, *he shall receive the crown of life.* (James 1:12, 13.) He immediately adds, taking the word in the latter sense, *Let no man say, when he is tempted, I am tempted of God: For God cannot be tempted with evil, neither tempts he any man: But every man is tempted when he is drawn away of his own lust,* or *desire,* ἐξελκόμενος— drawn out of God, in whom alone he is safe—*and enticed;* caught as a fish with bait. Then it is, when he is thus *drawn away and enticed,* that he properly enters into temptation. Then temptation covers him as a cloud; it overspreads his whole soul. Then how hardly shall he escape out of the snare! Therefore, we beseech God *not to lead us into temptation,* that is, (seeing God tempts no man) not to suffer us to be led into it. *But deliver us from evil:* Rather, *from the evil one,* ἀπὸ τοῦ πονηροῦ. Ὁ πονηρός is unquestionably *the wicked one,* emphatically so called, the prince and god of this world, who works with mighty power in the children of disobedience. But all those who are the children of God by faith are delivered out of his hands. He may fight against them; and so he will. But he cannot conquer, unless they betray their own souls. He may torment for a time, but he cannot destroy: For God is on their side, who will not fail, in the end, to *avenge his own elect, that cry unto him day and night.* Lord, when we are tempted, suffer us not to enter into temptation! Do you make a way for us to escape that the wicked one touch us not!

16. The conclusion of this divine prayer, commonly called the Doxology, is a solemn thanksgiving, a compendious acknowledgment of the attributes and works of God. *For yours is the kingdom*—the sovereign right of all things that are, or ever were, created; yes, your kingdom is an everlasting kingdom, and your dominion endures throughout all ages. *The power*—the executive power whereby you

govern all things in your everlasting kingdom, whereby you do whatsoever pleases you, in all places of your dominion. *And the glory*—the praise due from every creature, for your power, and the mightiness of your kingdom, and for all your wondrous works which you work from everlasting, and shall do, world without end, *forever and ever! Amen!* So be it!

[8]

A PLAIN ACCOUNT OF
GENUINE CHRISTIANITY 1753

SECTION I

1. I would consider, first, who is a Christian indeed? What does that term properly imply? It has been so long abused, I fear, not only to mean nothing at all, but what was far worse than nothing, to be a cloak for the vilest hypocrisy, for the grossest abominations and immoralities of every kind, that it is high time to rescue it out of the hands of wretches that are a reproach to human nature, to show determinately what manner of man he is to whom this name of right belongs.

2. A "Christian" cannot think of the Author of his being without abasing himself before him, without a deep sense of the distance between a worm of earth and him that *sits on the circle of the heavens.* In his presence he sinks into the dust, knowing himself to be less than nothing in his eye and being conscious, in a manner words cannot express, of his own littleness, ignorance, foolishness. So that he can only cry out, from the fulness of his heart, "O God, what is man? What am I?"

3. He has a continual sense of his dependence on the parent of good, for his being and all the blessings that attend it. To him he refers every natural and every moral endowment, with all that is commonly ascribed either to fortune or to the wisdom, courage, or merit of the possessor. And hence he acquiesces in whatsoever appears to be his will, not only with patience but with thankfulness. He willingly resigns all he is, all he has, to his wise and gracious disposal. The ruling temper of his heart is the most absolute submission and the tenderest gratitude to his sovereign benefactor. And this grateful love creates filial fear, an awful reverence toward him and an earnest care not to give place to any disposition, not to admit an action, word, or

thought, which might in any degree displease that indulgent power to whom he owes his life, breath, and all things.

4. And as he has the strongest affection for the fountain of all good, so he has the firmest confidence in him; a confidence which neither pleasure nor pain, neither life nor death, can shake. But yet this, far from creating sloth or indolence, pushes him on to the most vigorous industry. It causes him to put forth all his strength in obeying him in whom he confides; so that he is never faint in his mind, never weary of doing whatever he believes to be his will. And as he knows the most acceptable worship of God is to imitate him he worships, so he is continually laboring to transcribe into himself all his imitable perfections: in particular, his justice, mercy, and truth, so eminently displayed in all his creatures.

5. Above all, remembering that God is love, he is conformed to the same likeness. He is full of love to his neighbor: of universal love, not confined to one sect or party, not restrained to those who agree with him in opinions, or in outward modes of worship, or to those who are allied to him by blood or recommended by nearness of place. Neither does he love those only that love him, or that are endeared to him by intimacy of acquaintance. But his love resembles that of him whose mercy is over all his works. It soars above all these scanty bounds, embracing neighbors and strangers, friends and enemies; yes, not only the good and gentle but also the froward, the evil and unthankful. For he loves every soul that God has made, every child of man, of whatever place or nation. And yet this universal benevolence does in nowise interfere with a peculiar regard for his relations, friends, and benefactors, a fervent love for his country and the most endeared affection to all men of integrity, of clear and generous virtue.

6. His love to these, so to all mankind, is in itself generous and disinterested, springing from no view of advantage to himself, from no regard to profit or praise; no, nor even the pleasure of loving. This is the daughter, not the parent, of his affection. By experience he knows that *social love* (if it mean the love of our neighbor) is absolutely, essentially different from *self-love*, even of the most allowable kind, just as different as the objects at which they point. And yet it is sure that, if they are under due regulations, each will give additional force to the other, 'till they mix together never to be divided.

7. And this universal, disinterested love is productive of all right affections. It is fruitful of gentleness, tenderness, sweetness; of hu-

manity, courtesy, and affability. It makes a Christian rejoice in the virtues of all, and bear a part in their happiness at the same time that he sympathizes with their pains and compassionates their infirmities. It creates modesty, condescension, prudence—together with calmness and evenness of temper. It is the parent of generosity, openness, and frankness, void of jealousy and suspicion. It begets candor and willingness to believe and hope whatever is kind and friendly of every man; and invincible patience, never overcome of evil, but overcoming evil with good.

8. The same love constrains him to converse not only with a strict regard to truth but with artless sincerity and genuine simplicity, as one in whom there is no guile. And not content with abstaining from all such expressions as are contrary to justice or truth, he endeavors to refrain from every unloving word, either to a present or of an absent person; in all his conversation aiming at this, either to improve himself in knowledge or virtue, or to make those with whom he converses some way wiser, or better, or happier than they were before.

9. The same love is productive of all right actions. It leads him into an earnest and steady discharge of all social offices, of whatever is due to relations of every kind: to his friends, to his country and to any particular community whereof he is a member. It prevents his willingly hurting or grieving any man. It guides him into a uniform practice of justice and mercy, equally extensive with the principle whence it flows. It constrains him to do all possible good, of every possible kind, to all men; and makes him invariably resolved in every circumstance of life to do that, and that only, to others, which supposing he were himself in the same situation, he would desire they should do to him.

10. And as he is easy to others, so he is easy in himself. He is free from the painful swellings of pride, from the flames of anger, from the impetuous gusts of irregular self-will. He is no longer tortured with envy or malice, or with unreasonable and hurtful desire. He is no more enslaved to the pleasures of sense, but has the full power both over his mind and body, in a continued cheerful course of sobriety, of temperance and chastity. He knows how to use all things in their place and yet is superior to them all. He stands above those low pleasures of imagination which captivate vulgar minds, whether arising from what mortals term greatness, or novelty or beauty. All these too he can taste and still look upward, still aspire to nobler en-

joyments. Neither is he a slave to fame: popular breath affects not him; he stands steady and collected in himself.

11. And he who seeks no praise cannot fear dispraise. Censure gives him no uneasiness, being conscious to himself that he would not willingly offend and that he has the approbation of the Lord of all. He cannot fear want, knowing in whose hand is the earth and the fulness thereof and that it is impossible for him to withhold from one that fears him any manner of thing that is good. He cannot fear pain, knowing it will never be sent unless it be for his real advantage, and that then his strength will be proportioned to it, as it has always been in times past. He cannot fear death, being able to trust him he loves with his soul as well as his body, yes, glad to leave the corruptible body in the dust, 'till it is raised, incorruptible and immortal. So that, in honor or shame, in abundance or want, in ease or pain, in life or death, always and in all things, he has learned to be content, to be easy, thankful, joyful, happy.

12. He is happy in knowing there is a God—an intelligent Cause and Lord of all—and that he is not the produce either of blind chance or inexorable necessity. He is happy in the full assurance he has that this Creator and End of all things is a being of boundless wisdom, of infinite power to execute all the designs of his wisdom and of no less infinite goodness to direct all his power to the advantage of all his creatures. Nay, even the consideration of his immutable justice, rendering to all their due, of his unspotted holiness, of his all-sufficiency in himself, and of that immense ocean of all perfections which center in God from eternity to eternity, is a continual addition to the happiness of a Christian.

13. A farther addition is made thereto while, in contemplating even the things that surround him, that thought strikes warmly upon his heart—

These are your glorious works, Parent of Good! while he takes knowledge of the invisible things of God, even his eternal power and wisdom in the things that are seen, the heavens, the earth, the fowls of the air, the lilies of the field. How much more, while, rejoicing in the constant care which he still takes of the work of his own hand, he breaks out in a transport of love and praise, *O Lord our Governor! How excellent is your Name in all the earth; you that have set your glory above the heavens!* —while he, as it were, sees the Lord sitting upon his throne and ruling all things well; while he observes the general providence of God co-extended with his whole creation and surveys all the effects of it in the heavens and earth, as a well-pleased spectator; while he sees the wisdom and goodness of his general government descending to every particular, so presiding over the whole universe as over a single person, so watching over every single person as if he were the whole universe—how does he exult when he reviews the various traces of the Almighty Goodness in what has befallen himself in the several circumstances and changes of his own life, all which he now sees have been allotted to him and dealt out in number, weight, and measure. With what triumph of soul, in surveying either the general or particular providence of God, does he observe every line pointing out an hereafter, every scene opening into eternity?

14. He is peculiarly and inexpressibly happy in the clearest and fullest conviction: "This all-powerful, all-wise, all-gracious Being, this Governor of all, loves *me*. This lover of my soul is always with me, is never absent; no, not for a moment. And I love him: there is none in heaven but thee, none on earth that I desire beside thee! And he has given me to resemble himself; he has stamped his image on my heart. And I live unto him; I do only his will; I glorify him with my body and my spirit. And it will not be long before I shall die unto him, I shall die into the arms of God. And then farewell sin and pain, then it only remains that I should live with him forever."

15. This is the plain, naked portraiture of a Christian. But be not prejudiced against him for his name. Forgive his particularities of opinion and (what you think) superstitious modes of worship. These are circumstances but of small concern and do not enter into the essence of his character. Cover them with a veil of love and look at the substance: his tempers, his holiness, his happiness. Can calm reason conceive either a more amiable or a more desirable character?

Is it your own? Away with names! Away with opinions! I care not what you are called. I ask not (it does not deserve a thought) what opinion you are of, so you are conscious to yourself that you are the man whom I have been (however faintly) describing.

Do not you know you ought to be such? Is the Governor of the world well pleased that you are not?

Do you at least desire it? I would to God that desire may penetrate your inmost soul and that you may have no rest in your spirit 'till you are not only almost but altogether a Christian!

JOHN WESLEY

SECTION II

1. The second point to be considered is: what is real, genuine Christianity—whether we speak of it as a principle in the soul or as a scheme or system of doctrine?

Christianity, taken in the latter sense, is that system of doctrine which describes the character above recited, which promises it shall be mine (provided I will not rest till I attain) and which tells me how I may attain it.

2. First, it *describes* this character in all its parts, and that in the most lively and affecting manner. The main lines of this picture are beautifully drawn in many passages of the Old Testament. These are filled up in the New, retouched and finished with all the art of God.

The same we have in miniature more than once; particularly in the thirteenth chapter of the first Epistle to the Corinthians, and in that discourse which Saint Matthew records as delivered by our Lord at his entrance upon his public ministry.

3. Secondly, Christianity *promises* this character shall be mine if I will not rest till I attain it. This is promised both in the Old Testament and in the New. Indeed the New is, in effect, all a promise, seeing every description of the servants of God mentioned therein has the nature of a command, in consequence of those general injunctions: *Be you followers of me, as I am of Christ* (1 Cor. 11:1); *Be you followers of them who through faith and patience inherit the promises* (Heb. 6:12). And every command has the force of a promise, in virtue of those general promises: *A new heart will I give you, and I will put my Spirit within you, and cause you to walk in my statutes, and ye shall keep my judgments, and do them* (Ezek. 36:26–27). *This is the covenant that I will make after those days, says the Lord; I will put my laws into their minds and write them in their hearts* (Heb. 8:10). Accordingly, when it is said, *You shall love the Lord your God with all your heart, and with all your soul, and with all your mind* (Mt. 22:37); it is not only a direction what I shall do, but a promise of what God will do in me, exactly equivalent with what is written elsewhere: *The Lord your God will circumcise your heart, and the heart of your seed* (alluding to the custom then in use) *to love the Lord your God with all your heart, and with all your soul* (Deut. 30:6).

4. This being observed, it will readily appear to every serious person who reads the New Testament with that care which the importance of the subject demands that every particular branch of the preceding character is manifestly promised therein, either explicitly,

126

under the very form of a promise, or virtually, under that of a description or command.

5. Christianity tells me, in the third place, how I may attain the promise, namely, by faith.

But what is faith? Not an opinion, no more than it is a form of words; not any number of opinions put together, be they ever so true. A string of opinions is no more Christian faith than a string of beads is Christian holiness.

It is not an assent to any opinion, or any number of opinions. A man may assent to three or three-and-twenty creeds; he may assent to all the Old and New Testament (at least, as far as he understands them) and yet have no Christian faith at all.

6. The faith by which the promise is attained is represented by Christianity as a power wrought by the Almighty in an immortal spirit inhabiting a house of clay, to see through that veil into the world of spirits, into things invisible and eternal; a power to discern those things which with eyes of flesh and blood no man hath seen or can see, either by reason of their nature, which (though they surround us on every side) is not perceivable by those gross senses, or by reason of their distance, as being yet afar off in the bosom of eternity.

7. This is Christian faith in the general notion of it. In its more particular notion, it is a divine evidence or conviction wrought in my heart that God is reconciled to *me* through his Son, inseparably joined with a confidence in him as a gracious, reconciled Father, as for all things, so especially for all those good things which are invisible and eternal.

To believe (in the Christian sense) is, then, to walk in the light of eternity and to have a clear sight of, and confidence in, the Most High, reconciled to me through the Son of his love.

8. Now, how highly desirable is such a faith, were it only on its own account? For how little does the wisest of men know of anything more than he can see with his eyes? What clouds and darkness cover the whole scene of things invisible and eternal? What does he know even of himself as to his invisible part, what of his future manner of existence? How melancholy an account does the prying, learned philosopher (perhaps the wisest and best of all heathens), the great, the venerable Marcus Antoninus, give of these things? What was the result of all his serious researches, of his high and deep contemplations? "Either dissipation (of the soul as well as the body) into the common,

unthinking mass or reabsorption into the universal fire (the unintelligent source of all things) or some unknown manner of conscious existence, after the body sinks to rise no more." One of these three he supposed must succeed death; but which, he had no light to determine. Poor Antoninus—with all his wealth, his honor, his power, with all his wisdom and philosophy!

> What points of knowledge did he gain?
> That life is sacred all—and vain!
> Sacred how high, and vain how low?
> He could not tell—but died to know.

9. He died to know! And so must you, unless you are now a partaker of Christian faith. Oh, consider this! Nay, and consider, not only how little you know of the immensity of the things that are beyond sense and time, but how uncertainly do you know even that little! How faintly glimmering a light is that you have? Can you properly be said to *know* any of these things? Is that knowledge any more than bare conjecture? And the reason is plain. You have no senses suited to invisible or eternal objects. What *desiderata* then, especially to the rational, the reflecting part of mankind, are these: a more extensive knowledge of things invisible and eternal, a greater certainty in whatever knowledge of them we have, and, in order to both, faculties capable of discerning things invisible?

10. Is it not so? Let impartial reason speak. Does not every thinking man want a window, not so much in his neighbor's as in his own breast? He wants an opening there of whatever kind that might let in light from eternity. He is pained to be thus feeling after God so darkly, so uncertainly; to know so little of God and indeed so little of any beside material objects. He is concerned that he must see even that little, not directly, but in the dim, sullied glass of sense and, consequently, so imperfectly and obscurely that 'tis all a mere enigma still.

11. Now, these very *desiderata* faith supplies. It gives a more extensive knowledge of things invisible, showing what eye had not seen, nor ear heard, neither could it before enter into our heart to conceive. And all these it shows in the clearest light, with the fullest certainty and evidence, ἔλεγχος. For it does not leave us to receive our notices of them by mere reflection from the dull glass of sense, but resolves a thousand enigmas of the highest concern by giving faculties

suited to things invisible. Oh, who would not wish for such a faith, were it only on these accounts? How much more, if by this I may receive the promise, I may attain all that holiness and happiness?

12. So Christianity tells me and so I find it. May every real Christian say, "I now am assured that these things are so; I experienced them in my own breast. What Christianity (considered as a doctrine) promised is accomplished in my soul." And Christianity, considered as an inward principle, is the completion of all those promises. It is holiness and happiness, the image of God impressed on a created spirit; a fountain of peace and love springing up into everlasting life.

SECTION III

1. And this I conceive to be the strongest evidence of the truth of Christianity. I do not undervalue traditional evidence. Let it have its place and its due honor. It is highly serviceable in its kind and in its degree. And yet I cannot set it on a level with this.

It is generally supposed that traditional evidence is weakened by length of time, as it must necessarily pass through so many hands in a continued succession of ages. But no length of time can possibly affect the strength of this internal evidence. It is equally strong, equally new, through the course of seventeen hundred years. It passes now, even as it has done from the beginning, directly from God into the believing soul. Do you suppose time will ever dry up this stream? Oh no! It shall never be cut off.

Labitur et labetur in omne volubilis aevum
(It flows and goes on flowing through all the circling years.)

2. Traditional evidence is of an extremely complicated nature, necessarily including so many and so various considerations that only men of strong and clear understanding can be sensible of its full force. On the contrary, how plain and simple is this and how level to the lowest capacity. Is not this the sum: *One thing I know; I was blind, but now I see* —an argument so plain that a peasant, a woman, a child, may feel all its force.

3. The traditional evidence of Christianity stands, as it were, a great way off, and therefore, although it speaks loud and clear, yet

makes a less lively impression. It gives us an account of what was transacted long ago, in far distant times as well as places; whereas the inward evidence is intimately present to all persons, at all times and in all places. It is near you, in your mouth, and in your heart, if you believe in the Lord Jesus Christ. *This*, then, *is the record*, this is the evidence, emphatically so called, *that God has given unto us eternal life and this life is in his Son.*

4. If, then, it were possible (which I conceive it is not) to shake the traditional evidence of Christianity, still he that has the internal evidence (and every true believer has the witness or evidence in himself) would stand firm and unshaken. Still he could say to those who were striking at the external evidence, "Beat on the sack of Anaxagoras," but you can no more hurt *my* evidence of Christianity than the tyrant could hurt the spirit of that wise man.

5. I have sometimes been almost inclined to believe that the wisdom of God has, in most later ages, permitted the external evidence of Christianity to be more or less clogged and encumbered for this very end, that men (of reflection especially) might not altogether rest there, but be constrained to look into themselves also and attend to the light shining in their hearts.

Nay, it seems (if it may be allowed for us to pry so far into the reasons of the divine dispensations) that, particularly in this age, God suffers all kind of objections to be raised against the traditional evidence of Christianity that men of understanding (though unwilling to give it up, yet, at the same time they defend this evidence) may not rest the whole strength of their cause thereon but seek a deeper and firmer support for it.

6. Without this, I cannot but doubt whether they can long maintain their cause; whether, if they do not obey the loud call of God and lay far more stress than they have hitherto done on this internal evidence of Christianity, they will not, one after another, give up the external, and (in heart at least) go over to those whom they are now contending with; so that, in a century or two, the people of England will be fairly divided into real deists and real Christians. And I apprehend this would be no loss at all, but rather an advantage to the Christian cause. Nay, perhaps it would be the speediest, yea, the only effectual way of bringing all reasonable deists to be Christians.

7. May I be permitted to speak freely? May I, without offense, ask of you that are called Christians, what real loss would you sustain in giving up your present opinion that the Christian system is of

God? Though you bear the name, you are not Christians now: you have neither Christian faith nor love. You have no divine evidence of things unseen, you have not entered *into the holiest by the blood of Jesus.* You do not love God with all your heart; neither do you love your neighbor as yourself. You are neither happy nor holy. You have not learned in every state therewith to be content; to rejoice evermore, even in want, pain, death, and in everything to give thanks. You are not holy in heart: superior to pride, to anger, to foolish desires. Neither are you holy in life; you do not walk as Christ also walked. Does not the main of your Christianity lie in your opinion, decked with a few outward observances? For as to morality, even honest heathen morality—Oh, let me utter a melancholy truth!—many of those whom you style deists, there is reason to fear, have far more of it than you.

8. Go on, gentlemen, and prosper! Shame these nominal Christians out of that poor superstition which they call Christianity. Reason, rally, laugh them out of their dead, empty forms, void of spirit, of faith, of love. Convince them that such unmeaning pageantry—for such it manifestly is if there is nothing in the heart correspondent with the outward show—is absolutely unworthy, you need not say of God, but even of any man that is endued with common understanding. Show them that while they are endeavoring to please God thus, they are only beating the air. Know your time; press on; push your victories 'till you have conquered all that know not God. And then he, whom neither they nor you know now, shall rise and gird himself with strength and go forth in his almighty love, and sweetly conquer you all together.

9. Oh, that the time were come! How do I long for you to be partakers of the exceeding great and precious promises! How am I pained when I hear any of you using those silly terms which the men of form have taught you: calling the mention of the only thing you want "cant"; the deepest wisdom, the highest happiness, "enthusiasm"! What ignorance is this? How extremely despicable would it make you in the eyes of any but a Christian? But he cannot despise you, who loves you as his own soul, who is ready to lay down his life for your sake.

10. Perhaps you will say, "But this internal evidence of Christianity affects only those in whom the promise is fulfilled. It is no evidence to *me.*" There is truth in this objection. It does affect them chiefly, but it does not affect them only. It cannot, in the nature of

things, be so strong an evidence to others as it is to them. And yet it may bring a degree of evidence. It may reflect some light on you also.

For, first, you see the beauty and loveliness of Christianity, when it is rightly understood, and you are sure there is nothing to be desired in comparison of it.

Secondly, you know the scripture promises this and says it is attained by faith, and by no other way.

Thirdly, you see clearly how desirable Christian faith is, even on account of its own intrinsic value.

Fourthly, you are a witness that the holiness and happiness above described can be attained no other way. The more you have labored after virtue and happiness, the more convinced you are of this. Thus far, then, you need not lean upon other men; thus far you have personal experience.

Fifthly, what reasonable assurance can you have of things whereof you have not personal experience? Suppose the question were, can the blind be restored to sight? This you have not yourself experienced. How then will you know that such a thing ever was? Can there be an easier or surer way than to talk with one or some number of men who were blind but are now restored to sight? They cannot be deceived as to the fact in question; the nature of the thing leaves no room for this. And if they are honest men (which you may learn from other circumstances), they will not deceive you.

Now transfer this to the case before us. And those who were blind, but now see—those who were sick many years, but now are healed; those who were miserable, but now are happy—will afford *you* also a very strong evidence of the truth of Christianity; as strong as can be in the nature of things 'till you experience it in your own soul. And this, though it be allowed they are but plain men, and, in general, of weak understanding; nay, though some of them should be mistaken in other points and hold opinions which cannot be defended.

11. All this may be allowed concerning the primitive Fathers. I mean particularly Clemens Romanus, Ignatius, Polycarp, Justin Martyr, Irenaeus, Origen, Clemens Alexandrinus, Cyprian; to whom I would add Macarius and Ephraim Syrus.

I allow that some of these had not strong natural sense, that few of them had much learning, and none the assistances which our age enjoys in some respects above all that went before.

Hence I doubt not but whoever will be at the pains of reading over their writings for that poor end will find many mistakes, many weak suppositions, and many ill-drawn conclusions.

12. And yet I exceedingly reverence them, as well as their writings, and esteem them very highly in love. I reverence them, because they were Christians, such Christians as are above described. And I reverence their writings, because they describe true, genuine Christianity, and direct us to the strongest evidence of the Christian doctrine.

Indeed, in addressing the heathens of those times, they intermix other arguments—particularly, that drawn from the numerous miracles which were then performed in the Church, which they needed only to open their eyes and see daily wrought in the face of the sun.

But still they never relinquish this: "What the scripture promises, I enjoy. Come and see what Christianity has done here; and acknowledge it is of God."

I reverence these ancient Christians (with all their failings) the more, because I see so few Christians now; because I read so little in the writings of later times, and hear so little, of genuine Christianity; and because most of the modern Christians (so called), not content with being wholly ignorant of it, are deeply prejudiced against it, calling it "enthusiasm," and I know not what.

That the God of power and love may make both them, and you, and me, such Christians as those Fathers were, is the earnest prayer of, Reverend Sir,

Your real friend and servant,
John Wesley

[9]

WESLEY'S COVENANT SERVICE, DIRECTIONS FOR RENEWING OUR COVENANT WITH GOD
1780

I

Get these three Principles fixed in your hearts: that Things eternal are much more considerable than Things temporal; that Things not seen are as certain as the Things that are seen; that upon your present choice depends your eternal lot. Choose Christ and his ways, and you are blessed forever; refuse, and you are undone forever. And then,

II MAKE YOUR CHOICE

Turn either to the right-hand or to the left; lay both parts before you, with every link of each; Christ with his yoke, his cross and his crown; or the Devil with his wealth, his pleasure and curse: and then put yourselves to it thus; Soul, you see what is before you, what will you do? Which will you, either the crown or the curse? If you choose the crown, remember that the day you take this, you must be content to submit to the cross and yoke, the service and the sufferings of Christ, which are linked to it. What say you? Had you rather take the gains and pleasures of sin, and venture on the curse? Or will you yield yourself a servant to Christ, and so make sure the crown?

If your hearts fly off, and would fain waive the business, leave them not so. If you be unresolved, you are resolved; if you remain undetermined for Christ, you are determined for the Devil. Therefore give not off, but follow your hearts from day to day, let them not rest, till the matter be brought to an issue, and see that you make a good choice. This is your choosing the good part, God and the blessings of the world to come, for your portion and happiness; and in this is included your renouncing the world, and worldly happiness.

III EMBARK WITH CHRIST

Adventure yourselves with him; cast yourselves upon his Righteousness, as that which shall bring you to God: as a poor captive exile, that is cast upon a strange land, a land of robbers and murderers, where he is ready to perish, and having no hope, either of abiding there, or escaping home with life: and meeting at length with a pilot that offers to transport him safely home, he embarks with him, and ventures himself, and all he has in his vessel: do you likewise; you are exiles from the presence of God, and fallen into a land of robbers and murderers: your sins are robbers, your pleasures are robbers, your companions in sin are robbers and thieves: if you stay where you are, you perish, and escape home of yourselves you cannot: Christ offers, if you will venture with him, he will bring you home, and he will bring you to God: will you say now to him, *Lord Jesus, will you undertake for me? Will you bring me to God, bring me into the Land of Promise? With you will I venture myself; I cast myself upon you, upon your blood, upon your righteousness; I lay up all my hopes, and venture my whole interest, soul and body with you.*

This is closing with Christ as your Priest. And in this is included your renouncing your own righteousness; you can never, you will never cast yourselves on him alone, till all your hopes in yourselves have given up the ghost.

There are two things which must necessarily be supposed, in order to a sinner's coming to Christ. 1. *A deep sense of his sin and misery.* 2. *An utter despair of himself, and of all things else beside Christ.* Being

1. *A deep sense of his sin and misery.* No man will regard a Savior, that doth not see himself a sinner: the whole regard not the physician. Therefore it is said, That the Spirit of God, when he should come to christianize the world, should in the first place, *convince the world of sin* (John 16:8). He shall convince the world of sin; he shall demonstrate them sinners, bring up their sins before their eyes, bring home their sins upon their consciences, and make them see themselves, and

feel themselves the most vile and abominable of creatures: Sin hides itself from the Sinner's eyes, and all its vileness and deformity. But the Spirit of God plucks off the mantle, and makes Sin appear to be sin; makes all the Sinner's gods appear to be so many Devils; brings forth the blackness and filthiness of Sin into sight, makes the sinner see himself an unclean and abominable thing: and withal, he brings forth the guilt of Sin, sets all these Devils tormenting the Sinner, filling him with fear, and terror, and amazement: in this respect he is called the spirit of Bondage, that works fear and trouble in the heart: the Spirit's awakening a sleepy Sinner is a kind of wakening in hell. *Lord what am I? What mean these legions round about me? These chains and fetters that are upon me? What means this black roll before my eyes, of curses, and wrath, and woes? Lord, where am I? have I been playing, and sporting, and making merry, and my soul in such a case as this? But is there no hope of escaping out of this wretched state: I see there is no abiding thus, I am but a dead man, if I continue as I am. What may I do to be saved?*

When he is brought to this, there is some way made for his entertainment of Jesus: yet this is not all that is needful, but he must further be brought to

2. *An utter despair of himself, and of all things else beside Christ.* Being made sensible of his sin, and of his danger, a Sinner will look for help and deliverance; but he will look everywhere else, before he look unto Christ; nothing will bring a Sinner to Christ but absolute necessity: he will try to forsake his sins, will think of leaving his drunkenness, and becoming sober; of leaving his adulteries, and becoming chaste, and so see if by this means he may not escape. He will go to Prayers and Sermons, and Sacraments, and search out if there be no salvation in them: but all these, though they be useful in their places, yet looking no further, the Sinner sees there is no help in them; his Righteousness cannot help him, this is but rags; his duties cannot help him, these may be reckoned among his sins: Ordinances cannot help, these are but empty cisterns; and all tell him, *You knock at a wrong door; Salvation is not in us. Well, the Lord be merciful to me, says the sinner, What shall I do? Abide as I am, I dare not, and how to help myself I know not; my praying will not help me; if I give all my goods to the poor, if I should give my body to be burned, all this would not save my soul; woe is me, what shall I do, and whither shall I go?*

And now, being brought to this distress, to this utter loss, his despair drives him to the only source of hope that is left open. Then

Christ will be acceptable, when he sees none but Christ can help him: the Apostle tells us (Gal. 3:23), *We are kept under the Law, shut up unto the Faith, that should afterwards be revealed:* all other doors were shut up against us, there was no hope of escaping, but by that one door that was left open, *The Faith that was afterwards to be revealed.* As the besieged in a city, that have every gate blocked up, and but one difficult passage left open, by which there is any possibility of escaping, thither throng for the saving of their lives; they are shut up unto that door, to which (if there had been any other way open) they would never have come.

And as Christ will never be accepted, so can the Sinner never be received of him, till he lets go all other props, and trusts on him alone. Christ will have no sharer with him in the work of saving souls. *If you seek me, let these go their way,* as he said in another case: let not only your Sins go, but let your Righteousness go, all the refuge of lies wherein you have trusted; let all go, if you will have me to be a Refuge to you. I came not to call the Righteous; if I should, they would not come; or if they come, let them go as they came, let them go to their Righteousness in which they trust, and let naked, destitute Sinners, distressed Sinners, come to me, who am come to this end, to seek and to save them that are lost.

Sinners, Will you come now? Will you venture here? For this your adventuring on Christ, you have this threefold warrant:

a. God's Ordination. This is he, whom God the Father has appointed, and sent into the world, to bring back his exiles to himself, to save Sinners. This is he whom God the Father has sealed, has marked him out for that chosen person, in whom is salvation; has sealed him his commission, for the redeeming and reconciling the world to himself. As God said unto the three friends of Job, when he was angry with them, Job 42:8, *Go to my servant Job, and he shall offer sacrifice for you, he shall pray for you, for him will I accept:* so to Sinners, Go, says the Lord to my servant *Jesus,* he shall offer sacrifice for you, he shall make reconciliation for you, Isaiah 42:1, *Behold my Servant whom I uphold, my Elect in whom my soul delights: I have put my Spirit upon him, he shall bring forth judgment to the Gentiles.*

b. God's Command, 1 John 3:23, *This is his commandment, that we should believe on the Name of his Son Jesus Christ.*

c. The Promise of God, 1 Peter 2:6, *Behold, I lay in Sion a chief cornerstone, elect, precious: he that believes on him shall not be confounded.*

Now having this threefold warrant, the warrant of God's *Ordi-*

nation, Command, and *Promise,* you may be bold to adventure on Christ, and to apply yourselves to him thus; Lord Jesus, here I am, a poor captive exile, a lost creature, an enemy to God, under his wrath and curse: will you, Lord, undertake for me, reconcile me to God, and save my soul? Do not, Lord, refuse me, for if you refuse me, to whom then shall I go? Are you not he, and he alone, whom God the Father has sealed, the Savior of Sinners? The Lord God has sent me to you, has bid me come, he has commanded me to believe, and cast myself upon you. Lord Jesus, will you refuse to help a distressed creature, whom the Father has sent to you for your help? If I had come on my own head, or in my own name, you might well have put me back; but since I come at the command of the Father, reject me not; Lord, help me; Lord, save me. Are you not he concerning whom the Father has promised, *He that believes on him shall not be confounded?* I come, Lord; I believe, Lord; I throw myself upon your grace and mercy; I cast myself upon your blood and bowels, do not refuse me. I have nowhere else to go: here I will stay, I will not stir from your door; on you I will trust, and rest, and venture myself; God has laid my help on you, and on you I lay my hope for pardon, for life, for salvation; if I perish, I perish on your shoulders; if I sink, I sink in your vessel; if I die, I die at your door; bid me not go away, for I will not go.

IV RESIGN AND DELIVER UP YOURSELVES TO GOD IN CHRIST

Yield *yourselves to the* Lord, that is, as his servants, give up the dominion and government of yourselves to Christ. *Neither yield your members, as instruments of unrighteousness unto sin, but yield yourselves to God, as those that are alive from the dead, and your members, as instruments of righteousness unto God. To whom you yield yourselves servants to obey, his servants you are, to whom you obey.* Yield yourselves so to the Lord that you may henceforth be the Lord's; *I am yours,* says the Psalmist. Those that yield themselves to Sin, and the World, their hearts say, Sin I am yours; World, I am yours; Riches, I am yours; Pleasures, I am yours: I am yours, says the Psalmist; devoted to your fear, dedicated to your service; I am yours, save me; give yourselves to Christ, Sinners, be devoted to his fear.

And this giving yourselves to him must be such as supposes that you be heartily contented. 1. *That he appoint you your Work.* 2. *That he appoint you your Station.*

1. *That he appoint you your work;* that he put you to whatsoever he pleaseth: Servants, as they must do their Master's work, so they must be for any work their Master has for them to do: they must not pick and choose, this I will do, and that I will not do; they must not say this is too hard, or this is too mean, or this may be well enough let alone; good Servants, when they have chosen their Master, will let their Master choose their work, and will not dispute his will, do it.

Christ has many services to be done, some are more easy and honorable, others more difficult and disgraceful; some are suitable to our inclinations and interests, others are contrary to both: in some we may please Christ and please ourselves, as when he requires us to feed and clothe ourselves, to provide things honest for our maintenance, yes, and there are some spiritual duties that are more pleasing than others; as to rejoice in the Lord, to be blessing and praising of God, to be feeding ourselves with the delights and comforts of Religion; these are the sweet works of a Christian. But then there are other works wherein we cannot please Christ but by denying ourselves, as giving and lending, bearing and forbearing, reproving men for their sins, withdrawing from their company, witnessing against wickedness, when it will cost us shame and reproach; sailing against the wind; parting with our ease, our liberties, and accommodations for the Name of our Lord Jesus.

It is necessary, Beloved, to sit down and consider what it will cost you to be the Servants of Christ, and to take a thorough survey of the whole business of Christianity, and not engage hand over head, to you know not what.

First, See what it is that Christ expects, and then yield yourselves to his whole will: do not think of compounding, or making your own terms with Christ, that will never be allowed you.

Go to Christ, and tell him, Lord Jesus, if you will receive me into your house, if you will but own me as your Servant, I will not stand upon terms; impose upon me what conditions you please, write down your own articles, command me what you will, put me to any thing you see as good; let me come under your roof, let me be your Servant, and spare not to command me; I will be no longer my own, but give up myself to your will in all things.

JOHN WESLEY

2. *That he shall appoint you your station and condition;* whether it be higher or lower, a prosperous or afflicted state: be content that Christ should both choose your work, and choose your condition; that he should have the command of you, and the disposal of you: make me what you will, Lord, and set me where you will: let me be a vessel of silver or gold, or a vessel of wood or stone, so I be a vessel of honor: of whatsoever form or metal, whether higher or lower, finer or coarser, I am content; if I be not the head, or the eye, or the ear, one of the nobler and more honorable instruments you will employ, let me be the hand, or the foot, one of the most laborious, and lowest, and most contemptible of all the Servants of my Lord, let my dwelling be upon the dunghill, my portion in the wilderness, my name and lot among the hewers of wood, or drawers of water, among the door-keepers of your house; anywhere, where I may be serviceable; I put myself wholly into your hands: put me to what you will, rank me with whom you will; put me to doing, put me to suffering, let me be employed for you, or laid aside for you, exalted for you, or trodden under foot for you; let me be full, let me be empty, let me have all things, let me have nothing, I freely and heartily resign all to your pleasure and disposal.

This is closing with Christ, as your King and sovereign Lord; and in this is included your renouncing the Devil and his works, the Flesh and its lusts; together with your consenting to all the Laws and Ordinances of Christ, and his providential government.

Beloved, such a close with Christ as you have here been exhorted to is that wherein the essence of Christianity lies; when you have chosen the incorruptible crown, that is, when you have chosen God to be your portion and happiness; when you have adventured, and laid up your whole interest, and all your hopes with Christ, casting yourself wholly upon the Merits of his Righteousness; when you have understandingly and heartily resigned and given up yourselves to him, resolving forever to be at his command, and at his disposal; then you are Christians indeed, and never till then. Christ will be the Savior of none but his Servants; he is the Author of eternal salvation to those that obey him; Christ will have no Servants but by consent; his people are a willing people; and Christ will accept of no consent but in full, to all that he requires; he will be all in all, or he will be nothing.

V CONFIRM AND COMPLETE ALL THIS
BY SOLEMN COVENANT

Give yourselves to the Lord as his Servants, and bind yourselves to him as his Covenant-Servants.

Upon your entering into Covenant with God, the Covenant of God stands firm to you; God gives you leave, every man, to put in his own name into the Covenant-Grant; if it be not found there at last, it will be your own fault: if it be not there, there will be nothing found in the whole Covenant belonging unto you: if it be there, all is yours; if you have come into the Bond of the Covenant, you shall have your share in the Blessings of the Covenant. Deuteronomy 26:17–18, *You have avouched the Lord this day to be your God, to walk in his ways, and to keep his statutes, and his commandments, and his judgments, to hearken to his voice. And the Lord has avouched you this day to be his peculiar people, as he has promised you.* Observe it, the same day that they avouched the Lord to be their God, the same day the Lord avouched them to be his peculiar people; the same day that they engage to keep the commandments of God, the same day the Lord engages to keep his promise with them.

There is a twofold covenanting with God, *In Profession, in Reality*: an entering our names, or an engaging our hearts: the former is done in Baptism, by all that are baptized, who by receiving that Seal of the Covenant are visibly, or in Profession entered into it: the latter is also twofold.

1. VIRTUAL. Which is done by all those that have sincerely made that closure with God in Christ: those that have chosen the Lord, embarked with Christ, resigned up, and given themselves to the Lord are all engaged persons, and have virtually covenanted with him.

2. FORMAL. Which is our binding ourselves to the Lord by solemn vow or promise to stand to our choice. And this may be either only inward in the soul, or outward, and expressed either by words, lifting up of the hands, subscribing the hand, or the like: and that by how much the more express and solemn our covenanting with God is, by so much the more sensibly is it like to hold our hearts to him. Now that which I would persuade you to is this solemn and express covenanting with God. Providence has lately brought to my hand the advice of a dear Friend and faithful Laborer in the work of the Lord about this matter, together with an excellent form of words proposed

141

for the help of weak Christians, and aptly accommodated to all the substantials of our baptismal Covenant; which having found great acceptance with many, I do with zeal, for the establishing of souls in holiness and comfort, commend it to the use not only of young Converts, but of the more grown Christians that have not experienced this or the like course.

And in order to the putting this matter into practice, I shall first give you these few directions.

First, Set apart some time, more than once, to be spent in secret before the Lord.

a. In seeking earnestly his special assistance and gracious acceptance of you.

b. In considering distinctly all the conditions of the Covenant, as they have been laid before you.

c. In searching your hearts whether you either have already, or can now freely make such a closure with God in Christ, as you have been exhorted to. In special, consider what your sins are, and examine whether you can resolve to forgo them all. Consider what the laws of Christ are, how holy, strict, and spiritual, and whether you can upon deliberation make choice of them all (even those that most cross your interests and corrupt inclinations) as the rule of your whole life. Be sure you be clear in these matters, see that you do not lie unto God.

Secondly, Compose your spirits into the most serious frame possible, suitable to a transaction of so high importance.

Thirdly, Lay hold on the Covenant of God, and rely upon his promise of giving grace and strength, whereby you may be enabled to perform your promise. Trust not to your own strength, to the strength of your own resolutions, but take hold on his strength.

Fourthly, Resolve to be faithful. Having engaged your hearts, opened your mouths, and subscribed with your hands to the Lord, resolve in his strength never to go back.

Lastly, being thus prepared, on some convenient time set apart for the purpose, set upon the work; and in the most solemn manner possible, as if the Lord were visibly present before your eyes, fall down on your knees, and spreading forth your hands toward heaven, open your hearts to the Lord, in these or the like words.

SELECTED WRITINGS

(COVENANT PRAYER)

O Most dreadful God, for the passion of your Son, I beseech you to accept of your poor Prodigal now prostrating himself at your door: I have fallen from you by my Iniquity, and am by nature a Son of Death, and a thousandfold more the Child of Hell by my wicked practice; but of your infinite grace you have promised mercy to me in Christ if I will but turn to you with all my heart: therefore upon the call of your Gospel, I am now come in, and throwing down my weapons, submit myself to your mercy.

And because you require, as the condition of my peace with you, that I should put away my Idols, and be at defiance with all your enemies, which I acknowledge I have wickedly sided with against you, I here from the bottom of my heart renounce them all; firmly covenanting with you, not to allow myself in any known sin, but conscientiously to use all the means that I know you have prescribed for the death and utter destruction of all my Corruptions. And whereas I have formerly, inordinately and idolatrously let out my Affections upon the World, I do here resign my Heart to you that made it; humbly protesting before your glorious Majesty that it is the firm resolution of my heart, and that I do unfeignedly desire grace from you, that when you shall call me hereunto, I may practice this my Resolution, to forsake all that is dear to me in this World, rather than turn from you, to the ways of Sin: and that I will watch against all Temptations, whether of prosperity or adversity, lest they withdraw my heart from you; beseeching you also to help me against the temptations of Satan, to whose wicked suggestions I resolve, by your grace, never to yield. And because my own Righteousness is but menstruous rags, I renounce all confidence therein, and acknowledge that I am of myself a hopeless, helpless, undone creature, without righteousness or strength.

And forasmuch as you have, of your bottomless mercy, offered most graciously to me, wretched Sinner, to be again my God through Christ, if I would accept of you; I call heaven and earth to record this day that I do here solemnly avouch you for the Lord my God; and with all veneration bowing the neck of my soul under the feet of your most sacred Majesty, I do here take you the Lord Jehovah, Father, Son, and Holy Ghost, for my portion; and do give up myself, body and soul, for your Servant; promising and vowing to serve you in holiness and righteousness, all the days of my life. And since you have appointed the Lord Jesus Christ the only means of coming unto you I do here upon the bended knees of my soul accept of him as the only new and living way, by which Sinners may have access to you; and do solemnly join myself in a marriage-covenant to him.

O blessed Jesus, I come to you hungry, wretched, miserable, blind, and naked; a most loathsome, polluted wretch, a guilty, condemned malefactor, unworthy to wash the feet of the Servants of my Lord, much more to be solemnly married to the King of Glory; but since such is your unparalleled love, I do here with all my power accept you, and take you for my Head and Husband, for better, for worse, for richer, for poorer, for all times and conditions, to love, honor, and obey you before all others, and this to the death. I embrace you in all your offices: I renounce my own worthiness, and do here avow you for the Lord my Righteousness: I renounce my own wisdom, and do here take you for my only guide; I renounce my own will, and take your will for my law.

And since you have told me I must suffer if I will reign, I do here covenant with you to take my lot, as it falls, with you, and by your grace assisting to run all hazards with you, verily purposing that neither life nor death shall part between you and me.

And because you have been pleased to give me your holy Laws as the Rule of my life, and the way in which I should walk to your kingdom, I do here willingly put my neck under your yoke, and set my shoulder to your burden, and subscribing to all your laws as holy, just, and good, I solemnly take them as the Rule of my words, thoughts, and actions; promising that though my flesh contradict and rebel, I will endeavor to order and govern my whole life according to your direction, and will not allow myself in the neglect of any thing that I know to be my duty.

Now, Almighty God, Searcher of Hearts, you know that I make this Covenant with you this day, without any known guile or reservation, beseeching you, if you espy any flaw or falsehood therein, you would discover it to me, and help me to do it aright.

And now, glory be to you, O God the Father, whom I shall be bold from this day forward to look upon as my God and Father; that ever you should find out such a way for the recovery of undone Sinners. Glory be to you, O God the Son, who have loved me, and washed me from my sins in your own blood, and are now become my Savior and Redeemer. Glory be to you O God the Holy Ghost, who by the Finger of your almighty power have turned about my heart from Sin to God.

O dreadful Jehovah, the Lord God Omnipotent, Father, Son, and Holy Ghost, you are now become my Covenant-Friend, and I, through your infinite grace, am become your Covenant-Servant. Amen. So be it. And the Covenant which I have made on earth, let it be ratified in heaven.

(FINAL RUBRIC)

This Covenant I advise you to make, not only in heart, but in word; not only in word, but in writing; and that you would with all possible reverence spread the writing before the Lord as if you would present it unto him as your act and deed: and when you have done this, set your hand to it: keep it as a memorial of the solemn transactions that have passed between God and you, that you may have recourse to it in doubts and temptations.

FINIS.

[An example of a recent Covenant Service that could be used in any church today is included as an appendix at the end of this volume.]

[10]

A SHORT ACCOUNT OF
THE LIFE AND DEATH OF
THE REVEREND JOHN FLETCHER,
1786

HIS CHARACTER

1. I am sensible, it is the method of almost all writers, to place the character of a man at the conclusion of his life. But there seems to be a particular reason for varying from the usual practice in this place. The death of Mr. Fletcher (hardly to be paralleled in the present century) was so uncommon a display of the power and goodness of God in behalf of his highly favored servant that it is not proper for anything to come after it. It must needs therefore close the whole account.

2. From even the imperfect account which has been given of this great and good man, any discerning person may with very little difficulty extract his character. In general, it is easy to perceive that a more excellent man has not appeared in the Church for some ages. It is true, in several ages, and in several countries, many men have excelled in particular virtues and graces. But who can point out, in any age or nation, one that so highly excelled in all? one that was enabled in so large a measure to *put on the whole armor of God?* yea, so to *put on Christ* as to *perfect holiness in the fear of God?*

3. Yet there is a peculiar difficulty in giving a full account of either his life or his character, because we have scarce any light from himself. He was upon all occasions very uncommonly reserved in speaking of himself, whether in writing or conversation. He hardly ever said anything concerning himself, unless it slipped from him unawares. And among the great number of papers which he has left, there is scarce a page (except that single account of his conversion to God) relative either to his own inward experience or the transactions

146

of his life. So that the most of the information we have is gathered up, either from short hints scattered up and down in his letters, from what he had occasionally dropped among his friends, or from what one and another remembered concerning him. In writing the lives and characters of eminent men, the Roman Catholics have a great advantage over us. The pious members of the Church of Rome make a conscience of concealing anything from their Directors, but disclose to them all the circumstances of their lives, and all the secrets of their hearts: Whereas very few of the Protestants disclose to others, even their most intimate friends, what passes between God and their own souls; at least not of set purpose. Herein they forget, or at least disregard, that wise remark of the ancient writers (exactly agreeable to various passages that occur in the canonical Scriptures): "It is good to conceal the secrets of a King, but to declare the loving-kindness of the Lord."

4. This defect was indeed in some measure supplied by the entire intimacy which subsisted between him and Mrs. Fletcher. He did not willingly, much less designedly, conceal anything from her. They had no secrets with regard to each other, but had indeed one house, one purse, and one heart. Before her it was his invariable rule to think aloud; always to open the window in his breast. And to this we are indebted for the knowledge of many particulars which must otherwise have been buried in oblivion.

5. But, whatever the materials were, however complete our information, yet I am thoroughly sensible of my own inability to draw such a portrait as Mr. Fletcher deserves. I have no turn at all for panegyric: I have never accustomed myself to it. It gives me therefore no small satisfaction to find that this is in a great measure done to my hands. The picture is already drawn; and that by no mean pencil. All then which I shall attempt is to retouch Mrs. Fletcher's observations, and now and then to add a few articles, either from my own knowledge, or from the information of others.

6. The following are mostly her own words—for where they are clear and expressive, as they generally are, I do not think it right to alter them for altering's sake:

"Whatever he might be with regard to charity," said she, "he was no less eminent for his spirit of faith. Indeed he was not so much led by sights or impressions (which many mistake for faith) as abundance of people have been; but by a steady, firm reliance upon the love and truth and faithfulness of God. His ardent desire was, so to believe, as to be a partaker of all the great and precious promises; to be a witness of all that mind which was in Christ Jesus. And being conscious that he must be crucified with his Master, or never reign with Him, he gave himself up to Him, whom he continually set before him, to lie in his hand as the passive clay. He would often say, 'It is my business in all events to hang upon the Lord, with a sure trust and confidence, that he will order all things in the best time and manner. Indeed it would be nothing to be a believer, nay, in truth, there would be no room for faith, if everything were seen here. But against hope to believe in hope, to have a full confidence in that unseen power which so mightily supports us in all our dangers and difficulties—this is the believing which is acceptable to God.' Sometimes when I have expressed some apprehension of an approaching trial, he would answer, 'I do not doubt but the Lord orders all; therefore I leave everything to him.' In outward dangers, if they were ever so great, he seemed to know no shadow of fear. When I was speaking once, concerning a danger to which we were then particularly exposed, he answered, 'I know God always gives his angels charge concerning us: Therefore we are equally safe everywhere.'

"Not less eminent than his faith was his humility. Amid all his laying himself out for God, and for the good of souls, he ever preserved that special grace, the making no account of his own labors. He held himself and his own abilities in very low esteem; and seemed to have that word continually before his eyes, 'I am an unprofitable servant.' And this humility was so rooted in him as to be moved by no affront. I have seen many, even of the most provoking kind, offered him; but he received them as his proper portion; being so far from desiring the honor which comes of men, that he took pleasure in being little and unknown. Perhaps it might appear from some passages of his life that in this he even leaned to an extreme; for genuine humility does not require that any man should desire to be despised. Nay, we are to avoid it, so far as we possibly can, consistently with a good conscience; for that direction, 'Let no man despise thee,' concerns every man as well as Timothy.

"It is rare to meet with an eminent person that can bear an equal. But it was his choice and his delight to prefer everyone to himself. And this he did in so free and easy a manner that in him it appeared perfectly natural. He never willingly suffered any unkindness shown to him to be mentioned again; and if it was, he generally answered,

'Oh, let it drop; we will offer it in silence to the Lord.' And indeed the best way of bearing crosses is to consecrate all in silence to God.

"From this root of humility sprang such a patience as I wish I could either describe or imitate. It produced in him a most ready mind, which embraced every cross with alacrity and pleasure. For the good of his neighbor, nothing seemed hard, nothing wearisome. Sometimes I have been grieved to call him out of his study two or three times in an hour, especially when he was engaged in composing some of his deepest works; but he would answer, with his usual sweetness, 'O my dear, never think of that. It matters not, if we are but always ready to meet the will of God. It is conformity to the will of God that alone makes an employment excellent.' He never thought anything too mean, but sin; he looked on nothing else as beneath his character. If he overtook a poor man or woman on the road, with a burden too heavy for them, he did not fail to offer his assistance to bear part of it; and he would not easily take a denial. This therefore he has frequently done.

"In bearing pain he was most exemplary, and continued more and more so to the last. Nor was it least remarkable in the most humbling part of the ministry, the coming down to the capacities of the ignorant. Nevertheless he had a most resolute courage in the reproving of sin. To daring sinners he was a son of thunder; and no worldly considerations were regarded, whenever he believed God had given him a message to deliver to any of them.

"One considerable part of humility is to know our own place, and stand therein. Every member has its peculiar appointment in the human body, where the wise Master-builder has placed it; and it is well while each continues in its place. But, as every dislocated bone gives pain, and must continue so to do till it is replaced in its proper socket, so every dislocated affection must give pain to the soul till it is restored to its own place, till it is totally fixed in God, till we resign our whole selves to the disposal of infinite wisdom. This is the proper place of every rational creature; and in this place he invariably stood. Whatever he believed to be the will of God, he resolutely performed, though it were to pluck out a right eye, to lay his Isaac on the altar. When it appeared that God called him to any journey, he immediately prepared for it, without the least hesitation; although, for the last years of his life, he hardly ever traveled to any considerable distance without feeling some tendency to a relapse into his former distemper;

and it was usually some weeks after his return before he recovered his usual strength."

Humility continually produces meekness, and the latter bears an exact proportion to the former. I received a letter on this head but a few days since, which it may not be improper to subjoin:

Rev. Sir,

I was yesterday in company with several Clergymen, who, among other things, mentioned Mr. Fletcher, and seemed particularly anxious that in the account of his life a proper degree of caution should be observed in the panegyric that may be applied to his character. They say he was extremely passionate; and that there was in many instances an austere severity and rigor in his conduct to the young people under his care, particularly at Trevecka. As this information comes from a gentleman eminent for his knowledge of mankind, and universally esteemed as one of the greatest geniuses of the age, and one whose veracity has never been questioned, it will have no small weight in the learned world.

7. I am glad this information came to my hands in time, as it may now receive so sufficient an answer as will probably satisfy every candid and impartial reader.

Two things are here asserted concerning Mr. Fletcher: The First, that he was extremely passionate: The Second, that there was an austere severity and rigor in his conduct toward the young persons under his care, particularly at Trevecka. The former assertion is unquestionably true; such he was by nature. The latter I question much, with regard to his conduct at Tern, as well as at Trevecka. None can be a more competent witness of his conduct at Tern than Mr. Vaughan, who lived so long in the same house; and whose testimony concerning him has been so largely given in the preceding pages. But, waving this, can it possibly be supposed that either Mr. Hill or his sons, then verging toward manhood, would have borne the austere rigor and severity of a young man that received his bread from them? yea, and that year after year? Surely the supposition shocks all credibility.

8. Equally incredible is the assertion of his "austere severity and rigor" toward the young men at Trevecka. This is inconsistent with

the whole account given by Mr. Benson, an eye and ear witness of all his conduct. Had it been true in any degree, would it have been possible that he should have been so esteemed and beloved by those very young men? I cannot form the least conjecture whence such an assertion could arise unless it was invented by some young man after Mr. Fletcher was dismissed, in order to ingratiate himself with his patroness.

9. The farther account which Mr. Benson gives of him from personal knowledge is this: "Mr. Fletcher," says he, "was naturally a man of strong passions, and prone to anger in particular; insomuch that he has frequently thrown himself on the floor, and laid there most of the night bathed in tears, imploring victory over his own spirit. And he did not strive in vain; he did obtain the victory, in a very eminent degree. For twenty years and upwards before his death, no one ever saw him out of temper, or heard him utter a rash expression, on any provocation whatever. I have often thought the testimony that Bishop Burnet, in the History of his own Times, bears of Archbishop Leighton, might be borne of him with equal propriety: 'After an intimate acquaintance with the Archbishop for many years, and after being with him by night and by day, at home and abroad, in public and in private, on sundry occasions and in various affairs, I must say, I never heard an idle word drop from his lips, nor any which was not to the use of edifying. I never saw him in any temper in which I myself would not have wished to be found at death.' Any that has been intimately acquainted with Mr. Fletcher will say the same of him. But they that knew him best, will say it with the most assurance."

10. His "disengagements from the world, and love of the poor," Mrs. Fletcher joins together. "Never," says she, "did I behold any one more dead to the things of the world. His treasure was above; and so was his heart also. He always remembered that admonition of the Apostle, 'No man that wars entangles himself with the things of this life.' It was his constant endeavor to preserve a mind free and disencumbered; and he was exceeding wary of undertaking any business that might distract and hurry it. Yet, in his worldly concerns, knowing himself to be a steward for God, he would not through carelessness waste one penny. He likewise judged it to be his bounden duty to demand what he knew to be his right. And yet he could well reconcile this with that word, 'He that will have thy coat, let him have thy cloak also.' Indeed, whether he had less or more, it was the same

thing upon his own account, as he had no other use for it but to spread the gospel, and to assist the poor. And he frequently said, he never was happier than when he had given away the last penny he had in his house. If at any time I had gold in my drawers, it seemed to afford him no comfort. But if he could find a handful of small silver, when he was going out to see the sick, he would express as much pleasure over it as a miser would in discovering a bag of hid treasure. He was never better pleased with my employment than when he had set me to prepare food or physic for the poor. He was hardly able to relish his dinner if some sick neighbor had not a part of it; and sometimes, if any one of them was in want, I could not keep the linen in his drawers. On Sundays he provided for numbers of people who came from a distance to hear the word; and his house, as well as his heart, was devoted to their convenience: To relieve them that were afflicted in body or mind was the delight of his heart. Once a poor man, who feared God, being brought into great difficulties, he took down all the pewter from the kitchen shelves, saying, 'This will help you; and I can do without it. A wooden trencher will serve me just as well.' In epidemic and contagious distempers, when the neighbors were afraid to nurse the sick, he has gone from house to house, seeking some that were willing to undertake it. And when none could be found, he has offered his service, to sit up with them himself. But this was at his first setting out here. At present, there appears in many (and has done so for many years) a most ready mind to visit and relieve the distressed.

11. "He thoroughly complied with that advice
'Give to all something; to a good poor man,
Till thou change hands, and be where he began.'
I have heard him say that when he lived alone in his house, the tears have come into his eyes when one had brought him five or six insignificant letters, at three or four pence a piece; and perhaps he had only a single shilling in the house, to distribute among the poor to whom he was going. He frequently said to me, 'O Polly, can we not do without beer? Let us drink water, and eat less meat. Let our necessities give way to the extremities of the poor.'

12. "But with all his generosity and charity he was strictly careful to follow the advice of the Apostle, *Owe no man any thing.* He contracted no debt. While he gave all he had, he made it a rule to pay ready money for everything; believing this was the best way to keep the mind unencumbered and free from care. Meanwhile his sub-

stance, his time, his strength, his life, were devoted to the service of the poor. And, last of all, he gave me to them. For when we were married, he asked me solemnly whether I was willing to marry his parish. And the first time he led me among his people in this place, he said, 'I have not married this wife only for myself, but for you. I asked her of the Lord, for your comfort, as well as my own.' "

13. All his life, as well as during his illness, particularly at Newington and Brislington (as has been largely related), he was grateful in a very high degree to those who conferred the least benefit upon him; yea, or even endeavored so to do. One of these was Mr. Richard Edwards, of London, to whose care he was committed as a Leader when he was first admitted into the London Society. A lively sense of the kindness which Mr. Edwards then showed him, he retained to the end of his life. This he testified by repeated letters; one or two of which it may be well to transcribe.

Tern, Oct. 19, 1756

Dearest Brother,

This is to let you know, that (praise be to the Lord!) I am very well in body, and pretty well in soul. But I have very few Christian friends here. And God has been pleased to take away the chief of those few by a most comfortable death. And lately I heard that my aged father is gone the way of all flesh. But the glorious circumstances of his death make me ample amends for the sorrow which I felt. For some years, I have wrote to him with as much freedom as I could have done to a son, though not with so much effect as I wished. But last spring, God visited him with a severe illness, which brought him to a sense of himself. And, after a deep repentance, he died about a month ago, in the full assurance of faith. This has put several of my friends on thinking seriously, which affords me great cause of thankfulness. I am

Your unworthy brother and servant in the Lord,
JOHN FLETCHER.

14. Two years after he wrote to him as follows:
"I thank you for your encouraging observations. I want them, and

use them by the grace of God. When I received yours, I had not had one opportunity of preaching, so incensed were all the Clergy against me. One, however, let me have the use of his church, the Abbey church, at Shrewsbury. I preached in the forenoon with some degree of the demonstration of the Spirit. The congregation was very numerous; and I believe one half at least desired to hear me again. But the Minister would not let me have the pulpit any more. The next Sunday, the Minister of a neighboring parish lying a dying, I was sent for to officiate for him. He died a few days after, and the chief man in the parish offered to make interest that I might succeed him. But I could not consent. The next Sunday, I preached at Shewsbury again; but in another church. The next day I set out for Bristol, and was much refreshed among the brethren. As I returned I called at New-Kingswood, about sixteen miles from Bristol. The Minister offering me his church, I preached to a numerous congregation, gathered on half an hour's notice. I think the seed then sown will not be lost."

15. "Another uncommon talent which God had given him," says Mrs. Fletcher, "was a peculiar sensibility of spirit. He had a temper the most feeling of any I ever knew. Hardly a night passed over but some part of it was spent in groans for the souls and bodies committed to his care. I dreaded his hearing either of the sins or sufferings of any of his people before the time of his going to bed, knowing how strong the impressions would be on his mind, chasing the sleep from his eyes.

"And yet I have heard him speak of a time, twelve or fourteen years ago, when he was greatly tempted to think that he was not sensible enough of the afflictions of his fellow-creatures. He thought Christ bore our infirmities, and carried our sorrows; but, said he, 'I have not that Christ-like temper: I do not bear the sorrows of others.' After being for some time buffeted with this temptation, he prayed, that a measure of this spirit might be given him. Not long after, as he was visiting a poor sick family, so lively a sense of their affliction on a sudden fell upon his mind that he could scarce get home. As soon as he sat down in his house, his soul was penetrated with such a sense of the woes of mankind as utterly depressed and overcame him, and drank up his spirits, insomuch that he could not help himself, nor move from one chair to another. And he was no more able to walk or help himself than a newborn child. At the same time he seemed to lose the use of his memory, and of all his faculties. He thought,

'What is this? Is it a disease? Is it a stroke of the palsy? Rather, is it not an answer to my own ill-judged, though well-intended, prayer? Did I not ask a burden unsuitable to a finite, and capable of being borne only by an infinite, being?' He remained some hours in this situation. Then it came into his mind, 'If this is a purely natural event, the will of the Lord be done! But if it be the answer to an improper prayer, God will answer again by removing it.' He cried to the Lord, and was immediately restored to strength both of body and mind.

"When we were at Leeds, in the year 1784, I had another proof of the tender sensibility of his heart. Oh, how deeply was he affected concerning the welfare of his brethren! When any little disputes arose between them, his inmost soul groaned under the burden; and, by two or three o'clock in the morning, I was sure to hear him breathing out prayer for the peace and prosperity of Sion. When I observed to him I was afraid it would hurt his health, and wished him to sleep more, he would answer, 'O Polly, the cause of God lies near my heart!'

"Toward me his tenderness was exerted in its utmost extent. My soul, my body, my health, my ease and comfort, were his daily study. We had no thought, either past or present, which we purposely concealed from each other. My spiritual advancement was his constant endeavor; and to this he was continually stirring me up, inviting me to walk more closely with God; urging that thought, 'O my dear, let us pray for dying grace; for we shall not be long here.' His temporal affairs he committed solely to me, though he was always ready to assist me in the smallest matters.

"One article more remains to be spoken of, namely, his communion with God. Although he enjoyed this, more or less, at all times and in all places, yet I have frequently heard him observe that the seasons of his closest communion were always in his own house, or in the church; usually in the latter. It is much to be lamented that we have no account of it from his own pen. It was his constant endeavor to maintain an uninterrupted sense of the presence of God. In order to this, he was slow of speech, and had the greatest government of his words. Indeed he both acted, and spoke, and thought, as under the eye of God. And thus setting God always before him, he remained unmoved in all occurrences; at all times and on every occasion possessing inward recollection. Nor did I ever see him diverted therefrom on any occasion whatever, either going out or coming in, whether by ourselves or in company. Sometimes he took his journeys alone; but above a thousand miles I have traveled with him; during which neither change of company, place, nor the variety of circumstances which naturally occur in traveling ever seemed to make the least difference in his firm attention to the presence of God. To preserve this uniform habit of soul, he was so watchful and recollected that, to such as were unexperienced in these things, it might appear like insensibility. Although no one could converse in a more lively and sensible manner, even on natural things, when he saw it was to the glory of God; he was always striving to raise his own and every other spirit to a close and immediate intercourse with God. And I can say with truth, all his union with me was so intermingled with prayer and praise that every employment and every meal was, as it were, perfumed therewith."

16. I had concluded what I purposed to say concerning the character of Mr. Fletcher when I received a long letter from Mr. Benson, an extract of which I cannot withhold from the reader. For although most of the particulars hereof are contained in the preceding pages, yet as they are here placed in quite another order, and have also several new circumstances intermixed, I could not doubt of their being both agreeable and profitable to every person of piety.

"As to drawing the character of that great and good man," says Mr. Benson, "it is what I will not attempt: But if I can suggest anything that will assist you therein, I shall think my little labor well bestowed. With this view I have been looking over many of his letters, and observe in them all, what I have a thousand times observed in his conversation and behavior, the plainest marks of every Christian grace and virtue.

"Perhaps if he followed his Master more closely in one thing than another, it was in humility. It is one branch of poverty of spirit (another word for humility) to think meanly of ourselves. As he certainly thought meanly of himself, both as a Christian, as a Preacher, and as a writer, I need not say how he shone in all those characters; but he knew not that he shone in any of them. How low an opinion he had of himself as a Christian manifestly appears from his placing himself at the feet of all, and showing a continual desire to learn from every company he was in. He paid all due deference to the judgment of others, readily acknowledged whatever was good in them, and seemed to think himself the only person in whom there dwelt no excellency worth notice. Hence it was that he often wrote and spoke, as if he had not received that grace which he undoubtedly had received. And indeed he overlooked what he had attained, through the eager desire he had of higher and greater things. Many of his letters show how very meanly he thought of his own attainments as a Christian; through the continually increasing views which he had of the divine purity, and of the high degree of conformity thereto which is attainable even in this world.

"And however little he was in his own eyes as a Christian, he was equally so as a writer and a Preacher. In consequence of the mean opinion he had of his own abilities, he gladly offered what he wrote to be corrected by any friend, however inferior to himself. Thus in a letter, dated November 23, 1771, he says, 'I have sent a letter of fifty pages upon Antinomianism. I beg, upon my bended knees, you would revise and correct it. I have followed my light, small as it is. Put yours to mine.' What a mean opinion he had of his own writings appears from a letter written March 20, 1774: 'I do not repent of my having engaged in this controversy; for though I doubt my little publications cannot reclaim those who are confirmed in believing the lie of the day, yet they may here and there stop one from swallowing it at all, or at least from swallowing it so deeply.' Two years after, he says, 'I have almost run my race of scribbling; and I have preached as much as I could, though to little purpose; but I must not complain. If one person has received good by my ten years' labor, it is an honor for which I cannot be too thankful, if my mind were as low as it should be. Let us bless the Lord in all things.'

"As difficult as it is to think meanly of ourselves, it is still more difficult to be willing that others should think meanly of us. And how eminent he was in this appears from hence, that he was constantly upon his guard lest any expression should drop either from his lips or pen, which tended to make any one think well of him; either on account of his family, or learning, or parts, or usefulness. Yea, he took as much pains to conceal his excellencies as others do to show them; having the same desire to be little and unknown which many have to be known and esteemed.

"It would have remained a secret in this kingdom, even to his most intimate friends, that he was of so great a family, had not Mr. Ireland gone over with him to Switzerland, where he was surprised to find Mr. Fletcher's relations some of the first people in the country.

" '*Blessed are they that mourn*,' said the Lord Jesus. And this blessedness was as certainly his as the former. He was a man of a serious spirit; one that stood at the utmost distance from levity of every kind. Though he was constantly cheerful, as rejoicing in hope of his heavenly inheritance, yet had he too deep a sense of his own wants, and the wants of the Church of God, as also of the sins and miseries of mankind, to be at any time light or trifling. I have a letter before me, dated December, 1771, which at once gives us a picture of his seriousness, watchfulness, and earnestness; and contains advices well deserving the consideration of all that fear God. 'There is undoubtedly,' said he, 'such a thing as the full assurance of faith. Be not discouraged on account of thousands who stop short of it: It is our own fault if we do not attain. God would give us ample satisfaction if we did but deeply feel our wants. Both you and I want a deeper awakening, which will produce a death to outward things and speculative knowledge. Let us shut our eyes to the gilded clouds without us; let us draw inward, and search after God, if haply we may find him. Let us hold our confidence, though we are often constrained against hope to believe in hope. But let us not rest in our confidence, as thousands do; let it help us to struggle and wait till he come. Let us habituate ourselves to live inwardly. This will solemnize us, and prevent our trifling with the things of God. We may be thankful for what we have, without resting in it. We may strive, and yet not trust in our striving; but expect all from divine grace.'

"Four or five years after, he says, 'I send this to inquire after your welfare, and to let you know that though I am pretty well in body, yet I break fast. But I want to break faster in my spirit than I do. Yet, blessed be God, I have been in such pinching, grinding circumstances for near a year, by a series of providential and domestic trials, as have given me some deadly blows. I am not without hope of setting my eyes on you once more. Mr. Wesley kindly invites me to travel with him, and visit some of the societies. I feel an inclination to break one of my chains, parochial retirement, which may be a nest for self-indulgence. I leave the matter entirely to the Lord.'

"Meantime, he mourned, not only for himself and his friends, but also for the Church of God. 'The few professors,' says he, 'which I see in these parts, are so far from what I wish them to be that I cannot but cry out, Lord, how long will you give your heritage up to desolation? How long shall the Heathen say, *Where is now their* indwelling *God?*' In another letter he writes (dated May 8, 1776), 'I see so little fruit in these parts that I am almost disheartened. I am closely followed with the thought that faith in the dispensation of the Spirit is at a very low ebb. But it may be better in other places. I shall be glad to travel a little, to see the goodness of the land. May God make and keep us humble, loving, disinterested, and zealous!'

"These quotations give us not only an example of holy mourning, but likewise of hungering and thirsting after righteousness. In this he was peculiarly worthy our imitation. He never rested in anything he had either experienced or done in spiritual matters. But this one thing he did: *Forgetting those things that were behind, and reaching forth unto those things which were before,* he *pressed toward the mark for the prize of the high calling of God in Christ Jesus;* he was a true Christian racer, always on the stretch for higher and better things. Though his attainments, both in experience and usefulness, were above the common standard, yet the language of his conversation and behavior always was, *Not as though I had already attained, either were already perfected; but I follow after, if by any means I may apprehend that for which I am apprehended of Christ Jesus.* He had his eye upon a full conformity to the Son of God; or what the Apostle terms, *the measure of the stature of the fulness of Christ.* Nor could he be satisfied with anything less.

"And he was meek, like his Master, as well as lowly in heart. Not that he was so by nature, but of a fiery, passionate spirit. But so thoroughly had grace subdued nature, so fully was he renewed in the spirit of his mind, that, for many years before his death, I believe he was never observed by anyone, friend or foe, to be out of temper. And yet he did not want provocation, and that sometimes in a high degree; especially from those whose religious sentiments he thought it his duty to oppose. One of these, who once loved him so well as to be ready to pull out his eyes for him, was so exasperated on reading his *Second Check* that he wrote to him in the most bitter terms. But none of these things moved him; no, not in the least degree. The keenest word he used upon the occasion was, 'What a world, what a religious world we live in!'

"Hence arose his readiness to bear with the weaknesses, and forgive the faults, of others; the more remarkable, considering his flaming zeal against sin, and deep concern for the glory of God. Such hatred to sin, and such love to the sinner, I never saw joined together before. This very circumstance convinced me of the height of his grace, bearing so much of his Master's image, whose hatred to sin and love to sinners are equally infinite. He took all possible pains to detect what was evil in any of those that were under his care; pursuing it through all its turnings and windings, and stripping it of all its disguises. Yet none so ready to excuse when it was confessed, and to conceal it even from his most intimate friends.

"He never mentioned the faults of an absent person, unless absolute duty required it: And then he spoke with the utmost tenderness, extenuating, rather than aggravating. None could draw his picture more exactly that Saint Paul has done, in the thirteenth chapter of the first Epistle to the Corinthians. Every feature in that masterly piece of apostolic painting was found in him. Let all that knew him, especially his intimate friends, recollect the spirit and behavior of this servant of the God of love; and then let them judge whether I exaggerate, when I say, he *suffered long and was kind; he envied not; acted not rashly; was not puffed up; did not behave himself unseemly; sought not his own; was not easily provoked. He thought no evil, rejoiced not in iniquity, but rejoiced in the truth. He covered all things, believed all things, hoped all things, and endured all things.* It would be easy to enlarge on all these particulars, and show how they were exemplified in him. But waving this, I would only observe that, with regard to two of them—kindness to others, and not seeking his own—he had few equals. His kindness to others was such that he bestowed his all upon them; his time, his talents, his substance. His knowledge, his eloquence, his health, his money, were employed, day by day, for the good of mankind. He prayed, he wrote, he preached, he visited the sick and well, he conversed, he gave, he labored, he suffered, winter and summer, night and day; he endangered, nay, destroyed, his health, and, in the end, gave his life also for the profit of his neighbors, that they might be saved from everlasting death. He denied himself even such food as was necessary for him, that he might have to give to them that had none. And when he was constrained to change his manner of living, still his diet was plain and simple; and so were his clothing and furniture, that he might save all that was possible for his poor neighbors.

"He sought not his own in any sense; not his own honor, but the honor of God in all he said or did: He sought not his own interest, but the interest of his Lord; spreading knowledge, holiness, and happiness as far as he possibly could. He sought not his own pleasure, but studied to 'please all men, for their good to edification'; and to please him that had called him to his kingdom and glory. And yet it is certain, he found the greatest pleasure in pleasing God and his neighbor. For nothing could give a higher delight than this to his pious and benevolent mind.

"In the meantime, he was a man of peace, and spared no pains to restore it where it was broken. He gave numberless proofs of this amiable disposition. When we were at Trevecka, (to mention but one instance,) two of the students were bitterly prejudiced against each other. He took them into a room by themselves, reasoned with them, wept over them, and at last prevailed. Their hearts were broken; they were melted down; they fell upon each other's necks and wept aloud.

"The pains which he took to make peace at the Leeds Conference will not easily be forgotten. And although he could not prevail so far as might have been desired, yet his labor was not in vain.

"But I do not attempt his full character: I will only add, what the Apostle recommends to the Philippians was exactly copied by him. He was *blameless and harmless, a son of God, without rebuke, in the midst of a crooked and perverse generation; shining among them as a light in the world.*"

I think one talent wherewith God had endued Mr. Fletcher has not been sufficiently noted yet: I mean his courtesy; in which there was not the least touch either of art or affectation. It was pure and genuine, and sweetly constrained him to behave to everyone (although particularly to inferiors) in a manner not to be described, with so inexpressible a mixture of humility, love, and respect. This directed his words, the tone of his voice, his looks, his whole attitude, his every motion. This seems to be intended by Saint Paul, in those words, οὐκ ἀσχημονεῖ; not so well expressed in our translation by, "behaveth not itself unseemly." Do not the words literally mean, "is not ill bred?" "behaves on all occasions with decency and good breeding?" Certainly, so did Mr. Fletcher. Never did any man more perfectly suit his whole behavior to the persons and the occasion: So that one might apply to him, with great propriety, the words of the ancient poet:

Illum quicquid agit, quoquo vestigia tendit
Componit furtim, subsequiturque decor.

I cannot translate this; but I can give the English reader a parallel, and more than a parallel:

Grace was in all his steps, heaven in his eye,
In all his gestures sanctity and love.

ELEVEN LETTERS OF
SPIRITUAL COUNSEL
July 25, 1767 to February 24, 1791.

The Essential Point of Christian Holiness

TO MRS. BENNIS

Dublin, July 25, 1767

Dear Sister Bennis,

When you write to me, you have only to "think aloud," just to open the window in your breast. When we love one another, there is no need of either disguise or reserve. I love you, and I verily believe you love me; so you have only to write just what you feel.

The essential part of Christian holiness is giving the heart wholly to God; and certainly we need not lose any degree of that light and love which at first attend this: it is our own infirmity if we do; it is not the will of the Lord concerning us. Your present business is not to reason whether you should call your experience thus or thus, but to go straight to Him that loves you, with all your wants, how great or how many soever they are. Then all things are ready; help, while you ask, is given. You have only to receive it by simple faith. Nevertheless you will still be encompassed with numberless infirmities; for you live in an house of clay, and therefore this corruptible body will more or less press down the soul, yet not so as to prevent your rejoicing evermore and having a witness that your heart is all His. You may claim this: it is yours; for Christ is yours. Believe, and feel Him near.—My dear sister, adieu.

Yours affectionately,

SELECTED WRITINGS

To "Walk in Love" is the Essence of Christianity

TO PHILOTHEA BRIGGS

London, January 5, 1772

My Dear Philly,

It is not always a defect to mind one thing at a time. And an apt-ness so to do, to employ the whole vigour of the mind on the thing in hand, may answer excellent purposes. Only you have need to be exceeding wary, lest the thing you pursue be wrong. First, be well as-sured not only that it is good but that it is the best thing for you at that time; and then, whatsoever your hand findeth to do, do it with your might. But you have all things in one, the whole of religion con-tracted to a point, in that word. *"Walk in love," as Christ also loved us and gave Himself for us.* All is contained in humble, gentle, patient love. Is not this, so to speak, a divine contrivance to assist the narrow-ness of our minds, the scantiness of our understanding? Every right temper, and then all right words and actions, naturally branch out of love. In effect, therefore, you want nothing but this—to be filled with the faith that worketh by love.

You take no liberties that are not agreeable to, my dear Philly,

Yours affectionately,

Sanctification is a devoted Will, not necessarily Continuous Peace

TO MRS. BENNIS

London, January 18, 1774

My Dear Sister,

A will steadily and uniformly devoted to God is essential to a state of sanctification, but not an uniformity of joy or peace or happy communion with God. These may rise and fall in various degrees; nay, and may be affected either by the body or by diabolical agency, in a manner which all our wisdom can neither understand nor pre-

163

vent. As to wanderings, you would do right well to consider the sermon on Wandering Thoughts: you might likewise profit by Elizabeth Harper's *Journal,* whose experience much resembled yours, only she was more simple; and you may learn from her to go straight to God as a little child, and tell Him all your troubles and hindrances and doubts, and desire Him to turn them all to good. You are not sent to Waterford to be useless. Stir up the gift of God which is in you; gather together those that have been scattered abroad, and make up a band, if not a class or two. Your best way would be to visit from house to house. By this means you can judge of their conduct and dispositions in domestic life, and may have opportunity to speak to the young of the family. By motion you will contract warmth; by imparting life you will increase it in yourself.

As to the circumstance mentioned in the postscript of your last, I should think you would do well to exert yourself in that matter as much as possible. It will be a cross: take up that cross, bear your cross, and it will bear you; and if you do it with a single eye, it will be no loss to your soul.—I am, my dear sister,

Your affectionate brother,

Works increase Faith: Do Good, Don't Live in Solitude

TO MARY BISHOP

Reigate, November 30, 1774

My Dear Sister,

We so become all things to all, as not to hurt our own souls, when we first secure a single eye, a steady design, to please all for their good to edification, and then take care that our discourse be always good to the use of edifying and such as may minister grace to the hearers. But in order to this we have need to power from on high and of the wisdom that sitteth by the throne. This alone can give us to order our conversation aright, so as to profit both others and our own souls.

Before this can effectually be done, you must conquer your natural reserve, and exercise it only to those of whom you know nothing at all or of whom you know nothing good. Perhaps there is one occasion more on which it will be highly expedient, if not necessary—namely, when good persons (at least in some measure so) sink beneath their character, trifle away time, or indulge themselves in a conversation which has no tendency to improve either the speaker or the hearer.

I think it will not be best for you to go out less than you ever did. Suppose you have more faith and more love (as I would fain think you have), you certainly ought to go out more. Otherwise your faith will insensibly die away. It is *by works* only that it can be *made perfect*. And the more the love of solitude is indulged the more it will increase. This is a temptation common to men. In every age and country Satan has whispered to those who began to taste the powers of the world to come (as well as to Gregory Lopez), "Au desert!" Au desert! Most of our little flock at Oxford were tried with this, my brother and I in particular. Nay, but I say, "To the Bible! To the Bible!" And there you will learn, *as you have time, to do good unto all men:* to warn every man, to exhort every man as you have opportunity; although the greatest part of your care and labour should be laid out on those that are of the household of faith. Certainly you may continually do good to others without any ways endangering the salvation of your own soul. What at present you much want is simplicity, in the Archbishop of Cambray's sense of the word: that grace "whereby the soul casts off all unnecessary reflections upon itself." I wish I could say of you, as I did of a young person many years ago, when I sent her his little book,—

> In Art, in nature, can we find
> Colours to picture thee?
> Speak, Cambray's pen, for Sally's mind;
> She is simplicity.

—I am, my dear Miss Bishop,

Yours affectionately,

JOHN WESLEY

Christian Resignation and Love the Point, not Joy

TO MRS. BARTON

Bristol, July 29, 1777

My Dear Sister,

It is well that you have learned to say, *The Lord gave, and the Lord hath taken away.* Your child is gone but a little before you. How soon shall we overtake her! It is no way inconsistent with Christian resignation to ask conditionally, *Let this cup pass from me;* only with the addition, *Nevertheless, not as I will,* but as Thou wilt.

Rapturous joy, such as is frequently given in the beginning of justification or of entire sanctification, is a great blessing; but it seldom continues long before it subsides into calm, peaceful love. I believe, if Miss Hurrell were to spend a little time with you, it might be of great use to many. —I am, with love to Brother Barton,

Your affectionate brother,

Communion with God is not inconsistent with Business: Wesley's own experience

TO MISS MARCH

Near London, December 10, 1777

You do not at all understand my manner of life. Though I am always in haste, I am never in a hurry; because I never undertake any more work than I can go through with perfect calmness of spirit. It is true I travel four or five thousand miles in a year. But I generally travel alone in my carriage, and consequently am as retired ten hours in a day as if I was in a wilderness. On other days I never spend less than three hours (frequently ten or twelve) in the day alone. So there are few persons in the kingdom who spend so many hours secluded from all company. Yet I find time to visit the sick and the poor; and I must do it, if I believe the Bible, if I believe these are the marks whereby the Shepherd of Israel will know and judge His sheep at the great day; therefore, when there is time and opportunity for it, who can doubt but this is matter of absolute duty? When I was at Oxford, and lived almost like an hermit, I saw not how any busy man could be saved. I scarce thought it possible for a man to retain the Christian spirit amidst the noise and bustle of the world. God taught me better by my own experience. I had ten times more business in America (that is, at intervals) than ever I had in my life. But it was no hindrance to silence of spirit.

Mr. Boehm was Chaplain to Prince George of Denmark, Secretary to him and Queen Anne, principal manager of almost all the public charities in the kingdom, and employed in numberless private charities. An intimate friend, knowing this, said to him when they were alone, "Sir, are you not hurt by that amazing hurry of business? I have seen you in your office, surrounded with people, listening to one, dictating to another, and at the same time writing to a third; could you then retain a sense of the presence of God?" He answered, "All that company and all that business no more hindered or lessened my communion with God than if I had been all alone in a church kneeling before the communion table." Was it not the same case with him to whom Gregory Lopez said, "Go and be an hermit in Mexico"? I am concerned for you; I am sorry you should be content with lower degrees of usefulness and holiness than you are called to. But I cannot help it: so I submit; and am still, my dear Miss March,

Yours in sincere affection,

The Lord's Supper and Self-Knowledge

TO HIS NIECE SARAH WESLEY

Manchester, March 31, 1781

My Dear Sally,

The expression of *eating and drinking unworthily* has one, and only one, meaning affixed to it by St. Paul, who is the only inspired writer that uses that expression. He means by it that particular sin of which the Corinthians were then guilty—the snatching one before another his own supper, so that one was hungry and another was drunken. Now, it is certain you are in no danger of this any more than of committing murder. Deadness, coldness, wandering thoughts of various kinds are totally distinct from it. And now, when the worst of these occur, you may answer with pious Kempis, "Go, go, thou unclean spirit. These are not my thoughts but yours, and *you* shall answer for them to God."

God is now aiming, in all His dealings with you, to bring you to a knowledge of yourself as one in whom by nature dwells no good thing. And this He is particularly pursuing when you approach His Table. Were He to give you at that time remarkable joy or sweetness, it would not answer His design; neither were He to give you much contrition and brokenness of heart. Therefore He leaves you in great measure to your own dull, unfeeling heart, that you may know yourself in order to know Him. But nevertheless this is the way; walk thou in it, and in due time you shall reap if you faint not.

But you must needs have some companions in the way; for how can one be warm alone? I wish you to be acquainted with Miss Johnson, who lodges in Oxford Street at No. 368, and meets in Mrs. Thackeray's class. She is deeply mourning after God, whom she once knew and loved. She is of a tender, sensible temper; and I am certain your spirits would quickly take acquaintance with each other. You want a friend of your own sex and nearly your own age, and I know not one in London that would fit you better.

I pray God that you may resolutely choose Him for your portion; and am, my dear Sally,

Yours affectionately,

Christian Perfection and I Corinthians 13

TO ANN LOXDALE

Liverpool, April 12, 1782

My Dear Miss Loxdale,

I advised formerly my dear Jenny Cooper, and so I advise you, frequently to read and meditate upon the 13th chapter of the First

Epistle to the Corinthians. There is the true picture of Christian perfection! Let us copy after it with all our might. I believe it might likewise be of use to you to read more than once the *Plain Account of Christian Perfection.* Indeed, what is it more or less than humble, gentle, patient love! It is undoubtedly our privilege to "rejoice evermore", with a calm, still, heartfelt joy. Nevertheless this is seldom long at one stay. Many circumstances may cause it to ebb and flow. This, therefore, is not the essence of religion, which is no other than humble, gentle, patient love. I do not know whether all these are not included in that one word resignation. For the highest lesson our Lord (as man) learned on earth was to say, *Not as I will, but as You will.* May He confirm you more and more!

Yours most affectionately,

Inward Holiness, Works, Suffering; and our Future Reward

TO ANN BOLTON

Near London, December 15, 1786

My Dear Nancy,

There can be no possible reason to doubt concerning the happiness of that child. He did fear God, and according to his circumstances work righteousness. This is the essence of religion, according to St. Peter. His soul, therefore, was "darkly safe with God," although he was only under the Jewish Dispensation.

When the Son of Man shall come in his glory and assign every man his own reward, that reward will undoubtedly be proportioned, first to our inward holiness our likeness to God, secondly to our works, and thirdly to our sufferings; therefore for whatever you suffer in time, you will be an unspeakable gainer in eternity. Many of your sufferings, perhaps the greatest part, are now past; but the joy is to come! Look up, my dear friend, look up, and see the Crown before you! A little longer, and you shall drink of the rivers of pleasure that flow at God's right hand for evermore.—My dear Nancy, Adieu!

JOHN WESLEY

Holiness and Suffering

TO ANN BOLTON

Leeds, August 1, 1789

My Dear Sister,

I thank you for sending me so particular an account of your sister's death. "Right precious in the sight of the Lord is the death of His saints." It is well you have learned to say, *The Lord gave, and the Lord has taken away; blessed be the name of the Lord!* And you can say it even

When loss of friends ordained to know,—
Next pain and guilt, the sorest ill below.

But why does our Lord inflict this upon us? Not merely for His pleasure, but that we may be partakers of His holiness. It is true one grand means of grace is the doing the will of our Lord. But the suffering it is usually a quicker means and sinks us deeper into the abyss of love. It hath pleased God to lead you in the way of suffering from your youth up until now. For the present this is not joyous, but grievous; nevertheless it has yielded peaceable fruit. Your soul is still as a watered garden, as a field which the Lord has blessed. Cleave to Him still with full purpose of heart. To His tender care I commend you; and am

Yours affectionately,

Against Slavery

TO WILLIAM WILBERFORCE

Balam, February 24, 1791

Dear Sir,

Unless the divine power has raised you up to be as *Athanasius contra mundum*, I see not how you can go through your glorious enterprise in opposing that execrable villany which is the scandal of

170

religion, of England, and of human nature. Unless God has raised you up for this very thing, you will be worn out by the opposition of men and devils. But if God be for you, who can be against you? Are all of them together stronger than God? Oh, be not weary of well doing! Go on, in the name of God and in the power of his might, till even American slavery (the vilest that ever saw the sun) shall vanish away before it.

Reading this morning a tract written by a poor African, I was particularly struck by that circumstance that a man who has a black skin, being wronged or outraged by a white man, can have no redress; it being a "law" in all our colonies that the *oath* of a black against a white goes for nothing. What villainy is this?

That he who has guided you from youth up may continue to strengthen you in this and all things, is the prayer of, dear sir,

Your affectionate servant,

THE HYMNS
of
CHARLES WESLEY

[1]

PREFACE AND SELECTION OF HYMNS FROM THE *1780* HANDBOOK

THE PREFACE

1. For many years I have been importuned to publish such a hymn book as might be generally used in all our congregations, throughout Great Britain and Ireland. I have hitherto withstood the importunity, as I believed such a publication was needless, considering the various hymn books which my brother and I have published within these forty years last past: so that it may be doubted whether any religious community in the world has a greater variety of them.

2. But it has been answered, such a publication is highly needful upon this very account; for the greater part of the people, being poor, are not able to purchase so many books. And those that have purchased them are as it were bewildered in the immense variety. There is therefore still wanting a proper collection of hymns for general use, carefully made out of all these books; and one comprised in so moderate a compass as neither to be cumbersome nor expensive.

3. It has been replied, "You have such a collection already, (entitled, *Hymns and Spiritual Songs*)"—which I extracted several years ago, from a variety of hymn books. But it is objected: this is in the other extreme—it is abundantly too small. It does not, it cannot in so narrow a compass, contain variety enough—not so much as we want, among whom singing makes so considerable a part of the public service. What we want is a collection neither too large, that it may be cheap and portable, nor too small, that it may contain a sufficient variety for all ordinary occasions.

4. Such a hymn book you have now before you. It is not so large as to be either cumbersome or expensive. And it is large enough to contain such a variety of hymns as will not soon be worn threadbare. It is large enough to contain all the important truths of our most holy religion, whether speculative or practical; yea, to illustrate them all,

and to prove them both by Scripture and reason. And this is done in a regular order. The hymns are not carelessly jumbled together, but carefully ranged under proper heads, according to the experience of real Christians. So that this book is in effect a little body of experimental and practical divinity.

5. As but a small part of these hymns are of my composing, I do not think it inconsistent with modesty to declare that I am persuaded no such hymn book as this has yet been published in the English language. In what other publication of the kind have you so distinct and full an account of scriptural Christianity? Such a declaration of the heights and depths of religion, speculative and practical? So strong cautions against the most plausible errors, particularly those that are now most prevalent? And so clear directions for making our calling and election sure, for perfecting holiness in the fear of God?

6. May I be permitted to add a few words with regard to the poetry? Then I will speak to those who are judges thereof, with all freedom and unreserve. To these I may say, without offense: (a) In these hymns there is no doggerel, no botches, nothing put in to patch up the rhyme, no feeble expletives. (b) Here is nothing turgid or bombast on the one hand, nor low and creeping on the other. (c) Here are no *cant* expressions, no words without meaning. Those who impute this to us know not what they say. We talk common sense (whether they understand it or not) both in verse and prose, and use no word but in a fixed and determinate sense. (d) Here are (allow me to say) both the purity, the strength, and the elegance of the English language— and at the same time the utmost simplicity and plainness, suited to every capacity. Lastly, I desire men of taste to judge—these are the only competent judges—whether there is not in some of the following verses the true spirit of poetry, such as cannot be acquired by art and labor, but must be the gift of nature. By labor a man may become a tolerable imitator of Spenser, Shakespeare, or Milton, and may heap together pretty compound epithets, as "pale-eyed," "meek-eyed," and the like. But unless he is born a poet he will never attain the genuine *spirit of poetry.*

7. And here I beg leave to mention a thought which has been long upon my mind, and which I should long ago have inserted in the public papers, had I not been unwilling to stir up a nest of hornets. Many gentlemen have done my brother and me (though without naming us) the honor to reprint many of our hymns. Now they are perfectly welcome so to do, provided they print them just as they are.

HYMNS

But I desire they would not attempt to mend them—for really they are not able. None of them is able to mend either the sense or the verse. Therefore I must beg of them one of these two favors: either to let them stand just as they are, to take them for better for worse; or to add the true reading in the margin, or at the bottom of the page, that we may no longer be accountable either for the nonsense or for the doggerel of other men.

8. But to return. What is of infinitely more moment than the spirit of poetry is the spirit of piety. And I trust all persons of real judgment will find this breathing through the whole *Collection*. It is in this view chiefly that I would recommend it to every truly pious reader: as a means of raising or quickening the spirit of devotion, of confirming his faith, of enlivening his hope, and of kindling or increasing his love to God and man. When poetry thus keeps its place, as the handmaid of piety, it shall attain, not a poor perishable wreath, but a crown that fades not away.

ADORATION AND RETURN TO GOD

1   (1)   [1]

1 Oh, for a thousand tongues to sing[a]
      My dear Redeemer's praise!
  The glories of my God and King,[b]
      The triumphs of his grace!

2 My gracious Master, and my God,
      Assist me to proclaim,
  To spread through all the earth abroad[c]
      The honors of thy name.[d]

3 Jesus, the name that charms our fears,
      That bids our sorrows cease—

---

[a]Ps. 119:172 (BCP)
[b]Ps. 145:1 (BCP)
[c]Matt. 9:31
[d]Ps. 66:2

'Tis music in the sinner's ears,
    'Tis life, and health, and peace.

4 He breaks the power of canceled sin,
    He sets the prisoner free;[e]
  His blood can make the foulest clean—[f]
    His blood availed for me.[g]

5† Hear him, ye deaf; his praise, ye dumb,[h]
    Your loosened tongues employ;
  Ye blind, behold your Savior come,[i]
    And leap, ye lame, for joy!

6† Look unto him, ye nations, own[j]
    Your God, ye fallen race;
  Look, and be saved through faith alone,[k]
    Be justified by grace.

7 See all your sins on Jesus laid:[l]
    The Lamb of God was slain,[m]
  His soul was once an offering made[n]
    For every soul of man.

8† Awake from guilty nature's sleep,
    And Christ shall give you light,[o]
  Cast all your sins into the deep,[p]
    And wash the Ethiop white.[q]

---

[e]Isa. 61:1
[f]Isa. 1:18
[g]Gal. 2:20
[h]Matt. 11:4–5; Mark 7:37
[i]Isa. 35:4–5; Acts 3:8
[j]Isa. 45:22
[k]Eph. 2:8
[l]Isa. 53:6
[m]John 1:29; Rev. 5:6
[n]Isa. 53:10
[o]Eph. 5:14
[p]Mic. 7:19
[q]Jer. 13:23

9† With me, your chief, ye then shall know,
    Shall feel your sins forgiven;[r]
Anticipate your heaven below,
    And own that love is heaven.

HSP, 1740

2   (2)   [323]

1 Come, sinners to the gospel feast;[a]
    Let every soul be Jesu's guest;
    Ye need not one be left behind,
    For God hath bidden all mankind.

2 Sent by my Lord, on you I call;
    The invitation is to all:
    Come all the world; come, sinner, thou!
    All things in Christ are ready now.

3 Come, all ye souls by sin oppressed,
    Ye restless wanderers after rest;
    Ye poor, and maimed, and halt, and blind,
    In Christ a hearty welcome find.

4† Come, and partake the gospel feast,
    Be saved from sin, in Jesus rest;
    Oh, taste the goodness of your God,
    And eat his flesh, and drink his blood.

5† Ye vagrant souls, on you I call
    (Oh, that my voice could reach you all!):
    Ye all are freely justified,
    Ye all may live—for Christ hath died.

6† My message as from God receive:
    Ye all may come to Christ, and live.

---

[r]1 Tim. 1:15
[a]Luke 14:16–24

Oh, let his love your hearts constrain,
Nor suffer him to die in vain!

7 His love is mighty to compel;
His conqu'ring love consent to feel,
Yield to his love's resistless power,
And fight against your God no more.

8† See him set forth before your eyes,
That precious, bleeding sacrifice!
His offered benefits embrace,
And freely now be saved by grace!

9 This is the time: no more delay!
This is the acceptable day;
Come in, this moment, at his call,
And live for him who died for all!

Redemption H., 1747

3   (5)   [311]

1 Thy faithfulness, Lord,   Each moment we find,
So true to thy word,   So loving and kind!
Thy mercy so tender   To all the lost race,
The foulest offender   May turn and find grace.

2 The mercy I feel   To others I show;
I set to my seal   That Jesus is true:
Ye all may find favor,   Who come at his call;
Oh, come to my Savior;   His grace is for all.

3 To save what was lost   From heaven he came.
Come, sinners, and trust in Jesus' name!
He offers you pardon,   He bids you be free!
If sin is your burden,   Oh, come unto me!

4† Oh, let me commend   My Savior to you,
The publican's friend,   And advocate too;

For you he is pleading   His merits and death,
With God interceding   For sinners beneath.

5 Then let us submit   His grace to receive,
    Fall down at his feet,   And gladly believe;
    We all are forgiven   For Jesus's sake,
    Our title to heaven   His merits we take.

Hymns on God's Everlasting Love, 1741

DESCRIBING THE PLEASANTNESS OF RELIGION

4   (14)   [360]

1 Happy the man that finds the grace,
    The blessing of God's chosen race,
    The wisdom coming from above,
    The faith that sweetly works by love.

2 Happy beyond description he
    Who knows, the Savior died for me,
    The gift unspeakable obtains,
    And heavenly understanding gains.

3 Wisdom divine! Who tells the price
    Of wisdom's costly merchandise?
    Wisdom to silver we prefer,
    And gold is dross compared to her.

4 Her hands are filled with length of days,
    True riches, and immortal praise;
    Riches of Christ on all bestowed,
    And honor, that descends from God.

5 To purest joys she all invites,
    Chaste, holy, spiritual delights;
    Her ways are ways of pleasantness,
    And all her flowery paths are peace.

6 Happy the man who wisdom gains;
    Thrice happy who his guest retains;
    He owns, and shall forever own,
    Wisdom, and Christ, and heaven are one.

Redemption H., 1747

DESCRIBING THE GOODNESS OF GOD

5   (32)   [173]

1 Would Jesus have the sinner die?
      Why hangs he then on yonder tree?
    What means that strange expiring cry?
      (Sinners, he prays for you and me):
    "Forgive them, Father, Oh, forgive,
    They know not that by *me* they live!"

2† Adam descended from above
      Our loss of Eden to retrieve;
    Great God of universal love,
      If all the world through thee may live,
    In us a quickening spirit be,
    And witness thou hast died for me.

3 Thou loving, all-atoning Lamb,
      Thee, by thy painful agony,
    Thy bloody sweat, thy grief and shame,
      Thy cross, and Passion on the tree,
    Thy precious death and life, I pray,
    Take all, take all my sins away!

4 Oh, let me kiss thy bleeding feet,
      And bathe and wash them with my tears,
    The story of thy love repeat
      In every drooping sinner's ears;
    That all may hear the quick'ning sound,
    If I, ev'n I, have mercy found!

5 Oh, let thy love my heart constrain,
      Thy love for every sinner free,
  That every fallen soul of man
      May taste the grace that found out me;
  That all mankind with me may prove
  Thy sovereign, everlasting love.

HSP., 1742

6   (33)   [114]

1   Let earth and heaven agree,
         Angels and men be joined,
    To celebrate with me
        The Savior of mankind;
  T'adore the all-atoning Lamb,
  And bless the sound of Jesu's name.

2   Jesus, transporting sound!
         The joy of earth and heaven!
    No other help is found,
        No other name is given
  By which we can salvation have:
  But Jesus came the world to save.

3   Jesus, harmonious name!
         It charms the hosts above;
    They evermore proclaim,
        And wonder at his love;
  'Tis all their happiness to gaze,
  'Tis heaven to see our Jesu's face.

4   His name the sinner hears,
         And is from sin set free;
    'Tis music in his ears,
        'Tis life and victory;
  New songs do now his lips employ,
  And dances his glad heart for joy.

5 Stung by the scorpion sin
    My poor expiring soul
  The balmy sound drinks in,
    And is at once made whole.
 See there my Lord upon the tree!
 I hear, I feel, he died for me.

6 O unexampled love!
    O all-redeeming grace!
  How swiftly didst thou move
    To save a fallen race!
 What shall I do to make it known
 What thou for all mankind hast done!

7 Oh, for a trumpet-voice
    On all the world to call,
  To bid their hearts rejoice
    In him who died for all!
 For all my Lord was crucified,
 For all, for all my Savior died!

8† To serve thy blessed will,
    Thy dying love to praise,
  Thy counsel to fulfill,
    And minister thy grace,
 Freely what I receive to give,
 The life of heaven on earth I live.

Hymns on God's Everlasting Love (2nd series), [1742]

7 (36) [92]

1 Jesus, the name high over all
   In hell, or earth, or sky;
 Angels and men before it fall,
   And devils fear and fly.

2 Jesus, the name to sinners dear,
   The name to sinners given.

It scatters all their guilty fear,
    It turns their hell to heaven.

3 Jesus the prisoner's fetters breaks,
    And bruises Satan's head,
Power into strengthless souls it speaks,
    And life into the dead.

4 Oh, that the world might taste and see
    The riches of his grace!
The arms of love that compass me
    Would all mankind embrace.

5† Oh, that my Jesu's heavenly charms
    Might every bosom move!
Fly, sinners, fly into those arms
    Of everlasting love.

6 His only righteousness I show,
    His saving truth proclaim:
'Tis all my business here below,
    To cry, "Behold the Lamb!"

7 Happy, if with my latest breath
    I may but gasp his name!
Preach him to all, and cry in death,
    "Behold! behold the Lamb."

HSP, 1749, I

DESCRIBING DEATH

8   (45)   [956]

1 Come, let us anew   Our journey pursue,
    Roll round with the year,
And never stand still   Till the Master appear!
His adorable will   Let us gladly fulfill,

       And our talents improve
By the patience of hope and the labor of love.

2 Our life is a dream,   Our time as a stream
        Glides swiftly away,
And the fugitive moment refuses to stay.
The arrow is flown,   The moment is gone,
        The millennial year
Rushes on to our view, and eternity's here.

3 Oh, that each in the day   Of his coming may say,
       "I have fought my way through,
I have finished the work   Thou didst give me to do."
Oh, that each from his Lord   May receive the glad word,
       "Well and faithfully done:
Enter into my joy, and sit down on my throne."

Hymns for New Year's Day [1749]

PRAYING FOR A BLESSING

9   (83)   [363]

1   Spirit of faith, come down,
       Reveal the things of God,
And make to us the Godhead known,
       And witness with the blood:
       'Tis thine the blood t'apply,
       And give us eyes to see,
Who did for every sinner die
       Hath surely died for me.

2   No man can truly say
       That Jesus is the Lord
Unless thou take the veil away,
       And breathe the living word;
       Then, only then we feel
       Our interest in his blood,

And cry with joy unspeakable,
    Thou art my Lord, my God!

3   Oh, that the world might know
      The all-atoning Lamb!
Spirit of faith, descend, and show
      The virtue of his name;
      The grace which all may find,
      The saving power impart,
And testify to all mankind,
      And speak in every heart!

4   Inspire the living faith
      (Which whosoe'er receives,
The witness in himself he hath,
      And consciously believes),
      The faith that conquers all,
      And doth the mountain move,
And saves whoe'er on Jesus call,
      And perfects them in love.

Hymns of Petition and Thanksgiving, 1746

10   (85)   [305]

Before Reading the Scriptures

1 Come, Holy Ghost, our hearts inspire,
      Let us thine influence prove,
Source of the old prophetic fire,
      Fountain of life and love.

2 Come, Holy Ghost (for moved by thee
      The prophets wrote and spoke);
Unlock the truth, thyself the key,
      Unseal the sacred book.

3 Expand thy wings, celestial dove,
      Brood o'er our nature's night;

187

On our disordered spirits move,
    And let there now be light.

4   God through himself we then shall know,
        If thou within us shine;
    And sound, with all thy saints below,
        The depths of love divine.

HSP, 1740

DESCRIBING INWARD RELIGION

11   (92)   [362]

1   Author of faith, eternal Word,
        Whose spirit breathes the active flame,
    Faith, like its finisher and Lord,
        Today as yesterday the same;

2   To thee our humble hearts aspire,
        And ask the gift unspeakable;
    Increase in us the kindled fire,
        In us the work of faith fulfill.

3   By faith we know thee strong to save
        (Save us, a present Savior thou!)
    Whate'er we hope, by faith we have,
        Future and past subsisting now.

4   To him that in thy name believes
        Eternal life with thee is given;
    Into himself he all receives—
        Pardon, and holiness, and heaven.

5   The things unknown to feeble sense,
        Unseen by reason's glimmering ray,
    With strong commanding evidence
        Their heavenly origin display.

6 Faith lends its realizing light,
    The clouds disperse, the shadows fly;
Th'Invisible appears in sight,
    And God is seen by mortal eye.

HSP, 1740

12   (93)   [377]

1   How can a sinner know
      His sins on earth forgiven?
How can my gracious Savior show
      My name inscribed in heaven?
      What we have felt and seen
      With confidence we tell,
And publish to the sons of men
      The signs infallible.

2   We who in Christ believe,
      That he for us hath died,
We all his unknown peace receive,
      And feel his blood applied;
      Exults our rising soul,
      Disburdened of her load,
And swells unutterably full
      Of glory and of God.

3   His love surpassing far
      The love of all beneath,
We find within our hearts, and dare
      The pointless darts of death.
      Stronger than death or hell
      The mystic power we prove;
And conqu'rors of the world, we dwell
      In heaven, who dwell in love.

4†   We by his Spirit prove
      And know the things of God;

The things which freely of his love
    He hath on us bestowed:
    His Spirit to us he gave,
    And dwells in us, we know;
The witness in ourselves we have,
    And all his fruits we show.

5†   The meek and lowly heart
    That in our Savior was,
To us his Spirit does impart,
    And signs us with his cross:
    Our nature's turned, our mind
    Transformed in all its powers;
And both the witnesses are joined,
    The Spirit of God with ours.

6   Whate'er our pardoning Lord
    Commands, we gladly do,
And guided by his sacred Word
    We all his steps pursue.
    His glory our design,
    We live our God to please;
And rise, with filial fear divine,
    To perfect holiness.

HSP, 1749, II

PRAYING FOR LIGHT AND ASSURANCE

13   (130)   [349]

1 Jesu, if still the same thou art,
    If all thy promises are sure,
Set up thy kingdom in my heart,
    And make me rich, for I am poor:
To me be all thy treasures given,
The kingdom of an inward heaven.

HYMNS

2 Thou hast pronounced the mourners blest,
    And lo! for thee I ever mourn.
I cannot, no, I will not rest
    Till thou my only rest return;
Till thou, the Prince of peace, appear,
And I receive the Comforter.

3 Where is the blessedness bestowed
    On all that hunger after thee?
I hunger now, I thirst for God!
    See the poor fainting sinner, see,
And satisfy with endless peace,
And fill me with thy righteousness.

4 Ah, Lord!—if thou art in that sigh,
    Then hear thyself within me pray.
Hear in my heart thy Spirit's cry,
    Mark what my laboring soul would say,
Answer the deep, unuttered groan,
And show that thou and I are one.

5 Shine on thy work, disperse the gloom;
    Light in thy light I then shall see.
Say to my soul, "Thy light is come,
    Glory divine is risen on thee;
Thy warfare's past, thy mourning's o'er;
Look up, for thou shalt weep no more."

6† Lord, I believe the promise sure,
    And trust thou wilt not long delay;
Hungry, and sorrowful, and poor,
    Upon thy word myself I stay;
Into thine hands my all resign,
And wait till all thou art is mine!

HSP, 1740

CHARLES WESLEY

Wrestling Jacob

14   (136)   [339]

1   Come, O thou Traveler unknown,[a]
        Whom still I hold, but cannot see!
    My company before is gone,
        And I am left alone with thee;
    With thee all night I mean to stay,
    And wrestle till the break of day.

2   I need not tell thee who I am,
        My misery or sin declare;
    Thyself hast called me by my name,
        Look on thy hands, and read it there.
    But who, I ask thee, who art thou?
    Tell me thy name, and tell me now.

3   In vain thou strugglest to get free,
        I never will unloose my hold;
    Art thou the Man that died for me?
        The secret of thy love unfold:
    Wrestling, I will not let thee go
    Till I thy name, thy nature know.

4   Wilt thou not yet to me reveal
        Thy new, unutterable name?
    Tell me, I still beseech thee, tell;
        To know it now resolved I am:
    Wrestling, I will not let thee go
    Till I thy name, thy nature know.

5   What though my shrinking flesh complain
        And murmur to contend so long?
    I rise superior to my pain:
        When I am weak, then I am strong;
    And when my all of strength shall fail
    I shall with the God-man prevail.

---

[a]Gen. 32:24–32

6   Yield to me now—for I am weak,
        But confident in self-despair!
   Speak to my heart, in blessings speak,
        Be conquered by my instant prayer:
   Speak, or thou never hence shalt move,
   And tell me if thy name is *LOVE.*

7   'Tis Love! 'Tis Love! Thou diedst for me;
        I hear thy whisper in my heart.
   The morning breaks, the shadows flee,
        Pure Universal Love thou art:
   To me, to all, thy bowels move—
   Thy nature, and thy name, is *LOVE.*

8   My prayer hath power with God; the grace
        Unspeakable I now receive;
   Through faith I see thee face to face;
        I see thee face to face, and live!
   In vain I have not wept and strove—
   Thy nature, and thy name is *LOVE.*

9   I know thee, Savior, who thou art—
        Jesus, the feeble sinner's friend;
   Nor wilt thou with the night depart,
        But stay, and love me to the end:
   Thy mercies never shall remove,
   Thy nature, and thy name, is *LOVE.*

10   The Sun of Righteousness on me
        Hath rose with healing in his wings;
   Withered my nature's strength; from thee
        My soul its life and succor brings;
   My help is all laid up above:
   Thy nature, and thy name, is *LOVE.*

11   Contented now upon my thigh
        I halt, till life's short journey end;
   All helplessness, all weakness, I
        On thee alone for strength depend;

Nor have I power from thee to move:
Thy nature, and thy name, is *LOVE.*

12   Lame as I am, I take the prey,
        Hell, earth, and sin with ease o'ercome;
    I leap for joy, pursue my way,
        And as a bounding hart fly home,
    Through all eternity to prove,
    Thy nature, and thy name, is *LOVE.*

HSP, 1742

15   (180)   [477]

1   Son of God, if thy free grace
           Again hath raised me up,
      Called me still to seek thy face,
         And given me back my hope;
      Still thy timely help afford,
And all thy loving-kindness show;
      Keep me, keep me, gracious Lord,
        And never let me go.

2   By me, O my Savior, stand
          In sore temptation's hour;
      Save me with thine outstretched hand,
         And show forth all thy power;
      Oh, be mindful of thy word,
Thy all-sufficient grace bestow;
      Keep me, keep me, gracious Lord,
        And never let me go.

3   Give me, Lord, a holy fear,
         And fix it in my heart,
      That I may from evil near
         With timely care depart.
      Sin be more than hell abhorred
Till thou destroy the tyrant foe;

Keep me, keep me, gracious Lord,
And never let me go.

4   Never let me leave thy breast,
        From thee, my Savior, stray;
    Thou art my support and rest,
        My true and living way,
    My exceeding great reward,
In heaven above, and earth below:
    Keep me, keep me, gracious Lord,
        And never let me go.

HSP, 1742

FOR BELIEVERS REJOICING

16   (185)   [530]

1 Oft I in my heart have said,
      Who shall ascend on high?
  Mount to Christ my glorious head,
      And bring him from the sky?
  Borne on contemplation's wing,
      Surely I should find him there,
  Where the angels praise their King,
      And gain the morning star.

2 Oft I in my heart have said,
      Who to the deep shall stoop?
  Sink with Christ among the dead,
      From thence to bring him up?
  Could I but my heart prepare,
      By unfeigned humility,
  Christ would quickly enter there,
      And ever dwell with me.

3 But the righteousness of faith
      Hath taught me better things:

"Inward turn thine eyes" (it saith,
    While Christ to me it brings),
"Christ is ready to impart
    Life to all for life who sigh;
In thy mouth, and in thy heart,
    The word is ever nigh."

HSP, 1742

17   (191)   [7]

1   O heavenly King, Look down from above!
    Assist us to sing Thy mercy and love:
    So sweetly o'erflowing, So plenteous the store,
    Thou still art bestowing, And giving us more.

2   O God of our life, We hallow thy name!
    Our business and strife Is thee to proclaim;
    Accept our thanksgiving For creating grace;
    The living, the living Shall show forth thy praise.

3   Our Father and Lord, Almighty art thou;
    Preserved by thy word, We worship thee now,
    The bountiful donor Of all we enjoy!
    Our tongues to thine honor, And lives we employ.

4   But Oh! above all Thy kindness we praise,
    From sin and from thrall Which saves the lost race;
    Thy Son thou hast given A world to redeem,
    And bring us to heaven, Whose trust is in him.

5   Wherefore of thy love We sing and rejoice,
    With angels above We lift up our voice;
    Thy love each believer Shall gladly adore,
    Forever and ever, When time is no more.

HSP, 1742

HYMNS

18   (193)   [371]

1   And can it be that I should gain
       An interest in the Savior's blood?
  Died he for me, who caused his pain?[a]
       For me? Who him to death pursued?
  Amazing love! How can it be
  That thou, my God, shouldst die for me?

2   'Tis myst'ry all: th'Immortal dies!
       Who can explore his strange design?
  In vain the firstborn seraph tries
       To sound the depths of love divine.
  'Tis mercy all! Let earth adore!
  Let angel minds inquire no more.

3   He left his Father's throne above
       (So free, so infinite his grace!),
  Emptied himself of all but love,
       And bled for Adam's helpless race.
  'Tis mercy all, immense and free,
  For, O my God, it found out me!

4   Long my imprisoned spirit lay,
       Fast bound in sin and nature's night.
  Thine eye diffused a quick'ning ray;
       I woke; the dungeon flamed with light.
  My chains fell off, my heart was free,
  I rose, went forth, and followed thee.

5   No condemnation now I dread,
       Jesus, and all in him, is mine.
  Alive in him, my living head,
       And clothed in righteousness divine,
  Bold I approach th'eternal throne,
  And claim the crown, through Christ my own.

HSP, 1739

---

[a]Gal. 2:20

CHARLES WESLEY

19   (196)   [670]

I will sing with the spirit; I will sing with
the understanding also
1 Cor. 14:15

1   Jesus, thou soul of all our joys,
    For whom we now lift up our voice,
        And all our strength exert,
    Vouchsafe the grace we humbly claim,
    Compose into a thankful frame,
        And tune thy people's heart.

2   While in the heavenly work we join,
    Thy glory be our sole design,
        Thy glory, not our own;
    Still let us keep our end in view,
    And still the pleasing task pursue,
        To please our God alone.

3   The secret pride, the subtle sin,
    Oh, let it never more steal in,
        T'offend thy glorious eyes,
    To desecrate our hallowed strain,
    And make our solemn service vain,
        And mar our sacrifice.

4† To magnify thy awful name,
    To spread the honors of the Lamb,
        Let us our voices raise;
    Our souls and bodies' powers unite,
    Regardless of our own delight,
        And dead to human praise.

5† Still let us on our guard be found,
    And watch against the power of sound
        With sacred jealousy;
    Lest haply sense should damp our zeal,
    And music's charms bewitch and steal
        Our heart away from thee.

6† That hurrying strife far off remove,
  That noisy burst of selfish love
    Which swells the formal song;
  The joy from out our heart arise,
  And speak, and sparkle in our eyes,
    And vibrate on our tongue.

7† Then let us praise our common Lord,
  And sweetly join with one accord
    Thy goodness to proclaim;
  Jesus, thyself in us reveal,
  And all our faculties shall feel
    Thy harmonizing name.

8 With calmly reverential joy,
  Oh, let us all our lives employ
    In setting forth thy love;
  And raise in death our triumph higher,
  And sing, with all the heavenly choir,
    That endless song above.

HSP, 1749, II

20   (197)   [406]

1 My God, I am thine; What a comfort divine,
  What a blessing to know that my Jesus is mine!
  In the heavenly Lamb Thrice happy I am,
  And my heart it doth dance at the sound of his name.

2 True pleasures abound In the rapturous sound;
  And whoever hath found it hath paradise found.
  My Jesus to know, And feel his blood flow,
  'Tis life everlasting, 'tis heaven below!

3 Yet onward I haste To the heavenly feast;
  That, that is the fullness, but this is the taste;

And this I shall prove, Till with joy I remove
To the heaven of heavens in Jesus's love.

HSP, 1749, **I**

21   (201)   [98]

1   Thou hidden source of calm repose,
        Thou all-sufficient love divine,
    My help and refuge from my foes,
        Secure I am, if thou art mine:
    And lo! from sin, and grief, and shame,
    I hide me, Jesus, in thy name.

2   Thy mighty name salvation is,
        And keeps my happy soul above;
    Comfort it brings, and power, and peace,
        And joy, and everlasting love:
    To me with thy dear name are given
    Pardon, and holiness, and heaven.

3   Jesu, my all in all thou art,
        My rest in toil, my ease in pain;
    The med'cine of my broken heart,
        In war my peace, in loss my gain;
    My smile beneath the tyrant's frown,
    In shame my glory and my crown.

4   In want my plentiful supply,
        In weakness my almighty power;
    In bonds my perfect liberty,
        My light in Satan's darkest hour;
    In grief my joy unspeakable,
    My life in death, my heaven in hell.

HSP, 1749, **I**

22   (205)   [460]

1   Talk with us, Lord, thyself reveal,[a]
        While here o'er earth we rove;
    Speak to our hearts, and let us feel
        The kindling of thy love.

2   With thee conversing we forget
        All time, and toil, and care:
    Labor is rest, and pain is sweet
        If thou, my God, art here.

3   Here then, my God, vouchsafe to stay,
        And bid my heart rejoice;
    My bounding heart shall own thy sway,
        And echo to thy voice.

4   Thou callest me to seek thy face—
        'Tis all I wish to seek;
    To attend the whispers of thy grace,
        And hear thee inly speak.

5   Let this my every hour employ,
        Till I thy glory see,
    Enter into my Master's joy,
        And find my heaven in thee.

HSP, 1740

23   (209)   [263]

1   See how great a flame aspires,
        Kindled by a spark of grace!
    Jesu's love the nations fires,
        Sets the kingdoms on a blaze.
    To bring fire on earth he came;
        Kindled in some hearts it is;

[a]Luke 24:13–35

Oh, that all might catch the flame,
    All partake the glorious bliss!

2   When he first the work begun,
    Small and feeble was his day;
Now the word doth swiftly run,
    Now it wins its widening way.
More and more it spreads, and grows,
    Ever mighty to prevail;
Sin's strongholds it now o'erthrows,
    Shakes the trembling gates of hell.

3   Sons of God, your Savior praise!
    He the door hath opened wide;
He hath given the word of grace,
    Jesu's word is glorified.
Jesus, mighty to redeem,
    He alone the work hath wrought;
Worthy is the work of him,
    Him who spake a world from nought.

4   Saw ye not the cloud arise,
    Little as a human hand?
Now it spreads along the skies,
    Hangs o'er all the thirsty land!
Lo! the promise of a shower
    Drops already from above;
But the Lord will shortly pour
    All the spirit of his love!

HSP, 1749, I

24   (211)   [902]

1   All glory to God in the sky,[a]
    And peace upon earth be restored!

---

[a]Luke 2:6–14

HYMNS

O Jesus exalted on high,
    Appear our omnipotent Lord!
Who meanly in Bethlehem born,
    Didst stoop to redeem a lost race,
Once more to thy creatures return,
    And reign in thy kingdom of grace.

2 When thou in our flesh didst appear,
    All nature acknowledged thy birth;
Arose the acceptable year,
    And heaven was opened on earth.
Receiving its Lord from above,
    The world was united to bless
The giver of concord and love,
    The prince and the author of peace.

3 O wouldst thou again be made known!
    Again in thy spirit descend;
And set up in each of thine own
    A kingdom that never shall end.
Thou only art able to bless,
    And make the glad nations obey,
And bid the dire enmity cease,
    And bow the whole world to thy sway.

4 Come then to thy servants again,
    Who long thy appearing to know;
Thy quiet and peaceable reign
    In mercy establish below;
All sorrow before thee shall fly,
    And anger and hatred be o'er;
And envy and malice shall die,
    And discord afflict us no more.

5† No horrid alarum of war
    Shall break our eternal repose;
No sound of the trumpet is there,
    Where Jesus' Spirit o'erflows:
Appeased by the charms of thy grace

We all shall in amity join,
And kindly each other embrace,
And love with a passion like thine.

Nativity H., 1744

25   (212)   [17]

1   Meet and right it is to sing,
    In every time and place,
Glory to our heavenly King,
    The God of truth and grace.
Join we then with sweet accord,
    All in one thanksgiving join:
Holy, holy, holy, Lord,
    Eternal praise be thine!

2   Thee the firstborn sons of light,
    In choral symphonies,
Praise by day, day without night,
    And never, never cease;
Angels and archangels all
    Praise the mystic Three in One,
Sing, and stop, and gaze, and fall
    O'erwhelmed before thy throne.

3   Vying with that happy choir
    Who chant thy praise above,
We on eagles' wings aspire,
    The wings of faith and love;
Thee they sing with glory crowned,
    We extol the slaughtered Lamb;
Lower if our voices sound
    Our subject is the same.

4   Father, God, thy love we praise
    Which gave thy Son to die;
Jesus, full of truth and grace,
    Alike we glorify;

Spirit, Comforter divine,
    Praise by all to thee be given,
Till we in full chorus join,
    And earth is turned to heaven.

HSP, 1749, II

26   (213)   [—]

1 How happy, gracious Lord, are we,
  Divinely drawn to follow thee,
    Whose hours divided are
  Betwixt the mount and multitude;
  Our day is spent in doing good,
    Our night in praise and prayer.

2 With us no melancholy void,
  No period lingers unemployed
    Or unimproved below;
  Our weariness of life is gone
  Who live to serve our God alone,
    And only thee to know.

3 The winter's night, and summer's day,
  Glide imperceptibly away,
    Too short to sing thy praise;
  Too few we find the happy hours,
  And haste to join those heavenly powers
    In everlasting lays.

4 With all who chant thy name on high,
  And holy, holy, holy cry,
    A bright harmonious throng,
  We long thy praises to repeat,
  And restless sing around thy seat
    The new, eternal song.

HSP, 1749, II

CHARLES WESLEY

1 Hail, Father, Son, and Holy Ghost,
     One God in Persons Three;
  Of thee we make our joyful boast,
     Our songs we make of thee.

2 Thou neither canst be felt or seen;
     Thou art a spirit pure;
  Thou from eternity hast been,
     And always shalt endure.

3 Present alike in every place,
     Thy Godhead we adore;
  Beyond the bounds of time and space
     Thou dwell'st for evermore.

4 In wisdom infinite thou art,
     Thine eye doth all things see,
  And every thought of every heart
     Is fully known to thee.

5 Whate'er thou wilt in earth below
     Thou dost in heaven above;
  But chiefly we rejoice to know
     Th'Almighty God of love.

6 Thou lov'st whate'er thy hands have made;
     Thy goodness we rehearse,
  In shining characters displayed
     Throughout our universe.

7 Mercy, with love, and endless grace
     O'er all thy works doth reign;
  But mostly thou delight'st to bless
     Thy favorite creature, man.

8 Wherefore let every creature give
     To thee the praise designed;

But chiefly, Lord, the thanks receive,
The hearts of all mankind.

Hymns for Children, 1763

28   (238)   [—]

1   Holy as thee, O Lord, is none!
Thy holiness is all thy own;
A drop of that unbounded sea
Is ours, a drop derived from thee.

2   And when thy purity we share,
Thy only glory we declare;
And humbled into nothing, own
Holy and pure is God alone.

3   Sole self-existing God and Lord,
By all thy heavenly hosts adored,
Let all on earth bow down to thee,
And own thy peerless majesty;

4   Thy power unparalleled confess,
Established on the rock of peace,
The rock that never shall remove,
The rock of pure, almighty love!

Scripture H., 1762, I

29   (251)   [37]

1   Hail, holy, holy, holy Lord,
Whom One in Three we know;
By all thy heavenly host adored,
By all thy Church below.

2   One undivided Trinity
         With triumph we proclaim;
   Thy universe is full of thee,
         And speaks thy glorious name.

3   Thee, holy Father, we confess;
         Thee, holy Son, adore;
   Thee, Spirit of truth and holiness,
         We worship evermore.

4† The incommunicable right,
         Almighty God, receive,
   Which angel choirs, and saints in light,
         And saints embodied give.

5   Three Persons equally divine
         We magnify and love;
   And both the choirs ere long shall join
         To sing thy praise above.

6   Hail, holy, holy, holy Lord
         (Our heavenly song shall be),
   Supreme, essential One, adored
         In co-eternal Three!

Hymns on the Trinity, 1767

FOR BELIEVERS FIGHTING

30   (258)   [484]

Part I

1   Soldiers of Christ, arise,[a]
      And put your armor on,
   Strong in the strength which God supplies
      Through his eternal Son;

[a]Eph. 6:10–18

Strong in the Lord of hosts,
And in his mighty power,
Who in the strength of Jesus trusts
Is more than conqueror.

2   Stand then in his great might,
With all his strength endued,
But take to arm you for the fight
The panoply of God;
That having all things done,
And all your conflicts passed,
Ye may o'ercome through Christ alone
And stand entire at last.

3   Stand then against your foes
In close and firm array;
Legions of wily fiends oppose
Throughout the evil day;
But meet the sons of night,
But mock their vain design,
Armed in the arms of heavenly light,
Of righteousness divine.

4   Leave no unguarded place,
No weakness of the soul;
Take every virtue, every grace,
And fortify the whole;
Indissolubly joined,
To battle all proceed,
But arm yourselves with all the mind
That was in Christ your head.

HSP, 1749, I

FOR BELIEVERS PRAYING

31   (292)   [542]

1   Jesu, my strength, my hope,
On thee I cast my care,

With humble confidence look up,
    And know thou hear'st my prayer.
    Give me on thee to wait,
    Till I can all things do,
On thee almighty to create,
    Almighty to renew.

2†   I want a sober mind,
    A self-renouncing will
That tramples down and casts behind
    The baits of pleasing ill:
    A soul inured to pain,
    To hardship, grief, and loss,
Bold to take up, firm to sustain
    The consecrated cross.

3   I want a godly fear,
    A quick-discerning eye,
That looks to thee when sin is near
    And sees the tempter fly;
    A spirit still prepared
    And armed with jealous care,
Forever standing on its guard,
    And watching unto prayer.

4†   I want a heart to pray,
    To pray and never cease,
Never to murmur at thy stay,
    Or wish my sufferings less
    This blessing above all,
    Always to pray I want,
Out of the deep on thee to call,
    And never, never faint.

5   I want a true regard,
    A single, steady aim,
Unmoved by threat'ning or reward,
    To thee and thy great name;
    A jealous, just concern
    For thine immortal praise;

HYMNS

A pure desire that all may learn
　　And glorify thy grace.

6　　　I rest upon thy Word,
　　　　The promise is for me;
　　My succor, and salvation, Lord,
　　　　Shall surely come from thee.
　　　　But let me still abide,
　　　　Nor from thy hope remove,
　　Till thou my patient spirit guide
　　　　Into thy perfect love.

HSP, 1742

32　　(293)　　[549]

1　Lord, that I may learn of thee,
　Give me true simplicity;[a]
　Wean my soul, and keep it low,
　Willing thee alone to know.

2　Let me cast my reeds aside,
　All that feeds my knowing pride,
　Not to man, but God submit,
　Lay my reasonings at thy feet.

3　Of my boasted wisdom spoiled,
　Docile, helpless as a child,
　Only seeing in thy light,
　Only walking in thy might.

4　Then infuse the teaching grace,
　Spirit of truth and righteousness;
　Knowledge, love divine impart,
　Life eternal to my heart.

Scripture H., 1762, I

----

[a]Isa. 28:9

CHARLES WESLEY

FOR BELIEVERS WATCHING

33   (311)   [576]

1 Be it my only wisdom here,
   To serve the Lord with filial fear,
       With loving gratitude;
   Superior sense may I display
   By shunning every evil way,
       And walking in the good.

2 Oh, may I still from sin depart;
   A wise and understanding heart,
       Jesus, to me be given!
   And let me through thy Spirit know
   To glorify my God below,
       And find my way to heaven.

Scripture H., 1762, I

FOR BELIEVERS WORKING

34   (313)   [575]

1 Servant of all, to toil for man[a]
       Thou didst not, Lord, refuse;
   Thy Majesty did not disdain
       To be employed for us!

2 Thy bright example I pursue,
       To thee in all things rise;
   And all I think, or speak, or do,
       Is one great sacrifice.

3 Careless through outward cares I go,
       From all distraction free;

---

[a]Phil. 2:5–11

212

HYMNS

My hands are but engaged below—
My heart is still with thee.

HSP, 1739

35   (315)   [590]

1 Forth in thy name, O Lord, I go,
     My daily labor to pursue,
Thee, only thee resolved to know
     In all I think, or speak, or do.

2 The task thy wisdom has assigned
     Oh, let me cheerfully fulfill,
In all my works thy presence find,
     And prove thy acceptable will.

3 Thee may I set at my right hand
     Whose eyes my inmost substance see,
And labor on at thy command,
     And offer all my works to thee.

4 Give me to bear thy easy yoke,
     And every moment watch and pray,
And still to things eternal look,
     And hasten to thy glorious day;

5 For thee delightfully employ
     Whate'er thy bounteous grace hath given,
And run my course with even joy,
     And closely walk with thee to heaven.

HSP, 1749, I

36   (317)   [608]

1 Captain of Israel's host, and guide
     Of all who seek the land above,

Beneath thy shadow we abide,
    The cloud of thy protecting love:
Our strength thy grace, our rule thy Word,
Our end, the glory of the Lord.

2 By thy unerring Spirit led,
        We shall not in the desert stray;
    We shall not full direction need,
        Or miss our providential way;
    As far from danger as from fear,
    While love, almighty love, is near.

Scripture H., 1762, I

37   (318)   [386]

1 O thou who camest from above
        The pure celestial fire t'impart,
    Kindle a flame of sacred love
        On the mean altar of my heart!

2 There let it for thy glory burn
        With inextinguishable blaze,
    And trembling to its source return
        In humble love, and fervent praise.

3 Jesu, confirm my heart's desire
        To work, and speak, and think for thee;
    Still let me guard the holy fire,
        And still stir up thy gift in me;

4 Ready for all thy perfect will,
        My acts of faith and love repeat,
    Till death thy endless mercies seal
        And make the sacrifice complete.

Scripture H., 1762, I

HYMNS

38   (319)   [310]

1 When quiet in my house I sit,[a]
    Thy book be my companion still;
My joy thy sayings to repeat,
    Talk o'er the records of thy will,
And search the oracles divine
Till every heartfelt word be mine.

2 Oh, may the gracious words divine
    Subject of all my converse be;
So will the Lord his follower join,
    And walk and talk himself with me;
So shall my heart his presence prove,
And burn with everlasting love.

3 Oft as I lay me down to rest,
    Oh, may the reconciling word
Sweetly compose my weary breast,
    While on the bosom of my Lord,
I sink in blissful dreams away
And visions of eternal day.

4 Rising to sing my Savior's praise,
    Thee may I publish all day long,
And let thy precious word of grace
    Flow from my heart, and fill my tongue,
Fill all my life with purest love,
And join me to thy church above.

Scripture H., 1762, I

FOR BELIEVERS SUFFERING

39   (320)   [519]

1 Thee, Jesus, full of truth and grace,
    Thee, Savior, we adore;

---

[a] Deut. 6:7

Thee in affliction's furnace praise,
    And magnify thy power.

2 Thy power in human weakness shown
      Shall make us all entire;
  We now thy guardian presence own,
      And walk unburnt in fire.

3 Thee, Son of man, by faith we see,
      And glory in our Guide,
  Surrounded and upheld by thee,
      The fiery test abide.

4 The fire our graces shall refine
      Till, moulded from above,
  We bear the character divine,
      The stamp of perfect love.

HSP, 1749, **II**

40   (324)   [487]

1 Come on, my partners in distress,
  My comrades through the wilderness,
      Who still your bodies feel;
  Awhile forget your griefs and fears,
  And look beyond this vale of tears
      To that celestial hill.

2 Beyond the bounds of time and space
  Look forward to that heavenly place,
      The saints' secure abode;
  On faith's strong eagle pinions rise,
  And force your passage to the skies,
      And scale the mount of God.

3 Who suffer with our Master here,
  We shall before his face appear,
      And by his side sit down;

To patient faith the prize is sure,
And all that to the end endure
    The cross, shall wear the crown.

4   Thrice blessed bliss-inspiring hope!
It lifts the fainting spirits up,
    It brings to life the dead;
Our conflicts here shall soon be past,
And you and I ascend at last
    Triumphant with our head.

5   That great mysterious Deity
We soon with open face shall see;
    The beatific sight
Shall fill heaven's sounding courts with praise,
And wide diffuse the golden blaze
    Of everlasting light.

6   The Father shining on his throne,
The glorious, co-eternal Son,
    The Spirit, one and seven,
Conspire our rapture to complete,
And lo! we fall before his feet,
    And silence heightens heaven.

7   In hope of that ecstatic pause,
Jesu, we now sustain the cross,
    And at thy footstool fall,
Till thou our hidden life reveal,
Till thou our ravished spirits fill,
    And God is all in all.

HSP, 1749, **II**

FOR BELIEVERS SEEKING PERFECT LOVE

41   (333)   [—]

1   God of eternal truth and grace,
    Thy faithful promise seal!

Thy word, thy oath to Abraham's race,[a]
    In us, even us fulfill.

2 Let us, to perfect love restored,
    Thy image here receive;
  And in the presence of our Lord
    The life of angels live.

3 That mighty faith on me bestow
    Which cannot ask in vain,
  Which holds, and will not let thee go
    Till I my suit obtain.

4 Till thou into my soul inspire
    The perfect love unknown,
  And tell my infinite desire,
    Whate'er thou wilt, be done.

5 But is it possible that I
    Should live, and sin no more?
  Lord, if on thee I dare rely,
    The faith shall bring the power.

6 On me that faith divine bestow
    Which doth the mountain move;
  And all my spotless life shall show
    Th'omnipotence of love.

Scripture H., 1762

42   (334)   [550]

1 Oh, for a heart to praise my God,
    A heart from sin set free!
  A heart that always feels thy blood,
    So freely spilt for me!

---

[a]Mic. 7:20

HYMNS

2   A heart resigned, submissive, meek,
       My great Redeemer's throne,
  Where only Christ is heard to speak,
       Where Jesus reigns alone.

3   Oh! for a lowly, contrite heart,
       Believing, true, and clean,
  Which neither life nor death can part
       From him that dwells within.

4   A heart in every thought renewed,
       And full of love divine,
  Perfect, and right, and pure, and good—
       A copy, Lord, of thine!

5† Thy tender heart is still the same,
       And melts at human woe;
  Jesu, for thee distressed I am—
       I want thy love to know.

6† My heart, thou know'st, can never rest
       Till thou create my peace
  Till, of my Eden repossessed,
       From every sin I cease.

7† Fruit of thy gracious lips, on me
       Bestow that peace unknown,
  The hidden manna, and the tree
       Of life, and the white stone.

8   Thy nature, gracious Lord, impart;
       Come quickly from above;
  Write thy new name upon my heart,
       Thy new, best name of love!

HSP, 1742

219

43   (345)   [—]

1   Jesu, shall I never be[a]
    Firmly grounded upon thee?
    Never by thy work abide,
    Never in thy wounds reside?

2   Oh, how wavering is my mind,
    Tossed about with every wind!
    Oh, how quickly doth my heart
    From the living God depart!

3   Jesu, let my nature feel
    Thou art God unchangeable;
    Jah, Jehovah, great I AM,
    Speak into my soul thy name.

4   Grant that every moment I
    May believe, and feel thee nigh,
    Steadfastly behold thy face,
    'Stablished with abiding grace.

5   Plant and root, and fix in me
    All the mind that was in thee;
    Settled peace I then shall find—
    Jesu's is a quiet mind.

6   Anger I no more shall feel,
    Always even, always still;
    Meekly on my God reclined—
    Jesu's is a gentle mind.

7   I shall suffer, and fulfill
    All my Father's gracious will,
    Be in all alike resigned—
    Jesu's is a patient mind.

---

[a]Phil. 2:5

8 When 'tis deeply rooted here
   Perfect love shall cast out fear;
   Fear doth servile spirits bind—
   Jesu's is a noble mind.

9 When I feel it fixed within
   I shall have no power to sin;
   How shall sin an entrance find?
   Jesu's is a spotless mind.

10 I shall nothing know beside
   Jesus, and him crucified;
   I shall all to him be joined—
   Jesu's is a loving mind.

11 I shall triumph evermore,
   Gratefully my God adore,
   God so good, so true, so kind—
   Jesu's is a thankful mind.

12 Lowly, loving, meek, and pure,
   I shall to the end endure;
   Be no more to sin inclined—
   Jesu's is a constant mind.

13 I shall fully be restored
   To the image of my Lord,
   Witnessing to all mankind
   Jesu's is a perfect mind.

HSP, 1742

44   (348)   [465]

1 Open, Lord, my inward ear,
   And bid my heart rejoice!
   Bid my quiet spirit hear

Thy comfortable voice,
Never in the whirlwind found,
    Or where earthquakes rock the place;
Still and silent is the sound,
    The whisper of thy grace.

2 From the world of sin, and noise,
        And hurry, I withdraw;
For the small and inward voice
        I wait, with humble awe.
Silent am I now, and still,
        Dare not in thy presence move;
To my waiting soul reveal
        The secret of thy love.

3 Thou hast undertook for me,
        For me to death wast sold;
Wisdom in a mystery
        Of bleeding love unfold;
Teach the lesson of thy cross,
        Let me die with thee to reign,
All things let me count but loss
        So I may thee regain.

4 Show me, as my soul can bear,
        The depth of inbred sin,
All the unbelief declare,
        The pride that lurks within;
Take me, whom thyself has bought,
        Bring into captivity
Every high aspiring thought
        That would not stoop to thee.

5 Lord, my time is in thy hand,
        My soul to thee convert;
Thou canst make me understand,
        Though I am slow of heart;
Thine, in whom I love and move,
        Thine the work, the praise is thine,

Thou art wisdom, power, and love—
And all thou art is mine.

HSP, 1742

45   (351)   [387]

1 My God! I know, I feel thee mine,[a]
      And will not quit my claim
Till all I have is lost in thine,
      And all renewed I am.

2 I hold thee with a trembling hand,
      But will not let thee go
Till steadfastly by faith I stand,
      And all thy goodness know.

3† When shall I see the welcome hour
      That plants my God in me!
Spirit of health, and life, and power,
      And perfect liberty!

4 Jesu, thine all-victorious love
      Shed in my heart abroad!
Then shall my feet no longer rove,
      Rooted and fixed in God.

5† Love only can the conquest win,
      The strength of sin subdue
(Mine own unconquerable sin),
      And form my soul anew.

6† Love can bow down the stubborn neck,
      The stone to flesh convert;
Soften, and melt, and pierce, and break
      An adamantine heart.

---

[a]Rom. 4:13, etc.

7   Oh, that in me the sacred fire
      Might now begin to glow,
  Burn up the dross of base desire,
      And make the mountains flow!

8   Oh, that it now from heaven might fall,
      And all my sins consume!
  Come, Holy Ghost, for thee I call,
      Spirit of burning, come!

9   Refining fire, go through my heart,
      Illuminate my soul;
  Scatter thy life through every part,
      And sanctify the whole.
10† Sorrow and sin shall then expire,
      While, entered into rest,
  I only live my God t'admire—
      My God forever blest.

11† No longer then my heart shall mourn,
      While purified by grace
  I only for his glory burn,
      And always see his face.

12† My steadfast soul, from falling free,
      Shall then no longer move;
  But Christ be all the world to me,
      And all my heart be love.

HSP, 1740

46   (354)   [605]

1   Jesus, the gift divine I know,[a]
      The gift divine I ask of thee;
  That living water now bestow,
      Thy Spirit and thyself on me.

[a]John 4:10–15

HYMNS

Thou, Lord, of life the fountain art:
Now let me find thee in my heart!

2 Thee let me drink, and thirst no more
    For drops of finite happiness;
Spring up, O well, in heavenly power,
    In streams of pure, perennial peace,
In peace, that none can take away,
In joy, which shall forever stay.

3 Father, on me the grace bestow,
    Unblameable before thy sight,
Whence all the streams of mercy flow;
    Mercy, thy own supreme delight,
To me, for Jesu's sake impart,
And plant thy nature in my heart.

4 Thy mind throughout my life be shown,
    While listening to the wretch's cry,
The widow's and the orphan's groan,
    On mercy's wings I swiftly fly
The poor and helpless to relieve,
My life, my all for them to give.

5 Thus may I show thy Spirit within,
    Which purges me from every stain;
Unspotted from the world and sin
    My faith's integrity maintain,
The truth of my religion prove
By perfect purity and love.

Scripture H., 1762

47   (364)   [558]

1 Savior from sin, I wait to prove
    That Jesus is thy healing name,
To lose, when perfected in love,
    Whate'er I have, or can, or am;

225

I stay me on thy faithful word,
The servant shall be as his Lord.

2 Answer that gracious end in me
       For which thy precious life was given:
Redeem from all iniquity,
       Restore, and make me meet for heaven.
Unless thou purge my every stain,
Thy suffering and my faith are vain.

3† Didst thou not in the flesh appear
       Sin to condemn and man to save?
That perfect love might cast out fear?
       That I thy mind in me might have,
In holiness show forth thy praise,
And serve thee all my spotless days?

4 Didst thou not die that I might live
       No longer to myself, but thee?
Might body, soul, and spirit give
       To him who gave himself for me?
Come then, my Master, and my God!
Take the dear purchase of thy blood.

5 Thy own peculiar servant claim,
       For thy own truth and mercy's sake;
Hallow in me thy glorious name,
       Me for thine own this moment take,
And change, and thoroughly purify—
Thine only may I live and die.

HSP, 1742

48   (366)   [730]

1 Father of everlasting grace,
Thy goodness and thy truth we praise,
       Thy goodness and thy truth we prove;
Thou hast, in honor of thy Son,

The gift unspeakable sent down,
    The Spirit of life, and power, and love.

2 Send us the Spirit of thy Son
    To make the depths of Godhead known,
      To make us share the life divine;
    Send him the sprinkled blood t'apply,
    Send him our souls to sanctify,
      And show and seal us ever thine.

3 So shall we pray, and never cease,
    So shall we thankfully confess
      Thy wisdom, truth, and power, and love,
    With joy unspeakable adore,
    And bless, and praise thee evermore,
      And serve thee as thy hosts above.

4 Till added to that heavenly choir
    We raise our songs of triumph higher,
      And praise thee in a bolder strain,
    Out-soar the firstborn seraph's flight,
    And sing, with all our friends in light,
      Thy everlasting love to man.

Hymns of Petition and Thanksgiving, 1746

49   (374)   [431]

1 Love divine, all loves excelling,
    Joy of heaven, to earth come down,
    Fix in us thy humble dwelling,
    All thy faithful mercies crown!
    Jesu, thou art all compassion,
    Pure, unbounded love thou art;
    Visit us with thy salvation!
    Enter every trembling heart.

2 Come, almighty to deliver,
    Let us all thy grace receive;

Suddenly return, and never,
    Never more thy temples leave.
Thee we would be always blessing,
    Serve thee as thy hosts above,
Pray, and praise thee without ceasing,
    Glory in thy perfect love.

3 Finish then thy new creation,
    Pure and spotless let us be;
Let us see thy great salvation
    Perfectly restored in thee;
Changed from glory into glory,
    Till in heaven we take our place,
Till we cast our crowns before thee,
    Lost in wonder, love, and praise.

Redemption H., 1747

50   (379)   [568]

1 Since the Son hath made me free,
Let me taste my liberty;
Thee behold with open face,
Triumph in thy saving grace,
Thy great will delight to prove,
Glory in thy perfect love.

2 Abba, Father! hear thy child,
Late in Jesus reconciled;
Hear, and all the graces shower,
All the joy, and peace, and power,
All my Savior asks above,
All the life and heaven of love.

3† Lord, I will not let thee go
Till the blessing thou bestow;
Hear my Advocate divine!
Lo! to his my suit I join;

Joined to his it cannot fail—
Bless me; for I will prevail.

4 Heavenly Father, Life divine,
Change my nature into thine!
Move and spread throughout my soul,
Actuate, and fill the whole!
Be it I no longer now
Living in the flesh, but thou.

5 Holy Ghost, no more delay!
Come, and in thy temple stay!
Now thine inward witness bear,
Strong, and permanent, and clear;
Spring of life, thyself impart,
Rise eternal in my heart!

HSP, 1739

FOR MATURE BELIEVERS

51   (380)   [562]

Part I

1 God of all power, and truth, and grace,
    Which shall from age to age endure;
Whose word, when heaven and earth shall pass,
    Remains and stands forever sure:

2 That I thy mercy may proclaim,
    That all mankind thy truth may see;
Hallow thy great and glorious name,
    And perfect holiness in me.

3† Thy sanctifying spirit pour,
    To quench my thirst, and make me clean;

CHARLES WESLEY

Now, Father, let the gracious shower
    Descend, and make me pure from sin.

4† Oh, take this heart of stone away!
    Thy sway it doth not, cannot own:
In me no longer let it stay;
    Oh, take away this heart of stone!

5 Oh! that I now, from sin released,
    Thy word may to the utmost prove:
Enter into the promised rest,
    The Canaan of thy perfect love.

6† Father, supply my ev'ry need!
    Sustain the life thyself hast given;
Call for the never-failing bread,
    The manna that comes down from heaven.

7† The gracious fruits of righteousness,
    Thy blessing's unexhausted store,
In me abundantly increase,
    Nor let me ever hunger more!

8† Let me no more in deep complaint
    My leanness, Oh! my leanness, cry
Alone consumed with pining want,
    Of all my Father's children I.

9† The painful thirst, the fond desire,
    Thy joyous presence shall remove!
But my full soul shall still require
    A whole eternity of love.

HSP, 1742

HYMNS

52   (381)   [570]

Part II

1 Holy, and true, and righteous Lord,
   I wait to prove thy perfect will;
Be mindful of thy gracious word,
   And stamp me with thy spirit's seal.

2† Open my faith's interior eye:
   Display thy glory from above;
And all I am shall sink and die,
   Lost in astonishment and love!

3 Confound, o'erpower me by thy grace;
   I would be by myself abhorred:
All might, all majesty, all praise,
   All glory be to Christ my Lord!

4 Now let me gain perfection's height;
   Now let me into nothing fall;
Be less than nothing in thy sight,
   And feel that Christ is all in all!

HSP, 1742

53   (391)   [563]

1 Lord, I believe a rest remains
   To all thy people known;
A rest, where pure enjoyment reigns,
   And thou art loved alone.

2 A rest, where all our soul's desire
   Is fixed on things above;
Where fear, and sin, and grief expire,
   Cast out by perfect love.

3   Oh, that I now the rest might know,
      Believe, and enter in!
  Now, Savior, now the power bestow,
      And let me cease from sin!

4   Remove this hardness from my heart,
      This unbelief remove:
  To me the rest of faith impart,
      The sabbath of thy love.

5   I would be thine, thou know'st I would,
      And have thee all my own;
  Thee, O my all-sufficient good,
      I want, and thee alone.

6   Thy name to me, thy nature grant!
      This, only this, be given;
  Nothing beside my God I want,
      Nothing in earth or heaven.

7† Come, O my Savior, come away!
      Into my soul descend!
  No longer from thy creature stay,
      My author, and my end!

8† Come, Father, Son, and Holy Ghost,
      And seal me thine abode!
  Let all I am in thee be lost,
      Let all be lost in God!

HSP, 1740

54   (394)   [557]

1   What is our calling's glorious hope
      But inward holiness?
  For this to Jesus I look up,
      I calmly wait for this.

2 I wait, till he shall touch me clean,
   Shall life and power impart;
 Gives me the faith that casts out sin,
   And purifies the heart.

3 This is the dear redeeming grace,
   For every sinner free:
 Surely it shall on me take place,
   The chief of sinners, me.

4 From all iniquity, from all,
   He shall my soul redeem:
 In Jesus I believe, and shall
   Believe myself to him.

5 When Jesus makes my heart his home,
   My sin shall all depart:
 And lo! he saith, I quickly come,
   To fill and rule thy heart.

6 Be it according to thy word!
   Redeem me from all sin;
 My heart would now receive thee, Lord:
   Come in, my Lord, come in!

HSP, 1742

55 (395) [68]

1 None is like Jeshuron's God![a]
   So great, so strong, so high!
 Lo! he spreads his wings abroad,
   He rides upon the sky!
 Israel is his firstborn son;
   God, th' almighty God, is thine,
 See him in thy help come down,
   The excellence divine.

[a]Deut. 33:26–9

2 To thee the great Jehovah deigns
      To succor and defend;
Thee th' eternal God sustains,
      Thy maker and thy friend;
Sinner, what hast thou to dread?
      Safe from all impending harms,
Round thee and beneath are spread
      The everlasting arms.

3 God is thine; disdain to fear
      The enemy within;
God shall in thy flesh appear,
      And make an end of sin;
God the man of sin shall slay,
      Fill thee with triumphant joy;
God shall thrust him out, and say,
      Destroy them all, destroy!

4 All the struggle then is o'er
      And wars and fightings cease;
Israel then shall sin no more,
      But dwell in perfect peace.
All his enemies are gone;
      Sin shall have in him no part;
Israel now shall dwell alone,
      With Jesus in his heart.

5† In a land of corn and wine
      His lot shall be below;
Comforts there and blessings join,
      And milk and honey flow.
Jacob's well is in his soul;
      Gracious dew his heavens distil,
Fill his soul, already full,
      And shall forever fill.

6 Blest, O Israel, art thou!
      What people is like thee?
Saved from sin by Jesus now
      Thou art, and still shalt be.

Jesus is thy sevenfold shield,
    Jesus is thy flaming sword;
Earth, and hell, and sin shall yield
    To God's almighty word.

HSP., 1742

56   (403)   [560]

1 Jesus hath died, that I might live,
    Might live to God alone;
In him eternal life receive,
    And be in spirit one.

2 Savior, I thank thee for the grace,
    The gift unspeakable;
And wait with arms of faith t'embrace,
    And all thy love to feel.

3 My soul breaks out in strong desire,
    The perfect bliss to prove;
My longing heart is all on fire
    To be dissolved in love.

4 Give me thyself, from every boast,
    From every wish set free;
Let all I am in thee be lost—
    But give thyself to me!

5 Thy gifts, alas! cannot suffice,
    Unless thyself be given;
Thy presence makes my paradise,
    And where thou art is heaven!

HSP., 1742

CHARLES WESLEY

FOR MATURE BELIEVERS

57   (414)   [594]

1   Lord, in the strength of grace,
    With a glad heart and free,
 Myself, my residue of days,
    I consecrate to thee.[a]

2   Thy ransomed servant, I
    Restore to thee thy own;
 And from this moment live or die
    To serve my God alone.

Scripture H., 1762, I

58   (416)   [382]

1 Let him to whom we now belong,
   His sovereign right assert,
And take up every thankful song,
   And every loving heart.

2 He justly claims us for his own,
   Who bought us with a price;
The Christian lives to Christ alone,
   To Christ alone he dies.

3 Jesus, thine own at last receive!
   Fulfill our heart's desire!
And let us to thy glory live,
   And in thy cause expire.

4 Our souls and bodies we resign:
   With joy we render thee

---

[a]1 Chr. 39:5

HYMNS

Our all, no longer ours, but thine,
    To all eternity.

Hymns on the Lord's Supper, 1745

59   (417)   [572]

1   Behold the servant of the Lord!
        I wait thy guiding eye to feel,
    To hear and keep thy every word,
        To prove and do thy perfect will;
    Joyful from my own works to cease,
    Glad to fulfill all righteousness.

2   Me if thy grace vouchsafe to use,
        Meanest of all thy creatures, me,
    The deed, the time, the manner choose,
        Let all my fruit be found of thee:
    Let all my works in thee be wrought,
    By thee to full perfection brought.

3   My every weak, though good design,
        O'errule, or change as seems thee meet;
    Jesu, let all my work be thine!
        Thy work, O Lord, is all complete,
    And pleasing in thy Father's sight;
    Thou only hast done all things right.

4   Here then to thee thy own I leave;
        Mould as thou wilt thy passive clay:
    But let me all thy stamp receive;
        But let me all thy words obey:
    Serve with a single heart and eye,
    And to thy glory live and die.

HSP, 1749, I

60   (422)   [552]

1   Jesus, all-atoning Lamb,
    Thine, and only thine I am;
    Take my body, spirit, soul,
    Only thou possess the whole!

2   Thou my one thing needful be;
    Let me ever cleave to thee;
    Let me choose the better part;
    Let me give thee all my heart.

3   Fairer than the sons of men,
    Do not let me turn again,
    Leave the fountainhead of bliss,
    Stoop to creature-happiness.

4   Whom have I on earth below?
    Thee, and only thee, I know.
    Whom have I in heaven but thee?
    Thou art all in all to me.

5   All my treasure is above;
    All my riches is thy love.
    Who the worth of love can tell?
    Infinite, unsearchable!

6† Thou, O love, my portion art.
    Lord, thou knowst my simple heart:
    Other comforts I despise—
    Love be all my paradise.

7† Nothing else can I require;
    Love fills up my whole desire.
    All thy other gifts remove,
    Still thou giv'st me all in love.

HSP., 1749, I

HYMNS

61   (428)   [584]

1   Thou, Jesu, thou my breast inspire,
    And touch my lips with hallowed fire,
        And loose a stammering infant's tongue;
    Prepare the vessel of thy grace,
    Adorn me with the robes of praise,
        And mercy shall be all my song:
    Mercy for all who know not God,
    Mercy for all in Jesu's blood,
        Mercy, that earth and heaven transcends;
    Love, that o'erwhelms the saints in light,
    The length, and breadth, and depth, and height
        Of love divine, which never ends.

2   A faithful witness of thy grace,
    Well may I fill th' allotted space,
        And answer all thy great design;
    Walk in the works by thee prepared,
    And find annexed the vast reward,
        The crown of righteousness divine.
    When I have lived to thee alone,
    Pronounce the welcome word, "Well done!"
        And let me take my place above,
    Enter into my Master's joy,
    And all eternity employ
        In praise, and ecstasy, and love.

HSP., 1749, II

FOR BELIEVERS INTERCEDING FOR THE WORLD

62   (464)   [—]

At the Baptism of Adults

1   Come, Father, Son, and Holy Ghost,
        Honor the means ordained by thee!

239

Make good our apostolic boast,
    And own thy glorious ministry.

2 We now thy promised presence claim,
    Sent to disciple all mankind,
Sent to baptize into thy name
    We now thy promised presence find.

3 Father, in these reveal thy Son;
    In these for whom we seek thy face
The hidden mystery make known,
    The inward, pure, baptizing grace.

4 Jesus, with us thou always art;
    Effectuate now the sacred sign,
The gift unspeakable impart,
    And bless the ordinance divine.

5 Eternal Spirit, descend from high,
    Baptizer of our spirits thou!
The sacramental seal apply,
    And witness with the water now!

6 Oh, that the souls baptized therein
    May now thy truth and mercy feel,
May rise, and wash away their sin—
    Come, Holy Ghost, their pardon seal!

HSP, 1749, II

FOR THE SOCIETY, MEETING

63   (466)   [709]

1   And are we yet alive,
      And see each other's face?
Glory and praise to Jesus give
    For his redeeming grace!
    Preserved by power divine

To full salvation here,
Again in Jesu's praise we join,
And in his sight appear.

2   What troubles have we seen!
What conflicts have we passed!
Fightings without, and fears within,
Since we assembled last.
But out of all the Lord
Hath brought us by his love;
And still he doth his help afford,
And hide our life above.

3   Then let us make our boast
Of his redeeming power,
Which saves us to the uttermost,
Till we can sin no more;
Let us take up the cross
Till we the crown obtain,
And gladly reckon all things loss
So we may Jesus gain.

HSP, 1749, **II**

64   (473)   [718]

1   Jesu, we look to thee,
Thy promised presence claim,
Thou in the midst of us shalt be,
Assembled in thy name.

2   Thy name salvation is,
Which here we come to prove;
Thy name is life, and health, and peace,
And everlasting love.

3†   Not in the name of pride
Or selfishness we meet;

From nature's paths we turn aside,
    And worldly thoughts forget.

4   We meet the grace to take
      Which thou hast freely given;
We meet on earth for thy dear sake
    That we may meet in heaven.

5   Present we know thou art;
      But Oh! thyself reveal!
Now, Lord, let every bounding heart
    The mighty comfort feel!

6   Oh, may thy quick'ning voice,
      The death of sin remove,
And bid our inmost souls rejoice
    In hope of perfect love!

HSP, 1749, II

65   (474)   [719]

1 See, Jesu, thy disciples see,
      The promised blessing give!
Met in thy name, we look to thee,
    Expecting to receive.

2 Thee we expect, our faithful Lord,
      Who in thy name are joined;
We wait, according to thy word,
    Thee in the midst to find.

3 With us thou art assembled here,
      But Oh, thyself reveal!
Son of the living God, appear!
    Let us thy presence feel.

4† Breathe on us, Lord, in this our day,
      And these dry bones shall live;

Speak peace into our hearts, and say,
  "The Holy Ghost receive!"

5 Whom now we seek, Oh, may we meet!
    Jesus, the crucified,
Show us thy bleeding hands and feet,
    Thou who for us hast died.

6 Cause us the record to receive!
    Speak, and the tokens show:
"Oh, be not faithless, but believe
    In me who died for you!"

HSP, 1749, II

FOR THE SOCIETY, PRAYING

66   (496)   [716]

1   Thou God of truth and love,
      We seek thy perfect way,
    Ready thy choice t'approve,
      Thy providence obey,
Enter into thy wise design,
And sweetly lose our will in thine.

2   Why hast thou cast our lot
      In the same age and place?
    And why together brought
      To see each other's face,
To join with softest sympathy,
And mix our friendly souls in thee?

3   Didst thou not make us one,
      That we might one remain,
    Together travel on,
      And bear each other's pain,
Till all thy utmost goodness prove,
And rise renewed in perfect love?

243

4†   Surely thou didst unite
            Our kindred spirits here
That all hereafter might
            Before thy throne appear,
Meet at the marriage of the Lamb,
And all thy glorious love proclaim.

5   Then let us ever bear
            The blessed end in view,
And join with mutual care,
            To fight our passage through;
And kindly help each other on
Till all receive the starry crown.

6   Oh, may thy Spirit seal
            Our souls unto that day!
With all thy fulness fill,
            And then transport away—
Away to our eternal rest,
Away to our Redeemer's breast!

HSP, 1749, I

67   (499)   [—]

1   Jesu, with kindest pity see
The souls that would be one in thee,
If now accepted in thy sight
Thou dost our upright hearts unite,
Allow us, ev'n on earth to prove
The noblest joys of heavenly love!

2   Before thy glorious eyes we spread
The wish which doth from thee proceed;
Our love from earthly dross refine:
Holy, angelical, divine,
Thee let it its great Author show,
And back to the pure fountain flow.

3   A drop of that unbounded sea,
    O Lord, resorb it into thee,
    While all our souls, with restless strife,
    Spring up into eternal life,
    And lost in endless raptures, prove
    Thy whole immensity of love!

4   A spark of that ethereal fire,
    Still let it to its source aspire,
    To thee in every wish return,
    Intensely for thy glory burn,
    While all our souls fly up to thee,
    And blaze through all eternity.

HSP, 1749, II

68   (507)   [713]

(The Love-Feast)
Part III

1   Let us join ('tis God commands),
    Let us join our hearts and hands;
    Help to gain our calling's hope,
    Build we each the other up.
    God his blessing shall dispense,
    God shall crown his ordinance,
    Meet in his appointed ways,
    Nourish us with social grace.

2† Let us then as brethren love,
    Faithfully his gifts improve,
    Carry on the earnest strife,
    Walk in holiness of life.
    Still forget the things behind,
    Follow Christ in heart and mind;
    Toward the mark unwearied press,
    Seize the crown of righteousness!

245

3† Plead we thus for faith alone,
   Faith which by our works is shown;
   God it is who justifies,
   Only faith the grace applies,
   Active faith that lives within,
   Conquers earth, and hell, and sin,
   Sanctifies, and makes us whole,
   Forms the Savior in the soul.

4† Let us for this faith contend,
   Sure salvation is its end;
   Heaven already is begun,
   Everlasting life is won.
   Only let us persevere
   Till we see our Lord appear;
   Never from the rock remove,
   Saved by faith which works by love.

HSP, 1740

69   (515)   [598]

1 Holy Lamb, who thee confess,
   Followers of thy holiness,
   Thee they ever keep in view,
   Ever ask, "What shall we do?"

2 Governed by thy only will,
   All thy words we would fulfill,
   Would in all thy footsteps go,
   Walk as Jesus walked below.

3 While thou didst on earth appear,
   Servant to thy servants here,
   Mindful of thy place above,
   All thy life was prayer and love.

4 Such our whole employment be:
   Works of faith and charity,

Works of love on man bestowed,
Secret intercourse with God.

5 Early in the temple met,
Let us still our Savior greet;
Nightly to the mount repair,
Join our praying Pattern there.

6 There by wrestling faith obtain
Power to work for God again,
Power his image to retrieve,
Power like thee, our Lord, to live.

7 Vessels, instruments of grace,
Pass we thus our happy days
'Twixt the mount and multitude,
Doing or receiving good:

8 Glad to pray and labor on
Till our earthly course is run,
Till we on the sacred tree
Bow the head, and die like thee.

Family H., 1767

70   (518)   [749]

1 Come, let us use the grace divine,
   And all with one accord,[a]
In a perpetual covenant join
   Ourselves to Christ the Lord.

2 Give up ourselves, through Jesu's power,
   His name to glorify;
And promise in this sacred hour
   For God to live and die.

---

[a]Jer. 50:5

3 The covenant we this moment make
      Be ever kept in mind!
We will no more our God forsake,
      Or cast his words behind.

4 We never will throw off his fear
      Who hears our solemn vow;
And if thou art well pleased to hear,
      Come down, and meet us now!

5† Thee, Father, Son, and Holy Ghost,
      Let all our hearts receive!
Present with the celestial host,
      The peaceful answer give!

6 To each the covenant-blood apply
      Which takes our sins away;
And register our names on high,
      And keep us to that day!

Scripture H., 1762, **II**

FOR THE SOCIETY, PARTING

71   (520)   [712]

1 Blest be the dear, uniting love
      That will not let us part;
Our bodies may far off remove—
      We still are one in heart.

2 Joined in one spirit to our Head,
      Where he appoints we go,
And still in Jesu's footsteps tread,
      And show his praise below.

3 Oh, may we ever walk in him,
      And nothing know beside,

Nothing desire, nothing esteem,
    But Jesus crucified!

4 Closer and closer let us cleave
    To his beloved embrace,
Expect his fulness to receive,
    And grace to answer grace.

5 Partakers of the Savior's grace,
    The same in mind and heart,
Nor joy, nor grief, nor time, nor place,
    Nor life, nor death can part.

6† But let us hasten to the day
    Which shall our flesh restore,
When death shall all be done away,
    And bodies part no more!

HSP, 1742

72   (525)   [722]

1 Lift up your hearts to things above,[a]
    Ye followers of the Lamb,
And join with us to praise his love,
    And glorify his name;
To Jesu's name give thanks and sing,
    Whose mercies never end;
Rejoice! rejoice! the Lord is King!
    The King is now our Friend!

2 We for his sake count all things loss,
    On earthly good look down;
And joyfully sustain the cross
    Till we receive the crown.
Oh, let us stir each other up,

---

[a]Revelation 22:21

Our faith by works t'approve,
By holy, purifying hope,
  And the sweet task of love!

3† Love us, though far in flesh disjoined,
    Ye lovers of the Lamb;
  And ever bear us on your mind,
    Who think and speak the same;
  You on our minds we ever bear,
    Whoe'er to Jesus bow,
  Stretch out the arms of faith and prayer—
    And lo! we reach you now!

4 The blessings all on you be shed
    Which God in Christ imparts;
  We pray the spirit of our Head
    Into your faithful hearts:
  Mercy and peace your portion be,
    To carnal minds unknown,
  The hidden manna, and the tree
    Of life, and the white stone.

5† Let all who for the promise wait
    The Holy Ghost receive,
  And raised to our unsinning state
    With God in Eden live!
  Live till the Lord in glory come,
    And wait his heaven to share!
  He now is fitting up our home—
    Go on! we'll meet you there!

HSP, 1749, **II**

SELECTION OF HYMNS FROM
HYMNS ON THE LORD'S SUPPER
of 1745

I. AS IT IS A MEMORIAL OF
THE SUFFERING AND DEATH OF CHRIST

73   (8)   [—]

1   Come, to the supper come,
Sinners, there still is room;
Every soul may be his guest,
Jesus gives the general word;
Share the monumental feast,
Eat the supper of your Lord.

2   In this authentic sign
Behold the stamp Divine:
Christ revives his sufferings here,
Still exposes them to view;
See the Crucified appear,
Now believe he died for you.

74   (16)   [765]

1 Come, thou everlasting Spirit,
Bring to every thankful mind
All the Savior's dying merit,
All his sufferings for mankind;
True Recorder of his passion,
Now the living faith impart,

Now reveal his great salvation,
    Preach his gospel to our heart.

2   Come, thou Witness of his dying
     Come, Remembrancer Divine,
Let us feel thy power applying
     Christ to every soul and mine;
Let us groan thine inward groaning,
     Look on Him we pierced and grieve,
All receive the grace atoning,
     All the sprinkled blood receive.

75   (21)   [191]

1   God of unexampled grace,
     Redeemer of mankind,
Matter of eternal praise
     We in thy passion find:
Still our choicest strains we bring,
     Still the joyful theme pursue,
Thee the Friend of sinners sing,
     Whose love is ever new.

2   Endless scenes of wonder rise
     With that mysterious tree,
Crucified before our eyes
     Where we our Maker see:
Jesus, Lord, what hast thou done?
     Publish we the death Divine,
Stop, and gaze, and fall, and own
     Was never love like thine!

3   Never love nor sorrow was
     Like that my Jesus show'd
See him stretch'd on yonder cross,
     And crush'd beneath our load!
Now discern the Deity,

HYMNS

Now his heavenly birth declare;
    Faith cries out, 'Tis he, 'tis he,
      My God, that suffers there!

4† Jesus drinks the bitter cup,
      The winepress treads alone,
Tears the graves and mountains up
      By His expiring groan:
Lo! the powers of heaven he shakes;
      Nature in convulsions lies,
Earth's profoundest center quakes,
      The great *Jehovah* dies!

5† Dies the glorious Cause of all,
      The true eternal Pan,
Falls to raise us from our fall,
      To ransom sinful man:
Well may *Sol* withdraw his light,
      With the Sufferer sympathize,
Leave the world in sudden night,
      While his Creator dies.

6† Well may heaven be clothed with black,
      And solemn sackcloth wear,
Jesu's agony partake,
      The hour of darkness share:
Mourn th' astonied hosts above,
      Silence saddens all the skies,
Kindler of seraphic love,
      The God of angels dies.

7† O, my God, he dies for me,
      I feel the mortal smart!
See him hanging on the tree—
      A sight that breaks my heart!
Oh, that all to thee might turn!
      Sinners, ye may love him too;
Look on him ye pierced, and mourn
      For One who bled for you.

8† Weep o'er your Desire and Hope
    With tears of humblest love;
Sing, for Jesus is gone up,
    And reigns enthroned above!
Lives our Head, to die no more;
    Power is all to Jesus given,
Worship'd as he was before,
    Th' immortal King of heaven.

9† Lord, we bless thee for thy grace
    And truth, which never fail,
Hastening to behold thy face
    Without a dimming veil:
We shall see our heavenly King,
    All thy glorious love proclaim,
Help the angel choirs to sing
    Our dear triumphant Lamb.

II. AS IT IS A SIGN
AND A MEANS OF GRACE

76   (29)   [—]

1 O Thou who this mysterious bread
    Didst in *Emmaus* break,
Return, herewith our souls to feed,
    And to thy followers speak.

2 Unseal the volume of thy grace,
    Apply the gospel word,
Open our eyes to see thy face,
    Our hearts to know the Lord.

3 Of thee we commune still, and mourn
    Till thou the veil remove;
Talk with us, and our hearts shall burn
    With flames of fervent love.

4 Enkindle now the heavenly zeal
      And make thy mercy known,
  And give our pardon'd souls to feel
      That God and love are one.

77   (33)   [—]

1 Jesu, dear, redeeming Lord,
  Magnify thy Dying word;
  In thy ordinance appear,
  Come, and meet thy followers here.

2 In the rite thou hast enjoin'd
  Let us now our Savior find,
  Drink thy blood for sinners shed,
  Taste thee in the broken bread.

3 Thou our faithful hearts prepare,
  Thou thy pardoning grace declare;
  Thou that hast for sinners died,
  Show thyself the Crucified.

4 All the power of sin remove,
  Fill us with thy perfect love,
  Stamp us with the stamp Divine,
  Seal our souls forever thine.

78   (38)   [—]

1 Worthy the Lamb of endless praise,
      Whose double life we here shall prove,
  The pardoning and the hallowing grace,
      The dawning and the perfect love.

2 We here shall gain our calling's prize,
      The gift unspeakable receive,

And higher still in death arise,
    And all the life of glory live.

3 To make our right and title sure,
    Our dying Lord himself hath given,
His sacrifice did all procure,
    Pardon, and holiness, and heaven.

4 Our life of grace we here shall feel
    Shed in our loving hearts abroad,
Till Christ our glorious life reveal,
    Long hidden with himself in God.

5 Come, great Redeemer of mankind,
    We long thy open face to see;
Appear, and all who seek shall find
    Their bliss consummated in thee.

6 Thy presence shall the cloud dispart,
    Thy presence shall the life display;
Then, then our all in all thou art,
    Our fulness of eternal day!

79   (40)   [764]

1   Author of life Divine,
      Who hast a table spread,
    Furnish'd with mystic wine
      And everlasting bread,
Preserve the life thyself hast given,
And feed and train us up for heaven.

2   Our needy souls sustain
      With fresh supplies of love
    Till all thy life we gain,
      And all thy fulness prove,
And, strengthen'd by thy perfect grace,
Behold without a veil thy face.

HYMNS

80   (42)   [—]

1 Glory to him who freely spent
    His blood, that we might live,
And through this choicest instrument
    Doth all his blessings give.

2 Fasting he doth, and hearing bless,
    And prayer can much avail,
Good vessels all to draw the grace
    Out of salvation's well.

3 But none, like this mysterious rite
    Which dying mercy gave,
Can draw forth all his promised might
    And all his will to save.

4 This is the richest legacy
    Thou hast on man bestow'd:
Here chiefly, Lord, we feed on thee,
    And drink thy precious blood.

5 Here all thy blessings we receive,
    Here all thy gifts are given,
To those that would in thee believe
    Pardon, and grace, and heaven.

6 Thus may we still in thee be blest,
    Till all from earth remove,
And share with thee the marriage feast,
    And drink the wine above.

81   (43)   [760]

1   Savior, and can it be
    That thou shouldst dwell with me?
From thy high and lofty throne,
    Throne of everlasting bliss,

Will thy majesty stoop down
    To so mean a house as this?

2   I am not worthy, Lord,
      So foul, so self-abhorr'd,
Thee, my God, to entertain
    In this poor polluted heart:
I am a frail sinful man,
    All my nature cries, Depart!

3   Yet come, thou heavenly Guest,
    And purify my breast;
Come, thou great and glorious King,
    While before thy cross I bow,
With thyself salvation bring,
    Cleanse the house by entering now.

82   (53)   [—]

1   O God of truth and love,
    Let us thy mercy prove;
Bless thine ordinance Divine,
    Let it now effectual be,
Answer all its great design,
    All its gracious ends in me.

2   Oh, might the sacred word
    Set forth our dying Lord,
Point us to thy sufferings past,
    Present grace and strength impart,
Give our ravish'd souls a taste,
    Pledge of glory in our heart.

3   Come in thy Spirit down,
    Thine institution crown;
Lamb of God, as slain appear,
    Life of all believers thou
Let us now perceive thee near,
    Come, thou Hope of glory, now.

HYMNS

83   (57)   [—]

1 Oh the depth of love Divine,
       Th' unfathomable grace!
   Who shall say how bread and wine
       God into man conveys!
   How the bread his flesh imparts,
       How the wine transmits his blood,
   Fills his faithful people's hearts
       With all the life of God!

2 Let the wisest mortal show
       How we the grace receive,
   Feeble elements bestow
       A power not theirs to give.
   Who explains the wondrous way,
       How through these the virtue came?
   These the virtue did convey,
       Yet still remain the same.

3 How can heavenly spirits rise,
       By earthly matter fed,
   Drink herewith Divine supplies,
       And eat immortal bread?
   Ask the Father's Wisdom *how;*
       Him that did the means ordain!
   Angels round our altars bow
       To search it out in vain.

4 Sure and real is the grace
       The manner be unknown;
   Only meet us in thy ways,
       And perfect us in one.
   Let us taste the heavenly powers;
       Lord, we ask for nothing more:
   Thine to bless, 'tis only ours
       To wonder and adore.

84   (66)   [—]

1 Jesu, my Lord and God bestow
   All which thy sacrament doth show,
        And make the real sign
   A sure effectual means of grace,
   Then sanctify my heart, and bless,
        And make it all like thine.

2 Great is thy faithfulness and love,
   Thine ordinance can never prove
        Of none effect, and vain;
   Only do thou my heart prepare
   To find thy real presence there,
        And all thy fulness gain.

85   (72)   [767]

1 Come, Holy Ghost, thine influence shed,
        And realize the sign;
   Thy life infuse into the bread,
        Thy power into the wine.

2 Effectual let the tokens prove,
        And made, by heavenly art,
   Fit channels to convey thy love
        To every faithful heart.

86   (81)   [761]

1†   Jesu, we thus obey
        Thy last and kindest word,
   Here in thine own appointed way
        We come to meet our Lord:
        The way thou has enjoin'd
        Thou wilt therein appear;
   We come with confidence to find
        Thy special presence here.

2   Our hearts we open wide,
         To make the Savior room;
And lo! the Lamb, the Crucified,
         The sinner's Friend, is come!
         His presence makes the feast;
         And now our bosoms feel
The glory not to be exprest,
         The joy unspeakable.

3   With pure celestial bliss
         He doth our spirits cheer,
His house of banqueting is this,
         And he hath brought us here:
         He doth his servants feed
         With manna from above,
His banner over us is spread,
         His everlasting love.

4†   He bids us drink and eat
         Imperishable food,
He gives his flesh to be our meat,
         And bids us drink his blood:
         Whate'er th' Almighty can
         To pardon'd sinners give,
The fulness of our God made man
         We here with Christ receive.

         87   (89)   [—]

1 Ye faithful souls, who thus record
         The passion of that Lamb Divine,
  Is the memorial of your Lord
         A useless form, an empty sign?
  Or doth he here his life impart?
  What saith the witness in your heart?

2 Is it the dying Master's will
         That we should this persist to do?
  Then let him here himself reveal,

The tokens of his presence show,
Descend in blessings from above,
And answer by the fire of love.

3   Who thee remember in thy ways,
      Come, Lord, and meet and bless us here;
In confidence we ask the grace;
      Faithful and True, appear, appear,
Let all perceive thy blood applied,
Let all discern the Crucified.

4   'Tis done; the Lord sets to his seal,
      The prayer is heard, the grace is given
With joy unspeakable we feel
      The Holy Ghost sent down from heaven;
The altar streams with sacred blood,
And all the temple flames with God!

88   (91)   [—]

1   All-loving, all-redeeming Lord,
      Thy wandering sheep with pity see
Who slight thy dearest dying word,
      And will not thus remember thee:
To all who would perform thy will
The glorious promised truth reveal.

2   Can we enjoy thy richest love,
      Nor long that they the grace may share?
Thou from their eyes the scales remove,
      Thou th' eternal word declare,
Thy Spirit with thy word impart,
And speak the precept to their heart.

3   If chiefly here thou mayst be found,
      If now, even now, we find thee here,
Oh, let their joys like ours abound,
      Invite them to the royal cheer,

Feed with imperishable food,
And fill their raptured souls with God.

4 Jesu, we will not let thee go,
  But keep herein our fastest hold,
Till thou to them thy counsel show,
  And call and make us all one fold,
One hallow'd undivided bread,
One body knit to thee our Head.

III. THE SACRAMENT A PLEDGE OF HEAVEN

89 (94) [—]

1 Oh, what a soul-transporting feast
  Doth this communion yield!
Remembering here thy passion past,
  We with thy love are fill'd.

2 Sure instrument of present grace
  Thy sacrament we find,
Yet higher blessings it displays,
  And raptures still behind.

3 It bears us now on eagle's wings,
  If thou the power impart,
And thee our glorious earnest brings
  Into our faithful heart.

4 Oh, let us still the earnest feel,
  Th' unutterable peace,
This loving Spirit be the seal
  Of our eternal bliss!

CHARLES WESLEY

90   (99)   [—]

1 Whither should our full souls aspire,
At this transporting feast?
They never can on earth be higher,
Or more completely blest.

2 Our cup of blessing from above
Delightfully runs o'er,
Till from these bodies they remove
Our souls can hold no more.

3 To heaven the mystic banquet leads;
Let us to heaven ascend,
And bear this joy upon our heads
Till it in glory end.

4 Till all who truly join in this
The marriage supper share,
Enter into their Master's bliss,
And feast forever there.

91   (101)   [—]

1 How glorious is the life above,
Which in this ordinance we *taste;*
That fulness of celestial love,
That joy which shall forever last!

2 That heavenly life in Christ conceal'd
These earthen vessels could not bear,
The part which now we find reveal'd
No tongue of angels can declare.

3 The light of life eternal darts
Into our souls a dazzling ray,
A drop of heaven o'erflows our hearts,
And deluges the house of clay.

4   Sure pledge of ecstasies unknown
      Shall this Divine communion be;
  The ray shall rise into a sun,
      The drop shall swell into a sea.

IV. THE HOLY EUCHARIST AS IT IMPLIES A SACRIFICE

92   (116)   [771]

1   Victim Divine, thy grace we claim
      While thus thy precious death we show;
  Once offer'd up, a spotless Lamb,
      In thy great temple here below,
  Thou didst for all mankind atone,
  And standest now before the throne.

2   Thou standest in the holiest place,
      As now for guilty sinners slain;
  Thy blood of sprinkling speaks, and prays,
      All-prevalent for helpless man;
  Thy blood is still our ransom found,
  And spreads salvation all around.

3† The smoke of thy atonement here
      Darken'd the sun and rent the veil.
  Made the new way to heaven appear,
      And show'd the great Invisible;
  Well pleased in thee our God look'd down,
  And call'd his rebels to a crown.

4† He still respects thy sacrifice,
      Its savor sweet doth always please;
  The offering smokes through earth and skies,
      Diffusing life, and joy, and peace;
  To these thy lower courts it comes,
  And fills them with divine perfumes.

5 We need not now go up to heaven,
       To bring the long-sought Savior down;
   Thou art to all already given,
       Thou dost even now thy banquet crown:
   To every faithful soul appear,
   And show thy real presence here!

                 93   (125)   [723]

1 O God of our forefathers, hear,
       And make thy faithful mercies known;
   To thee through Jesus we draw near,
       Thy suffering, well-beloved Son,
   In whom thy smiling face we see,
   In whom thou art well pleased with *me*.

2 With solemn faith we offer up,
       And spread before thy glorious eyes
   That only ground of all our hope
       That precious bleeding Sacrifice,
   Which brings thy grace on sinners down,
   And perfects all our souls in one.

3 Acceptance through his only name,
       Forgiveness in his blood we have;
   But more abundant life we claim
       Through him who died our souls to save,
   To sanctify us by his blood,
   And fill with all the life of God.

4 Father, behold thy dying Son,
       And hear his blood that speaks above;
   On us let all thy grace be shown,
       Peace, righteousness, and joy, and love;
   Thy kingdom come to every heart,
   And all thou hast, and all thou art.

HYMNS

V. CONCERNING THE SACRIFICE OF OUR PERSONS

94   (129)   [—]

1   See where our great High-Priest
    Before the Lord appears,
And on his loving breast
    The tribes of *Israel* bears,
Never without his people seen,
The Head of all believing men!

2   With him, the Cornerstone,
    The living stones conjoin;
Christ and his church are one,
    One body and one vine;
For us he uses all his powers,
And all he has, or is, is ours.

3   The motions of our Head
    The members all pursue,
By his good Spirit led
    To act, and suffer too
Whate'er he did on earth sustain,
Till glorious all like him we reign.

95   (130)   [—]

1   Jesu, we follow Thee,
    In all thy footsteps tread,
And pant for full conformity
    To our exalted Head;

    We would, we would partake
    Thy every state below,
And suffer all things for thy sake,
    And to thy glory do.

2   We in thy birth are born,
    Sustain thy grief and loss,

267

Share in thy want, and shame, and scorn,
    And die upon thy cross.

    Baptized into thy death
    We sink into thy grave,
Till thou the quickening Spirit breathe,
    And to the utmost save.

3   Thou said'st, "Where'er I am
    There shall my servant be";
Master, the welcome word we claim
    And die to live with thee.

    To us who share thy pain,
    Thy joy shall soon be given,
And we shall in thy glory reign,
    For thou art now in heaven.

VI.   AFTER THE SACRAMENT

96   (164)   [—]

1   Sons of God, triumphant rise,
    Shout th' accomplish'd Sacrifice!
    Shout your sins in Christ forgiven,
    Sons of God, and heirs of heaven!

2   Ye that round our altars throng,
    Listening angels, join the song:
    Sing with us, ye heavenly powers,
    Pardon, grace, and glory ours!

3   Love's mysterious work is done!
    Greet we now th' accepted Son,
    Heal'd and quicken'd by his blood,
    Join'd to Christ, and one with God.

4   Christ, of all our hopes the seal;
    Peace Divine in Christ we feel,

Pardon to our souls applied:
Dead for all, for me he died!

5 Sin shall tyrannize no more,
Purged its guilt, dissolved its power;
Jesus makes our hearts his throne,
There he lives, and reigns alone.

6 Grace our every thought controls,
Heaven is open'd in our souls,
Everlasting life is won,
Glory is on earth begun.

7 Christ in us; in him we see
Fulness of the Deity.
Beam of the Eternal Beam;
Life Divine we taste in him!

8 Him we only taste below;
Mightier joys ordain'd to know,
Him when fully ours we prove,
Ours the heaven of perfect love!

97   (166)   [—]

1 Happy the saints of former days,
    Who first continued in the word,
A simple, lowly, loving race,
    True followers of their lamblike Lord.

2 In holy fellowship they lived,
    Nor would from the commandment move
But every joyful day received
    The tokens of expiring Love.

3 Not then above their Master wise,
    They simply in his paths remain'd,
And call'd to mind his sacrifice
    With steadfast faith and love unfeign'd.

4 From house to house they broke the bread
   Impregnated with life Divine,
 And drank the Spirit of their Head
   Transmitted in the sacred wine.

5 With Jesu's constant presence blest,
   While duteous to his dying word,
 They kept the Eucharistic feast,
   And supp'd in *Eden* with their Lord.

6 Throughout their spotless lives was seen
   The virtue of this heavenly food;
 Superior to the sons of men,
   They soar'd aloft, and walk'd with God.

7 Oh, what a flame of sacred love
   Was kindled by the altar's fire!
 They lived on earth like those above,
   Glad rivals of the heavenly choir.

8 Strong in the strength herewith received,
   And mindful of the Crucified,
 His confessors for him they lived,
   For him his faithful martyrs died.

9 Their souls from chains of flesh released,
   By torture from their bodies driven,
 With violent faith the kingdom seized,
   And fought and forced their way to heaven.

10 Where is the pure primeval flame,
   Which in their faithful bosom glow'd?
 Where are the followers of the Lamb,
   The dying witnesses for God?

11 Why is the faithful seed decreased,
   The life of God extinct and dead?
 The daily sacrifice is ceased,
   And charity to heaven is fled.

12   Sad mutual causes of decay,
        Slackness and vice together move;
    Grown cold, we cast the means away,
        And quench the latest spark of love.

13   The sacred signs Thou didst ordain,
        Our pleasant things, are all laid waste;
    To men of lips and hearts profane,
        To dogs and swine and heathens cast.

14   Thine holy ordinance contemn'd
        Hath let the flood of evil in,
    And those who by thy name are named
        The sinners unbaptized outsin.

15   But canst thou not Thy work revive
        Once more in our degenerate years?
    Oh, wouldst thou with thy rebels strive,
        And melt them into gracious tears.

16   Oh, wouldst thou to thy church return,
        For which the faithful remnant sighs,
    For which the drooping nations mourn!
        Restore the daily sacrifice.

17   Return, and with thy servants sit
        Lord of the sacramental feast;
    And satiate us with heavenly meat,
        And make the *world* thy happy guest.

18   Now let the spouse, reclined on thee,
        Come up out of the wilderness,
    From every spot and wrinkle free,
        And wash'd and perfected in grace.

19   Thou hear'st the pleading Spirit's groan,
        Thou know'st the groaning Spirit's will:
    Come in thy gracious kingdom down,
        And all thy ransom'd servants seal.

20 Come quickly, Lord, the Spirit cries,
        The number of thy saints complete;
    Come quickly, Lord, the bride replies,
        And make us all for glory meet;

21 Erect thy tabernacle here,
        The *New Jerusalem* send down,
    Thyself amidst thy saints appear,
        And seat us on thy dazzling throne.

22 Begin the great millennial day;
        Now, Savior, with a shout descend,
    Thy standard in the heavens display,
        And bring the joy which ne'er shall end.

[3]

SELECTION OF OTHER HYMNS
BY CHARLES WESLEY

FELLOWSHIP

98   (500)   [745]

1   All praise to our redeeming Lord,
        Who joins us by his grace,
    And bids us, each to each restored,
        Together seek his face.

2   He bids us build each other up;
        And, gathered into one,
    To our high calling's glorious hope
        We hand in hand go on.

3   The gift which he on one bestows,
        We all delight to prove;
    The grace through every vessel flows,
        In purest streams of love.

4   Even now we think and speak the same,
        And cordially agree;
    Concentered all, through Jesu's name,
        In perfect harmony.

5   We all partake the joy of one,
        The common peace we feel,
    A peace to sensual minds unknown,
        A joy unspeakable.

6   And if our fellowship below
        In Jesus be so sweet,

What heights of rapture shall we know,
When round his throne we meet!

Redemption H, 1747

ADORATION

99   (568)   [270]

1   My heart is full of Christ, and longs[a]
        Its glorious matter to declare!
Of him I make my loftier songs,
        I cannot from his praise forbear;
My ready tongue makes haste to sing
The glories of my heavenly King.

2   Fairer than all the earthborn race,
        Perfect in comeliness thou art;
Replenished are thy lips with grace,
        And full of love thy tender heart:
God ever blest! we bow the knee,
And own all fulness dwells in thee.

3   Gird on thy thigh the Spirit's sword,
        And take to thee thy power divine;
Stir up thy strength, almighty Lord,
        All power and majesty are thine;
Assert thy worship and renown;
O all-redeeming God, come down!

4   Come, and maintain thy righteous cause,
        And let thy glorious toil succeed;
Dispread the victory of thy cross,
        Ride on, and prosper in thy deed;

---

[a]Psalm 45

Through earth triumphantly ride on,
 And reign in every heart alone.

Psalms and Hymns I, 1743

100   (654)   [383]

1 Being of beings, God of love!
      To thee our hearts we raise;
   Thy all-sustaining power we prove,
      And gladly sing thy praise.

2 Thine, only thine, we pant to be;
      Our sacrifice receive;
   Made, and preserved, and saved by thee,
      To thee ourselves we give.

3 Heavenward our every wish aspires;
      For all thy mercies' store,
   The sole return thy love requires
      Is that we ask for more.

4 For more we ask; we open then
      Our hearts to embrace thy will;
   Turn, and revive us, Lord, again,
      With all thy fulness fill.

5 Come, Holy Ghost, the Savior's love
      Shed in our hearts abroad!
   So shall we ever live, and move,
      And be, with Christ in God.

HSP, 1739

CHARLES WESLEY

JUDGMENT

101   (66)   [264]

1 Lo! He comes with clouds descending,
    Once for favored sinners slain;
  Thousand thousand saints attending,
    Swell the triumph of his train:
      Hallelujah!
  God appears on earth to reign.

2 Every eye shall now behold him
    Robed in dreadful majesty;
  Those who set at nought and sold him,
    Pierced and nailed him to the tree,
      Deeply wailing,
  Shall the true Messiah see.

3 The dear tokens of his passion
    Still his dazzling body bears;
  Cause of endless exultation
    To his ransomed worshipers;
      With what rapture
  Gaze we on those glorious scars!

4 Yea, Amen! let all adore thee,
    High on thy eternal throne;
  Savior, take the power and glory
    Claim the kingdom for thine own;
      Jah, Jehovah,
  Everlasting God, come down!

Intercession H, 1758

CHRIST'S PERSON

102   (143)   [110]

1 Jesu, Lover of my soul,
    Let me to thy bosom fly,

While the nearer waters roll,
    While the tempest still is high:
Hide me, O my Savior, hide,
    Till the storm of life be past!
Safe into the haven guide,
    Oh, receive my soul at last!

2   Other refuge have I none,
    Hangs my helpless soul on thee;
Leave, ah! leave me not alone,
    Still support and comfort me:
All my trust on thee is stayed,
    All my help from thee I bring;
Cover my defenseless head
    With the shadow of thy wing.

3   Thou, O Christ, art all I want
    More than all in thee I find!
Raise the fallen, cheer the faint,
    Heal the sick, and lead the blind;
Just and holy is thy name,
    I am all unrighteousness;
False and full of sin I am,
    Thou art full of truth and grace.

4   Plenteous grace with thee is found,
    Grace to cover all my sin,
Let the healing streams abound;
    Make and keep me pure within:
Thou of life the fountain art,
    Freely let me take of thee,
Spring thou up within my heart,
    Rise to all eternity.

HSP I, 1740

103   (169)   [—]

1   Jesus, the all-restoring Word,
    My fallen spirit's hope,

After thy lovely likeness, Lord,
    Ah, when shall I wake up?

2 Thou, O my God, thou only art
    The Life, the Truth, the Way;
Quicken my soul, instruct my heart,
    My sinking footsteps stay.

3 Of all thou hast in earth below,
    In heaven above, to give,
Give me thy only love to know,
    In thee to walk and live.

4 Fill me with all the life of love;
    In mystic union join
Me to thyself, and let me prove
    The fellowship divine.

5 Open the intercourse between
    My longing soul and thee,
Never to be broke off again
    To all eternity.

HSP I, 1740

104   (228)   [457]

1 Thou Shepherd of Israel, and mine,[a]
    The joy and desire of my heart,
For closer communion I pine,
    I long to reside where thou art:
The pasture I languish to find
    Where all, who their Shepherd obey,
Are fed, on thy bosom reclined,
    And screened from the heat of the day.

---

[a]Canticles 1:7

2   Ah! show me that happiest place,
     The place of thy people's abode,
  Where saints in an ecstasy gaze,
     And hang on a crucified God;
  Thy love for a sinner declare,
     Thy passion and death on the tree:
  My spirit to Calvary bear,
     To suffer and triumph with thee.

3   'Tis there, with the lambs of thy flock,
     There only, I covet to rest,
  To lie at the foot of the rock,
     Or rise to be hid in thy breast;
  'Tis there I would always abide,
     And never a moment depart,
  Concealed in the cleft of thy side,
     Eternally held in thy heart.

Scripture H, 1762

CHRIST'S BIRTH

105   (683)   [117]

1   Hark how all the welkin rings,
    "Glory to the King of kings,
    Peace on earth, and mercy mild,
    God and sinners reconciled!"

2   Joyful, all ye nations, rise,
    Join the triumph of the skies;
    Universal Nature, say,
    "Christ the Lord is born to-day!"

3   Christ, by highest heaven adored,
    Christ, the everlasting Lord,
    Late in time behold him come,
    Offspring of a virgin's womb.

4 Veil'd in flesh, the Godhead see,
   Hail the' Incarnate Deity!
   Pleased as man with men to' appear
   Jesus, our *Immanuel* here!

5 Hail the heavenly Prince of Peace!
   Hail the Sun of Righteousness!
   Light and life to all he brings,
   Risen with healing in his wings.

6 Mild he lays his glory by,
   Born—that man no more may die,
   Born—to raise the sons of earth,
   Born—to give them second birth.

7† Come, Desire of Nations, come
    Fix in us thy humble home;
    Rise, the woman's conquering Seed,
    Bruise in us the serpent's head.

8† Now display thy saving power,
    Ruin'd nature now restore;
    Now in mystic union join
    Thine to ours, and ours to thine.

9† *Adam's* likeness, Lord, efface
    Stamp thy image in its place;
    Second *Adam* from above,
    Reinstate us in Thy love.

10† Let us thee, though lost, regain,
     Thee, the Life, the Inner Man:
     Oh! to all Thyself impart,
     Form'd in each believing heart.

HSP II, 1739

HYMNS

106   (684)   [134]

1 Glory be to God on high,
        And peace on earth descend!
   God comes down, he bows the sky,
        And shows himself our friend:
   God the invisible appears!
        God, the blest, the great I AM,
   Sojourns in this vale of tears,
        And Jesus is his name.

2 Him the angels all adored,
        Their Maker and their King;
   Tidings of their humbled Lord
        They now to mortals bring.
   Emptied of his majesty,
        Of his dazzling glories shorn,
   Being's source begins to be,
        And God himself is born!

3 See the eternal Son of God
        A mortal Son of man;
   Dwelling in an earthly clod,
        Whom heaven cannot contain!
   Stand amazed, ye heavens, at this!
        See the Lord of earth and skies;
   Humbled to the dust he is,
        And in a manger lies.

4 We, the sons of men, rejoice,
        The Prince of peace proclaim;
   With heaven's host lift up our voice,
        And shout Immanuel's name:
   Knees and hearts to him we bow;
        Of our flesh and of our bone,
   Jesus is our brother now,
        And God is all our own.

Nativity H, 1746

CHARLES WESLEY

107   (685)   [142]

1   Let earth and heaven combine,
          Angels and men agree,
       To praise in songs divine
          The incarnate Deity,
       Our God contracted to a span,
       Incomprehensibly made man.

2   He laid his glory by
          He wrapped him in our clay;
       Unmarked by human eye,
          The latent Godhead lay;
       Infant of days he here became,
       And bore the mild Immanuel's name.

3   Unsearchable the love
          That hath the Savior brought;
       The grace is far above
          Or man or angel's thought;
       Suffice for us that God, we know,
       Our God, is manifest below.

4   He deigns in flesh to appear,
          Widest extremes to join;
       To bring our vileness near,
          And make us all divine:
       And we the life of God shall know,
       For God is manifest below.

5   Made perfect first in love,
          And sanctified by grace,
       We shall from earth remove,
          And see his glorious face:
       Then shall his love be fully showed,
       And man shall then be lost in God.

Nativity H, 1746

282

HYMNS

108   (686)   [135]

1 Stupendous height of heavenly love,
       Of pitying tenderness divine!
   It brought the Savior from above,
       It caused the springing day to shine
   The Sun of righteousness to appear,
   And gild our gloomy hemisphere.

2 God did in Christ himself reveal,
       To chase our darkness by his light,
   Our sin and ignorance dispel,
       Direct our wandering feet aright,
   And bring our souls, with pardon blest,
   To realms of everlasting rest.

3 Come then, O Lord, thy light impart,
       The faith that bids our terror cease:
   Into thy love direct our heart,
       Into thy way of perfect peace;
   And cheer the souls of death afraid,
   And guide them through the dreadful shade.

4 Answer thy mercy's whole design,
       My God incarnated for me;
   My spirit make thy radiant shrine,
       My light and full salvation be,
   And through the shades of death unknown
   Conduct me to thy dazzling throne.

Hymns on 4 Gospels, 1762

109   (688)   [242]

1 Come, thou long-expected Jesus,
       Born to set thy people free,
   From our fears and sins release us,
       Let us find our rest in thee.

283

Israel's strength and consolation,
    Hope of all the earth thou art;
Dear Desire of every nation,
    Joy of every longing heart.

2 Born thy people to deliver,
     Born a child and yet a king,
Born to reign in us forever,
     Now thy gracious kingdom bring:
By thine own eternal Spirit
     Rule in all our hearts alone;
By thine all-sufficient merit
     Raise us to thy glorious throne.

Nativity H, 1746

110   (689)   [141]

1 To us a child of royal birth,
     Heir of the promises, is given;
The Invisible appears on earth,
     The Son of man, the God of heaven.

2 A Savior born, in love supreme
     He comes our fallen souls to raise;
He comes his people to redeem
     With all his plenitude of grace.

3 The Christ, by raptured seers foretold,
     Filled with the eternal Spirit's power,
Prophet, and Priest, and King behold,
     And Lord of all the worlds adore.

4 The Lord of hosts, the God most high,
     Who quits his throne on earth to live,
With joy we welcome from the sky,
     With faith into our hearts receive.

Hymns on 4 Gospels, 1762

HYMNS

CHRIST'S RESURRECTION, ASCENSION

111   (716)   [204]

1 "Christ, the Lord is risen to-day,"
  Sons of men and angels say!
  Raise your joys and triumphs high:
  Sing, ye heavens; thou earth reply.

2 Love's redeeming work is done;
  Fought the fight, the battle won:
  Lo! the sun's eclipse is o'er,
  Lo! he sets in blood no more!

3 Vain the stone, the watch, the seal,
  Christ hath burst the gates of hell:
  Death in vain forbids his rise,
  Christ hath opened Paradise.

4 Lives again our glorious King!
  Where, O death, is now thy sting!
  Once he died our souls to save;
  Where's thy victory, boasting grave!

5 Soar we now where Christ hath led,
  Following our exalted Head:
  Made like him, like him we rise,
  Ours the cross, the grave, the skies.

6 King of glory! Soul of bliss!
  Everlasting life is this,
  Thee to know, thy power to prove,
  Thus to sing, and thus to love.

HSP I, 1739

112   (718)   [221]

1 Hail the day that sees him rise,
  Ravished from our wishful eyes!

CHARLES WESLEY

    Christ, awhile to mortals given,
    Re-ascends his native heaven.

2   There the pompous triumph waits:
    "Lift your heads, eternal gates;
    Wide unfold the radiant scene;
    Take the King of glory in!"

3† Circled round with angel powers,
    Their triumphant Lord, and ours,
    Conqueror over death and sin;
    "Take the King of glory in!"

4   Him though highest heaven receives,
    Still he loves the earth he leaves;
    Though returning to his throne,
    Still he calls mankind his own.

5   See, he lifts his hands above!
    See, he shows the prints of love!
    Hark, his gracious lips bestow
    Blessings on his Church below!

6† Still for us his death he pleads:
    Prevalent he intercedes;
    Near himself prepares our place,
    Harbinger of human race.

7† Master (will we ever say)
    Taken from our head today:
    See thy faithful servants, see,
    Ever gazing up to thee.

8   Grant, though parted from our sight,
    High above yon azure height,
    Grant our hearts may thither rise,
    Following thee beyond the skies.

9† Ever upward let us move,
    Wafted on the wings of love;

Looking when our Lord shall come,
Longing, gasping after home.

10† There we shall with thee remain,
Partners of thy endless reign;
There thy face unclouded see,
Find our heaven of heavens in thee.

HSP I, 1739

CHRIST'S KINGDOM

113   (745)   [787]

1   Lord of the harvest, hear
              Thy needy servants cry;
Answer our faith's effectual prayer,
              And all our wants supply.

2   On thee we humbly wait,
              Our wants are in thy view:
The harvest truly, Lord, is great,
              The laborers are few.

3   Convert, and send forth more
              Into thy Church abroad,
And let them speak thy word of power,
              As workers with their God.

4   Give the pure gospel word,
              The word of general grace;
Thee let them preach, the common Lord,
              Savior of human race.

5   Oh, let them spread thy name,
              Their mission fully prove,
Thy universal grace proclaim,
              Thy all-redeeming love.

6†   On all mankind forgiven
        Empower them still to call,
And tell each creature under heaven
        That thou hast died for all.

HSP II, 1742

114   (749)   [814]

1   Head of thy church, whose Spirit fills,
        And flows through every faithful soul
Unites in mystic love, and seals
        Them one, and sanctifies the whole;

2† Less than the least of saints, I join
        My littleness of faith to theirs;
O King of all, thine ear incline,
        Accept our much availing prayers.

3   Come, Lord, the glorious Spirit cries,
        And souls beneath the altar groan;
Come, Lord, the bride on earth replies,
        And perfect all our souls in one.

4   Pour out the promised gift on all,
        Answer the universal *Come*,
The fulness of the gentiles call,
        And take thine ancient people home.

5   To thee let all the nations flow,
        Let all obey the gospel word,
Let all their bleeding Savior know,
        Fill'd with the glory of the Lord.

6   Oh, for thy truth and mercy's sake,
        The purchase of thy passion claim,
Thine heritage the gentiles take,
        And cause the world to know thy name.

7† Thee, Lord, let every tongue confess,
  Let every knee to Jesus bow:
O all redeeming Prince of peace,
  We long to see thy kingdom now.

8† Hasten that kingdom of thy grace,
  And take us to our heavenly home,
And let us now behold thy face:
  Come, glorious God, to judgment come!

HSP II 1, 1749

HOLY SPIRIT

115   (754)   [275]

1 Jesus, we on the word depend,
  Spoken by thee while present here,
"The Father in my name shall send
  The Holy Ghost, the Comforter."

2 That promise made to Adam's race,
  Now, Lord, in us, even us, fulfill;
And give the Spirit of thy grace,
  To teach us all thy perfect will.

3 That heavenly Teacher of mankind,
  That Guide infallible impart,
To bring thy sayings to our mind,
  And write them on our faithful heart.

4 He only can the words apply
  Through which we endless life possess,
And deal to each his legacy,
  His Lord's unutterable peace.

5 That peace of God, that peace of thine,
  Oh, might he now to us bring in,

And fill our souls with power divine,
    And make an end of fear and sin;

6 The length and breadth of love reveal,
    The height and depth of Deity;
And all the sons of glory seal,
    And change, and make us all like thee!

Hymns for Whit Sunday, 1746

116   (758)   [277]

1 Granted is the Savior's prayer,
Sent the gracious Comforter;
Promise of our parting Lord,
Jesus now to heaven restored;

2 Christ, who now gone up on high
Captive leads captivity;
While his foes from him receive
Grace, that God with man may live.

3 God, the everlasting God,
Makes with mortals his abode;
Whom the heavens cannot contain,
He vouchsafes to dwell in man.

4 Never will he thence depart,
Inmate of a humble heart;
Carrying on his work within,
Striving till he casts out sin.

5 There he helps our feeble moans,
Deepens our imperfect groans,
Intercedes in silence there,
Sighs the unutterable prayer.

6 Come, divine and peaceful Guest,
Enter our devoted breast;

HYMNS

Life divine in us renew,
Thou the Gift, and Giver too!

HSP II, 1739

TUMULT

117   (859)   [426]

1 Ye servants of God,   Your Master proclaim,
   And publish abroad   His wonderful name:
   The name all-victorious   Of Jesus extol;
   His kingdom is glorious,   And rules over all.

2† The waves of the sea   Have lift up their voice,
   Sore troubled that we   In Jesus rejoice;
   The floods they are roaring,   But Jesus is here;
   While we are adoring   He always is near.

3† Men, devils engage,   The billows arise,
   And horribly rage,   And threaten the skies:
   Their fury shall never   Our steadfastness shock,
   The weakest believer   Is built on a Rock.

4 God ruleth on high,   Almighty to save,
   And still he is nigh,   His presence we have;
   The great congregation   His triumph shall sing,
   Ascribing salvation   To Jesus our King.

5 Salvation to God   Who sits on the throne!
   Let all cry aloud,   And honor the Son!
   Our Jesus' praises   The angels proclaim,
   Fall down on their faces,   And worship the Lamb.

6 Then let us adore,   And give Him his right,
   All glory, and power,   And wisdom, and might,
   All honor and blessing,   With angels above,
   And thanks never ceasing,   And infinite love.

Hymns in a Tumult, 1745

CHARLES WESLEY

INFANT BAPTISM

118   (893)   [—]

1 Jesus, in earth and heaven the same,
        Accept a parent's vow,
   To thee baptized into thy name,
        I bring my children now;
   Thy love permits, invites, commands,
        My offspring to be blessed;
   Lay on them, Lord, thy gracious hands,
        And hide them in thy breast.

2 To each the hallowing Spirit give
        Even from their infancy;
   Into thy holy church receive
        Whom I devote to thee;
   Committed to thy faithful care,
        Protected by thy blood,
   Preserve by thine unceasing prayer,
        And bring them all to God.

Hymns on 4 Gospels, 1762

FUNERALS

119   (53)   [—]

1 Glory be to God on high,
   God in whom we live and die,
   God, who guides us by his love,
   Takes us to his throne above!
   Angels that surround his throne
   Sing the wonders he hath done,
   Shout, while we on earth reply,
   Glory be to God on high!

2 God of everlasting grace,
   Worthy thou of endless praise,

Thou hast all thy blessings shed
On the living and the dead:
Thou wast here their sure defense,
Thou hast borne their spirits hence,
Worthy thou of endless praise,
God of everlasting grace.

3　Thanks be all ascribed to thee,
Blessing, power, and majesty,
Thee, by whose almighty name
They their latest foe o'ercame;
Thou the victory hast won,
Saved them by thy grace alone,
Caught them up thy face to see,
Thanks be all ascribed to thee!

4　Happy in thy glorious love,
We shall from the vale remove,
Glad partakers of our hope,
We shall soon be taken up;
Meet again our heavenly friends,
Blest with bliss that never ends,
Joined to all thy hosts above,
Happy in thy glorious love!

Redemption H, 1747

MORNING HYMN

120　(963)　[924]

1　Christ, whose glory fills the skies,
　　Christ, the true, the only Light,
Sun of righteousness, arise,
　　Triumph o'er the shades of night;
Day-spring from on high, be near;
Day-star, in my heart appear!

2   Dark and cheerless is the morn,
       Unaccompanied by thee:
Joyless is the day's return,
       Till thy mercy's beams I see:
Till thou inward light impart,
Glad my eyes, and warm my heart.

3   Visit then this soul of mine,
       Pierce the gloom of sin and grief;
Fill me, Radiancy Divine!
       Scatter all my unbelief:
More and more thyself display,
Shining to the perfect day!

HSP I, 1740

GOD'S UNIVERSAL LOVE

Part I
121   (39)   [75]

1   Father, whose everlasting love
       Thy only Son for sinners gave,
Whose grace to all did freely move,
       And sent him down a world to save;

2   Help us thy mercy to extol,
       Immense, unfathom'd, unconfined;
To praise the Lamb who died for all,
       The general Savior of mankind.

3   Thy undistinguishing regard
       Was cast on Adam's fallen race;
For all thou hast in Christ prepared
       Sufficient, sovereign, saving grace.

4†   Jesus hath said, we all shall hope,
       Preventing grace for all is free:

"And I, if I be lifted up,
    I will draw all men unto Me."

5† What soul those drawings never knew?
    With whom hath not thy Spirit strove?
We all must own that God is true,
    We all may feel that God is love.

6† O all ye ends of earth, behold
    The bleeding, all-atoning Lamb!
Look unto him for sinners sold,
    Look and be saved through Jesu's name.

7† Behold the Lamb of God, who takes
    The sins of all the world away!
His pity no exception makes;
    But all that will receive him, may.

8 A world he suffer'd to redeem;
    For all he hath th' atonement made:
For those that will not come to him
    The ransom of his life was paid.

Hymns on God's Everlasting Love, 1741

A PLAIN ACCOUNT
of
CHRISTIAN PERFECTION

1. WHAT I purpose in the following papers is to give a plain and distinct account of the steps by which I was led, during a course of many years, to embrace the doctrine of Christian Perfection. This I owe to the serious part of mankind, those who desire to know all *the truth as it is in Jesus.* And these are only concerned in questions of this kind. To these I would nakedly declare the thing as it is: endeavoring all along to show from one period to another, both *what I thought and why I thought so.*

2. In the year 1725, being in the twenty-third year of my age, I met with Bishop Taylor's *Rule and Exercises of Holy Living and Dying.* In reading several parts of this book, I was exceedingly affected, that part in particular which relates to *purity of intention.* Instantly I resolved to dedicate *all my life* to God, *all* my thoughts, and words, and actions, being thoroughly convinced, there was no medium; but that *every part* of my life (not *some* only) must either be a sacrifice to God, or myself, that is, in effect, to the devil.

Can any serious person doubt of this or find a medium between serving God and serving the devil?

3. In the year 1726, I met with Kempis's *Christian's Pattern.* The nature and extent of *Inward Religion,* the religion of the heart, now appeared to me in a stronger light than ever it had done before. I saw that giving even *all my life* to God (supposing it possible to do this, and go no farther) would profit me nothing, unless I *gave my heart,* yea *all my heart,* to him. I saw that "simplicity of intention, and purity of affection," *one design* in all we speak or do, and *one desire* ruling all our tempers, are indeed "the wings of the soul," without which she can never ascend to the mount of God.

4. A year or two after, Mr. Law's *Christian Perfection* and *Serious Call* were put into my hands. These convinced me more than ever of the absolute impossibility of being *half a Christian.* And I determined thro' his grace (the absolute necessity of which I was deeply sensible of) to be *all-devoted* to God, to give him *all* my soul, my body, and my substance.

Will any considerate man say that this is carrying matters *too far?* or that anything *less* is due to him who has given himself for us, than to give him ourselves; *all* we have, and *all* we are?

5. In the year 1729, I began not only to read, but to *study* the Bible, as the one, the only standard of truth, and the only model of pure religion. Hence I saw, in a clearer and clearer light, the indispensable necessity of having *the mind which was in Christ,* and of *walking as*

Christ also walked, even of having, not *some part* only, but all the mind which was in him; and of walking as he walked, not only in *many* or in *most* respects, but in *all* things. And this was the light, wherein at this time I generally considered religion, as a *uniform* following of Christ, an *entire* inward and outward conformity to our master. Nor was I afraid of anything more than of *bending* this rule to the experience of myself, or of other men, of allowing myself in any *the least* disconformity to our grand Exemplar.

6. On January 1, 1733, I preached before the University, in St. Mary's Church, on *the circumcision of the heart,* an account of which I gave in those words: "It is that habitual disposition of soul, which in the sacred writings is termed holiness, and which directly implies the being cleansed from sin, from all filthiness both of flesh and spirit, and by consequence, the being endued with those virtues which were in Christ Jesus; the being so *renewed in the image of our mind* as to be *perfect as our Father in heaven is perfect."*

In the same sermon I observed: *"Love is the fulfilling of the law, the end of the commandment.* It is not only the first and great command, but all the commandments in one. *Whatsoever things are just, whatsoever things are pure, if there be any virtue, if there be any praise,* they are all comprised in this one word, love. In this is perfection, and glory, and happiness. The royal law of heaven and earth is this: *Thou shalt love the Lord thy God with all thy heart, and with all thy soul, and with all thy mind, and with all thy strength.* The one perfect good shall be your one ultimate end. One thing shall ye desire for its own sake, the fruition of him who is all in all. One happiness shall ye propose to your souls, even a union with him that made them; the having *fellowship with the Father and the Son;* the being *joined to the Lord in one spirit.* One design you are to pursue to the end of time, the enjoyment of God in time and in eternity. Desire other things so far as they tend to this: love the creature, as it leads to the Creator. But in *every step* you take, be this the glorious point that terminates your view. Let every affection, and thought, and word, and action, be subordinate to this. Whatever you desire or fear, whatever you seek or shun, whatever you think, speak, or do, be it in order to your happiness in God, the sole end, as well as source, of your being."

I concluded in these words: "Here is the sum of *the perfect law,* the circumcision of the Heart. Let the spirit return to God that gave it, with the whole train of its affections. Other Sacrifices from us he would not, but the living sacrifice of the heart has he chosen. Let it be *continually* offered up to God, through Christ, in flames of holy love. And let no creature be suffered to share with him, for he is a jealous God. His throne will he not divide with another: he will reign without a rival. Be no design, no desire admitted there, but what has him for its ultimate object. This is the way wherein those children of God once walked, who being dead still speak to us, 'Desire not to live but to praise his name: let *all* your thoughts, words, and works tend to his glory.' 'Let your Soul be filled with so entire a love to him that you may love nothing but for his sake.' 'Have a *pure intention* of heart, a steadfast regard to his glory in all your actions.' For then, and not 'till then, is that mind in us which was also in Christ Jesus, when in *every* motion of our heart, in *every* word of our tongue, in *every* work of our hands, we 'pursue nothing but in relation to him, and in subordination to his pleasure'; When we too neither think, nor speak, nor act, to fulfill *our own will, but the will of him that sent us;* When, *whether* we *eat or drink, or whatever* we *do,* we *do it all to the glory of God."*

It may be observed, this sermon was composed the first of all my writings which have been published. This was the view of religion I then had, which even then I scrupled not to term *perfection.* This is the view I have of it now, without any material addition or diminution. And what is there here, which any man of understanding, who believes the Bible, can object to? What can he deny, without flatly contradicting the scripture? what retrench, without taking from the word of God?

7. In the same sentiment did my brother and I remain (with all those young gentlemen in derision termed *Methodists*) 'till we embarked for America, in the latter end of 1735. It was the next year, while I was at Savannah, that I wrote the following lines:

Is there a thing beneath the sun
    That strives with thee my heart to share?
Ah tear it thence, and *reign alone,*
    The Lord of *every motion* there!

In the beginning of the year 1738, as I was returning from thence, the cry of my heart was

O grant that nothing in my soul
    May dwell, but thy *pure love alone!*

301

O may thy love *possess me whole,*
    My joy, my treasure, and my crown;
Strange fires far from my heart remove:
My *every act, word, thought, be love!*

I never heard that any one objected to this. And indeed who can object? Is not this the language, not only of every believer, but of every one that is truly awakened? But what have I written to this day, which is either stronger or plainer?

8. In August following, I had a long conversation with Arvin Gradin, in Germany. After he had given me an account of his experience, I desired him to give me, in writing, a definition of *the full assurance of faith,* which he did in the following words:

Requies in sanguine Christi; firma fiducia in Deum et persuasio de gratia divina; tranquillitas mentis summa atque serenitas et pax; cum absentia omnis desiderii carnalis, et cessatione peccatorum etiam internorum.

"Repose in the blood of Christ; a firm confidence in God and persuasion of his favor; the highest tranquillity, serenity, and peace of mind; with a deliverance from *every fleshly desire,* and a *cessation of all, even inward, sins.*"

This was the first account I ever heard from any living man, of what I had before learned myself from the oracles of God, and had been praying for (with the little company of my friends) and expecting for several years.

9. In 1739 my brother and I published the volume *Hymns and Sacred Poems.* In many of these we declared our sentiments strongly and explicitly.

Turn the full stream of nature's tide:
    Let *all* our actions tend
To thee, their source: thy love the guide,
    Thy glory be the end.
Earth then a scale to heaven shall be:
    Sense shall point out the road:
The creatures *all* shall lead to thee,
    And all we taste be God.

CHRISTIAN PERFECTION

Again:

> Lord, arm me with thy Spirit's might,
>   Since I am call'd by thy great name:
> In thee my wandering thoughts unite,
>   Of *all* my works be thou the aim:
> Thy love attend me all my days,
> And my *sole business* be thy praise.

Again:

> Eager for thee I ask and pant,
>   So strong the principle divine,
> Carries me out with sweet constraint,
>   'Till *all my hallow'd soul* be thine;
> Plung'd in the Godhead's deepest sea,
> And lost in thine immensity!

Once more:

> Heavenly Adam, life divine,
> Change my nature into thine:
> Move and spread throughout my soul,
> *Actuate* and *fill the whole.*

It would be easy to cite many more passages to the same effect. But these are sufficient to show beyond contradiction what our sentiments then were.

10. The first tract I ever wrote expressly on this subject was published in the latter end of this year. That none might be prejudiced before they read it, I gave it the indifferent title of *The Character of a Methodist.* In this I described *a perfect Christian,* placing in the front, *Not as tho' I had already attained.* Part of it I subjoin, without any alteration:

"A *Methodist* is one who loves the Lord his God with all his heart, with all his soul, with all his mind, and with all his strength. God is the joy of his heart and the desire of his soul which is continually crying out, *Whom have I in Heaven but you; and there is none upon earth whom I desire besides you. My God and my all! You are the strength of my heart, and my portion forever.* He is therefore happy in God, yea always

303

happy, as having in him a well of water springing up into everlasting life, and overflowing his soul with peace and joy. *Perfect love* having now *cast out fear*, he *rejoices evermore*. Yea, his joy is full, and all his bones cry out, *Blessed be the God and Father of our Lord Jesus Christ, who according to his abundant mercy has begotten me again unto a living hope of an inheritance incorruptible and undefiled, reserved in heaven for me*.

"And he who has this *hope*, thus *full of immortality, in everything gives thanks;* as knowing *this* (whatsoever it is) *is the will of God in Christ Jesus concerning him.* From him, therefore he cheerfully receives all, saying: *Good is the will of the Lord;* and whether he gives or takes away, equally *blessing the name of the Lord.* Whether in ease or pain, whether in sickness or health, whether in life or death, he *gives thanks* from the ground of the heart, to him who orders it for good; into whose hands he has wholly committed his body and soul, *as into the hands of a faithful Creator.* He is therefore anxiously *careful for nothing*, as having *cast all his care on him that cares for him;* and *in all things* resting on him, after *making* his *request known to him with thanksgiving.*

"For indeed he *prays without ceasing;* at all times the language of his heart is this: *Unto you is my mouth, though without a voice; and my silence speaks unto you.* His heart is lifted up to God at all times, and in all places. In this he is never hindered, much less interrupted, by any person or thing. In retirement or company, in leisure, business, or conversation, his heart is ever with the Lord. Whether he lie down or rise up, *God is in all his thoughts;* He *walks with God* continually; having the loving eye of his soul fixed on him, and everywhere *seeing him that is invisible.*

"And loving God, he *loves his neighbor as himself;* he loves every man as his own soul. He loves his enemies, yea, and the enemies of God. And if it be not in his power to *do good to them that hate him*, yet he ceases not to *pray for them*, tho' they spurn his love, and still *despitefully use him and persecute him.*

"For he is *pure in heart.* Love has purified his heart from envy, malice, wrath, and every unkind temper. It has cleansed him from pride, whereof *only comes contention;* and he has now *put on bowels of mercies, kindness, humbleness of mind, meekness, long-suffering.* And indeed all possible ground for contention on his part is cut off. For none can take from him what he desires: Seeing he *loves not the world, nor* any of *the things of the world;* but *all* his *desire is unto God, and to the remembrance of his name.*

"Agreeable to this his one desire is the one design of his life, namely, *to do not his own will, but the will of him that sent him.* His one intention at all times and in all places is not to please himself, but him whom his soul loves. He has a single eye. And because his *eye is single, his whole body is full of light. The whole is light, as when the bright shining of a candle does enlighten the house.* God reigns alone; all that is in the soul is *holiness to the Lord.* There is not a motion in his heart but is according to his will. Every thought that arises points to him, and is *in obedience to the law of Christ.*

"And the *tree is known by its fruits.* For as he loves God, so he *keeps his commandments:* Not only *some,* or *most* of them, but ALL, from the least to the greatest. He is not content to *keep the whole law, and offend in one point,* but has in all points a *conscience void of offense, toward God, and toward man.* Whatever God has forbidden he avoids, whatever God has enjoined he does. He *runs the way of God's commandments,* now he has *set* his *heart at liberty.* It is his glory and joy so to do: It is his daily crown of rejoicing, to *do the will of* God *on earth as it is done in heaven.*

"All the commandments of God he accordingly keeps, and that with all his might. For his obedience is in proportion to his love, the source from whence it flows. And therefore loving God with all his heart, he serves him with all his strength. He continually *presents* his soul and *body a living sacrifice, holy, acceptable to God:* Entirely and without reserve, devoting himself, all he has, all he is, to his glory. All the talents he has, he constantly employs according to his master's will; every power and faculty of his soul, every member of his body.

"By consequence, *whatsoever he does, it is all to the glory of God.* In all his employments of every kind, he not only *aims* at this (which is implied in having a single eye), but actually *attains* it. His business and his refreshments, as well as his prayers, all serve to this great end. Whether he *sit in the house, or walk by the way,* whether he lie down or rise up, he is promoting in all he speaks, or does, the one business of his life. Whether he put on his apparel, or labor, or eat and drink, or divert himself from too wasting labor, it all tends to advance the glory of God, by peace and goodwill among men. His one invariable rule is this: *Whatsoever you do in word or deed, do it all in the name of the Lord Jesus, giving thanks to God even the Father through him.*

"Nor do the customs of the world at all hinder his *running the race which is set before him.* He cannot, therefore, *lay up treasures upon earth,* no more than he can take fire into his bosom. He cannot *speak evil* of his neighbor, any more than he can lie either for God or man. He cannot utter an unkind word of anyone, for love keeps the door of his lips. He cannot *speak idle words; no corrupt conversation* ever *comes out of his mouth,* as is all that is not *good to the use of edifying,* not fit to *minister grace to the hearers.* But *whatsoever things are pure, whatsoever things are lovely, whatsoever things* are justly *of good report,* he thinks, speaks, and acts, *adorning the doctrine of God our Savior in all things."*

These are the very words wherein I largely declared, for the first time, my sentiments of Christian Perfection. And is it not easy to see: That this is the very point at which I aimed all along from the year 1725; and more determinately from the year 1730, when I began to be *homo unius libri,* a man of one book, regarding none, comparatively, but the Bible? Is it not easy to see: That this is the very same doctrine which I believe and teach at this day; not adding one point either to that inward or outward holiness, which I maintained eight and thirty years ago? And it is the same which by the grace of God I have continued to teach from that time 'till now; as will appear to every impartial person, from the extracts subjoined below.

11. I do not know that any writer has made any objection against that tract, to this day. And for some time I did not find much opposition upon the head; at least, not from serious persons. But after a time a cry arose, and (what a little surprised me) among religious men, who affirmed, not that I stated perfection wrong, but that "there is no perfection on earth." Nay, and fell vehemently on my brother and me for affirming the contrary. We scarce expected so rough an attack from these; especially as we were clear on justification by faith, and careful to ascribe the whole of salvation to the mere grace of God. But what most surprised us was that we were said to "dishonor Christ," by asserting that he *saves to the uttermost;* by maintaining he will reign in our hearts *alone,* and subdue *all things* to himself.

12. I think it was in the latter end of the year 1740 that I had a conversation with Dr. Gibson, then Bishop of London, at Whitehall. He asked me what I meant by *Perfection?* I told him without any disguise or reserve. When I ceased speaking, he said, "Mr. Wesley, if this be all you mean, publish it to all the world. If anyone then can confute what you say, he may have free leave." I answered, "My Lord, I will," and accordingly wrote and published the sermon *Christian Perfection.*

In this I endeavored to show, (A) In what sense Christians *are not,* (B) in what sense they *are perfect.*

CHRISTIAN PERFECTION

A. In what sense they are not: They *are not perfect* in *knowledge.* They are not free from *ignorance;* no, nor from *mistake.* We are no more to expect any living man to be *infallible* than to be omniscient. They are not free from *infirmities,* such as weakness or slowness of understanding, irregular quickness or heaviness of imagination. Such in another kind are impropriety of language, ungracefulness of pronunciation, to which one might add a thousand nameless defects, either in conversation or in behavior. From such infirmities as these none are perfectly freed 'till their spirits return to God. Neither can we expect, 'till then, to be wholly freed from *temptation:* for *the servant is not above his master.* But neither in this sense is there any *absolute perfection* on earth. There is no *perfection of degrees;* none which does not admit of a continual increase.

B. In what sense then are they *perfect?* Observe, we are not now speaking of babes in Christ, but adult Christians. But even babes in Christ are so far perfect as not to *commit sin.* This Saint John affirms expressly, and it cannot be disproved by the examples of the Old Testament. For what if the holiest of the ancient Jews did *sometimes commit sin?* We cannot infer from hence that "all Christians do and must commit sin as long as they live."

But does not the scripture say: *A just man* sins seven *times a day?* It does not. Indeed it says: *A just man falls seven times.* But this is quite another thing. For, first, the words *a day* are not in the text. Secondly, here is no mention of *falling into sin* at all. What is here mentioned is *falling into temporal affliction.*

But elsewhere Solomon says, *There is no man that sins not.* Doubtless thus it was in the days of Solomon; yea, "and from Solomon to Christ there was *then* no man that sinned not." But whatever was the case of those under the law, we may safely affirm with Saint John, that since the Gospel was given, *he that is born of God sins not.*

The privileges of *Christians* are in no wise to be measured by what the Old Testament records concerning those who were under the *Jewish* dispensation; seeing *the fulness of time* is now *come, the Holy Ghost is* now *given,* the great *salvation* of God is now *brought* to men *by the revelation of Jesus Christ.* The kingdom of heaven is now set up on earth, concerning which the spirit of God declared of old time (so far is David from being the pattern or standard of Christian Perfection), *He that is feeble among them at that day shall be as David, and the house of David shall be as the angel of the Lord before them* (Zech. 12:8).

But the Apostles themselves committed sin—Peter by *dissembling,*

Paul by his *sharp contention* with Barnabas. Suppose they did, will you argue thus: If two of the Apostles once committed sin, then *all other Christians* in *all ages* do and must commit sin *as long as they live?* Nay, God forbid we should thus speak. No necessity of sin was laid upon *them;* the grace of God was surely sufficient for them. And it is sufficient for *us* at this day.

But Saint James says, *In many things we offend all.* True: but who are the persons here spoken of? Why, those *many masters* or teachers whom God had not sent. Not the Apostle himself, nor any real Christian. That in the word *we* (used by a figure of speech, common in all other, as well as the inspired writings) the Apostle could not possibly include himself, or any other true believer, appears, first, from the ninth verse: *Therewith bless we God, and therewith curse we men.* Surely not *we apostles!* Not *we believers!* Secondly, from the words preceding the text: *My brethren, be not many masters,* or *teachers, knowing that* we *shall receive the greater condemnation: for in many things we offend all. We!* Who? Not the apostles, nor true believers, but they who were to *receive the greater condemnation,* because of those many offenses. Nay, thirdly, the verse itself proves that *we offend all* cannot be spoken either of all men, or all Christians. For in it immediately follows the mention of a man *who offends not,* as the *we* first mentioned did: from whom, therefore, he is professedly contradistinguished, and pronounced a *perfect man.*

But Saint John himself says, *If we say that we have no sin, we deceive ourselves;* and, *if we say we have not sinned, we make him a liar, and his word is not in us.*

I answer, (a) The tenth verse fixes the sense of the eighth. *If we* say *we have no sin* in the former, being explained by *If we say we have not sinned,* in the latter verse: (b) The point under consideration is not whether we have or have not sinned heretofore; and neither of these verses asserts that we do sin or commit sin *now.* (c) The ninth verse explains both the eighth and tenth. *If we confess our sins, he is faithful and just, to forgive us our sins, and to cleanse us from all unrighteousness.* As if he had said, I have before affirmed, *The blood of Christ cleanses from all sin.* And no man can say, I need it not; I have no sin to be cleansed from. *If we say we have no sin,* that *we have not sinned, we deceive ourselves,* and *make* God a liar. But *if we confess our sins, he is faithful and just,* not only *to forgive us our sins,* but also to *cleanse us from all unrighteousness,* that we may *go and sin no more.* In conformity therefore both to the doctrine of Saint John, and the whole tenor of the

New Testament, we fix this conclusion: A Christian is so far perfect as not to commit sin.

This is the glorious privilege of every Christian, yea, tho' he be but a babe in Christ. But it is only of grown Christians it can be affirmed they are in such a sense perfect, as secondly, to be freed from evil thoughts and evil tempers. First, from evil or sinful thoughts. Indeed, whence should they spring? *Out of the heart of man*, if at all, *proceed evil thoughts.* If therefore, the heart be no longer evil, then evil thoughts no longer proceed out of it. For, *a good tree cannot bring forth evil fruit.*

And as they are freed from evil thoughts, so likewise from evil tempers. Every one of these can say with Saint Paul, *I am crucified with Christ: nevertheless I live: yet not I, but Christ lives in me:* words that manifestly describe a deliverance from inward as well as from outward sin. This is expressed both negatively, *I live not*—my evil nature, the body of sin is destroyed; and positively, *Christ lives in me*, and therefore all that is holy, and just, and good. Indeed both these, *Christ lives in me*, and *I live not*, are inseparably connected. For what communion has light with darkness, or Christ with Belial?

He, therefore, who lives in these Christians has *purified their hearts by faith:* Insomuch that *every one* that has Christ in him, *the hope of glory, purifies himself even as he is pure.* He is purified from pride: for Christ was lowly in heart. He is pure from desire and self-will: for Christ desired only to do the will of his Father. And he is pure from anger, in the common sense of the word: for Christ was meek and gentle. I say, in the common sense of the word, for he is *angry* at sin while he is grieved for the sinner. He feels a displeasure[1] at every offense against God, but only tender compassion to the offender.

Thus does Jesus save his people from their sins, not only from outward sins, but from the sins of their hearts. "True," say some, "but not 'till death, not in this world." Nay, Saint John says: *Herein is our love made perfect, that we may have boldness in the day of judgment; because, as he is, so are we in this world.* The Apostle here, beyond all contradiction, speaks of himself and other living Christians, of whom he flatly affirms that not only at or after death, but *in this world* they are as their Master.

Exactly agreeable to this are his words in the first chapter: *God is light, and in him is no darkness at all. If we walk in the light, as he is*

---

[1]"Displacency" in the original text.

in the light, we have fellowship one with another, and the blood of Jesus Christ his Son cleanses us from all sin. And again: *If we confess our sins, he is faithful and just to forgive us our sins, and to cleanse us from all unrighteousness.* Now, it is evident, the Apostle here speaks of deliverance wrought *in this world.* For he says not, the blood of Christ *will cleanse* (at the hour of death, or in the day of judgment), but it *cleanses,* at the time present, *us* living Christians, *from all sin.* And it is equally evident that if *any* sin remain, we are not cleansed from *all* sins. If any unrighteousness remain in the soul, it is not cleansed from *all* unrighteousness. Neither let any say that this relates to justification only, or the cleansing us from the guilt of sin: first, because this is confounding together what the Apostle clearly distinguishes, who mentions first, *to forgive us our sins,* and then, *to cleanse us from all unrighteousness;* secondly, because this is asserting justification by works in the strongest sense possible: It is making all inward, as well as all outward holiness, necessarily previous to justification. For if the cleansing here spoken of is no other than the cleansing us from the guilt of sin, then we are not cleansed from guilt, that is, not justified, unless on condition of *walking in the light as he is in the light.* It remains, then, that Christians are saved *in this world* from all sin, from *all unrighteousness;* that they are now in such a sense perfect as *not to commit sin,* and to be freed from evil thoughts and evil tempers.

It could not be but that a discourse of this kind, which directly contradicted the favorite opinion of many who were esteemed by others, and possibly esteemed themselves, some of the best of Christians (whereas if these things were so, they were not Christians at all) should give no small offense. Many answers or animadversions therefore were expected, but I was agreeably disappointed. I do not know that any appeared, so I went quietly on my way.

13. Not long after, I think in the spring, 1741, we published a second volume of hymns. As the doctrine was still much misunderstood, and consequently misrepresented, I judged it needful to explain yet farther upon the head; which was done in the preface to it as follows:

"This great gift of God, the salvation of our souls, is no other than the image of God fresh stamped on our hearts. It is a *renewal in the spirit of our minds, after the likeness of him that created them.* God has now laid *the axe unto the root of the tree, purifying their hearts by faith,* and 'cleansing all the thoughts of their hearts by the inspiration of his Holy Spirit.' Having this hope, that they shall see God as he is, they *purify themselves even as he is pure;* and are *holy, as he that has called them is holy, in all manner of conversation. Not that they have already attained* all that they shall attain, *either are already* (in this sense) *perfect.* But they daily *go on from strength to strength; beholding* now, *as in a glass, the glory of the Lord, they are changed into the same image, from glory to glory, by the spirit of the Lord.*

"And *where the spirit of the Lord is, there is liberty;* such liberty *from the law of sin and death* as the children of this world will not believe, tho' a man declare it unto them. *The Son has made them free* who are thus *born of God,* from that great root of sin and bitterness, *Pride.* They feel that *all* their *sufficiency is of God;* that it is he alone who *is in all their thoughts* and *works in them both to will and to do of his good pleasure.* They feel that *it is not* they *that speak, but the Spirit of* their Father *who speaks* in them; and that whatsoever is done by their hands, *the Father who is in them, he does the works.* So that God is to them all in all, and they are as nothing in his sight. They are freed from *self-will,* as desiring nothing but the holy and perfect will of God: not supplies in want, not ease in pain, nor life, or death, or any creature, but continually crying in their inmost soul, *Father, thy will be done.* They are freed from *evil thoughts* so that they cannot enter into them, no not for a moment. Aforetime when an evil thought came in, they looked up and it vanished away. But now it does not come in, there being no room for this in a soul which is full of God. They are freed from wanderings in prayer. Whensoever they pour out their hearts in a more immediate manner before God, they have *no thought* of anything past, or absent, or to come but of God alone. In times past they had wandering thoughts dart in, which yet fled away like smoke; but now that smoke does not rise at all. They have no *fear* or *doubt,* either as to their state in general, or as to any particular action. The *unction from the Holy One* teaches them every hour what they shall do, and what they shall speak. Nor therefore have they any need to *reason* concerning it. They are *in one sense* freed from temptations, for tho' numberless temptations *fly about them,* yet they trouble them not. At all times their soul is even and calm, their heart is steadfast and unmovable. Their peace, flowing as a river, *passes all understanding,* and they *rejoice with joy unspeakable and full of glory.* For they *are sealed by the Spirit unto the day of redemption,* having the witness in themselves, that *there is laid up for them a crown of righteousness, which the Lord will give* them *in that day.*

"Not that every one is a child of the devil, 'till he is thus renewed

in love. On the contrary, whoever has *a sure confidence in God that,
through the merits of Christ, his sins are forgiven,* he is a child of God, and
if he abide in him, an heir of all the promises. Neither ought he in
any wise to *cast away* his *confidence,* or to deny the faith he has received, because it is weak, or because it is *tried with fire,* so that his
soul is *in heaviness through manifold temptations.*

"Neither dare we affirm, as some have done, that *all this salvation*
is given *at once.* There is indeed an *instantaneous* (as well as a *gradual*)
work of God in his children; and there wants not, we know, a cloud
of witnesses who have received, in one moment, either a clear sense
of the forgiveness of their sins, or the abiding witness of the Holy
Spirit. But we do not know a single instance, in any place, of a person's receiving *in one and the same moment* remission of sins, the abiding witness of the Spirit, and a new, a clean heart.

"Indeed, how God *may* work, we cannot tell: but the general
manner wherein he *does* work is this: Those who once trusted in
themselves, that they were righteous, that they were *rich, and increased
in goods, and had need of nothing,* are by the Spirit of God applying his
word convinced that they are poor and naked. All the things that they
have done are brought to their remembrance, and set in array before
them, so that they see the wrath of God hanging over their heads, and
feel that they deserve the damnation of hell. In their trouble they cry
unto the Lord, and he shows them that he has taken away their sins,
and opens the kingdom of heaven in their hearts, *righteousness, and
peace and joy in the Holy Ghost.* Sorrow and pain are fled away, and *sin
has no more dominion over* them. Knowing they are *justified freely*
through faith in his blood, they *have peace with God through Jesus Christ;*
they *rejoice in hope of the glory of God,* and *the love of God is shed abroad
in their hearts.*

"In this peace they remain for days, or weeks, or months, and
commonly suppose that they shall not know war any more; 'till some
of their old enemies, their bosom sins, or the sin which *did* most easily
beset them (perhaps anger or desire), assault them again, and thrust
sore at them that they may fall. Then arises fear that they should not
endure to the end, and often doubt whether God has not forgotten
them, or whether they did not deceive themselves in thinking their
sins were forgiven. Under these clouds, especially if they reason with
the devil, they go *mourning* all the day long. But it is seldom long before their Lord answers for himself, sending them the Holy Ghost to
comfort them, to bear witness continually with their spirits, that they

are the children of God. Then they are indeed *meek* and gentle and teachable, even as a little child. And now first do they see the ground of their heart, which God before would not disclose unto them, lest the soul should fail before him, and the spirit which he had made. Now they see all the hidden abominations there, the depths of pride, self-will, and hell; yet having the witness in themselves: thou art an heir of God, a joint-heir with Christ; even in the midst of this fiery trial, which continually heightens both the strong sense they then have of their inability to help themselves and the inexpressible *hunger* they feel *after* a full renewal in his image, in *righteousness and true holiness.* Then God is mindful of the desire of them that fear him, and gives them a single eye, and a pure heart. He stamps upon them his own image and superscription; he creates them anew in Christ Jesus; he comes unto them with his Son and Blessed Spirit, and fixing his abode in their souls, brings them into the *rest* which *remains for the people of God."*

Here I cannot but remark: (a) That this is the strongest account we ever gave of Christian Perfection; indeed, too strong in more than one particular; (b) that there is nothing which we have since advanced upon the subject, either in verse or prose, which is not either directly or indirectly contained in this preface. So that whether our present doctrine be right or wrong, it is, however, the same which we taught from the beginning.

14. I need not give additional proofs of this by multiplying quotations from the volume itself. It may suffice to cite part of one hymn only, the last in that volume:

Lord, I believe a rest remains
    To all thy people known,
A rest where *pure enjoyment* reigns,
    And thou art *lov'd alone:*

A rest where *all our* soul's *desire*
    Is fixed on things above:
Where doubt, and pain, and fear expire,
    Cast out by *perfect love.*

From *every evil motion* freed
    (The Son hath made us free),

313

JOHN WESLEY

On all the pow'rs of hell we tread
    In glorious liberty.

Safe in the way of life, above
    Death, earth and hell we rise:
We find, when *perfected in love,*
    Our long-sought Paradise.

Oh, that I now the rest might know,
    Believe, and enter in!
Now, Savior, *now* the power bestow,
    And let me cease from sin!

Remove this hardness from my heart,
    This *unbelief* remove;
To me the rest of *faith* impart,
    The sabbath of thy love.

Come, O my Savior, come away!
    Into my soul descend!
No longer from thy creature stay,
    My author and my End.

The bliss thou hast for me prepar'd
    No longer be delay'd:
Come, my exceeding great reward,
    For whom I first was made.

Come, Father, Son, and Holy Ghost,
    And seal me thine abode!
Let all I am in thee be lost:
    Let all be lost in God.

Can anything be more clear than: (a) that here also is as *full* and *high* a salvation as we have ever spoken of? (b) that this is spoken of as receivable by mere *faith,* and as hindered only by *unbelief?* (c) that this faith, and consequently the salvation which it brings, is spoken of as given *in an instant?* (d) that it is supposed that instant may be *now;* that we need not stay another moment; that *now,* the very *now, is the accepted time! Now is the day of* this full *salvation?* And, lastly, that if any speak otherwise, he is the person that brings *new* doctrine among us?

15. About a year after, namely in the year 1742, we published another volume of hymns. The dispute being now at the height, we spoke upon the head more largely than ever before. Accordingly an abundance of the hymns in this volume treat expressly on this subject. And so does the preface, which, as it is short, it may not be amiss to insert entire.

"(A) Perhaps the general prejudice against Christian Perfection may chiefly arise from a misapprehension of the nature of it. We willingly allow, and continually declare, there is *no such perfection* in this life as implies either a dispensation from doing good, and attending all the ordinances of God, or a freedom from ignorance, mistake, temptation, and a thousand infirmities necessarily connected with flesh and blood.

"(B) First, we not only allow, but earnestly contend, that there is no perfection in this life which implies any dispensation from attending all the ordinances of God, or from *doing good unto all men while we have time*, though *especially unto the household of faith*. We believe that not only the babes in Christ who have newly found redemption in his blood but those also who are *grown up into perfect men* are indispensably obliged, as often as they have opportunity, *to eat bread and drink wine in remembrance of him*, and to *search the Scriptures*; by *fasting*, as well as temperance, *to keep their bodies under, and bring them into subjection*; and above all, to pour out their souls in *prayer*, both secretly and in the great congregation.

"(C) We secondly believe that there is *no such perfection* in this life as implies an entire deliverance: either from ignorance or mistake, in things not essential to salvation; or from manifold temptations; or from numberless infirmities, wherewith the corruptible body more or less presses down the soul. We cannot find any ground in scripture to suppose that any inhabitant of a house of clay is wholly exempt, either from bodily infirmities, or from ignorance of many things; or to imagine any is incapable of mistake, or falling into divers temptations.

"(D) But whom then do you mean by *one that is perfect?* We mean one in whom *is the mind which was in Christ*, and who so *walks as Christ also walked*; a man *that has clean hands and a pure heart*, or that is *cleansed from all filthiness of flesh and spirit*; one in whom is *no occasion of stumbling*, and who accordingly *does not commit sin*. To declare this a little more particularly: We understand by that scriptural expression, *a perfect man*, one in whom God has fulfilled his faithful word, *from all your filthiness and from all your idols will I cleanse you. I will also save you from all your uncleannesses.* We understand hereby one whom God has *sanctified throughout, in body, soul, and spirit;* one who *walks in the light as he is in the light, in whom is no darkness at all: the blood of Jesus Christ his son having cleansed him from all sin.*

"(E) This man can now testify to all mankind, *I am crucified with Christ: nevertheless I live: yet not I, but Christ lives in me.* He is *holy as God who called* him *is holy,* both in heart and *in all manner of conversation.* He *loves the Lord his God with all his heart,* and serves him *with all his strength.* He *loves his neighbor,* every man, *as himself;* yea, *as Christ loves us;* them in particular that *despitefully use him, and persecute him, because they know not the Son, neither the Father.* Indeed his soul is all love, filled with *bowels of mercies, kindness, meekness, gentleness, long-suffering.* And his life agrees thereto, full of *the work of faith, the patience of hope, the labor of love. And whatsoever he does, either in word or deed, he does it all in the name,* in the love and power, *of the Lord Jesus.* In a word, he does *the will* of God *on earth, as it is done in heaven.*

"(F) This it is to be a perfect man, to be *sanctified throughout:* even 'to have a heart so all-flaming with the love of God (to use Archbishop Usher's words) as continually to offer up every thought, word, and work as a spiritual sacrifice, acceptable to God through Christ.' In every thought of our hearts, in every word of our tongues, in every work of our hands, *to show forth his praise, who has called us out of darkness into his marvelous light.* O that both we, and all who seek the Lord Jesus in sincerity, may thus *be made perfect in one!*"

This is the doctrine which we preached from the beginning, and which we preach this day. Indeed, by viewing it in every point of light, and comparing it again and again, with the word of God on the one hand, and the experience of the children of God on the other, we saw farther into the nature and properties of Christian Perfection. But still there is no contrariety at all between our first and our last sentiments. Our first conception of it was: It is to have *the mind which was in Christ,* and to *walk as he walked,* to have *all* the mind that was in him, and *always* to walk as he walked. In other words, to be inwardly and outwardly devoted to God, *all devoted* in heart and life. And we have the same conception of it now, without either addition or diminution.

CHRISTIAN PERFECTION

16. The hymns concerning it in this volume are too numerous to transcribe. I shall cite only a part of three.

Savior from sin, I wait to prove
    That Jesus is thy healing name:
To lose, when perfected in love,
    Whate'er I have, or can, or am:
I stay me on thy faithful word,
"The servant shall be as his Lord."

Answer that gracious end in me
    For which thy precious life was given:
Redeem from *all iniquity,*
    Restore and make me meet for heaven.
Unless thou purge my *every stain,*
Thy suffering and my faith is vain.

Didst thou not die that I might live
    No longer to myself, but thee?
Might body, soul, and spirit give
    To Him who gave himself for me?
Come then, my Master, and my God,
Take the dear purchase of thy blood.

Thy own peculiar servant claim,
    For thy own truth and mercy's sake:
Hallow in me thy glorious name:
    Me for thine own *this moment* take:
And change and *thoroughly purify:*
Thine only may I live and die.

Chose from the world if now I stand,
    Adorn'd with righteousness divine;
If, brought into the promis'd land
    I justly call the savior mine:
The sanctifying spirit pour
    To quench my thirst and wash me clean:
Now, Savior, let the gracious shower
    Descend, and make me *pure from sin.*

JOHN WESLEY

Purge me from *every sinful blot;*
 My idols all be cast aside:
Cleanse me from *ev'ry evil thought,*
 From *all* the filth of self and pride.
The hatred of the carnal mind
 Out of my flesh *at once* remove!
Give me a tender heart, resign'd,
 And pure, and full of faith and love.

O that I *now* from sin releas'd,
 Thy word might to the utmost prove:
Enter into thy promis'd rest!
 The *Canaan* of thy *perfect love!*
Now let me gain perfection's height!
 Now let me into nothing fall!
Be less than nothing in my sight,
 And feel that Christ is all in all.

Lord, I believe, thy work of grace
 Is perfect in the soul:
His heart is pure who sees thy face,
 His spirit is made whole.

From *every sickness* by thy word,
 From every foul disease
Sav'd, and to *perfect health* restored,
 To *perfect holiness.*

He walks in glorious liberty,
 To sin *entirely dead:*
The Truth, the Son hath made him free,
 And he is free indeed.

Throughout his soul thy glories shine,
 His soul is *all renew'd,*
And deck'd in righteousness divine,
 And clothed and *fill'd with God.*

This is the rest, the life, the peace,
 Which all thy people prove:

Love is the bond of perfectness,
    And *all* their soul is love.

O joyful sound of gospel-grace!
    Christ shall in me appear:
I, even I, shall see his face;
    I shall be holy *here!*

He visits now the house of clay:
    He shakes his future home,
O wouldst thou, Lord, on *this glad day*
    Into thy temple come!

Come, O my God, thyself reveal,
    Fill all this mighty void!
Thou only canst my spirit fill;
    Come, O my God, my God!

Fulfill, fulfill my large desires,
    Large as infinity!
Give, give me all my soul requires,
    All, all that is in thee!

17. On Monday, June 25, 1744, our first conference began, six clergymen and all our preachers being present. The next morning we seriously considered the doctrine of sanctification, or perfection. The questions asked concerning it and the substance of the answers given were as follows:

Q. What is it to be *sanctified?*
A. To be renewed in the image of God, *in righteousness and true holiness.*

Q. What is implied in being a *perfect Christian?*
A. The loving God with all our heart, and mind, and soul (Deut. 6:5).

Q. Does this imply that *all inward sin* is taken away?
A. Undoubtedly: or how can we be said to be *saved from all our uncleanness?* (Ezek. 36:29).

319

JOHN WESLEY

Our second conference began August 1, 1745. The next morning we spoke of sanctification, as follows:

Q. When does inward sanctification begin?
A. In the moment a man is justified. Yet sin remains in him; yea, the seed of all sin, 'till he is *sanctified throughout.* From that time a believer gradually dies to sin, and grows in grace.

Q. Is this ordinarily given 'till a little before death?
A. It is not, to those who expect it no sooner.

Q. But may we expect it sooner?
A. Why not? For although we grant: (1) that the generality of believers whom we have hitherto known were not so sanctified 'till near death; (2) that few of those to whom Saint Paul wrote his Epistles were so at that time; nor (3) he himself at the time of his writing his former Epistles; yet all this does not prove that we may not be so today.

Q. In what manner should we preach sanctification?
A. Scarce at all to those who are not pressing forward; to those who are, always by way of promise, always *drawing* rather than *driving.*

Our third conference began Tuesday, May 13, 1746.
In this we carefully read over the minutes of the two preceding conferences, to observe whether anything contained therein might be retrenched or altered on mature consideration. But we did not see cause to alter in any respect what we had agreed upon before.
Our fourth conference began on Tuesday, June 16, 1747. As several persons were present who did not believe the doctrine of perfection, we agreed to examine it from the foundation.
In order to do this, it was asked:

How much is allowed by our brethren who differ from us with regard to entire sanctification?
A. They grant: (1) that everyone must be entirely sanctified in the article of death; (2) that 'till then a believer daily grows in grace, comes nearer and nearer to perfection; (3) that we ought to be continually pressing after it, and to exhort all others so to do.

CHRISTIAN PERFECTION

Q. What do we allow them?

A. We grant: (1) that many of those who have died in the faith, yea the greater part of those we have known, were not *perfected in love,* 'till a little before their death; (2) that the term *sanctified* is continually applied by Saint Paul to all that were justified; (3) that by this term alone, he rarely, if ever, means "saved from all sin"; (4) that, consequently, it is not proper to use it in that sense, without adding the word *wholly, entirely,* or the like; (5) that the inspired writers almost continually speak of or to those who were justified, but very rarely of, or to, those who were wholly sanctified; (6) that, consequently, it behooves us to speak almost continually of the state of justification, but more rarely, "at least in full and explicit terms, concerning entire sanctification."

Q. What, then, is the point where we divide?

A. It is this: Should we expect to be saved from *all sin* before the article of death?

Q. Is there any clear scripture *promise* of this, that God will save us from *all sin?*

A. There is: *He shall redeem Israel from* all *his sins* (Ps. 130:8).

This is more largely expressed in the prophecy of Ezekiel: *Then will I sprinkle clean water upon you, and you shall be clean; from* all *your filthiness and from* all *your idols will I cleanse you. I will also save you from* all *your uncleannesses* (36:25, 29). No promise can be more clear. And to this the Apostle plainly refers in that exhortation: *Having these promises, let us cleanse ourselves from all filthiness of flesh and spirit, perfecting holiness in the fear of God* (2 Cor. 7:1). Equally clear and express is that ancient promise: *The Lord your God will circumcise your heart, and the heart of your seed, to love the Lord your God with all your heart and with all your soul* (Deut. 30:6).

Q. But does any *assertion* answerable to this occur in the New Testament?

A. There does, and that laid down in the plainest terms. So 1 John 3:8: *For this purpose, the Son of God was manifested, that he might destroy the works of the devil; the works of the devil,* without any limitation or restriction; but all sin is *the work of the devil.* Parallel to which is the assertion of Saint Paul, Ephesians 5:25–27: *Christ loved the church and gave himself for it that he might present it to himself a glorious church, not having spot or wrinkle, or any such thing, but that it might be holy and without blemish.*

And to the same effect is his assertion in the eighth chapter of Romans, verses 3, 4: *God sent his Son—that the righteousness of the law might be fulfilled in us, who walk not after the flesh, but after the spirit.*

Q. Does the New Testament afford any further ground for expecting to be saved from *all sin?*

A. Undoubtedly it does, both in those *prayers* and *commands* which are equivalent to the strongest assertions.

Q. What *prayers* do you mean?

A. Prayers for entire sanctification, which, were there no such thing, would be mere mockery of God. Such, in particular are: (1) *Deliver us from evil.* Now when this is done, when we are delivered from all evil, there can be no sin remaining. (2) *Neither pray I for these alone, but for them also who shall believe on me through their word: that they all may be one, as you, Father, are in me and I in you, that they also may be one in us: I in them, and you in me, that they may be made perfect in one* (John 17:20, 21, 23). (3) *I bow my knees unto the God and Father of our Lord Jesus Christ, that he would grant you that you being rooted and grounded in love, may be able to comprehend with all saints what is the breadth, and length, and depth, and height, and to know the love of Christ which passes knowledge. That you may be filled with all the fulness of God* (Eph. 3:14ff.). (4) *The very God of peace sanctify you wholly. And I pray God, your whole spirit, soul and body may be preserved blameless, unto the coming of our Lord Jesus Christ* (1 Thess. 5:23).

Q. What *command* is there to the same effect?

A. (1) *Be you perfect, as your Father who is in heaven is perfect* (Mt. 5:48). (2) *You shall love the Lord your God with all your heart, and with all your soul, and with all your mind* (Mt. 22:37). But if the love of God fill *all the heart*, there can be no sin there.

Q. But how does it appear that this is to be done before the article of death?

A. (1) From the very nature of a command, which is not given to the dead but to the living. Therefore, *you shall love God with all your heart* cannot mean, you shall do this when you die, but while you live. (2) From express texts of scripture. (a) *The grace of God that brings salvation has appeared to all men, teaching us, that having renounced ungodly and worldly lusts, we should live soberly, righteously, and godly in this present world: looking for the glorious appearing of our Lord Jesus Christ, who gave himself for us that he might redeem us from* all iniquity, *and purify unto himself a peculiar people, zealous of good works* (Tit. 2:11–14). (b) *He has raised up a horn of salvation for us to perform the mercy promised to our fathers; the oath which he swore to our father Abraham, that he would grant unto us, that we being delivered out of the hands of our enemies should serve him without fear, in holiness and righteousness before him, all the days of our life* (Luke 1:69ff.).

Q. Is there any *example* in scripture of persons who had attained to this?

A. Yes, Saint John, and all those of whom he says: *Herein is our love made perfect, that we may have boldness in the day of judgment, because as he is, so are we in this world* (1 John 4:17).

Q. Can you show one such example now? Where is he that is thus perfect?

A. To some that make this inquiry one might answer: If I knew one here, I would not tell *you,* for you do not inquire out of love. You are like Herod. You seek the young child only to slay it.

But more directly we answer. There are many reasons why there should be few, if any, *indisputable* examples. What inconveniences would this bring on the person himself, set as a mark for all to shoot at? And how unprofitable would it be to gainsayers! *For if they hear not Moses and the prophets,* Christ and his apostles, *neither would they be persuaded though one rose from the dead.*

Q. Are we not apt to have a secret distaste to any who say they are saved from all sin?

A. 'Tis very possible we may, and that upon several grounds: partly from a concern for the good of souls who may be hurt, if these are not what they profess; partly from a kind of explicit envy at those who speak of higher attainments than our own; and partly from our natural slowness and unreadiness of heart to believe the works of God.

JOHN WESLEY

Q. Why may we not continue in the joy of faith 'till we are *perfected in love?*

A. Why, indeed? Since holy grief does not quench this joy, since even while we are under the cross, while we deeply partake of the sufferings of Christ, we may rejoice with joy unspeakable.

From these extracts it undeniably appears, not only what was mine and my brother's judgment, but what was the judgment of all the preachers in connection with us, in the years 1744, 1745, 1746, and 1747. Nor do I remember that in any one of these conferences we had one dissenting voice; but whatever doubts anyone had when we met, they were all removed before we parted.

18. In the year 1749 my brother printed two volumes of *Hymns and Sacred Poems*. As I did not see these before they were published, there were some things in them which I did not approve of. But I quite approved of the main of the hymns on this head, a few verses of which are subjoined.

Come, Lord, be manifested here,
    And *all the devil's works* destroy!
Now, without sin in me appear,
    And fill with everlasting joy:
Thy beatific face display,
Thy presence is the perfect day!

Swift to my rescue come,
    Thy own *this moment* seize!
Gather my wandering spirit home,
    And keep in perfect peace.
Suffer'd no more to rove
    O'er all the earth abroad,
Arrest the prisoner of thy love,
    And shut me up in God.

Thy pris'ners release, vouchsafe us thy peace;
And our sorrows and sins *in a moment* shall cease,
That moment be now! Our petition allow,
Our *present* Redeemer and Comforter thou!

CHRISTIAN PERFECTION

From this inbred sin deliver:
Let the yoke Now be broke;
   Make me thine forever.

Partner of thy perfect nature,
Let me be Now in thee
   A new sinless creature.
Turn me, Lord, and turn me *now*,
To thy yoke my spirit bow:
Grant me now the pearl to find
Of a meek and quiet mind.
Calm, Oh, calm my troubled breast;
Let me gain that second rest:
From my works forever cease,
Perfected in holiness.

Come in *this* accepted *hour*,
   Bring thy heavenly kingdom in!
Fill us with the glorious power
   Rooting out the seeds of sin.

Come, thou dear Lamb, for sinners slain,
   Bring in the cleansing flood:
Apply, to wash out *every stain*,
   Thine efficacious blood.

Oh, let it sink into our soul
   Deep as the inbred sin:
Make every wounded spirit whole,
   And every leper clean!

   Pris'ners of hope arise
   And see your Lord appear!
Lo! on the wings of love he flies,
   And brings redemption near.
   Redemption in his blood
   He calls you to receive:
Come unto me, the pardoning God:
   Believe, he cries, believe!

Jesus, to thee we look,
   'Till sav'd from sin's remains,
Reject the inbred tyrant's yoke,
   And cast away his chains.
   Our nature shall no more
   O'er us dominion have:
By faith we apprehend the power
   Which shall for ever save.

Jesu, our life, in us appear,
   Who daily die thy death:
Reveal thyself the finisher:
   Thy quick'ning spirit breathe!
Unfold the hidden mystery!
   The second gift impart!
Reveal thy glorious self in me:
   In every waiting heart.

In him we have peace, In him we have power!
Preserv'd by his grace Throughout the dark hour;
In all our temptations He keeps us to prove
His utmost salvation, His fulness of love.
Pronounce the glad word, And bid us be free!
Ah, hast thou not, Lord, A blessing for me?
The peace thou hast given, *This moment* impart,
And open thy heaven, O Love, in my heart!

A second edition of these hymns was published in the year 1752, and that without any other alteration than that of a few literal mistakes.

I have been the more large in these extracts because hence it appears, beyond all possibility of exception, that to this day, both my brother and I maintained: (1) that Christian Perfection is that love of God and our neighbor which implies deliverance from *all sin;* (2) that this is received merely *by faith;* (3) that it is given *instantaneously,* in one moment; (4) that we are to expect it (not at death, but) *every moment:* that *now* is the accepted time, *now* is the day of this salvation.

19. At the conference in the year 1759, perceiving some danger

that a diversity of sentiments should insensibly steal in among us, we again largely considered this doctrine. And soon after I published *Thoughts on Christian Perfection*, prefaced with the following advertisement:

"The following tract is by no means designed to gratify the curiosity of any man. It is not intended to prove the doctrine at large, in opposition to those who explode and ridicule it; no, nor to answer the numerous objections against it, which may be raised even by serious men. All I intend here is simply to declare what are my sentiments on this head: what Christian Perfection does, according to my apprehension, include, and what it does not; and to add a few practical observations and directions relative to the subject."

As these thoughts were at first thrown together by way of question and answer, I let them continue in the same form. They are just the same that I have entertained for above twenty years.

Q. What is Christian Perfection?
A. The loving God with all our heart, mind, soul, and strength. This implies that no wrong temper, none contrary to love, remains in the soul; and that all the thoughts, words, and actions are governed by pure love.

Q. Do you affirm that this perfection excludes all infirmities, ignorance, and mistake?
A. I continually affirm quite the contrary, and always have done so.

Q. But how can every thought, word, and work be governed by pure love, and the man be subject at the same time to ignorance and mistake?
A. I see no contradiction here: "A man may be filled with pure love, and still be liable to mistake." Indeed I do not expect to be freed from actual mistakes 'till this mortal puts on immortality. I believe this to be a natural consequence of the soul's dwelling in flesh and blood. For we cannot now *think* at all, but by the mediation of those bodily organs which have suffered equally with the rest of our frame. And hence we cannot avoid sometimes *thinking wrong* 'till this corruptible shall have put on incorruption.

But we may carry this thought further yet. A mistake in judgment may possibly occasion a mistake in practice. For instance: Mr. de Renty's mistake touching the nature of mortification, arising from prejudice of education, occasioned that practical mistake, his wearing an iron girdle. And a thousand such instances there may be, even in those who are in the highest state of grace. Yet, where every word and action springs from love, such a mistake is not properly *a sin*. However, it cannot bear the rigor of God's justice, but needs the atoning blood.

Q. What was the judgment of all our brethren who met at Bristol in August 1758, on this head?

A. It was expressed in these words: (1) everyone may mistake as long as he lives; (2) a mistake in *opinion* may occasion a mistake in *practice;* (3) every such mistake is a transgression of the perfect law; (4) therefore, every such mistake, were it not for the blood of atonement, would expose to eternal damnation; (5) it follows that the most perfect have continual need of the merits of Christ, even for their actual transgressions, and may say, for themselves, as well as for their brethren: *Forgive us our trespasses.*

This easily accounts for what might otherwise seem to be utterly unaccountable, namely, that those who are not offended when we speak of the highest degree of love, yet will not hear of living *without sin*. The reason is, they know all men are liable to mistake, and that in practice as well as in judgment. But they do not know, or do not observe, that this is not sin, if love is the sole principle of action.

Q. But still if they live without sin, does not this exclude the necessity of a Mediator? At least is it not plain that they stand no longer in need of Christ in his priestly office?

A. Far from it. None feel their need of Christ like these; none so entirely depend upon him. For Christ does not give life to the soul separate from, but in and with himself. Hence his words are equally true of all men, in whatsoever state of grace they are: *As the branch cannot bear fruit of itself, except it abide in the vine, no more can you, except you abide in me; without* (or separate from) *me, you can do nothing.*

In every state we need Christ in the following respects: (1) whatever grace we receive, it is a free gift from him; (2) we receive it as his purchase, merely in consideration of the price he paid; (3) we have this grace not only *from* Christ, but *in* him. For our perfection is not like that of a tree, which flourishes by the sap derived from its own root, but, as was said before, like that of a branch, which united to the vine, bears fruit; but severed from it, *is dried up and withered;* (4) all our blessings, temporal, spiritual, and eternal, depend on his intercession for us, which is one branch of his priestly office, whereof therefore we have always equal need; (5) the best of men still need Christ, in his priestly office, to atone for their omissions, their shortcomings (as some not improperly speak), their mistakes in judgment and practice, and their defects of various kinds. For these are all deviations from the perfect law, and consequently need an atonement. Yet that they are not properly sins, we apprehend may appear from the words of Saint Paul: *He that loves has fulfilled the law; for love is the fulfilling of the law* (Rom. 13:10). Now mistakes, and whatever infirmities necessarily flow from the corruptible state of the body, are no way contrary to love; nor therefore, in the scripture sense, *sin.*

To explain myself a little further on this head: (a) not only *sin properly so called,* that is, a voluntary transgression of a known law, but sin, improperly so called, that is, an involuntary transgression of a divine law, known or unknown, needs the atoning blood. (b) I believe there is no such perfection in this life, as excludes these involuntary transgressions, which I apprehend to be naturally consequent on the ignorance and mistakes inseparable from mortality. (c) Therefore *sinless perfection* is a phrase I never use, lest I should *seem* to contradict myself. (d) I believe a person filled with the love of God is still liable to these involuntary transgressions. (e) Such transgressions you may call *sins,* if you please; I do not, for the reasons above mentioned.

Q. What advice would you give to those that do, and those that do not, call them so?

A. Let those that do not call them *sins* never think that themselves, or any other persons, are in such a state as that they can stand before infinite justice without a mediator. This must argue either the deepest ignorance, or the highest arrogance and presumption.

Let those who do call them so beware how they confound these *defects* with *sins,* properly so called. But how will they avoid it? How will these be distinguished from those, if they are all promiscuously called *sins?* I am much afraid, if we should allow any *sins* to be consistent with perfection, few would confine the idea to those *defects,* concerning which only the assertion could be true.

Q. But how can a liableness to mistake coexist[2] with perfect love? Is not a person who is perfected in love every moment under its influence? And can any mistake flow from pure love?

A. I answer: (a) many mistakes *may* coexist[3] with pure love; (b) some may accidentally *flow* from it—I mean love itself may incline us to mistake. The pure love of our neighbor springing from the love of God *thinks no evil, believes and hopes all things.*

Now this very temper, unsuspicious, ready to believe and hope the best of all men, may occasion our thinking some men better than they really are. Here, then, is a manifest mistake, accidentally *flowing* from pure love.

Q. How shall we avoid setting perfection too high or too low?

A. By keeping to the Bible, and setting perfection just as high as the scripture does. It is nothing higher and nothing lower than this: The pure love of God and man, the loving God with all our heart and soul, and our neighbor as ourselves. It is love governing the heart and life, running through all our tempers, words, and actions.

Q. Suppose one had attained to this, would you advise him to speak of it?

A. At first, perhaps, he would scarce be able to refrain, the fire would be so hot within him: his desire to declare the loving-kindness of the Lord, carrying him away like a torrent. But afterwards he might; and then it would be advisable not to speak of it to them that know not God. 'Tis most likely it would only provoke them to contradict and blaspheme, nor to others, without some particular reason, without some good in view. And then he should have especial care to avoid all appearance of boasting; to speak with the deepest humility and reverence, giving all the glory to God.

Q. But would it not be better to be entirely silent? Not to speak of it at all?

A. By silence he might avoid many crosses, which will naturally and necessarily ensue, if he simply declare, even among believers, what God has wrought in his soul. If, therefore, such a one were to confer with flesh and blood, he would be entirely silent. But this

---

[2]"Consist" in the original text.
[3]*Ibid.*

could not be done with a clear conscience, for undoubtedly he ought to speak. *Men* do not light a candle to put it under a bushel; much less does the all-wise God. He does not raise such a monument of his power and love to hide it from all mankind. Rather he intends it as a general blessing to those who are simple of heart. He designs thereby not barely the happiness of that individual person, but the animating and encouraging others, to follow after the same blessing. His will is *that many shall see it* and rejoice, *and put their trust in the Lord.* Nor does any thing under heaven more quicken the desires of those who are justified than to converse with those whom they believe to have experienced a still higher salvation. This places that salvation full in their view, and increases their hunger and thirst after it; an advantage which must have been entirely lost, had the person so saved buried himself in silence.

Q. But is there no way to prevent these crosses, which usually fall on those who speak of being thus saved?

A. It seems they cannot be prevented altogether, while so much of nature remains even in believers. But something might be done, if the preacher in every place would: (a) Talk freely with all who speak thus; and (b) labor to prevent the unjust or unkind treatment of those, in favor of whom there is reasonable proof.

Q. What is reasonable proof? How may we certainly know one that is saved from all sin?

A. We cannot *infallibly* know one that is thus saved (no, nor even one that is justified), unless it should please God to endow us with the miraculous discernment of spirits. But we apprehend these would be sufficient proofs to any reasonable man, and such as would leave little room to doubt, either the truth or depth of the work: (a) If we had clear evidence of his exemplary behavior, for some time before this supposed change. This would give us reason to believe he would not *lie for God,* but speak neither more nor less than he felt. (b) If he gave a distinct account of the time and manner wherein the change was wrought, with sound speech which could not be reproved. And (c) if it appeared that all his subsequent words and actions were holy and unblamable.

The short of the matter is this: (a) I have abundant reason to believe this person will not lie; (b) he testifies before God, "I feel no sin, but all love; I pray, rejoice, and give thanks without ceasing; and I have as clear an inward witness that I am fully renewed, as that I am justified." Now, if I have nothing to oppose to this plain testimony, I ought in reason to believe it.

It avails nothing to object, "But I know several things wherein he is quite mistaken." For it has been allowed that all who are in the body are liable to mistake, and that a mistake in judgment may sometimes occasion a mistake in practice (tho' great care is to be taken that no ill use be made of this concession). For instance, even one that is perfected in love may mistake with regard to another person, and may think him, in a particular case, to be more or less faulty than he really is. And hence he may speak to him with more or less severity than the truth requires. And in this sense (tho' that be not the primary meaning of St. James): *In many things we offend all.* This therefore is no proof at all that the person so speaking is not perfect.

Q. But is it not a proof, if he is *surprised* or *fluttered* by a noise, a fall, or some sudden danger?

A. It is not: For one may start, tremble, change color, or be otherwise disordered in body, while the soul is calmly stayed on God, and remains in perfect peace. Nay, the mind itself may be deeply distressed, may be exceeding sorrowful, may be perplexed and pressed down by heaviness and anguish, even to agony, while the heart cleaves to God by perfect love, and the will is wholly resigned to him. Was it not so with the Son of God himself? Does any child of man endure the distress, the anguish, the agony, which he sustained? And yet he *knew no sin.*

Q. But can any one who has a pure heart prefer pleasing to unpleasing food? Or use any pleasure of sense which is not strictly necessary? If so how do they differ from others?

A. The difference between these and others in taking pleasant food is (a) They need none of these things to make them happy; for they have a spring of happiness within. They see and love God. Hence they rejoice evermore, and in everything give thanks. (b) They may use them, but they do not seek them. (c) They use them sparingly, and not for the sake of the thing itself. This being premised, we answer directly: Such a one may use pleasing food, without the danger which attends those who are not saved from sin. He may prefer it to unpleasing, though equally wholesome, food as a means of increasing thankfulness, with a single eye to God, who gives us all things richly to enjoy. On the same principle, he may smell a flower, or eat a bunch of grapes or take any other pleasure which does not lessen, but increases his delight in God. Therefore neither can we say that one perfected in love would be incapable of marriage, and of worldly business. If he were called thereto, he would be more capable than ever, as being able to do all things without hurry or concern,[4] without any distraction of spirit.

Q. But if two perfect Christians had children, how could they be born in sin, since there was none in the parents?

A. It is a possible, but not a probable case: I doubt whether it ever was or ever will be. But waving this, I answer, sin is entailed upon me, not by *immediate generation,* but by my first parent. *In Adam all died; by the disobedience* of one, *all men were made sinners:* All men without exception who were in his loins, when he ate the forbidden fruit.

We have a remarkable illustration of this in gardening. Grafts on a crab-stock bear excellent fruit. But sow the kernels of this fruit, and what will be the event? They produce as mere crabs as ever were eaten.

Q. But what does the perfect one do more than others? More than the common believers?

A. Perhaps nothing: so may the providence of God have hedged him in, by outward circumstances. Perhaps not so much, though he desires and longs to spend and be spent for God; at least not externally, he neither speaks so many words, nor does so many works. As neither did our Lord himself speak so many words, or do so many, no nor so great works, as some of his Apostles (John 14:12). But what then? This is no proof that he has not more grace: and by this God measures the outward work. Hear him. *Verily I say unto you, this poor widow has cast in more than them all.* Verily this poor man, with his few broken words, has spoke more than them all. Verily this poor woman, that has given a cup of cold water, has done more than them all! Oh, cease to *judge according to appearance,* and learn to *judge righteous judgments.*

---

[4]"Carefulness" in original text.

JOHN WESLEY

Q. But is not this a proof against him? I feel no power either in his words or prayer.

A. It is not: for perhaps that is your own fault. You are not likely to feel any power therein, if any of these hindrances lie in the way: (a) Your own *deadness* of soul. The dead pharisees felt *no power* even in his words, who *spoke as never man spoke;* (b) the *guilt* of some unrepented sin, lying upon the conscience; (c) *prejudice* toward him of any kind; (d) your *not believing* that state to be attainable, wherein he professes to be; (e) *ungodliness* to think or own he has attained it; (f) overvaluing or idolizing him; (g) overvaluing yourself and your own judgment. If any of these is the case, what wonder is it that you feel no power in anything he says? But do not others feel it? If they do, your argument falls to the ground. And if they do not, do none of these hindrances lie in their way too? You must be certain of this before you can build any argument thereon. And even then your argument will prove no more than that grace and gifts do not always go together.

"But he does not come up to my idea of a perfect Christian." And perhaps no one ever did, or ever will. For your idea may go beyond, or at least beside the scriptural account. It may include more than the Bible includes therein, or however something which that does not include. Scripture perfection is pure love filling the heart and governing all the words and actions. If your idea includes any thing more or any thing else, it is not scriptural; and then no wonder that a scripturally-perfect Christian does not come up to it.

I fear many stumble on this stumbling block. They include as many ingredients as they please, not according to scripture, but their own imagination, in their idea of one that is perfect; and then readily deny anyone to be such, who does not answer that imaginary idea.

The more care should we take to keep the simple, scriptural account continually in our eye. Pure love reigning alone in the heart and life, this is the whole of scriptural perfection.

Q. When may a person judge himself to have attained this?

A. When after having been fully convinced of inbred sin, by a far deeper and clearer conviction than he experienced before justification, and after having experienced a gradual mortification of it, he experiences a total death to sin, and an entire renewal in the love, and image of God, so as to rejoice evermore, to pray without ceasing, and in everything give thanks. Not that "to feel all love and no sin" is a sufficient proof. Several have experienced this for a time, before their souls were fully renewed. None therefore ought to believe that the work is done, till there is added the testimony of the spirit, witnessing his entire sanctification, as clearly as his justification.

Q. But whence is it that some imagine they are thus sanctified, when in reality they are not?

A. It is hence: They do not judge by all the preceding marks, but either by part of them, or by others, that are ambiguous. But I know no instance of a person attending to them all, and yet deceived in this matter. I believe there can be none in the world. If a man be deeply and fully convinced, after justification, of inbred sin; if he then experience a gradual mortification of sin, and afterwards an entire renewal in the image of God; if to this change immensely greater than that wrought when he was justified be added a clear direct witness of the renewal: I judge it as impossible this man should be deceived herein, as that God should lie. And if one whom I know to be a man of veracity testify these things to me, I ought not, without some sufficient reason, to reject his testimony.

Q. Is this death to sin, and renewal in love, gradual or instantaneous?

A. A man may be dying for some time; yet he does not, properly speaking, die, till the instant the soul is separated from the body; and in that instant he lives the life of eternity. In like manner, he may be dying to sin for some time; yet he is not dead to sin, 'till sin is separated from his soul. And in that instant he lives the full life of love. And as the change undergone when the body dies is of a different kind, and infinitely greater than any we had known before, yea, such as 'till then it is impossible to conceive, so the change wrought when the soul dies to sin is of a different kind, and infinitely greater than any before, and than any conceive 'till he experiences it. Yet he still grows in grace, in the knowledge of Christ, in the love and image of God; and will do so, not only 'till death, but to all eternity.

Q. How are we to wait for this change?

A. Not in careless indifference, or indolent inactivity; but in vigorous, universal obedience, in a zealous keeping of all the commandments, in watchfulness and painfulness, in denying ourselves and taking up our cross daily, as well as in earnest prayer and fasting, and a close attendance on all the ordinances of God. And if any man dream of attaining it any other way (yea or of keeping it, when it is attained, when he has received it even in the largest measure) he deceiveth his own soul. 'Tis true we receive it by simple faith. But God does not, will not give that faith, unless we seek it with all diligence, in the way which he has ordained.

This consideration may satisfy those who enquire why so few have received the blessing. Enquire, how many are seeking it in this way? And you have a sufficient answer.

Prayer especially is wanting. Who continues instant therein? Who wrestles with God for this very thing? So you have not because you ask not, or because you ask amiss, namely, "That you may be renewed before you die." Before you die! Will that content you? Nay, but ask that it may be done now! Today! While it is called today! Do not call this "setting God a time." Certainly today is his time as well as tomorrow. Make haste man, make haste! Let

> Thy soul break out in strong desire
>   The perfect bliss to prove!
> Thy longing heart be all on fire
>   To be dissolv'd in love!

Q. But, may we continue in peace and joy, till we are perfected in love?

A. Certainly we may; for the kingdom of God is not divided against itself. Therefore let not believers be discouraged, from *rejoicing in the Lord always.* And yet we may be sensibly pained at the sinful nature that still remains in us. It is good for us to have a piercing sense of this, and a vehement desire to be delivered from it. But this should only incite us the more zealously to fly every moment to our strong helper, the more earnestly to *press forward to the mark, the prize of our high calling in Christ Jesus.* And when the sense of our sin most abounds, the sense of his love should much more abound.

Q. How should we treat those who think they have attained?

A. Examine them candidly, and exhort them to pray fervently, that God would show them all that is in their hearts. The most earnest exhortations to abound in every grace, and the strongest cautions to avoid all evil, are given throughout the New Testament, to those who are in the highest state of grace. But this should be done with the utmost tenderness, and without any harshness, sternness, or sourness. We should carefully avoid the very appearance of anger, unkindness or contempt. Leave it to Satan thus to tempt, and to his children to cry out, *Let us examine him with despitefulness and torture, that we may know his meekness and prove his patience.* If they are faithful to the grace given, they are in no danger of perishing thereby: no not if they remain in that mistake, 'till their spirit is returning to God.

Q. But what hurt can it do to deal harshly with them?

A. Either they are mistaken or they are not. If they are, it may destroy their souls. This is nothing impossible, no, nor improbable. It may so enrage or so discourage them that they will sink, and rise no more. If they are not mistaken, it may grieve those whom God has not grieved, and do much hurt unto our own souls. For undoubtedly he that touches them touches as it were the apple of God's eye. If they are indeed full of his spirit, to behave unkindly or contemptuously to them is doing no little despite to the spirit of grace. Hereby likewise we feed and increase in ourselves evil surmising and many wrong tempers. To instance only one. What self-sufficiency is this, to set ourselves up for inquisitors-general, for peremptory judges in these deep things of God? Are we qualified for the office? Can we pronounce in all cases how far infirmity reaches? What may, and what may not be resolved into it? What may in all circumstances, and what may not, consist with perfect love? Can we precisely determine how it will influence the look, the gesture, the tone of voice? If we can, doubtless we are the men, *and wisdom shall die with us.*

Q. But if they are displeased at our not believing them, is not this a full proof against them?

A. According as that displeasure is: If they are angry, it is a proof against them; if they are grieved, it is not. They ought to be grieved, if we disbelieve a real work of God, and thereby deprive ourselves of the advantage we might have received from it. And we may easily mistake this grief for anger, as the outward expressions of both are much alike.

Q. But is it not well to find out those who fancy they have attained, when they have not?

A. It is well to do it by mild, loving examination. But it is not well to triumph even over these. It is extremely wrong, if we find such an instance, to rejoice, as if we had found great spoils. Ought we not rather to grieve, to be deeply concerned, to let our eyes run down with tears? Here is one who seemed to be a living proof of God's power to save to the uttermost, but alas! It is not as we hoped! He is weighed in the balance and found wanting! And is this matter of joy? Ought we not to rejoice a thousand times more if we can find nothing but pure love?

"But he is deceived." What then? It is a harmless mistake, while he feels nothing but love in his heart. It is a mistake which generally argues great grace, a high degree both of holiness and happiness. This should be a matter of real joy to all that are simple of heart: not the mistake itself, but the height of grace which for a time occasions it. I rejoice that the soul is always happy in Christ, always full of prayer and thanksgiving. I rejoice that he feels no unholy temper but the pure love of God continually. And I will rejoice, if sin is suspended, 'till it is totally destroyed.

Q. Is there no danger then in a man's being thus deceived?

A. Not at the time that he feels no sin. There was danger before, and there will be again, when he comes into fresh trials. But so long as he feels nothing but love animating all his thoughts, and words and actions, he is in no danger: he is not only happy, but safe, *under the shadow of the Almighty.* And, for God's sake, let him continue in that love as long as he can; meantime, you may do well to warn him of the danger that *will be,* if his love grow cold and sin revive, even the danger of casting away hope, and supposing, that, because he hath not attained yet, therefore he never shall.

Q. But what if none have attained it yet? What if all, who think so are deceived?

A. Convince me of this, and I will preach it no more. But understand me right: I do not build any doctrine on this or that person. This or any other man may be deceived, and I am not moved. But if there are none made perfect yet, God has not sent *me* to preach perfection.

Put a parallel case. For many years I have preached, *There is a peace of God, which passes all understanding.* Convince me that this word has fallen to the ground, that in all these years none have attained this peace, that there is no living witness of it at this day, and I will preach it no more.

"Oh, but several persons have died in that peace." Perhaps so: but I want living witnesses. I cannot indeed be infallibly certain that this or that person is a witness. But if I were certain there are none such, I must have done with this doctrine.

"You misunderstand me. I believe some, who died in his love, enjoyed it long before their death. But I was not certain that their former testimony was true, 'till some hours before they died."

You had not an infallible certainty then. And a reasonable certainty you might have had before; such a certainty, as might have quickened and comforted your own soul, and answered all other Christian purposes. Such a certainty as this any candid person may have, suppose there be any living witness, by talking one hour with that person in the love and fear of God.

Q. But what does it signify, whether any have attained it or no, seeing so many scriptures witness for it?

A. If I were convinced that none in England had attained what has been so clearly and strongly preached by such a number of Preachers, in so many places, and for so long a time; I should be clearly convinced that we had all mistaken the meaning of those scriptures. And therefore for the time to come, I too must teach, that "sin will remain till death."

20. In the year 1762, there was a great increase of the word of God in London. Many, who had hitherto cared for none of these things, were deeply convinced of their lost estate. Many found redemption in the blood of Christ; not a few backsliders were healed. And a considerable number of persons believed that God had saved them from *all sin.* Easily foreseeing that Satan would be endeavoring to sow tares among the wheat, I took much pains to apprise them of the danger, particularly with regard to *pride* and *enthusiasm.* And while I stayed in town, I had reason to hope they continued both humble and sober-minded. But almost as soon as I was gone, enthusiasm broke in. Two or three began to take their own imagination for impression from God, and thence to suppose that they should *never*

die. And these laboring to bring others into the same opinion occasioned much noise and confusion. Soon after, the same persons, with a few more, ran into other extravagancies, fancying they could not be tempted, that they should feel no more pain, and that they had the gift of prophecy, and of discerning of spirits. At my return to London in Autumn, some of them stood reproved; but others were got above instruction. Meantime, a flood of reproach came upon *me* almost from every quarter; from themselves, because I was checking them on all occasions; and from others, "because, they said, I did not check them." However, the hand of the Lord was not stayed, but more and more sinners were convinced: while others were almost daily converted to God, and others enabled to love him *with all their heart*.

21. About this time, a friend at some distance from London wrote to me as follows:

"Be not over alarmed that Satan sows tares among the wheat of Christ! It ever has been so, especially on any remarkable outpouring of his Spirit; and ever will be so, till he is chained up for a thousand years. Till then he will always *ape*, and endeavor to *counteract* the work of the Spirit of Christ.

"One melancholy effect of this has been that a world, who is always asleep in the arms of the evil one, has ridiculed every work of the Holy Spirit.

"But what can real Christians do? Why, if they would act worthy of themselves, they should (a) pray that every deluded soul be delivered; (b) endeavor to reclaim them in the spirit of meekness; (c) take the utmost care, both by prayer and watchfulness, that the delusion of others may not lessen their zeal in seeking after that *universal holiness* of soul, body, and spirit, *without which no man shall see the Lord*.

"Indeed this *complete new creature* is mere madness to a mad world. But it is notwithstanding the *will* and *wisdom* of God. May we all seek after it!

"But some who maintain this doctrine in its full extent are too often guilty of limiting the Almighty. He dispenses his gifts just as he pleases; therefore it is neither *wise* nor *modest* to affirm that a person must be a believer for any length of time, before he is capable of receiving a *high degree* of the *spirit of holiness*.

"God's *usual method* is one thing, but his *sovereign pleasure* is another. He has wise reasons both for hastening and retarding his work; sometimes he comes suddenly and unexpected; sometimes not 'till we have *long* looked for him.

CHRISTIAN PERFECTION

"Indeed it has been my opinion for many years that one great cause why men make so little improvement in the divine life is their own *coldness, negligence,* and *unbelief.* And yet I here speak of *believers.*

"May the spirit of Christ give us a right judgment in all things, and *fill* us *with all the fulness of God,* that so we may be *perfect and entire, wanting nothing.*"

22. About the same time, five or six honest enthusiasts foretold the world was to end on the 28th of February. I immediately withstood them, by every possible means, both in public and private. I preached expressly upon the subject, both at West Street and Spittlefields. I warned the Society, again and again, and spoke severally to as many as I could, and I saw the fruit of my labor. They made exceeding few converts; I believe scarce thirty in our whole Society. Nevertheless they made abundance of noise, gave huge occasion of offense to those who take care to improve to the uttermost every occasion against *me,* and greatly increased both the number and courage of those who opposed Christian Perfection.

23. Some questions, now published by one of these, induced a plain man to write the following *Queries,* humbly proposed to those who deny perfection to be attainable in this life.

A. Has there not been a larger measure of the Holy Spirit given under the Gospel than under the Jewish dispensation? If not, in what was the *spirit not given* before Christ was glorified? (John 7:39).

B. Was that *glory which followed the sufferings of Christ* (1 Pet. 1:11) an external glory, or an internal, *viz.* the glory of holiness?

C. Has God anywhere in scripture commanded us more than he has promised to us?

D. Are the promises of God respecting holiness to be fulfilled in this life, or only in the next?

E. Is a Christian under any other laws than those which God promises to *write in our hearts?* (Jer. 31:31ff.; Heb. 8:10).

F. In what sense is *the righteousness of the law fulfilled in those who walk not after the flesh, but after the spirit?* (Rom. 8:4).

G. Is it impossible for anyone in this life to *love God with all his heart, and mind, and soul, and strength?* And is the Christian under any law which is not fulfilled in this love?

H. Does the soul's *going out of the body* effect its purification from indwelling sin?

I. If so, is it not something else, not *the blood of Christ, which cleanses it from all sin?*

341

J. If his blood cleanses us from all sin, while the soul and body are united, is it not *in this life?*

K. If when that union ceases, is it not *in the next?* And is not this too late?

L. If in the article of death; what situation is the soul in, when it is neither *in the body,* nor *out* of it?

M. Has Christ anywhere taught us to pray for what he never designs to give?

N. Has he not taught us to pray, *your will be done on earth as it is done in heaven?* And is it not done perfectly in heaven?

O. If so, has he not taught us to pray for *Perfection on earth?* Does he not then design to give it?

P. Did not Saint Paul pray according to the will of God, when he prayed that the Thessalonians might be *sanctified wholly, and preserved* (in this world, not the next, unless he was praying for the dead) *blameless in body, soul, and spirit, unto the coming of Jesus Christ?*

Q. Do you sincerely desire to be freed from indwelling sin in this life?

R. If you do, did not God give you that desire?

S. If so, did he not give it you to mock you, since it is impossible it should ever be fulfilled?

T. If you have not sincerity enough even to desire it, are you not disputing about matters too high for you?

U. Do you ever pray God to *cleanse the thoughts of your heart, that you may perfectly love him?*

V. If you neither desire what you ask, nor believe it attainable, pray you not as a fool prays?

God help you to consider these questions calmly and impartially!

24. In the latter end of this year, God called to himself that burning and shining light, Jane Cooper. As she was both a living and dying witness of Christian Perfection, it will not be at all foreign to the subject to add a short account of her death, with one of her own letters, containing a plain and artless relation of the manner wherein it pleased God to work that great change in her soul.

May 2, 1761

I believe while memory remains in me, gratitude will continue. From the time you preached on Gal. 5:5, I saw clearly the true state of my soul. That sermon described my heart, and what it wanted to be truly happy. You read Mr. M's letter, and it described the religion which I desired. From that time the prize appeared in view, and I was enabled to follow hard after it. I was kept watching unto prayer, sometimes in much distress, at other times in patient expectation of the blessing. For some days before you left London, my soul was stayed on a promise I had applied to me in prayer, *The Lord whom you seek shall suddenly come to his temple.* I believed he would, and that he would sit there as a refiner's fire. The Tuesday after you went, I thought I could not sleep, unless he fulfilled his word that night. I never knew as I did then the force of these words, *Be still and know that I am God.* I became nothing before him, and enjoyed perfect calmness in my soul. I knew not, whether he had destroyed my sin; but I desired to know, that I might praise him. Yet I soon found the return of unbelief, and groaned, being burdened. On Wednesday I went to London, and sought the Lord without ceasing. I promised, if he would save me from sin, I would praise him. I could part with all things so I might win Christ. But I found all these pleas to be nothing worth, and that if he saved *me,* it must be freely, for his own name's sake. On Thursday I was so much tempted that I thought of destroying myself, or never conversing more with the people of God. And yet I had no doubt of his pardoning love: but, t'was worse than death my God to love, and not my God alone. On Friday my distress was deepened. I endeavored to pray and could not. I went to Mrs. D who prayed for me, and told me it was the death of nature. I opened the Bible, on *The fearful and unbelieving shall have their part in the lake that burns with fire and brimstone.* I could not bear it. I opened again on Mark 16:6–7: *Be not affrighted: you seek Jesus of Nazareth—Go your way; tell his disciples he goes before you into Galilee: there shall you see him.* I was encouraged and enabled to pray, believing I should see Jesus at home. I returned that night and found Mrs. G. She prayed for me; and the Predestinarian had no plea, but *Lord, you are no respecter of persons.* He proved he was not, by blessing *me.* I was in a moment enabled to lay hold on Jesus, and found salvation by simple faith. He assured me, the Lord, the King was in the midst of me, and that I should see evil no more. I now blessed him who had visited and redeemed me, and was become my *wisdom, righteousness, sanctification and redemption.* I saw Jesus altogether lovely, and knew he was mine in all his offices. And, glory be to him! he now reigns in my heart without a rival. I find no will but his. I feel no pride; nor any affection but what is placed on him. I know, it is by faith I stand, and that watching unto prayer must be the guard of faith. I am happy in God this moment, and I believe for the next. I have often read the chapter you mention (1 Cor. 13) and compared my heart and life with it. In so doing, I feel my shortcomings, and the need I have of the atoning blood. Yet I dare not say, I do not feel a measure of the love there described, though I am not all I shall be. I desire to be lost in that *love which passes knowledge.* I see *the just shall live by faith:* and unto me, who am less than the least of all saints, is this grace given. If I were an archangel, I should veil my face before him, and let silence speak his praise!

The following account is given by one who was an eye and ear witness of what she relates.

A. "In the beginning of November, she seemed to have a foresight of what was coming upon her, and used frequently to sing these words:

When pain o'er this weak flesh prevails,
With lamb-like patience arm my breast.

"And when she sent to me, to let me know she was ill, she wrote in her note, I suffer the will of Jesus. All he sends is sweetened by his love. I am as happy as if I heard a voice say,

For me my elder brethren stay,
And angels beckon me away,
And *Jesus* bids me come!

B. "Upon my telling her, 'I cannot choose life or death for you,' she said, 'I asked the Lord that if it was his will, I might die first. And he told me, you should survive me, and that you should close my eyes.' When we perceived it was the smallpox, I said to her 'My dear, you will not be frighted if I tell you what is your distemper.' She said, 'I *cannot* be frighted at *his* will.'

C. "The distemper was soon very heavy upon her. But so much the more was her faith strengthened. Tuesday, Nov. 19, she said to me, 'I have been worshiping before the throne in a glorious manner, my soul was so let into God.' I said, 'Did the Lord give you any particular promise?' 'No,' replied she: 'it was all

That sacred awe that dares not move
And all the silent heaven of love.'

D. "On Thursday, upon my asking, 'What have you to say to me?' She said, 'Nay, nothing but what you know already: God is love.' I asked, 'Have you any particular promise?' She replied, 'I do not seem to want any, I can live without. I shall die a lump of deformity, but shall meet you all glorious. And meantime I shall still have fellowship with your spirit.'

E. "Mr. M asked, 'what she thought the most excellent *way* to walk in, and what were its chief *hindrances?*' She answered, 'The greatest hindrance is generally from the natural constitution. It was mine, to be reserved, to be very quiet, to suffer much, and to say little. Some may think one *way* more excellent, and some another. But the thing is to live in the will of God. For some months past, when I have been particularly devoted to this, I have felt such a guidance of his Spirit, and *the unction which I have received from the Holy One has so taught me of all things, that I needed not any man should teach me, save as this anointing teaches.*'

F. "On Friday morning she said, 'I believe I shall die.' She then sat up in her bed and said, 'Lord, I bless you that you are ever with me, and all you have is mine. Your love is greater than my weakness, greater than my helplessness, greater than my unworthiness. Lord you *say to corruption, you are my sister!* And glory be to you, O *Jesus,* you are my brother. Let me *comprehend with all saints, the length, and breadth, and depth, and height of your love!* Bless these: (some that were present) let them be every moment exercised in all things, as you would have them to be.'

G. "Some hours after it seemed as if the agonies of death were just coming upon her. But her face were full of smiles of triumph, and she clapped her hands for joy. Mrs. C said, 'My dear, you are more than conqueror, through the blood of the Lamb.' She answered, 'Yes, O yes, sweet *Jesus! O death, where is your sting!*' She then lay as in a doze for some time. Afterwards she strove to speak, but could not. However, she testified her love, by shaking hands with all in the room.

H. "Mr. W then came. She said, 'Sir, I did not know that I should live to see you. But I am glad the Lord has given me this opportunity, and likewise power to speak to you. I love you. You have always preached the strictest doctrine; and I loved to follow it. Do so still, whoever is pleased or displeased.' He asked, 'Do you *now* believe you are saved from sin?' She said, 'Yes; I have had no doubt of it for many months. That I ever had was because I did not abide in the faith. I now feel I have kept the faith; and perfect love casts out all fear. As to you, the Lord promised me, your latter works should exceed your former, though I do not live to see it. I have been a great *enthusiast*, as they term it, these six months; but never lived so near the heart of Christ in my life. You, Sir, desire to comfort the hearts of hundreds, by following that simplicity your soul loves.'

I. "To one who had received the love of God under her prayer, she said, 'I feel I have not followed a cunningly devised fable; for I am as happy as I can live. Do you press on, and stop not short of the mark.' To Miss M she said, 'Love Christ; he loves you. I believe I shall see you at the right hand of God. But *as one star differs from another star in glory, so shall it be in the resurrection.* I charge you, in the presence of God, meet me in that day all glorious within. Avoid all conformity to the world. You are robbed of many of your privileges. I know I shall be found blameless. Do you labor to be found of him *in peace, without spot.*'

J. "Saturday morning she prayed nearly as follows: 'I know, my Lord, my life is prolonged, only to do your will. And though I should never eat or drink more' (she had not swallowed anything for near eight and twenty hours) your will be done. I am willing to be kept so a twelvemonth: *Man lives not by bread alone.* I praise you that there is not a shadow of complaining in our streets. In that sense we know not what sickness means. Indeed, Lord, *neither life nor death nor things present, nor things to come, no, nor any creature, shall separate us from your love* one moment. Bless these, that there may be no lack in their souls. I believe there shall not. I pray in faith.'

"On Sunday and Monday she was lightheaded, but sensible at times. It then plainly appeared her heart was still in heaven. One said to her, 'Jesus is our mark.' She replied, 'I have but one mark, I am all spiritual.' Miss M said to her, 'You dwell in God.' She answered, 'Altogether.' A person asked her, 'Do you love me?' She said, 'Oh, I love Christ: I love my Christ.' To another she said, 'I shall not long be here, Jesus is precious: very precious indeed.' She said to Miss M: 'The Lord is very good, he keeps my soul above all.' For fifteen hours before she died, she was in strong convulsions; her sufferings were extreme. One said, 'You are made perfect through sufferings.' She said, 'More and more so.' After lying quite some time, she said, 'Lord, you are strong!' Then pausing a considerable space, she uttered her last words, 'My Jesus is all in all to me: glory be to him through time and eternity.' After this, she lay still for about half an hour, and then expired without a sigh or groan."

25. The next year, the number of those who believed they were saved from sin still increasing, I judged it needful to publish, chiefly for their use, *Farther Thoughts on Christian Perfection.*

Q. (1) How is *Christ the end of the law for righteousness to everyone that believes?* (Rom. 10:4).

A. In order to understand this, you must understand what law is here spoken of. And this, I apprehend, is: (a) The Mosaic law, the whole Mosaic dispensation, which Saint Paul continually speaks of as one, though containing three parts, the political, moral, and ceremonial; (b) the Adamic law, that given to Adam in innocence, properly called "the law of works." This is in substance the same with the Angelic law, being common to angels and men. It required that man should use to the glory of God all the powers with which he was created. Now he was created free from any defect, either in his understanding, or his affections. His body was then no clog to the mind; it did not hinder his apprehending all things clearly, judging truly concerning them, and reasoning justly, if he reasoned at all. I say "if he reasoned," for possibly he did not. Perhaps he had no need of reasoning, 'till his corruptible body pressed down the mind, and impaired its native faculties. Perhaps 'till then the mind saw every truth that offered as directly as the eye now sees the light.

Consequently this law, proportioned to his original powers, required that he should always think, always speak, and always act precisely right, in every point whatever. He was well able so to do. And God could not but require the service he was able to pay.

But Adam fell: and his incorruptible body became corruptible;

and ever since it is a clog to the soul, and hinders its operations. Hence, at present no child of man can at all times apprehend clearly, or judge truly. And where either the judgment or apprehension is wrong, it is impossible to reason justly. Therefore it is as natural for a man to err[5] as to breathe; and he can no more live without the one than without the other. Consequently no man is able to perform the service, which the Adamic law requires.

And no man is obliged to perform it: God does not require it of any man. *For Christ is the end of the Adamic*, as well as the *Mosaic law*. By his death he has put an end to both: he has abolished both the one and the other with regard to man; and the obligation to observe either the one or the other is vanished away. Nor is any man living bound to observe the *Adamic*, more than the *Mosaic* law.

In the room of this, *Christ* has established another, namely, the law of faith. Not everyone that does, but every one that believes, now receives righteousness, in the full sense of the word, that is, he is justified, sanctified, and glorified.

Q. (2) Are we then dead *to the law?*

A. We *are dead to the law, by the body of Christ given for us* (Rom. 7:4), to the *Adamic*, as well as *Mosaic* law. We are wholly freed therefrom by his death: that law expiring with him.

Q. (3) How then are we *not without law to God, but under the law to Christ* (1 Cor. 9:21)?

A. We are without that law. But it does not follow that we are without any law. For God has established another law in its place, even the law of faith. And we are all under this law to God and to Christ. Both our Creator and our Redeemer require us to observe it.

Q. (4) Is love the fulfilling of this law?

A. Unquestionably it is. *The whole law, under which we now are, is fulfilled by love* (Rom. 13:9–10). Faith working or animated by love is all that God now requires of man. He has substituted not sincerity, but love, in the room of angelic perfection.

Q. (5) How is *love the end of the commandment* (1 Tim. 1:5)?

A. It is the end of every commandment of God. It is the point

---

[5]"Mistake" in original text.

aimed at by the whole, and every part of the Christian institution. The foundation is faith, purifying the heart, the end love, preserving a good conscience.

Q. (6) What love is this?
A. The *loving the Lord our God with all our heart, mind, soul, and strength:* and the *loving our neighbor,* every man as ourselves, as our own souls.

Q. (7) What are the fruits or properties of this love?
A. Saint Paul informs us at large: *Love is long-suffering.* It suffers all the wickedness of the children of the world. And that not for a little time only, but as long as God pleases. In all it sees the hand of God, and willingly submits thereto. Meantime *it is kind.* In all, and after all it suffers, it is soft, mild, tender, benign. *Love envies not:* it excludes every kind and degree of envy out of the heart: *Love acts not rashly,* in a violent headstrong manner, nor passes any rash or severe judgment. It *does not behave itself indecently,* is not rude, does not act out of character; *seeks not her own* ease, pleasure, honor or profit; *is not provoked;* expels all anger from the heart; *thinks no evil;* casts out all jealousy, suspiciousness, readiness to believe evil; *rejoices not in iniquity;* yea, weeps at the sin or folly of its bitterest enemies; *but rejoices in the truth,* in the holiness and happiness of every child of man. *Love covers all things,* speaks evil of no man; *believes all things* that tend to the advantage of another's character. *It hopes all things,* whatever may extenuate the faults which cannot be denied, and it *endures all things,* which God can permit, or men and devils inflict. This is *the law of Christ, the perfect law, the law of liberty.*
And this distinction between the *law of faith* (or love) and *the law of works* is neither a *subtle,* nor an unnecessary distinction. It is plain, easy, and intelligible to any common understanding. And it is absolutely necessary, to prevent a thousand doubts and fears, even in those who do *walk in love.*

Q. (8) But do *we* not *in many things offend all,* yea, the best of us, even against this law?
A. In one sense we do not, while all our tempers and thoughts, and words and works, spring from love. But in another we do, and shall do, more or less, as long as we remain in the body. For neither love nor the *unction of the Holy One* makes us infallible. Therefore

349

through unavoidable defect of understanding, we cannot but mistake in many things. And these mistakes will frequently occasion something wrong, both in our temper, and words and actions. From mistaking his character, we may love a person less than he really deserves. And by the same mistake we are unavoidably led to speak or act with regard to that person, in such a manner as is contrary to this law, in some or other of the preceding instances.

Q. (9) Do we not then need Christ, even on this account?

A. The holiest of men still need Christ, as their prophet, as *the light of the world.* For he does not give them light, but from moment to moment: the instant he withdraws, all is darkness. They still need Christ as their king. For God does not give them a stock of holiness. But unless they receive a supply every moment, nothing but unholiness would remain. They still need Christ as their priest, to make atonement for their holy things. Even perfect holiness is acceptable to God only through Jesus Christ.

Q. (10) May not then the very best of men adopt the dying martyr's confession, "I am in myself *nothing but sin, darkness, hell;* but you are my light, my holiness, my heaven?"

A. Not exactly. But the best of men may say, "You are my light, my holiness, my heaven. Through my union with you, I am full of light, of holiness and happiness. And *if I were left to myself, I should be* nothing but sin, darkness, hell."

But to proceed. The best of men need Christ as their priest, their atonement, their advocate with the Father; not only as the continuance of their every blessing depends on his death and intercession, but on account of their coming short of the law of love. For every man living does so. You who *feel all love,* compare yourselves with the preceding description. Weigh yourselves in this balance, and see if you are not wanting in many particulars.

Q. (11) But if all this is consistent with Christian Perfection, that perfection is not freedom from all sin: seeing *sin is the transgression of the law.* And the perfect transgress the very law they are under. Besides, they need the atonement of Christ. And he is the atonement of nothing but sin. Is then the term *sinless perfection* proper?

A. It is not worth disputing about. But observe, in what sense the persons in question need the atonement of Christ. They do not need him to reconcile them to God *afresh*, for they are reconciled. They do not need him to *restore* the favor of God, but to *continue* it. He does not procure pardon for them anew, but *ever lives to make intercession for them.* And *by one offering, he has perfected forever them that are sanctified* (Heb. 10:14).

For want of duly considering this, some deny that they need the atonement of Christ. Indeed exceeding few: I do not remember to have found five of them in England. Of the two, I would sooner give up perfection. But we need not give up either one or the other. The perfection I hold: *Love rejoicing evermore, praying without ceasing, and in everything giving thanks,* is well consistent with it; if any hold a perfection, which is not, they must look to it.

Q. (12) Does then Christian Perfection imply any more than *sincerity?*

A. Not if you mean by that word, love filling the heart, expelling pride, anger, desire, self-will; rejoicing evermore, praying without ceasing, and in everything giving thanks. But I doubt few use *sincerity* in this sense. Therefore I think the old word is best.

A person may be *sincere* who has all his natural tempers, pride, anger, lust, self-will. But he is not *perfect*, till his heart is cleansed from these, and all its other corruptions.

To clear this point a little farther: I know many that love God with all their heart. He is their one desire, their one delight, and they are continually happy in him. They love their neighbor as themselves. They feel as sincere, fervent, constant a desire for the happiness of every man, good or bad, friend or enemy, as for their own. They rejoice evermore, pray without ceasing, and in everything give thanks. Their souls are continually streaming up to God, in holy joy, prayer, and praise. This is a point of fact; and this is plain, sound, scriptural experience.

But even these souls dwell in a shattered body, and are so pressed down thereby that they cannot always exert themselves as they would, by thinking, speaking, and acting *precisely right.* For want of better bodily organs, they must at times think, speak, or act wrong; not indeed through a defect of *love*, but through a defect of *knowledge*. And while this is the case, notwithstanding that defect, and its consequences, they fulfill the law of love.

Yet as even in this case, there is not a full conformity to the perfect law, so the most perfect do on this very account need the blood

351

of atonement, and may properly for themselves, as well as for their brethren say: *Forgive us our trespasses.*

Q. (13) But if Christ has put an end to that law, what need of any atonement for their transgressing it?

A. Observe in what sense he has *put an end* to it, and the difficulty vanishes. Were it not for the *abiding merit* of his death, and his *continual intercession* for us, that law would condemn us still. These therefore we still need, for every transgression of it.

Q. (14) But can one that is saved from sin be tempted?

A. Yes: for *Christ was tempted.*

Q. (15) However, what you call temptation, I call the corruption of the heart. And how will you distinguish one from the other?

A. In some cases it is impossible to distinguish without the *direct witness* of the Spirit. But in general one may distinguish thus:

One commends me. Here is a temptation to pride. But instantly my soul is humbled before God. And I feel no pride, of which I am as sure as that pride is not humility.

A man strikes me. Here is a temptation to anger. But my heart overflows with love. And I feel no anger at all, of which I can be as sure as that love and anger are not the same.

A woman solicits me. Here is a temptation to lust. But in the instant I shrink back. And I feel no desire or lust at all, of which I am as sure as that my hand is cold or hot.

Thus it is, if I am tempted by a *present* object: and it is just the same if when it is absent the devil recalls a commendation, an injury, or a woman to my mind. In the instant the soul repels the temptation, and remains filled with pure love.

And the difference is still plainer when I compare my present state with my past, wherein I felt temptation and corruption too.

Q. (16) But how do you *know* that you are sanctified, saved from your inbred corruption?

A. I can know it no otherwise than I know that I am justified. *Hereby know we that we are of God,* in either sense, *by the Spirit he has given us.*

We know it by *the witness,* and by *the fruit* of the spirit. And first, by *the witness.* As when we were justified, the *Spirit bore witness with our spirit* that our sins were forgiven; so when we were sanctified, he bore witness that they were taken away. Indeed the witness of sanctification is not always clear at first (as neither is that of justification); neither is it afterward, always the same, but like that of justification, sometimes stronger and sometimes fainter. Yea, and sometimes it is withdrawn. Yet in general, the latter testimony of the Spirit is both as clear and as steady as the former.

Q. (17) But what need is there of it, seeing sanctification is a *real change*, not a *relative* only, like justification?

A. But is the new birth a *relative* change only? Is not this a *real* change? Therefore if we need no witness of our sanctification, because it is a *real* change, for the same reason we should need none that we are born of or are the children of God.

Q. (18) But does not sanctification shine by its own light?

A. And does not the new birth too? Sometimes it does. And so does sanctification: at others it does not. In the hour of temptation Satan clouds the work of God, and injects various doubts and reasonings, especially in those who have either very weak or very strong understandings. At such times there is absolute need of that witness: without which the work of sanctification not only could not be discerned, but could no longer subsist. Were it not for this, the soul could not then abide in the love of God; much less could it rejoice evermore, and in everything give thanks. In these circumstances therefore, a *direct testimony* that we are sanctified is necessary in the highest degree.

"But I have no *witness* that I am saved from sin. And yet I have no doubt of it." Very well. As long as you have no doubt, it is enough; when you have, you will need that witness.

Q. (19) But what scripture makes mention of any such thing, or gives any reason to expect it?

A. That scripture, 1 Corinthians 2:12: *We have received not the spirit that is of the world, but the Spirit which is of God, that we may know the things which are freely given us of God.*

Now surely sanctification is one of *the things which are freely given us of God.* And no possible reason can be assigned why this should be excepted, when the Apostle says, *We receive the Spirit* for this very end, *that we may know the things which are* thus *freely given us.*

Is not the same thing implied in that well-known scripture, Romans 8:16: *The spirit itself witnesseth with our spirit, that we are the children of God?* Does he only witness the want of this to those who are children of God in the lowest sense? Nay, but to those also who are such in the highest sense. And does he not witness that they are such in the highest sense? What reason have we to doubt it?

What if a man were to affirm (as indeed many do) that this witness belongs *only to the highest* class of Christians? Would not you answer, the Apostle makes no restriction. Therefore doubtless it belongs to all the children of God. And will not the same answer hold, if any affirm, that it belongs *only to the lowest* class?

Consider likewise, 1 John 5:19: *We know that we are of God.* How? *By the Spirit that he has given us.* Nay, *hereby we know that he abides in us.* And what ground have we, either from scripture or reason, to exclude the witness, any more than the fruit of the Spirit, from being here intended? By this then also *we know that we are of God,* and *in what sense* we are so; whether we be babes, young men or fathers, we know in the same manner.

Not that I affirm that all young men, or even fathers, have this testimony every moment. There may be intermissions of the direct testimony that they are thus born of God. But those intermissions are fewer and shorter as they grow up in Christ. And some have the testimony of both their justification and sanctification, without any intermission at all; which I presume more might have, did they walk humbly and closely with God.

Q. (20) May not some of them have a testimony from the Spirit, that they shall not finally fall from God?

A. They may. And this persuasion, that *neither life nor death shall separate them from* him, far from being hurtful, may in some circumstances be extremely useful. These therefore we should in no wise grieve, but earnestly encourage them to *hold the beginning of their confidence steadfast to the end.*

Q. (21) But have any a testimony from the Spirit, that they shall *never sin?*

A. We know not what God may vouchsafe to some particular persons. But we do not find any general state described in scripture, from which a man cannot draw back to sin. If there were any state wherein this was impossible, it would be that of these who are *sanctified*, who are *fathers in Christ, who rejoice evermore, pray without ceasing*, and *in everything give thanks*. But it is not impossible for these to draw back. They who are *sanctified*, yet may fall and perish (Heb. 10:29). Even *fathers in Christ* need that warning. *Love not the world* (1 John 2:15). They who *rejoice, pray*, and *give thanks without ceasing* may nevertheless *quench the Spirit* (1 Thes. 5:16ff.). Nay, even they who are *sealed unto the day of redemption* may yet *grieve the Holy Spirit of God* (Eph. 4:30).

Although therefore God may give such a witness to some particular persons, yet it is not to be expected by Christians in general, there being no scripture whereon to ground such an expectation.

Q. (22) By what *fruit of the spirit* may we *know that we are of* God, even in the highest sense?

A. By *love, joy, peace* always abiding; by invariable *long-suffering*, patience, resignation; by *gentleness*, triumphing over all provocation; by *goodness*, mildness, sweetness, tenderness of spirit; by *fidelity*, simplicity, godly sincerity; by *meekness*, calmness, evenness of spirit; by *temperance*, not only in food and sleep, but in all things natural and spiritual.

Q. (23) But what great matter is there in this? Have we not all this when we are justified?

A. What! *Total resignation* to the will of God, without any mixture of self-will? *Gentleness*, without any touch of anger, even the moment we are provoked? *Love* to God, without the least love to the creature, but in and for God, excluding *all* pride? Love to man, excluding *all* envy, *all* jealousy, and rash judging? *Meekness*, keeping the whole soul inviolably calm? And *temperance* in all things? Deny that any ever came up to this, if you please; but do not say all who are justified do.

Q. (24) But some who are newly justified do; what then will you say to these?

A. If they really do, I will say they are sanctified, saved from sin in that moment; and that they never need lose what God has given, or feel sin any more.

But certainly this is an exempt case. It is otherwise with the generality of those that are justified: They feel in themselves more or less pride, anger, self-will, a heart bent to backsliding. And till they have gradually mortified these, they are not fully renewed in love.

Q. (25) But is not this the case of all that are justified? Do they not *gradually* die to sin and grow in grace, till at, or perhaps a little before death, God perfects them in love?

A. I believe this is the case of most, but not all.

God usually gives a considerable *time* for men to receive *light,* to grow in *grace,* to *do and* suffer his will before they are either justified or sanctified. But he does not invariably adhere to this. Sometimes he *cuts short his work.* He does the work of many years in a few weeks: perhaps in a week, a day, an hour. He justifies or sanctifies both those who have *done* or *suffered* nothing, and who have not had *time* for a gradual growth either in *light* or *grace.* And *may* he *not do what* he *will with his own? Is your eye evil, because he is good?*

It need not therefore be affirmed over and over, and proved by forty texts of scripture, either that most men are perfected in love *at last,* that there is a *gradual work* of God in the soul; or that, generally speaking, it is a *long time,* even many years, before sin is destroyed. All this we know. But we know likewise that God *may,* with man's good leave, *cut short his work,* in whatever degree he pleases, and do the usual work of many years in a moment. He does so, in many instances. And yet there is a *gradual* work, both *before* and *after* that moment. So that one may affirm, the work is *gradual,* another, it is *instantaneous,* without any manner of contradiction.

Q. (26) Does Saint *Paul* mean any more by being *sealed with the Spirit,* than being *renewed in love?*

A. Perhaps in one place, 2 Corinthians 1:22, he does not mean so much. But in another, Ephesians 1:13, he seems to include both the fruit and the witness; and that in a higher degree than we experience, even, when we are first *renewed in love,* God *seals us with the Spirit of promise,* by giving us *the full assurance of hope;* such a confidence of receiving all the promises of God as excludes the possibility of doubting: with that Holy Spirit, by universal holiness, stamping the whole image of God on our hearts.

Q. (27) But how can those who are thus *sealed grieve the Holy Spirit of God?*

CHRISTIAN PERFECTION

A. Saint Paul tells you very particularly, (a) by such conversation as is not profitable, not to the use of edifying, not apt to minister grace to the hearers; (b) by relapsing into bitterness or want of kindness; (c) by wrath, lasting displeasure, or want of tenderheartedness; (d) by anger, however soon it is over, want of instantly forgiving one another; (e) by clamor or brawling, loud, harsh, rough speaking; (f) by evil-speaking, whispering, tale-bearing; needlessly mentioning the fault of an absent person, though in ever so soft a manner.

Q. (28) What do you think of those in London who seem to have been lately *renewed in love?*
A. There is something very peculiar in the experience of the greatest part of them. One would expect that a believer should first be filled with love, and thereby emptied of sin: whereas these were emptied of sin first, and then filled with love. Perhaps it pleased God to work in this manner, to make his work more plain and undeniable, and to distinguish it more clearly from that overflowing love which is often felt even in a justified state.

It seems likewise most agreeable to the great promise, Ezekiel 36:25, 26, *From all your filthiness I will cleanse you; a new heart also will I give you, and a new spirit will I put within you.*

But I do not think of them all alike: there is a wide difference between some of them and others. I think most of them with whom I have spoken have much faith, love, joy, and peace. Some of these I believe are renewed in love, and have the *direct witness* of it: and they manifest the *fruit* above described, in all their words and actions. Now let any man call this what he will. It is what I call *Perfection.*

But some who have much love, peace, and joy, yet have not the direct witness. And others who think they have are nevertheless manifestly wanting in the fruit. How many I will not say, perhaps one in ten, perhaps more or fewer. But some are undeniably wanting, in long-suffering, Christian resignation. They do not see the hand of God in whatever occurs, and cheerfully embrace it. They do not in everything give thanks, and rejoice evermore. They are not happy, at least not always happy. For sometimes they complain. They say, "This or that is *hard!*"

Some are wanting in *gentleness.* They resist evil, instead of turning the other cheek. They do not receive reproach with gentleness; no, nor even reproof. Nay, they are not able to bear contradiction, without the appearance, at least, of resentment. If they are reproved, or contradicted, though mildly, they do not take it well. They behave with more distance and reserve than they did before. If they are reproved or contradicted harshly, they answer it with harshness, with a loud voice, or with an angry tone, or in a sharp and surly manner. They speak sharply or roughly, when they reprove others, and behave roughly to their inferiors.

Some are wanting in *goodness*. They are not kind, mild, sweet, amiable, soft, and loving at all times, in their spirit, in their words, in their look and air, in the whole tenor of their behavior; and that to all, high and low, rich and poor, without respect of persons: particularly to them that are out of the way, to opposers, and to those of their own household. They do not long, study, endeavor by every means, to make all about them happy. They can see them uneasy, and not be concerned; perhaps they make them so; and then wipe their mouths and say, "Why, they deserve it; it is their own fault."

Some are wanting in *fidelity,* a nice regard to truth, simplicity, and godly sincerity. Their love is hardly *without dissimulation;* something like guile is found in their mouth. To avoid roughness, they lean to the other extreme. They are smooth to an excess, so as scarce to avoid a degree of fawning, or of seeming to mean what they do not.

Some are wanting in *meekness,* quietness of spirit, composure, evenness of temper. They are up and down, sometimes high, sometimes low; their mind is not well balanced. Their affections are either not in due proportion, they have too much of one, too little of another; or they are not duly mixed and tempered together, so as to counterpoise each other. Hence there is often a jar. Their soul is out of tune, and cannot make the true harmony.

Some are wanting in *temperance*. They do not steadily use that kind and degree of food which they know, or might know, would most conduce to the health, strength, and vigor of the body. Or they are not temperate in sleep; they do not rigorously adhere to what is best both for body and mind. Otherwise they would constantly go to bed and rise early, and at a fixed hour. Or they sup late, which is good for neither body nor soul. Or they use neither fasting nor abstinence. Or they prefer (which is so many sorts of intemperance) that preaching, reading, or conversation, which gives them transient joy and comfort, before that which brings godly sorrow, or *instruction in righteousness.* Such joy is not sanctified: It does not tend to and terminate in the crucifixion of the heart. Such faith doth not center in God, but rather in itself.

So far all is plain. I believe you have faith, and love, and joy, and peace. You who are particularly concerned, know each for yourself, that you are wanting in the respect above-mentioned. You are wanting either in long-suffering, gentleness, or goodness; either in fidelity, meekness, or temperance. Let us not then, on either hand, fight about words. In the thing we clearly agree.

You have not what I call perfection. If others will call it so, they may. However hold fast what you have, and earnestly pray for what you have not.

Q. (29) Can those who are perfect grow in grace?
A. Undoubtedly they can. And that not only while they are in the body, but to all eternity.

Q. (30) Can they fall from it?
A. I am well assured they can. Matter of fact puts this beyond dispute. Formerly we thought, one saved from sin could not fall. Now, we know the contrary. We are surrounded with instances of those who lately experienced all that I mean by perfection. They had both the *fruit* of the spirit and the *witness.* But they have now lost both. Neither does anyone stand, by virtue of anything that is implied in the *nature* of the state. There is no such *height* or *strength* of holiness as it is impossible to fall from. If there be any that *cannot fall,* this wholly depends on the promise and faithfulness of God.

Q. (31) Can those who fall from this state recover it?
A. Why not? We have many instances of this also. Nay, it is an exceeding common thing for persons to lose it more than once, before they are established therein.

It is therefore to guard them who are saved from sin, from every occasion of stumbling, that I give the following advices. But first I shall speak plainly concerning the work itself.

I esteem this late work to be of God, probably the greatest now upon earth. Yet like all others, this also is mixed with much human frailty. But these weaknesses are far less than might have been expected, and ought to have been joyfully borne by all that loved and followed after righteousness. That there have been a few weak, warm-headed men is no reproach to the work itself, no just ground for accusing a multitude of sober-minded men, who are patterns of strict holiness. Yet (just contrary to what ought to have been) the opposition is great, the helps few. Hereby many are hindered from seeking faith and holiness by the false zeal of others, and some who at first began to run well are turned out of the way.

Q. (32) What is the first advice that you would give them?

A. Watch and pray continually against pride. If God has cast it out, see that it enter no more: It is full as dangerous as desire. And you may slide back into it unawares, especially if you think there is no danger of it. "Nay, but I ascribe all I have to God." So you may, and be proud nevertheless. For it is pride, not only to ascribe anything we have to ourselves, but to think we have what we really have not. Mr. L for instance, ascribed all the light he had to God, and so far he was humble. But then he thought he had more light than any man living. And this was palpable pride. So you ascribe all the knowledge you have to God, and in this respect you are humble. But if you think you have more than you really have, or if you think you are so taught of God as no longer to need man's teaching, pride lies at the door. Yes, you have need to be taught, not only by Mr. M-n, by one another, by Mr. M-d, or me, but by the weakest preacher in *London:* yea, by all men. For God sends by whom he will send.

Do not therefore say to any who would advise or reprove you, "You are blind: you cannot teach me." Do not say, "This is your *wisdom,* your *carnal reason*"; but calmly weigh the thing before God.

Always remember, much grace does not imply much light. These do not always go together. As there may be much light where there is little love, so there may be much love where there is little light. The heart has more heat than the eye, yet it cannot see. And God has wisely tempered the members of the body together, that none may say to another, *I have no need of you.*

To imagine none can teach you but those who are themselves saved from sin is a very great and dangerous mistake. Give not place to it for a moment. It would lead you into a thousand other mistakes, and that irrecoverably. No: *Dominion* is not *founded upon grace,* as the madmen of the last age talked. Obey and regard *them that are over you in the Lord,* and do not think you know better than them. Know their place, and *your own;* always remembering much love does not imply much light.

The not observing this has led some into many mistakes, and into the appearance, at least, of pride. Oh, beware of the appearance, and the thing. Let there *be in you that* lowly *mind, which was in Christ Jesus.*

And *be you* likewise *clothed with humility*. Let it not only fill, but cover you all over. Let modesty and self-diffidence appear in all your words and actions. Let all you speak and do show that you are little, and base, and mean, and vile in your own eyes.

As one instance of this, be always ready to own any fault you have been in. If you have at any time thought, spoke, or acted wrong, be not backward to acknowledge it. Never dream that this will hurt the cause of God; no, it will further it. Be therefore open and frank, when you are taxed with anything: Do not seek either to evade or disguise it. But let it appear just as it is, and you will thereby not hinder, but adorn the Gospel.

Q. (33) What is the second advice, which you would give them?
A. Beware of that daughter of pride, *enthusiasm!* Oh, keep at the utmost distance from it; give no place to a heated imagination. Do not hastily ascribe things to God. Do not easily suppose dreams, voices, impressions, visions, or revelations to be from God. They may be from him. They may be from nature. They may be from the devil. Therefore *believe not every spirit, but try the spirits whether they be of God.* Try all things by the written word, and let all bow down before it. You are in danger of enthusiasm every hour, if you depart ever so little from scripture; yea, or from the plain literal meaning of any text, taken in connection with the context. And so you are, if you despise or lightly esteem reason, knowledge, or human learning, every one of which is an excellent gift of God, and may serve the noblest purposes.

I advise you, never to use the words *wisdom, reason,* or *knowledge* by way of reproach. On the contrary, pray that you yourself may abound in them more and more. If you mean *worldly* wisdom, *useless* knowledge, *false* reasoning, say so; and throw away the chaff, but not the wheat.

One general inlet to enthusiasm is expecting the end without the means; the expecting knowledge, for instance, without searching the scriptures, and consulting the children of God; the expecting spiritual strength without constant prayer, and steady watchfulness; the expecting any blessing without hearing the word of God at every opportunity.

Some have been ignorant of this device of Satan. They have left off searching the scriptures. They said, "God writes all the scripture on my heart. Therefore I have no need to read it." Others thought they had not so much need of hearing, and grew so slack in attending the morning preaching. Oh, take warning, you who are concerned herein. You have listened to the voice of a stranger. Fly back to Christ, and keep in the good old way, which was *once delivered to the saints,* the way that even a heathen bore testimony of: "That the Christians rose early every day to sing hymns to Christ as God."

The very desire of *growing in grace* may sometimes be an inlet of enthusiasm. As it continually leads us to seek *new grace,* it may lead us unawares to seek something else new, besides *new degrees* of love to God and man. So it has led some to seek and fancy they had received gifts of a *new kind,* after a new heart, as: (a) the loving God with all our mind; (b) with all our soul; (c) with all our strength; (d) oneness with God; (e) oneness with Christ; (f) having our life hid with Christ in God; (g) being dead with Christ; (h) rising with him; (i) the sitting with him in heavenly places; (j) the being taken up into his throne; (k) the being in the new Jerusalem; (l) the seeing the tabernacle of God come down among men; (m) the being dead to all works; (n) the not being liable to death, pain, grief, or temptation.

One ground of many of these mistakes is the taking every fresh strong application of any of these scriptures to the heart, to be a gift of a *new kind:* not knowing that several of these scriptures are not fulfilled yet; that most of the others are fulfilled when we are justified; the rest, the moment we are sanctified. It remains only to experience them in *higher degrees.* This is all we have to expect.

Another ground of these and a thousand mistakes is the not considering deeply that love is the highest gift of God, humble, gentle, patient love; that all visions, revelations, manifestations whatever, are little things compared to love; and that all the gifts above-mentioned are either the same with, or infinitely inferior to it.

It were well you should be thoroughly sensible of this: The heaven of heavens is love. There is nothing higher in religion; there is, in effect, nothing else; if you look for anything but *more love,* you are looking wide of the mark, you are getting out of the royal way. And when you are asking others, have *you* received this or that blessing? If you mean anything but *more love,* you mean wrong; you are leading them out of the way, and putting them upon a false scent. Settle it then in your heart; that from the moment God has saved you from all sin, you are to aim at nothing more, but more of that love described in the thirteenth of the Corinthians. You can go no higher than this, till you are carried into Abraham's bosom.

I say yet again, beware of *enthusiasm.* Such is, the imagining you have the gift of *prophesying*, or of *discerning of spirits*, which I do not believe one of you has; no, nor ever had yet. Beware of judging people to be either right or wrong, by your own *feelings*. This is no scriptural way of judging. Oh, keep close to *the law and the testimony!*

Q. (34) What is the third?

A. Beware of Antinomianism, *making void the law*, or any part of it *through faith*. Enthusiasm naturally leads to this; indeed they can scarce be separated. This may steal upon you in a thousand forms, so that you cannot be too watchful against it. Take heed of everything, whether in principle or practice, which has any tendency thereto. Even that great truth, that Christ *is the end of the law*, may betray us into it, if we do not consider that he has adopted every point of the moral law, and grafted into it the law of love. Beware of thinking, "Because I am filled with love, I need not have *so much* holiness. Because I pray always, therefore I need no *set time* for private prayer; because I watch always, therefore I need no particular self-examination." Let us *magnify the law*, the whole written word, *and make it honorable*. Let this be our voice, *I prize your commandments, above gold or precious stones. Oh, what love have I unto your law. All the day long is my study in it!* Beware of *Antinomian books*, particularly the works of Dr. Crisp, and Mr. Saltmarsh. They contain many excellent things. And this makes them the more dangerous. Oh, be warned in time! Do not play with fire; do not put your hand on the hole of a cockatrice den! I entreat you, beware of *bigotry*. Let not your love or beneficence be confined to *Methodists* (so called) only; much less to that very small part of them who seem to be renewed in love; or to those who believe yours and their report; Oh, make not this your *shibboleth*. Beware of *stillness: ceasing*, in a wrong sense, *from your own works*. To mention one instance out of many, "You have received, says one, a great blessing. But you began to *talk* of it, and to *do* this and that. So you lost it. You should have been *still*."

Beware of *self-indulgence*, yea, and making a virtue of it, laughing at *self-denial*, and *taking up the cross daily*, at fasting or abstinence. Beware of *censoriousness*: thinking or calling them that anyways oppose *you*, whether in judgment or practice, *blind, dead, fallen*, or "enemies to the work." Once more, beware of *solifidianism*: crying nothing but "believe, believe" and condemning those as *ignorant* or *legal* who speak in a more scriptural way. At certain seasons indeed, it may be right to treat of nothing but repentance, or merely of faith, or altogether of holiness; but in general our call is to declare the whole counsel of God, and to prophesy according to the analogy of faith. The written word treats of the whole, and every particular branch of righteousness, descending to its minutest branches, as to be sober, courteous, diligent, patient, to honor all men. So likewise the Holy Spirit works the same in our hearts, not merely creating desires after holiness in general, but strongly inclining us to every particular grace, leading us to every individual part of *whatsoever is lovely*. And this with the greatest propriety; for as *by works faith is made perfect*, so the completing or destroying the work of faith, and enjoying the favor, or suffering the displeasure of God, greatly depends on every single act of obedience or disobedience.

Q. (35) What is the fourth?

A. Beware of *sins of omission*; lose no opportunity of doing good in any kind. Be zealous of good works; willingly omit no work, neither of piety or mercy. Do all the good you possibly can to the bodies and souls of men. Particularly, *you shall in any wise reprove your neighbor, and not suffer sin upon him*. Be *active*. Give no place to indolence or sloth; give no occasion to say, "You are idle, you are idle." Many will say so still; but let your whole spirit and behavior refuse the slander. Be always employed: lose no shred of time; gather up the fragments, that none be lost. And whatsoever your hand finds to do, do it with your might. *Be slow to speak*, and wary in speaking. *In a multitude of words there needs not sin*. Do not talk much: neither long at a time. Few can converse profitably above an hour. Keep at the utmost distance from pious chitchat, from religious gossiping.

Q. (36) What is the fifth?

A. Beware of *desiring* anything but God. Now you desire nothing else. Every other desire is driven out: see that none enter again. *Keep yourself pure, let your eye remain single, and your whole body shall be full of light*. Admit no desire of pleasing food, or any other pleasure of sense; no desire of pleasing the eye or the imagination, by anything grand, or new, or beautiful; no desire of money, of praise, or esteem; of happiness in *any creature*. You may bring these desires back; but you *need* not; you need feel them no more. Oh, stand fast in the liberty wherewith Christ has made you free.

Be patterns to all of denying yourselves and taking up your cross daily. Let them see that you make no account of any pleasure which does not bring you nearer to God, nor regard any pain which does; that you simply aim at pleasing him, whether by doing or suffering; that the constant language of your heart, with regard to pleasure or pain, honor or dishonor, riches or poverty, is

All's alike to me, so I
In my Lord may live and die!

Q. (37) What is the sixth?

A. Beware of *schism,* of making a rent in the church of Christ. That inward disunion, the members ceasing to have a reciprocal love *one for another* (1 Cor. 12:25) is the very root of all contention, and every outward separation. Beware of everything tending thereto. Beware of a dividing spirit; shun whatever has the least aspect that way. Therefore say not, *I am of Paul or of Apollos;* the very thing which occasioned the schism at Corinth. Say not, "This is *my* preacher, the best preacher in England. Give me him, and take all the rest." All this tends to breed or foment division, to disunite those whom God hath joined. Do not expel, or run down any preacher. Do not exalt anyone above the rest, lest you hurt both him and the cause of God. On the other hand do not bear hard upon any by reason of some incoherency or inaccuracy of expression; no, nor for some mistakes, were they really such.

Likewise if you would avoid schism, observe every *rule* of the *Society,* and of the *bands,* for conscience sake. Never omit meeting your class or band; never absent yourself from any public meeting. These are the very sinews of our Society; and whatever weakens, or tends to weaken our regard for these, or our exactness in attending them, strikes at the very root of our community. As one says, "That part of our economy, the private weekly meetings for prayer, examination, and particular exhortation, has been the greatest means of deepening and confirming every blessing that was received by the word preached, and of diffusing it to others who could not attend the public ministry; whereas, without this religious connection and intercourse, the most ardent attempts by mere preaching have proved of no lasting use."

Suffer not one thought of separating from your brethren, whether their opinions agree with yours or not. Do not dream that any man sins in not believing *you,* in not taking *your word;* or that this or that *opinion* is essential to the work, and both must stand or fall together.

Beware of *impatience, of contradiction*. Do not condemn or think hardly of those who cannot see just as you see, or who judge it their duty to contradict you, whether in a great thing or a small. I fear some of us have thought hardly of others, merely because they contradicted what we affirmed. All this tends to division. And by everything of this kind, we are teaching them an evil lesson against ourselves.

Oh, beware of touchiness, or testiness, not bearing to be spoken to; starting at the least word; and flying from those who do not implicitly receive mine or another's sayings!

Expect contradiction and opposition, together with crosses of various kinds. Consider the words of Saint Paul, *To you it is given in the behalf of Christ*, for his sake, as a fruit of his death and intercession for you, *not only to believe, but also to suffer for his sake* (Phil. 1:10). *It is given!* God *gives* you this opposition or reproach; it is a fresh token of his love. And will you disown the giver? Or spurn his gift and count it a misfortune? Will you not rather say, "*Father, the hour is come that you should be glorified.* Now you give your child to suffer something for you. *Do with me according to your will.*" Know that these things, far from being hindrances to the work of God, or to your soul, unless by your own fault, are not only unavoidable in the course of providence, but profitable, yea necessary for you. Therefore receive them from God (not from chance) with willingness, with thankfulness. Receive them from men with humility, meekness, yieldingness, gentleness, sweetness. Why should not even your outward *appearance* and *manner* be soft? Remember the character of Lady Cutts: "It was said of the Roman Emperor, Titus, never anyone came displeased from him. But it might be said of her, never anyone went displeased to her. So secure were all of the kind and favorable reception which they would meet with from her."

Beware of tempting others to separate from *you*. Give no offense which can possibly be avoided; see that your practice be in all things suitable to your profession, adorning the doctrine of God our Savior. Be particularly careful in speaking of yourself; you may not indeed deny the work of God; but speak of it, when you are called thereto, in the most inoffensive manner possible. Avoid all magnificent, pompous words. Indeed you need give it no *general* name. Neither "perfection, sanctification, the second blessing, nor the having attained." Rather speak of the *particulars*, which God has wrought for you. You may say, "At such a time I felt a change which I am not able to express. And since that time I have not felt pride, or self-will, or anger, or unbelief: nor anything but a fulness of love, to God and to all mankind." And answer any other plain question that is asked with modesty and simplicity.

And if any of you should at any time fall from what you now are, if you should again feel pride or unbelief, or any temper from which you are now delivered; do not deny, do not hide, do not disguise it at all, at the peril of your soul. At all events go to one in whom you can confide, and speak just what you feel. God will enable him to speak a word in season, which shall be health to your soul. And surely he will again lift up your head, and cause the bones that have been broken to rejoice.

Q. (38) What is the last advice that you would give them?

A. Be exemplary in all things: particularly in outward things (as in *dress*), in *little* things, in the laying out of your money (avoiding every needless expense), in deep, steady seriousness, and in the solidity and usefulness of all your conversation. So shall you be *a light shining in a dark place.* So shall you daily *grow in grace,* till *an entrance be ministered unto you abundantly into the everlasting kingdom of our Lord Jesus Christ.*

Most of the preceding advices are strongly enforced in the following reflections, which I recommend to your deep and frequent consideration, next to the holy scriptures.

A. The sea is an excellent figure of the fulness of God, and that of the blessed Spirit. For as the rivers all return into the sea, so the bodies, the souls, and the good works of the righteous return into God, to live there in his eternal repose.

Although all the graces of God depend on his mere bounty, yet is he pleased generally to attach them to the prayers, the instructions, and the holiness of those with whom we are. By strong, though invisible attractions, he draws some souls through their intercourse with others.

The sympathies formed by grace far surpass those formed by nature.

The truly devout show that passions as naturally flow from true as from false love, so deeply sensible are they of the goods and evils of those whom they love for God's sake. But this can only be comprehended by those who understand the language of love.

The bottom of the soul may be in repose, even while we are in many outward troubles; just as the bottom of the sea is calm, while the surface is strongly agitated.

The *best helps to growth in grace* are the ill usage, the affronts, and the losses which befall us. We should receive them with all thankfulness, as preferable to all others, were it only on this account, that our will has no part therein.

The readiest way to escape from our sufferings is to be willing they should endure as long as God pleases.

If we suffer persecution and affliction in a right manner, we attain a larger measure of conformity to Christ, by a due improvement of one of these occasions, than we could have done merely by imitating his mercy, in abundance of good works.

One of the greatest evidences of God's love to those that love him is to send them afflictions with grace to bear them.

Even in the greatest afflictions, we ought to testify to God that in receiving them from his hand, we feel pleasure in the midst of the pain, from being afflicted by him who loves us, and whom we love.

The readiest way which God takes to draw a man to himself is to afflict him in that he loves most, and with good reason; and to cause this affliction to arise from some good action done with a single eye; because nothing can more clearly show him the emptiness of what is most lovely and desirable in the world.

B. True *resignation* consists in a thorough conformity to the whole will of God, who wills and does all (excepting sin) which comes to pass in the world. In order to this we have only to embrace all events, good and bad, as his will.

In the greatest afflictions which can befall the just, either from heaven or earth, they remain immovable in peace and perfectly submissive to God, by an inward, loving regard to him, uniting in one all the powers of their souls.

We ought quietly to suffer whatever befalls us, to bear the defects of others, and our own, to confess them to God in secret prayer, or with groans which cannot be uttered; but never to speak a sharp or peevish word, nor to murmur or repine; but thoroughly willing that God should treat you in the manner that pleases him. We are his lambs, and therefore ought to be ready to suffer, even to the death, without complaining.

We are to bear with those we cannot amend, and to be content with offering them to God. This is true resignation. And since he has borne our infirmities, we may well bear those of each other for his sake.

To abandon all, to strip oneself of all, in order to seek and to follow Jesus Christ, naked to Bethlehem, where he was born; naked to the hall where he was scourged; and naked to Calvary, where he died on the cross, is so great a mercy that neither the thing nor the knowledge of it is given to any, but through faith in the Son of God.

C. There is no love of God without patience, and no patience without *lowliness* and sweetness of spirit.

Humility and patience are the surest proofs of the increase of love.

Humility alone unites patience with love, without which it is impossible to draw profit from suffering; or indeed to avoid complaint, especially when we think we have given no occasion for what men make us suffer.

True humanity is a kind of self-annihilation; and this is the center of all virtues.

A soul returned to God ought to be attentive to everything which is said to him on the head of salvation, with a desire to profit thereby.

Of the sins which God has pardoned, let nothing remain but a deeper humility in the heart, and a stricter regulation in our words, in our actions, and in our sufferings.

D. The bearing men, and suffering evils in *meekness* and silence, is the sum of a Christian life.

God is the first object of our love; its next office is to bear the defects of others. And we should begin the practice of this amid our own household.

We should chiefly exercise our love toward them who most shock, either our way of thinking, or our temper, or our knowledge, or the desire we have that others should be as virtuous as we wish to be ourselves.

E. God hardly gives his Spirit even to those whom he has established in grace, if they do not *pray* for it on all occasions, not only once, but many times.

God does nothing but in answer to prayer; and even they who have been converted to God without praying for it themselves (which is exceeding rare) were not without the prayers of others. Every new victory which a soul gains is the effect of a new prayer.

On every occasion of uneasiness, we should retire to prayer, that we may give place to the grace and light of God, and then form our resolutions, without being in any pain about what success they may have.

In the greatest temptations, a single look to Christ, and the barely pronouncing his name, suffice to overcome the wicked one so it be done with confidence and calmness of spirit.

God's command, to *pray without ceasing,* is founded on the necessity we have of his grace, to preserve the life of God in the soul, which can no more subsist one moment without it than the body can without air.

Whether we think of or speak to God, whether we act or suffer for him, all is prayer, when we have no other object than his love, and the desire of pleasing him.

All that a Christian does, even in eating and sleeping, is prayer, when it is done in simplicity, according to the order of God, without either adding to or diminishing from it by his own choice.

Prayer continues in the desire of the heart, tho' the understanding be employed on outward things.

In souls filled with love, the desire to please God is a continual prayer.

As the furious hate which the devil bears us is termed the roaring of the lion, so our vehement love may be termed crying after God.

God only requires of his adult children that their hearts be truly purified, and that they offer him continually the wishes and vows that naturally spring from perfect love. For these desires, being the genuine fruits of love, are the most perfect prayers that can spring from it.

F. It is scarce conceivable how *straight the way* is, wherein God leads them that follow him; and how dependent on him we must be, unless we are wanting in our faithfulness to him.

It is hardly credible of how great consequence before God the smallest things are, and what great inconveniences sometimes follow those which appear to be light faults.

As a very little dust will disorder a clock, and the least sand will obscure our sight, so the least grain of sin which is upon the heart will hinder its right motion toward God.

We ought to be in the church as the saints are in heaven, and in the house as the holiest men are in the church; doing our work in the house as we pray in the church, worshiping God from the ground of the heart.

CHRISTIAN PERFECTION

We should be continually laboring to cut off all the useless things that surround us. And God usually retrenches the superfluities of our souls in the same proportion as we do those of our bodies.

The best means of resisting the devil is to destroy whatever of the world remains in us, in order to raise for God upon its ruins a building all of love. Then shall we begin in this fleeting life to love God as we shall love him in eternity.

We scarce conceive how easy it is to rob God of his due in our friendship with the most virtuous persons, until they are torn from us by death. But if this loss produce lasting sorrow, that is a clear proof that we had before two treasures, between which we divided our heart.

G. If after having renounced all, we do not *watch* incessantly, and beseech God to accompany our vigilance with his, we shall be again entangled and overcome.

As the most dangerous winds may enter at little openings, so the devil never enters more dangerously than by little unobserved incidents which seem to be nothing, yet insensibly open the heart to great temptation.

It is good to renew ourselves from time to time by *closely examining* the state of our souls, as if we had never done it before. For nothing tends more to the full assurance of faith than to keep ourselves by this means in humility, and the exercise of all good works.

To continual watchfulness and prayer ought to be added continual employment. For grace fills a vacuum as well as nature, and the devil fills whatever God does not fill.

There is no faithfulness like that which ought to be between a guide of souls, and the person directed by him. They ought continually to regard each other, in God, and closely to examine themselves, whether all their thoughts are pure, and all their words directed with Christian discretion. Other affairs are only the things of men; but these are peculiarly the things of God.

H. The words of Saint Paul: *No man can call Jesus Lord, but by the Holy Ghost*, show us the necessity of eyeing God in our *good works*, and even in our minutest thoughts, knowing that none are pleasing to him but those which he forms in us and with us. From hence we learn that we cannot serve him unless he use our tongue, hands, and heart, to do by himself and his Spirit whatever he would have us to do.

If we were not utterly impotent, our good works would be our

371

own property; whereas now they belong wholly to God, because they proceed from him and his grace; while raising our works, and making them all divine, he honors himself in us through them.

One of the principal rules of religion is to lose no occasion of serving God. And since he is invisible to our eyes, we are to serve him in our neighbor, which he receives as if done to himself in person, standing visibly before us.

God does not love men that are inconstant, nor good works that are intermitted. Nothing is pleasing to him but what has a resemblance of his own immutability.

A constant attention to the work which God entrusts us with is a mark of solid piety.

Love fasts when it can, and as much as it can. It leads to all the ordinances of God, and employs itself in all the outward works whereof it is capable. It flies as it were, like Elijah over the plain, to find God upon his holy mountain.

God is so great that he communicates greatness to the least thing that is done for his service.

Happy are they who are sick; yea or lose their life for having done a good work.

God frequently conceals the part which his children have in the conversion of other souls. Yet one may boldly say: That person who long groans before him for the conversion of another, whenever that soul is converted to God, is one of the chief causes of it.

Charity cannot be practiced right unless, first, we exercise it the moment God gives the occasion; and secondly, retire the instant after, to offer it to God by humble thanksgiving. And this for three reasons, first: to render him what we have received from him; the second: to avoid the dangerous temptation, which springs from the very goodness of these works; and the third: to unite ourselves to God, in whom the soul expands itself in prayer, with all the graces we have received, and the good works we have done; to draw from him new strength against the bad effects which these very works may produce in us, if we do not make use of the antidotes which God has ordained against these poisons. The true means to be filled anew with the riches of grace is thus to strip ourselves of it; and without this, it is extremely difficult not to grow faint in the practice of good works.

Good works do not receive their last perfection 'till they, as it were, lose themselves in God. This is a kind of death to them, resembling that of our bodies, which will not attain their highest life, their immortality, 'till they lose themselves in the glory of our souls, or rather of God, wherewith they shall be filled. And it is only what they had of earthly and mortal, which good works lose by this spiritual death.

Fire is the symbol of love; and the love of God is the principle and the end of all our good works. But truth surpasses figure, and the fire of divine love has this advantage over material fire, that it can re-ascend to its source, and raise thither with it all the good works which it produces. And by this means it prevents their being corrupted by pride, vanity, or any evil mixture. But this cannot be done otherwise than by making these good works in a spiritual manner die in God, by a deep gratitude, which plunges the soul in him as in an abyss, with all that it is, and all the grace and works for which it is indebted to him: a gratitude whereby the soul seems to empty itself of them, that they may return to their source, as rivers seem willing to empty themselves when they pour themselves with all their waters into the sea.

When we have received any favor from God, we ought to retire, if not into our closets, into our hearts, and say, "I come, Lord, to restore to you what you have given, and I freely relinquish it, to enter again into my own nothingness. For what is the most perfect creature in heaven or earth in your presence, but a void capable of being filled with you and by you, as the air which is void and dark is capable of being filled with the light of the sun, who withdraws it every day to restore it the next, there being nothing in the air that either appropriates this light or resists it. O give me the same faculty of receiving and restoring your grace and good works! I say yours, for I acknowledge the root from which they spring is in you, and not in me."

26. In the year 1764, upon a review of the whole subject, I wrote down the sum of what I had observed, in the following short propositions.

A. There is such a thing as *perfection;* for it is again and again mentioned in scripture.

B. It is not so early as justification; for justified persons are to *go on to perfection* (Heb. 6:1).

C. It is not so late as death, for Saint Paul speaks of living men that were perfect (Phil. 3:15).

D. It is not *absolute.* Absolute perfection belongs not to man, nor to angels, but to God alone.

E. It does not make a man *infallible:* none is infallible, while he remains in the body.

F. Is it *sinless?* It is not worth while to contend for a term. It is *salvation from sin.*

G. It is *perfect love* (1 John 4:18). This is the *essence* of it: its *properties,* or inseparable fruits, are *rejoicing evermore, praying without ceasing, and in everything giving thanks* (1 Thes. 5:16ff.).

H. It is *improvable.* It is so far from lying in an indivisible point, from being incapable of increase, that one perfected in love may grow in grace far swifter than he did before.

I. It is *amissible*, capable of being lost, of which we have numerous instances. But we were not thoroughly convinced of this 'till five or six years ago.

J. It is constantly both preceded and followed by a *gradual* work.

K. But is it in itself instantaneous, or not? In examining this, let us go on step by step.

An *instantaneous change* has been wrought in some believers: None can deny this.

Since that change, they enjoy *perfect love.* They *rejoice evermore, pray without ceasing, and in everything give thanks.* Now this is all that I mean by perfection. Therefore these are witnesses of the perfection which I preach.

"But in some this change was not instantaneous." They did not perceive the instant, when it was wrought. It is often difficult to perceive the instant when a man dies. Yet there is an instant in which life ceases. And if even sin ceases, there must be a last moment of its existence, and a first moment of our deliverance from it.

"But if they have this love now, they will lose it." They may; but they need not. And whether they do or no, they have it now; they now experience what we teach. They now are *all love.* They *now* rejoice, pray, and praise without ceasing.

"However, sin is only *suspended* in them; it is not *destroyed.*" *Call* it which you please. They are *all love* today; and they take no thought for the morrow.

"But this doctrine has been much abused." So has that of justification by faith. But that is no reason for giving up, either this or any other scriptural doctrine! When you wash your child, as one speaks, "throw away the water, but do not throw away the child."

"But those who think they are saved from sin, say they have no need of the merits of Christ." They say just the contrary. Their language is,

CHRISTIAN PERFECTION

> Ev'ry moment, Lord, I want
> The merit of thy death!

They never before had so deep, so unspeakable a conviction of the need of Christ in all his offices as they have now.

Therefore all our preachers should make a point of *preaching perfection* to believers constantly, strongly, and explicitly.

And all believers should *mind this one thing*, and continually agonize for it.

27. I have now done what I proposed. I have given a plain and simple account of the manner wherein I first received the doctrine of perfection, and the sense wherein I received, and wherein I do receive and teach it to this day. I have declared the whole, and every part of what I mean by that scriptural expression. I have drawn the picture of it at full length, without either disguise or covering. And I would now ask any impartial person: What is there so frightful therein? Whence is all this outcry, which, for these twenty years and upwards, has been made throughout the kingdom; as if all Christianity were destroyed, and all religion torn up by the roots? Why is it that the very name of *Perfection* has been cast out of the mouths of Christians; yea, exploded and abhorred, as if it contained the most pernicious heresy? Why have the preachers of it been hooted at, like mad dogs, even by men that fear God; nay, and by some of their own children, some whom they, under God, had begotten through the Gospel? What *reason* is there for this? Or what *pretense?* Reason, sound reason there is none. It is impossible there should; but *pretenses* there are, and those in great abundance. Indeed there is ground to fear that with some who treat us thus, it is a mere pretense; that it is no more than a copy of their countenance, from the beginning to the end. They wanted, they sought occasion against *me;* and here they found what they sought. "This is Mr. *Wesley's* doctrine. He preaches perfection!" He does; yet this is not *his* doctrine, any more than it is *yours;* or anyone else's that is a Minister of *Christ.* For it is *his* doctrine, particularly, emphatically his: It is the doctrine of Jesus Christ. Those are *his* words, not mine: *You shall therefore be perfect, as your Father who is in heaven is perfect.* And who says, you shall not? Or at least, not till your soul is separated from the body? It is the doctrine of Saint Paul, the doctrine of Saint James, of Saint Peter, and Saint John; and no otherwise Mr. Wesley's than as it is the doctrine of everyone who

preaches the pure and the whole Gospel. I tell you, as plain as I can speak, where and when I found this. I found it in the oracles of God, in the Old and New Testaments; when I read them with no other view or desire but to save my own soul. But whose-soever this doctrine is, I pray you, what harm is there in it? Look at it again; survey it on every side and that with the closest attention. In one view it is purity of intention, dedicating all the life to God. It is the giving God all our heart; it is desire and design ruling all our tempers. It is the devoting, not a part, but all our soul, body, and substance to God. In another view, it is all the mind which was in Christ, enabling us to walk as Christ walked. It is the circumcision of the heart from all filthiness, all inward as well as outward pollution. It is a renewal of the heart in the whole image of God, the full likeness of him that created it. In yet another, it is the loving God with all our heart, and our neighbor as ourselves. Now take it in which of these views you please (for there is no material difference) and this is the whole and sole perfection, as a train of writings prove to a demonstration, which I have believed and taught for these forty years, from the year 1725 to the year 1765.

28. Now let this *perfection* appear in its native form, and who can speak one word against it? Will any dare to speak against loving the Lord our God with all our heart, and our neighbor as ourselves? Against a renewal of heart, not only in part, but in the whole image of God? Who is he that will open his mouth against being cleansed from all pollution both of flesh and spirit? Or against having all the mind that was in Christ, and walking in all things as Christ walked? What man who calls himself a Christian has the hardiness to object to the devoting, not a part, but all our soul, body, and substance to God? What serious man would oppose the giving God all our heart, and the having one design ruling all our tempers? I say, again, let this perfection appear in its own shape, and who will fight against it? It must be *disguised*, before it can be *opposed*. It must be *covered* with a bearskin first, or even the wild beasts of the people will scarce be induced to *worry* it. But whatever these do, let not the children of God any longer fight against the image of God. Let not members of Christ say anything against having the whole mind that was in Christ. Let not those who are alive to God oppose the dedicating all our life to him. Why should you, who have his love shed abroad in your heart, withstand the giving him all your heart? Does not all that is within you cry out: "Oh, who that loves can love enough?" What pity that

those who desire and design to please him should have any other design or desire? Much more that they should dread, as a fatal delusion, yea, abhor, as an abomination to God, the having this one desire and design ruling every temper! Why should *devout* men be afraid of devoting all their soul, body, and substance to God? Why should those who love Christ count it a damnable error, to think we may have all the mind that was in him? We allow, we contend, that we are *justified freely*, through the righteousness and the blood of Christ. And why are you so hot against us, because we expect likewise, to be *sanctified wholly* through his Spirit? We look for no favor either from the open servants of sin, or from those who have only the form of religion. But how long will you, who worship God in spirit, who are *circumcised with the circumcision not made with hands*, set your battle in array against those who seek an entire *circumcision of heart*, who thirst to be cleansed *from all filthiness of flesh and spirit*, and to *perfect holiness in the fear of God*? Are we your enemies because we look for a full deliverance from that *carnal mind, which is enmity against God*? Nay, we are your brethren, your fellow-laborers in the vineyard of our Lord, your companions in the kingdom and patience of Jesus. Although this we confess (if we are fools therein, yet as fools bear with us), we do expect to love God with all our heart, and our neighbor as ourselves. Yea, we do believe that he will in this world so "cleanse the thoughts of our hearts, by the inspiration of his Holy Spirit, that we shall perfectly love him, and worthily magnify his holy name."

A SERVICE
for
SUCH AS WOULD MAKE *or* RENEW THEIR COVENANT WITH GOD

[A Modern Adaptation]

A Hymn may be sung here or after the Lord's Prayer.

Minister: Let us pray.

Almighty God, unto whom all hearts be open, all desires known, and from whom no secrets are hid, cleanse the thoughts of our hearts by the inspiration of your Holy Spirit, that we may perfectly love you, and worthily magnify your holy Name; through Christ our Lord.

People: Amen.

Minister and People: Our Father, who are in heaven, hallowed by your name; your kingdom come; your will be done in earth as it is in heaven. Give us this day our daily bread. And forgive us our trespasses as we forgive them that trespass against us. And lead us not into temptation, but deliver us from evil. For yours is the kingdom, the power, and the glory, forever and ever. Amen.

Minister: Dearly beloved: Of old time the people called of God dedicated themselves to him in a Covenant of law and promise, the shadow of better things to come. We are called to a life in Christ, in whom we are redeemed from sin and consecrated to God, having been admitted into the New Covenant of love which our Lord instituted and sealed with his own blood, that it might remain forever.

On the one side this Covenant is the gracious promise of God in Christ, that he will fulfill in us, and for us, and through us, all that he has declared in Him who is the same yesterday, today, and forever. "He that spared not his own Son, but delivered him up for us all, how shall he not also with him freely give us all things?" We know that our God abides faithful, for we have abundantly proved that his grace is sufficient for us.

On our part the Covenant means that we willingly engage ourselves to live no more unto ourselves, but to him who loved us and gave himself for us.

"I beseech you therefore, brethren, by the mercies of God, that you present your bodies a living sacrifice, holy, acceptable unto God, which is your reasonable service." "For the love of Christ constrains us, because we thus judge that one died for all, therefore all died; and he died for all, that they who live should no longer live unto themselves, but unto him who for their sakes died and rose again."

381

APPENDIX

We know well that in the past we have not fulfilled all our part in this Covenant. We have been more willing to claim its promises than to be held by its bonds. We are ignorant and frail; too often we have been wayward and willfully disobedient. Yet God has had long patience with us; his mercy endures forever.

From time to time we renew our vows of consecration, especially when we gather at the table of the Lord; but on this day we meet expressly, as generations of our fathers have met, that we may sacredly and earnestly renew that Covenant which bound them and binds us to God.

Let us then draw near to God, thankfully remembering his mercies and examining ourselves by the light of his Spirit, that we may see wherein we have transgressed or fallen short. Then, having considered what is the hope of our calling, let us give ourselves anew to him.

ADORATION

Here all shall kneel

Minister: Let us adore the Father, the God of love who created us;
  Who every moment preserves and sustains us;
  Who has loved us with an everlasting love, and given us the light of the knowledge of his glory in the face of Jesus Christ.

People: We praise you, O God, we acknowledge you to be the Lord.

Minister: Let us glory in the grace of our Lord Jesus Christ;
  Who, though he was rich, yet for our sakes became poor;
  Who was tempted in all points like as we are, yet without sin;
  Who was obedient unto death, even the death of the cross;
  Who was dead, and lives forevermore;
  Who opened the kingdom of heaven to all believers;
  Who will yet make all things new.

People: To him be glory and dominion forever.

APPENDIX

Minister: Let us rejoice in the fellowship of the Holy Spirit, the Lord and Giver of Life, by whom we are born into the family of God, and made members of the body of Christ, one fellowship in him;

Whose witness confirms us;

Whose wisdom teaches us;

Whose power enables us;

Who waits to do for us exceeding abundantly above all that we ask or think.

People: Breathe you within our hearts, most Holy Spirit.

THANKSGIVING

Here all shall stand

Minister: Let us give thanks to God for his manifold mercies.

O God our Father, the fountain of all goodness, who has been gracious to us, not only in the year that is past but through all the years of our lives: we give you thanks for your loving kindness which has filled our days and brought us to this time and place.

People: We praise your Holy Name.

Minister: You have given us life and reason, and set us in a world which is bright with your beauty. You have comforted us with kindred and friends, and ministered to us through the hands and minds of our fellows.

People: We praise your Holy Name.

Minister: You have set in our hearts a hunger for you, and given us your peace. You have redeemed us and called us to a high calling in Christ Jesus. You have given us a place in the fellowship of your Spirit and the witness of your Church.

People: We praise your Holy Name.

APPENDIX

Minister: In darkness you have been light to us; in adversity and temptation a rock of strength; in our joys the very spirit of joy; in our labors the all-sufficient reward.

People: We praise your Holy Name.

Minister: You have remembered us when we have forgotten you, followed us even though we fled from you, met us with forgiveness when we turned back to you. For all your long-suffering and the abundance of your grace,

People: We praise your Holy Name.

Minister: For these and all your mercies, known or unknown, remembered or forgotten,

People: We praise your Holy Name.

CONFESSION

Minister: Let us now examine ourselves before God, humbly confessing our sins and looking for his promised forgiveness, watching our hearts, lest by self-deceit we shut ourselves out from his presence.

Here all shall kneel
O God our Father, who has set forth the way of life for us in your beloved Son: we confess with shame our slowness to learn of him, our reluctance to follow him. You have spoken and called, and we have not given heed; your beauty has shone forth and we have been blind; you have stretched your hands to us through our fellows and we have passed by. We have taken great benefits with little thanks; we have been unworthy of your changeless love.

People: Have mercy upon us and forgive us, O Lord.

Minister: Forgive us, we beseech you, the poverty of our worship, the formality and selfishness of our prayers, our inconstancy and little faith, our neglect of fellowship, our hesitating witness for Christ, our false pretenses and our willful ignorance of your ways.

APPENDIX

People: Have mercy upon us and forgive us, O Lord.

Minister: Forgive us wherein we have wasted our time or abused our gifts. Forgive us if we have excused our evildoing or evaded our responsibilities. Forgive us that we have been unwilling to overcome evil with good, that we have drawn back from the cross.

People: Have mercy upon us and forgive us, O Lord.

Minister: Forgive us that so little of your love has reached others through us. We have borne too easily wrongs and sufferings that were not our own. We have been thoughtless in our judgments, hasty in condemnation, grudging in forgiveness.

People: Forgive us as we forgive others, O Lord.

Minister: Most Holy Father, our sins are such as sent our Lord to his cross. We have no ground where we can stand before you save the greatness of the mercy revealed in that cross.

People: Nothing in my hands I bring,
    Simply to Thy cross I cling.

Minister and People: Have mercy upon me, O God, according to your loving kindness; according to the multitude of your tender mercies, blot out my transgressions. Create in me a clean heart, O God, and renew a right spirit within me.

Minister: As the heaven is high above the earth, so great is his mercy toward them that fear him. As far as the east is from the west, so far has he removed our transgressions from us.
    God is light, and in him is no darkness at all. If we walk in the light as he is in the light, we have fellowship one with another, and the blood of Jesus his Son cleanses us from all sin. If we say we have no sin, we deceive ourselves, and the truth is not in us. If we confess our sins, he is faithful and righteous to forgive us our sins, and to cleanse us from all unrighteousness.

People: Amen.

APPENDIX

Then all shall stand and sing Hymn 338 (M.H.B.)

My Savior, how shall I proclaim,
How pay the mighty debt I owe?
Let all I have and all I am,
Ceaseless to all thy glory show.

Too much to thee I cannot give;
Too much I cannot do for thee;
Let all thy love, and all thy grief
Graven on my heart forever be.

THE COVENANT

Minister: And now, beloved, let us bind ourselves with willing bonds to our Covenant God, and take the yoke of Christ upon us.

This taking of his yoke upon us means that we are heartily content that he shall appoint us our place and work, and that he alone shall be our reward.

Christ has many services to be done; some are easy, others more difficult; some bring honor, others bring reproach; some are suitable to our natural inclinations and temporal interests, others are contrary to both. In some we may please Christ and please ourselves; but there are others in which we cannot please Christ except by denying ourselves. Yet the power to do this is assuredly given us in Christ. We can do all things in him who strengtheneth us.

Search your hearts, therefore, whether you can now freely make a sincere and unreserved dedication of yourselves to God.

Make the Covenant of God your own. Engage yourself to him. Resolve to be faithful. Having engaged your heart to the Lord, resolve, not in your own strength, nor in the power of your own resolutions, but in his might, never to go back.

Let us commune with God in silent prayer.

SILENT PRAYER

Then shall the Minister say in the name of all:
O Lord God, Holy Father, who has called us through Christ to

APPENDIX

be partakers in this gracious Covenant, we take upon ourselves with joy the yoke of obedience, and engage ourselves, for love of you, to seek and do your perfect will. And as you have shown us him who is the Way, the Truth, and the Life, we will follow our Lord whithersoever he goes. We are no longer our own, but yours.

And here all the people shall join:
I am no longer my own, but yours. Put me to what you will, rank me with whom you will; put me to doing, put me to suffering; let me be employed for you or laid aside for you, exalted for you or brought low for you; let me be full, let me be empty; let me have all things, let me have nothing; I freely and heartily yield all things to your pleasure and disposal.

And now, O glorious and blessed God, Father, Son, and Holy Spirit, you are mine, and I am yours. So be it. And the Covenant which I have made on earth, let it be ratified in heaven.

Here shall follow a Hymn, the Collection for the Poor, and the Service of Holy Communion.

BENEDICTION

Minister: Now unto him that is able to keep you from falling, and to present you faultless before the presence of his glory with exceeding joy, to the only wise God our Savior, be glory and majesty, dominion and power, now and ever.

People: Amen.

Minister: The grace of our Lord Jesus Christ, and the love of God, and the communion of the Holy Spirit, be with you all.

People: Amen.

BIBLIOGRAPHY

Abbey, C. J., and Overton, J. H. *The English Church in the Eighteenth Century.* London: Longmans, Green & Co., 1887.

Asbury, H. *A Methodist Saint: The Life of Bishop Asbury.* New York: A. A. Knopf, 1927.

Baker, F. *A Union Catalogue of the Publications of John and Charles Wesley.* Duke University Divinity School, North Carolina, 1966.

————. *Charles Wesley as Revealed by His Letters.* Wesley Historical Society Lecture, no. 14. London, 1948.

————. *John Wesley and the Church of England.* London: Epworth, 1970.

Bengel, J. A. *Gnomon of the New Testament.* Edited by M. E. Bengel, completed by J. C. F. Steudel. 2 vols., 7th ed. Edinburgh, 1877.

Bett, H. *The Spirit of Methodism.* London: Epworth, 1937.

Bowmer, J. C. *The Sacrament of the Lord's Supper in Early Methodism.* London: Epworth, 1951.

Cannon, W. *The Theology of John Wesley.* New York: Abingdon, 1946.

Cell, G. C. *The Rediscovery of John Wesley.* New York: Henry Holt & Co., 1935.

Church, L. F. *The Early Methodist People.* London: Epworth, 1948.

Coulter, E. M., and Saye, A. B., eds. *A List of the Early Settlers of Georgia.* Athens, Georgia, 1949.

Davey, C. J. *The March of Methodism.* London: Epworth, 1951.

Davies, Horton. *Worship and Theology in England. From Watts and Wesley to Maurice, 1690–1850.* Princeton University Press, 1961.

Davies, R. E. *Methodism.* London: Epworth, 1976.

————, and Rupp, G., eds. *A History of the Methodist Church in Great Britain,* vol. I. London: Epworth, 1965.

Deschner, J. *Wesley's Christology.* Dallas, 1960.

Doughty, W. L. *John Wesley, His Conferences and His Preachers.* Wesley Historical Society Lecture, no. 10. London, 1944.

389

————. *John Wesley, Preacher.* London: Epworth, 1955.

Edwards, M. L. *Family Circle: A Study of the Epworth Household in Relation to John and Charles Wesley.* London: Epworth, 1949.

————. *John Wesley and the Eighteenth Century.* London: Epworth, 1955.

————. *My Dear Sister. The Story of John Wesley and the Women in His Life.* Leeds: Penwork, 1980.

Fletcher, J. *Collected Works.* 8 vols. Edited by J. Benson. London, 1806.

Flew, R. N. *The Hymns of Charles Wesley: A Study of Their Structure.* London, 1963.

————. *The Idea of Perfection in Christian Theology.* London: Oxford University Press, 1934.

Form of Discipline for the Ministers, Preachers and Members of the Methodist Episcopal Church in America, Considered and Approved at a Conference Held at Baltimore . . . 27th of December, 1784. Elizabeth-Town, N.J., 1788.

Gill, F. C. *John Wesley's Prayers.* London: Epworth, 1951.

————. *Selected Letters of John Wesley.* London: Epworth, 1956.

Green, R. *The Works of John and Charles Wesley: A Bibliography.* London: C. H. Kelly, 1896.

Green, V. H. H. *The Young Mr. Wesley.* London: Edward Arnold, 1961.

Halevy, E. *The Birth of Methodism in England.* Translated and edited by B. Semmel. Chicago: University of Chicago Press, 1971.

Harrison, A. W. *The Separation of Methodism from the Church of England.* Wesley Historical Society Lecture, no. 11. London, 1945.

Harrison, G. E. *Son to Susanna.* London: Nicholson & Watson, 1937.

Herbert, T. W. *John Wesley as Editor and Author.* Princeton University Press, 1940.

Hildebrandt, F. *From Luther to Wesley.* London: Lutterworth, 1951.

————. *Christianity According to the Wesleys.* London: Epworth, 1956.

Hodges, H. A., and A. M. Allchin. *A Rapture of Praise.* London: Hodder and Stoughton, 1966.

Holt, I. L. *The Methodists of the World.* New York: Methodist Church Board of Missions and Church Extension, 1950.

Hunter, F. *John Wesley and The Coming Comprehensive Church.* Wesley Historical Society lecture, no. 33. London, 1968.

Hutton, J. E. *History of the Moravian Church.* 2nd ed. Moravian Pub. Off., 1909.

Jackson, T. *Life of Charles Wesley.* 2 vols. London: Mason, 1841.

BIBLIOGRAPHY

————, ed. *Lives of the Early Methodist Preachers*. 6 vols. London, 1871–1872.

Jaeger, W. *Two Rediscovered Works of Ancient Christian Literature: Gregory of Nyssa and Macarius*. Leiden: E. J. Brill, 1954.

Lecky, W. E. H. *A History of England in the Eighteenth Century*, vol. III. London: Longmans, 1892.

Kay, J. A. *Wesley's Prayers and Praises*. London: Epworth, 1958.

Lawton, G. *Shropshire Saint*. London: Epworth, 1960.

Lawton, J. S. *Miracles and Revelation*. London: Lutterworth, 1959.

Lee, U. *John Wesley and Modern Religion*. Nashville, Tenn.: Cokesbury, 1936.

————. *The Lord's Horseman*. London: Hodder & Stoughton, 1956.

Lindstrom, H. *Wesley and Sanctification*. Stockholm: Nya Bokförlags Aktiebolaget, 1946.

Lyles, A. M. *Methodism Mocked*. London: Epworth, 1960.

Manning, B. L. *The Hymns of Wesley and Watts*. London: Epworth, 1942.

Methodist Hymn Book. London: Methodist Conference Office, 1933.

Munk, Robert C. *John Wesley. His Puritan Heritage*. London: Epworth, 1966.

Nuelsen, J. L. *John Wesley and the German Hymn*. Translated by T. Parry, S. H. Moore, and A. Holbrook. Calverley: Holbrook, 1972.

Ollard, S. L., and Walker, P. C. *Archbishop Herring's Visitation Returns*, vol. I. 1743.

Orcibal, J. "Les Spirituels francais et espagnols chez John Wesley et ses contemporains." *Revue de l'Histoire des Religions*, vol. 139, 1951.

Outler, A. C. *John Wesley*. New York: Oxford University Press, 1964.

Parris, J. R. *John Wesley's Doctrine of the Sacraments*. London: Epworth, 1963.

Peters, J. L. *Christian Perfection and American Methodism*. New York: Abingdon, 1956.

Piette, M. *John Wesley in the Evolution of Protestantism*. New York: Sheed and Ward, 1937.

Pollock, J. C. *George Whitefield and the Great Awakening*. London: Hodder and Stoughton, 1973.

Pudney, J. *John Wesley and His World*. London: Thames & Hudson, 1978.

Rack, H. D. *The Future of John Wesley's Methodism*. London: Lutterworth, 1965.

BIBLIOGRAPHY

Rattenbury, J. E. *The Evangelical Doctrines of Charles Wesley's Hymns.* London: Epworth, 1941.

———. *The Eucharistic Hymns of John and Charles Wesley.* London: Epworth, 1948.

Sangster, W. E. *The Path to Perfection.* London: Hodder & Stoughton, 1943.

Schmidt, M. *John Wesley, a Theological Biography,* vols. I and II. Translated by N. P. Goldhawk. London: Epworth, 1962, 1971.

Semmel, B. *The Methodist Revolution.* London: Heinemann, 1974.

Sidney, E. *The Life, Ministry and Selections from the Remains of the Rev. Samuel Walker, B.A., formerly of Truro, Cornwall.* London: Baldwin and Cradock, 1835.

Simon, J. S. *John Wesley and the Religious Societies.* London: Epworth, 1921.

———. *John Wesley and the Methodist Societies.* London: Sharp, 1923.

———. *John Wesley and the Advance of Methodism.* London: Epworth, 1925.

———. *John Wesley, the Master Builder.* London: Epworth, 1927.

———. *John Wesley, the Last Phase.* London: Epworth, 1934.

Southey, R. *Life of Wesley,* vol. II. New ed. London, 1925.

Sweet, W. W. *Religion on the American Frontier, IV. The Methodists, 1783–1840.* New York: Cooper Square, 1946.

Sykes, N. *Church and State in England in the Eighteenth Century.* Historical Association Pamphlet 78, Cambridge, 1934.

Todd, J. M. *John Wesley and the Catholic Church.* London: Hodder and Stoughton, 1958.

Towlson, C. W. *Moravian and Methodist.* London: Epworth, 1957.

Tripp, D. *The Renewal of the Covenant in the Methodist Tradition.* London: Epworth, 1969.

Tuttle, R. G. *John Wesley, His Life and Theology.* Michigan: Zundervan Pub., 1979.

Tyerman, L. *Life and Times of Rev. John Wesley, M.A.* 3 vols. London: Hodder & Stoughton, 1870–1871.

Vallins, G. H. *The Wesleys and the English Language.* London: Epworth, 1957.

Wakefield, G. *Methodist Devotion. The Spiritual Life in the Methodist Tradition.* London: Epworth, 1966.

———. *Fire of Love. The Spirituality of John Wesley.* London: Darton, Longman and Todd, 1976.

Watson, P. S. *The Message of the Wesleys.* London: Epworth, 1964.

BIBLIOGRAPHY

Wearmouth, F. R. *Methodism and the Common People of the Eighteenth Century.* London: Epworth, 1945.

Wesley, Charles. *Journal.* 2 vols. Edited by T. Jackson. London: Mason, 1849.

———. *Journal.* Edited by J. Telford and R. Culley. London, 1909.

Wesley, Charles, and Wesley, John. *Poetical Works.* Edited by G. Osborn. 13 vols. London: Wesleyan Methodist Conference Office, 1868–1872.

Wesley, John. *Works.* 3rd ed., with last corrections of the author. Edited by T. Jackson. London: Mason, 1829–1831.

———. *Journal.* Standard ed. Edited by N. Curnock. 8 vols. London: R. Culley, 1909–1916.

———. *Letters.* Standard ed. Edited by J. Telford. 8 vols. London: Epworth, 1931.

Wesley, John. *Standard Sermons.* Edited by E. H. Sugden. 2 vols. London: Epworth, 1921.

———. *A Christian Library. Consisting of Extracts from and Abridgements of the Choicest Pieces of Practical Divinity, Which Have Been Publish'd in the English Tongue.* 50 vols. Bristol, 1749–1755.

Whitehead, J. *The Life of the Rev. John Wesley, M.A.* 2 vols. London, 1793–1796.

Williams, C. *John Wesley's Theology Today.* Paper. Nashville, Tenn.: Abingdon, 1972.

Wiseman, F. L. *Charles Wesley and His Hymns.* London: Epworth, 1938.

INDEX TO PREFACE
FOREWORD AND INTRODUCTION

INDEX

Predestination, 37, 43.
Psalms, 4.
Puritans, xv, 5, 39, 59.

Quesnel, 10.
Quietism, 13, 21, 27, 28.

Rattenbury, J.E., 1–2.
Raikes, Robert, 58.
Reason, and hymns, 38; and
    spirituality, xiii, xv, 6, 7, 8, 45.
Reformation, 3, 48.
Religion, and doctrine, 8; as inward,
    xvii, 5, 9, 10, 19, 62; and
    practices, 11; and renewal, 7; as
    social, 58, 62; and Wesleys, xiii,
    5, 8, 21, 24, 44.
Repentance, xiii, xv, 43.
Revival, 18th Century, 26, 40, 48;
    Methodist, xiv, 1, 3, 11, 14, 26,
    34, 37, 39, 44, 61, 69; popular,
    xvii; Protestant, 39; streams of,
    26, 40, 48, 61.
Richter, 17, 66.
Ritchie, Elizabeth, xiii.
Robson, George B., 73.
Romaine, 42.
Rothe, J., 66.

Sacraments, xx, 3, 5, 12, 14, 15, 19,
    27, 28, 29, 30, 32, 33, 43, 55, 60,
    62, 63.
Sacrifice, of Christ, 31; of Church,
    31; of Eucharist, 28–33; of
    ourselves, 29.
Saints, xiii, 40, 60, 69.
Salvation, and Christ, xvi, 20, 33;
    and dispensations, 43–44; and
    faith, 36; fruits of, 36; order of,
    xv, xvii, 33; and works, 43.
Sanctification, 8, 11, 47, 48, 50, 52,
    60, 64.
Saye, A.B., 16.
Scheffler, J., 18, 66.
Scougal, Henry, xiv.
Scupoli, Lorenzo, xiv, 10, 11.
Self, and assurance, 46; -awareness,
    53; -consciousness, xiii;

-examination, xiv; -knowledge,
    xv.
Sidney, Edwin, 54.
Sin, 20, 43, 44, 48, 50, 53–54.
Sinners, and Christ, xvi, 24, 38.
Smith, John, 5.
Social Concern, xvii, xx, 13, 15, 19,
    35–36, 44, 50, 56, 58, 59, 61, 63,
    64.
Social Gospel, 63.
Soteriology, xvi.
Southey, R., 53.
Spangenberg, 16, 19, 66.
Spirituality, Anglican, 2, 3, 5, 12,
    25–27, 56; Christian, 4, 13, 42,
    50; Eastern, xiv, 12, 48; and
    Methodist Revival, 26, 28, 36,
    37; Protestant, 3, 4, 11, 12, 13,
    48; Roman, 3, 4, 10, 11, 13, 30;
    Western, 2, 10, 12.
Spirituality, Wesleyan, development
    of, 11, 15, 16, 17, 23, 26, 43, 60;
    and discipline, xiv, 15, 55; and
    doctrine, 2, 3, 8, 11; and
    eucharist, 2, 13, 14, 28–31; and
    hymns, 4, 19, 27–33, 37, 43,
    46–53, 54, 61, 62; integral, 26,
    28, 59, 63, 64; inward, 13, 19, 22,
    23, 44, 46, 47, 56, 58, 60, 64; life
    of, 8–9, 23, 46; and liturgy, 2, 3,
    13, 14, 19, 27; outward, 13, 23,
    36, 44, 56, 58, 59, 60, 61, 64; and
    reason, xiii, xv, 6, 7, 8, 45; and
    sacraments, 3, 14, 19, 27, 28, 32,
    33; and scripture, 6, 7, 9–10, 42;
    universal, xvii, 43, 45, 50, 56, 63.
Sykes, N., 25.

Tauler, J., 10.
Taylor, Jeremy, xiv, 9.
Telford, J., 69.
Tersteegen, G., 66.
Theology, Arminian, 37, 43; and
    Calvinism, 21, 43; Moravian, 27;
    of Reformation, 48; Wesleyan,
    2, 6, 16, 31, 37, 41, 43.
Thomson, 40.
Todd, J.M., 2, 9, 30.

399

INDEX

Trinity, 8.
Tripp, D., 59.

Vasey, 55.
Vazeille, Mrs., 2.
Venn of Huddersfield, 40.
Voltaire, 40.

Walker, P.C., 26.
Walker, Samuel, 42, 43, 44, 46, 50, 54, 55.
Watson, P.S., 58.
Wesley, Charles; and doctrine, xiv-xv; and Georgia, 1, 15, 19, 23, 24; *Hymns* of xv, xvi, xix, 1, 4, 5, 19, 24, 27–33, 35, 37, 43, 46–53, 61, 62, 63, 69–72; life of, 1, 3, 6, 11, 23, 24, 57; style of, xvii, 1, 70.
Wesley, John, and Aldersgate, 3, 20, 21, 22, 26; conversion of, 9, 20; and Georgia, xiv, 1, 15, 16, 19, 20, 21, 23, 34, 35; life of, 1, 4-23, 55, 57; myths about, 6; as organizer, 7, 11, 12, 16, 34, 36, 37, 60; and preaching, xv, xvi, 2, 6, 7, 34, 39.
Wesley, John, Works of, *Christian Library*, 10, 12; *A Collection of Prayers*, xiv; *An Earnest Appeal*, 8; editions, 65–69; *A Farther Appeal*, 8; *Forms of Prayer*, xix, 15, 65; *Journal*, 7, 20, 21, 22, 36, 66–67; letters, 5, 12, 44, 55, 58, 69; *Life of Fletcher*, 69; *Notes on the New Testament*, 61; pamphlets, 58; *Plain Account of*

Christian Perfection, xv, 7, 9, 10, 43, 72–73; *Plain Account of Genuine Christianity*, 12, 44, 56, 57, 68; *Scheme of Self-Examination*, xix, 15, 65; sermons, 14, 21, 34, 48, 50, 56, 58, 59, 61, 67; *A Short History*, 13, 21; translations by, xix, 1, 15, 16–19, 27, 63, 66.
Wesley, Samuel, 5, 25.
Wesley, Susanna, 5.
Wesleys, cf. also Spirituality (Wesleyan); Arminianism of, 37–42; 53, 60, 63; differences between, 2; and doctrine, xv, 3, 4, 8, 37, 43, 45, 54, 61, 62, 70; influences on, xiv, xix, 3, 5, 8–9, 10, 12, 26, 34, 35; and Scripture, xiv, 5, 6, 7, 9–10, 11, 12, 36, 63, 70, 73; and social concerns, xvii, 13, 15, 19, 35–36, 44, 56, 58, 61, 63; vision of, xvii, 3, 55, 68.
Whatcoat, 55.
Whitefield, George, 15, 22, 33, 34, 37.
Whitehead, J., 57, 67.
Wilberforce, William, xix, 58.
Will, cf. also God; 8, 13, 43, 54.
William of St. Thierry, xv.
Williams, William, 25.
Winckler, 18, 66.
Word, the, 47.
Works, and faith, 22; good-, 22, 59; and holiness, 13, 44, 64; and salvation, 43.
Worship, 53, 56, 61, 63.

Zinzendorf, 17, 18, 21, 27, 66.

INDEX TO TEXTS

INDEX

INDEX

INDEX

Galatians, 2:20, 178, 197; 5:5, 342.
Genesis, 32:24–32, 192.
George, Prince of Denmark, 167.
Gerhard, Paulus, 93.
Gibson, Bishop, 306.
God, adoration of, 177, 206, 207, 221, 382; attributes of, 86, 113, 119; blessing of, 112, 139, 157, 158, 181, 206, 210, 227, 230, 245, 250, 258, 293, 308, 331, 361, 362, 365; children of, 83, 91, 92, 112, 116, 119, 161, 164, 202, 228, 230, 268, 290, 301, 311, 312, 313, 316, 353, 354, 361, 376; commands, 80, 81, 100, 101, 102, 115, 117, 126, 137, 138, 141, 190, 213, 245, 258, 305, 315, 322, 336, 348, 370, 372; communion with, 155, 163, 166, 167; as Creator, 81, 83, 112, 117, 119, 121, 122, 124, 125, 206, 234, 300, 304, 310, 348, 376, 382, 383; debt to, 117, 373; dedication to, 78, 85, 95, 96, 121, 125, 138, 149, 162, 163, 199, 205, 211, 224, 232, 235, 236, 239, 247, 292, 299, 301, 305, 316, 376, 377, 381, 382, 386; desire for, 78, 81, 85, 91, 96, 125, 214, 218, 230, 231, 300, 303, 304, 313, 319, 333, 336, 351, 364, 370, 376, 377, 383; elect of, 82, 115, 119, 137, 176; face of, 95, 217, 240, 266, 293; fear of, 146, 152, 158, 169, 176, 194, 210, 212, 248, 313, 321, 339, 375, 377, 385; as friend, 234, 281; gifts of, 82, 92, 106, 107, 109, 115, 117, 164, 227, 245, 273, 310, 340, 353, 361, 362, 366, 373; and glory, 78, 79, 109, 111, 113, 115, 117, 120, 125, 144, 156, 159, 177, 191, 202, 207, 212, 229, 281, 289, 292, 301, 302, 305, 312, 330, 347, 366, 373, 381, 382; goodness (kindness) of, 81, 83, 85, 115, 117, 124, 125, 146, 147, 179, 182, 196, 206, 221, 226, 243, 330, 356, 367, 383, 385; hand of, 81, 83, 85, 91, 93, 112, 115, 169, 206, 349, 357, 368, 384; heirs of, 313; help of, 91, 103, 162, 164, 342; image of, 83, 86, 94, 104, 122, 125, 129, 169, 218, 221, 247, 278, 280, 310, 311, 313, 319, 334, 335, 356, 376; Kingdom of, 82, 107, 114, 115, 119, 120, 266, 270, 271, 289, 291, 336, 381; knowledge of, 80, 83, 96, 109, 111, 113, 114, 124, 128, 131, 168, 186, 188, 189, 205, 206, 211, 227, 330, 343, 353, 382; light of, 89, 90, 92, 96, 97, 127, 309, 316, 384, 385; love for, 79, 80, 81, 82, 83, 89, 90, 91, 95, 96, 97, 109, 112, 114, 121, 124, 125, 126, 131, 168, 177, 208, 231, 236, 270, 300, 301, 303, 304, 305, 312, 313, 316, 321, 322, 326, 329, 330, 332, 338, 339, 340, 341, 342, 343, 349, 351, 355, 362, 367, 368, 369, 370, 371, 376, 377, 381, 387; love of, 82, 83, 91, 92, 93, 94, 112, 113, 117, 125, 131, 147, 162, 188, 196, 200, 204, 206, 211, 214, 222, 227, 239, 243, 258, 259, 266, 275, 283, 292, 293, 294, 301, 302, 304, 312, 319, 327, 330, 331, 335, 338, 346, 353, 366, 368, 373, 376, 382, 383, 384, 385, 387; name of, 81, 82, 94, 113, 114, 115, 170, 171, 208, 229, 240, 293, 301, 303, 304, 377, 381, 383, 384; nature of, 113, 225, 229, 303; offending of, 111, 180, 198, 305, 309, 377; pleasing of, 104, 111, 112, 115, 116, 118, 120, 125, 131, 139, 148, 160, 170, 190, 198, 237, 248, 265, 266, 301, 349, 356, 357, 365, 368, 370, 371, 372, 377; power of, 91, 92, 95, 113, 114, 117, 119, 120, 122, 124, 145, 146, 170, 171, 207, 229, 275, 293, 331, 338, 381; praise of, 81, 82, 94, 95, 120, 124, 139, 204, 205, 206, 208, 217, 218, 226, 227, 292, 293, 301, 303, 316, 343, 351, 382, 383, 384; presence of, 95, 113, 121, 125, 135, 142, 155, 156, 162, 167, 201, 218, 222, 230, 240, 346, 373,

INDEX

others, 180, 316; works of, 79, 109, 123, 166, 225, 364.
Messiah, 276.
Methodists, 301, 303, 363; Society of, 365.
Micah, 7:19, 178; 7:20, 218.
Milton, J., 176.
Moravians, 104.
Mortification, 78, 328, 334, 335, 356.
Moses, 323; law of, 347, 348.
Mysticism, 102, 104, 280, 288.

Nelson, Mr., 101.

Obedience, 87; of angels, 115; of Christ, 114, 382; to Christ, 140, 144, 203, 237, 260, 305; to Church, 86, 360; to God, 80, 81, 83, 102, 103, 122, 130, 138, 243, 278, 364, 387; the Gospel, 288; and salvation, 102, 140; universal, 335.
Ordination, 103.
Origen, 132.

Papists, 100, 101.
Pardon, 82, 106, 138, 180, 188, 190, 200, 240, 255, 257, 261, 268, 269, 283, 325, 343, 369.
Passions, 80, 90, 151, 159, 367.
Patience, 82, 84, 89, 94, 110, 121, 123, 126, 149, 163, 169, 186, 211, 217, 316, 337, 343, 344, 355, 362, 364, 369, 377, 382.
Paul, 78, 160, 161, 167, 308, 309, 320, 321, 329, 342, 347, 349, 356, 357, 366, 371, 373, 375.
Peace, 105, 129, 161, 163, 181, 191, 200, 202, 219, 220, 225, 228, 241, 243, 250, 265, 266, 268, 273, 279, 280, 281, 283, 289, 304, 311, 312, 318, 322, 324, 326, 332, 336, 338, 339, 346, 355, 357, 383.
Perfection, of Christians, 78, 88, 122, 159, 165, 168–169, 231, 259, 299, 303, 306, 307, 309, 310, 311, 313, 315, 316, 319, 322, 325–328, 330, 334, 338, 341, 342, 347, 350, 351,

357, 359, 372, 373, 375, 376; doctrine of, 299, 310, 313, 316, 319, 320, 327, 338–340, 346, 374–376; of love, 82, 187, 216–218, 221, 225, 226, 228, 230, 231, 242–244, 255, 269, 282, 304, 309, 313, 314, 317–319, 321, 323, 324, 330, 332–337, 342, 346, 356, 370, 374, 377, 381; and sin, 315, 319, 321–323, 326–329, 331, 333, 349, 350, 352, 373, 374.
Peter, 169, 307, 375.
1 Peter, 1:11, 341; 2:6, 137.
2 Peter, 1:4, 106.
Philippians, 1:10, 366; 2:5, 220; 2:5–11, 212; 3:15, 373.
Piety, 177, 364, 372.
Polycarp, 132.
Prayer, ceaseless, 100, 112, 210, 227, 228, 304, 334, 351, 355, 360, 361, 363, 370, 371, 374; and Christ, 342; communal, 108; Covenant-, 143; and distractions, 311; ejaculatory, 85, 89; and fervor, 85, 88, 336; forms of, 77, 111; for help, 86, 92, 287; improper, 155; of intercession, 77, 87; lacking, 336; Lord's-, 111–120, 381; mental, 104; for others, 83; of petition, 77, 111, 115, 116; private, 79, 85, 102, 110, 315, 363; public, 79, 85, 86, 102, 315; of thanksgiving, 77, 86; times of, 77, 79, 363; and virtue, 85, 86.
Preaching, 154, 157, 160, 185, 287, 319, 320, 324, 331, 338, 339, 341, 342, 346, 358, 362, 365, 375, 376.
Predestinarians, 343.
Presbyterians, 106.
Pride, 99, 123, 131, 198, 211, 222, 241, 304, 311, 313, 318, 339, 344, 351, 352, 355, 356, 360, 361, 367.
Promise, of Christ, 190, 191, 211, 241, 242, 250, 257, 262, 288, 290, 312, 318, 320, 321, 345, 346; of Christianity, 126–133; and covenant, 381, 382; of God, 137,